EARLY INTERVENTION SERVICES FOR INFANTS, TODDLERS, AND THEIR FAMILIES

PATRICIA MULHEARN BLASCO
Portland State University

ALLYN AND BACON
Boston ▪ London ▪ Toronto ▪ Sydney ▪ Tokyo ▪ Singapore

Senior Editor: *Virginia Lanigan*
Editorial Assistant: *Jennifer Connors*
Composition Buyer: *Linda Cox*
Manufacturing Buyer: *Suzanne Lareau*
Marketing Manager: *Brad Parkins*
Editorial-Production Service: *P. M. Gordon Associates*
Editorial-Production Administrator: *Deborah Brown*
Cover Administrator: *Kristina Mose-Libon*

Copyright © 2001 by Allyn and Bacon
A Pearson Education Company
160 Gould Street
Needham Heights, Massachusetts 02494

Internet: www.abacon.com

Library of Congress Cataloging-in-Publication Data
Blasco, Patricia M.
    Early intervention services for infants, toddlers, and their families / Patricia M. Blasco.
      p. cm.
    Includes bibliographical references and index.
    ISBN 0-205-19443-5
    1. Handicapped children—Services for. 2. Child development. 3. Early childhood education. I. Title.
    HV888.B583   2000
    362.4'048'083—dc21

                                                     99-049319

Printed in the United States of America

10 9 8 7 6 5 4 3 2   05 04 03

To all the children and families I have worked with over the years

*And especially to the memory of Marc Borror and Michelle O'Connor,
toddlers who both died before the age of three
and inspired my love for working with young children and their families*

BRIEF CONTENTS

CONTENTS

CHAPTER THREE

Living in Our World: The First Year 63

With Jolene Pearson

CHAPTER SEVEN

Curriculum and Teaching Strategies in Early Intervention   191

CHAPTER EIGHT

Medical Considerations   213

Peter A. Blasco, M.D.

CHAPTER NINE

Models of Collaboration for Early Intervention: Laying the Groundwork   259

Virginia Buysse and Patricia W. Wesley

CHAPTER TEN

Technology and the Future   295

Deborah J. Kravik

Working with and caring for infants and toddlers is different from working with and caring for preschoolers. This fact has been obvious for years to early childhood professionals, but its implications still seem to elude the public and many operators of early child care programs. Recent research provides compelling evidence that the quality of child care programs for infants and toddlers is generally poorer than that of child care programs for preschoolers. This gap reflects in part a lack of societal commitment to our youngest citizens, in part a belief that what happens to an infant is not really so important in the grand scheme of things, and in part a lack of knowledge about what constitutes appropriate caregiving for infants and toddlers.

When infants and toddlers have or are at risk for disabilities, working with and caring for them poses an even more complex set of challenges. Professionals entering the field who want to work with very young children with disabilities need a broad range of exposure to topics as well as specific skills if they are to be adequately prepared. In this text, Patricia M. Blasco has identified much of the complexity underlying infant intervention programs and has presented this information in a readable and understandable fashion.

First, the text recognizes that professionals need a fundamental grounding in normal infant development. However, this is not the traditional view of development in terms of the attainment of specific milestones, but rather a portrayal of development that captures its interactive nature and the underlying goals that the infant is trying to achieve as he or she progresses through these milestones. Second, the text acknowledges the complex and multiple settings in which infants are cared for and in which services are provided. Hospitals, homes, and child care centers are probably the most common settings, and the roles that professionals will play in each setting will differ considerably. Third, the text emphasizes the importance of research in the biological realm, and that an understanding of both behavior and biology is essential in order to design appropriate interventions. Finally, the text establishes the importance of intervention in the context of families and family caregiving.

Throughout the text, Dr. Blasco has provided numerous examples of situations or events that help to bring points to life. Though brief, these "snapshots" give us insights into the unique experiences of children, families, and infants as they grow, live, and interact with various service systems. They show us the very real challenges faced by both families and professionals and remind us of the importance of an early intervention system that is both comprehensive and personal.

No single text will be sufficient to prepare individuals for work with infants and their parents. These skills ultimately will need to be developed and refined in the context of ongoing relationships and experiences. The present text, however, provides the necessary foundation in both information and insights into the world of practice. Blasco's efforts are a real contribution to the field and should help ensure that the next generation of practitioners is ready for the inevitable challenges it will face.

Don Bailey

The inspiration and motivation for this book came from my years of work with bright, competent service providers who for a variety of reasons return to pursue their education in graduate school. We were engaged in a mutual learning experience as we tried to understand the many new issues and trends in working with very young children and their families. In teaching these students, I was often frustrated by the lack of a teaching textbook that adequately linked research and practice in the field of early services and intervention.

This text combines a firm theoretical/philosophical orientation to both normal and atypical development of infants and toddlers with practical ideas for teaching and working with families. I worked with several assumptions while preparing this book:

- Service providers need a firm foundation in typical child development before they can understand and develop programs for children who have unique needs.
- Family members must be acknowledged as partners in making decisions about all aspects of their children's education
- Sensitivity to diversity must be addressed in all aspects of early intervention (e.g., referral, service delivery, curriculum, and evaluation).
- Children with disabilities are best served in their natural environments.
- A team, including family members and service providers, is jointly responsible for designing and implementing services for young children with disabilities.
- Ethical standards must be upheld and maintained by the team and related service providers.
- Service providers must be advocates for children and their families.

Many graduate students in the field of early childhood intervention come from a variety of backgrounds, including education, special education, nursing, occupational and physical therapy, and treatment of communication disorders. Many of these professionals have been prepared within the limited scope of their fields and often feel the need to expand their general knowledge about infants, toddlers, and families.

Service providers work in a variety of settings as team members, but dwindling resources can affect the ability of the team to function appropriately. Service providers may need to engage in more role releasing and job sharing. Textbooks currently available tend to represent the literature from one or two disciplines, but rarely include work from all applied fields. This approach makes it difficult for students to understand the underlying premises that guide each discipline. By reflecting more than one philosophical approach, this text offers students the opportunity to think critically about practices and to make decisions regarding appropriate interventions.

This book was written to integrate research with actual practice in the field of early intervention. In my classes, students would challenge me by asking questions such as, "We know what mastery motivation is, but how do we encourage it on a home visit?" In this text, I answer this and similar questions.

EARLY INTERVENTION SERVICES

The focus of this book is on providing services to infants and toddlers with disabilities and their families. I deliberately introduce the term *early intervention services* because of the multiple meanings of *early intervention* in today's society. For example, it has also been used to describe interventions for young, first-time offenders in our penal system. Furthermore, although early childhood services are available for children from birth to age eight, the focus of this textbook is on birth to age three. In textbooks that span the period from birth to age eight, there tends to be greater emphasis on the later years, and the information on birth to age three is not represented in depth across the many disciplines serving young children and their families. In addition, most textbooks continue to divide chapters according to developmental domains of early childhood (e.g., cognitive, social-emotional, motor). But the organization of this text follows the currently recommended practice of teaching across domains to enhance the holistic development of the child rather than concentrate on isolated skills.

CHAPTER ORGANIZATION

The first chapter presents a historical perspective on the programs serving young children that formed the present framework for service delivery. In this chapter, a family-centered approach to services is emphasized. Chapters 2 through 4 examine development from prebirth through year three. These chapters discuss typical development as well as the major disabilities that are often diagnosed during those years. The remaining chapters focus more directly on service delivery. Chapter 5 explores screening and assessment for infants and toddlers with disabilities. The importance of understanding standardized assessment protocols and methods of reliability and validity is underscored. This chapter highlights the current trend toward naturalistic and observational methods of gathering data. Chapter 6 addresses service delivery for young children in the natural environment. Chapter 7 considers strategies for teaching along with the curriculum guidelines currently used in the field of early intervention. Chapter 8 focuses on the medical issues prevalent among infants and young children who are referred for services. Chapter 9 discusses models of collaboration for service providers working in many different agencies. Chapter 10 addresses the use of assistive technology for young children with disabilities.

ACKNOWLEDGMENTS

I would like to thank all the students who have helped with this book through their ideas and insights into early intervention practices, particularly Asha Lateef Williams, Tara Layne, and Nigel Pierce. Many of these students were graduate students at the University of St. Thomas in St. Paul, Minnesota, as well as students at Bowie State University in Bowie, Maryland. I would also like to acknowledge the following reviewers: Virginia Buysse, University of North Carolina at Chapel Hill; Amy G. Dell, Trenton State College; Rebecca R. Fewell, University of Miami School of Medicine; Marie F. Fritz, Indiana State University; and Phillip L. Safford, Case Western Reserve University.

In addition, I would like to thank Don Bailey for his willingness to write the foreword and Sharon Walsh for her assistance with Part C of IDEA.

Some of the photographs in this text were contributed by Dan Grogan and Deborah Kravik. Many thanks.

My appreciation goes to Kimberly Brown, Danielle King, Naomi Mimnaugh, Halili Thompson, and A. Tasa Lehman from Portland State University for their assistance with typing the multiple revisions to this book. I would also like to thank my colleagues who patiently waited for this book to be completed after two cross-continental moves by the author. Thanks also to Deborah Brown of Allyn and Bacon and Joe Barron of P. M. Gordon Associates for shepherding the manuscript through production.

Finally I would like to thank my children, Margaret and Peter, who were my most important focus of attention for the past eight years, and my husband, Peter, whose support, in addition to his writing and editing, was instrumental in the completion of this book.

CHAPTER ONE

AN EVOLUTIONARY PERSPECTIVE ON EARLY SERVICES

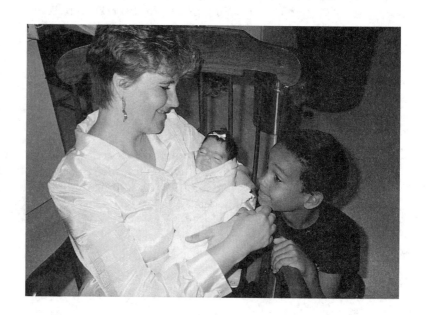

OBJECTIVES

- To provide a philosophical framework of early education and services for young children from birth to age three and their families
- To provide an understanding of the evolution of family-guided services for young children from birth to age three
- To provide insight into the response of families experiencing the birth and recent diagnosis of a child with a disability
- To describe the Individualized Family Service Plan (IFSP) through the experiences of one family
- To describe service coordination and the importance of coordinating services across disciplines
- To view early intervention within an ecological framework
- To discuss the efficacy of early intervention services
- To discuss the future of early intervention services

PHILOSOPHICAL FRAMEWORK

Many authors will argue that there are inherent philosophical differences between early childhood education and early childhood special education, but both fields share a common origin: the pursuit of better education for all young children. Early childhood education in this country can be traced to European roots. There are many people who helped shape the future of early childhood education, and a comprehensive review of all contributors is beyond the scope of this book. However, contributions of several key persons will be discussed.

In the eighteenth century the French philosopher Jean-Jacques Rousseau (1712–1778) argued that young children would benefit from an integrated curriculum that enhanced all the natural senses. He also believed children learned differently from adults by experiencing developmental stages (Essa, 1999).

Rousseau in turn influenced Friedrich Froebel, who in the early 1800s developed the concept of a kindergarten or "children's garden," where children could play and develop under the supervision of nurturing adults, an idea that forms the basis for recommended practices in early childhood today. As Froebel's beliefs became a part of the practice in American kindergartens, new voices argued for a more progressive approach to education led by John Dewey (1859–1952) and his colleagues. Early educators such as Dewey believed that children learned through both intrinsic motivation from within themselves and external motivation from the environment. Dewey's progressive approach to education continues to be reflected today through recommended practices by organizations such as the National Association for the Education of Young Children (NAEYC) and the Division for Early Childhood (DEC). His belief in the tandem process of intrinsic and external motivation is echoed in the works of Jean Piaget (1896–1980) and Lev Vygotsky (1896–1934).

1

Maria Montessori (1870–1952) was the first Italian woman to receive a doctorate in medicine. She was primarily interested in children and influenced by the work of Jean-Marc-Gaspard Itard and his student, Edouard Séguin. Both of these men believed that children learn through the senses. Their seminal work, *The Wild Boy of Aveyron,* is the account of a boy who grew up with little human contact and never learned to talk. Séguin and Itard developed a series of didactic materials that Montessori adapted when she opened her first school, Casa dei Bambini (The Children's House), to serve young children from disadvantaged areas of Rome. (Most publications list the opening of *Casa dei Bambini* as 1907, but some believe it was established in 1906.) Montessori also had an interest in helping children with mental disabilities. She believed that all children need to explore the world through their senses and that the teacher's role was primarily that of an observer/facilitator (Essa, 1999).

Montessori believed in a "prepared environment" where everything has a purpose and where materials are placed on shelves in specific order of difficulty, from simple to complex. She made the analogy between a sponge absorbing liquid and a child's mind absorbing learning. It is easy to see in Montessori's ideas the origin of many practices in special education today, particularly with children who have sensory impairments. With today's renewed emphasis on the plasticity of the human brain during the first three years of life, we can appreciate the importance of her original work.

Early education in the United States was established through nursery schools that promoted Dewey's philosophy in terms of exploratory learning and social engagement. These nursery schools primarily served children ages three to five from middle- and upper-income families who could afford the tuition. Infants and toddlers, by contrast, were studied behaviorally, in psychology laboratories associated with universities, as early as the 1880s (Rosenblith, 1992). These studies provided the foundation for understanding infant growth and development.

Although nursery schools for upper-class and middle-class children flourished, it was not until the 1960s and the federally declared War on Poverty that care for infants and toddlers outside the home was promoted. One of the most influential programs to advance early education for young children at risk was Project Head Start, founded in 1965 to remove children from the "cycle of poverty."

X Educational and child development experts believed that prekindergarten education for disadvantaged children would lead to successful entry into formal education. An assumption behind the Head Start program was that children from impoverished environments were at risk for intellectual growth due to factors such as poor nutrition, lack of stimulation, and lack of educational opportunities.

Head Start also established a precedent for federal assistance to programs for young children and their families. In 1972, the Economic Opportunity Amendments (PL 92-424) required Head Start to reserve 10 percent of its enrollment slots for children with disabilities. As of 1998, 13 percent of children enrolled in Head Start had diagnosed disabilities. In 1994, the reauthorization of the Head Start Act established a new Early Head Start program for low-income families with infants and toddlers. Today, 600 projects provided Early Head Start child development and family support services for 35,000 children under the age of three. These projects include partnerships with early intervention services (Head Start Bureau, 1999). For a comprehensive history of the Head Start Program, see Zigler and Muenchow (1992).

The Head Start Bureau provides training and assistance to ensure program quality. Through its efforts, child-to-adult ratios, group size, average daily attendance, and percent of teachers with degrees have improved significantly. In 1998, Head Start was reauthorized by Congress. The current goals include establishing a seamless program from birth to compulsory school age and strengthening Early Head Start to meet the developmental needs of the youngest children (National Head Start Association, 1999).

CHILDREN WITH DISABILITIES

Programs that serve infants and toddlers with disabilities have been available to families in the United States for several decades. Early residential facilities for children and adults who were deaf and/or blind were established as early as 1800. For example, the Perkins Institute for the Blind founded by Samuel Gridley Howe in the 1800s (Peterson, 1987) continues to serve as a resource for early intervention.

Early programs for children with disabilities were also linked to local Associations for Retarded Citizens (ARC) or mental health agencies, but they were developed and run on shoestring budgets. Federal assistance to the parents of such children started as early as 1965, when PL 89-313, the amendment to the Elementary and Secondary Education Act (ESEA), gave states supplementary funds that could be applied to programs for children ages birth to five. In 1968, PL 90-538, the Handicapped Children's Early Education Assistance Act (HCEEAA), created the Handicapped Early Education Program (HCEEP) to provide federal assistance in developing experimental programs for young children with disabilities. Under the HCEEP Model Demonstration Programs, federal grants were distributed to model projects throughout the United States for a period of three years (Peterson, 1987). Today, this program operates under the auspices of the Office of Special Education and Rehabilitative Services (OSERS) at the U.S. Department of Education.

Many of these early programs involved parents as teachers of their children. The goal of early intervention was to teach the child developmental skills, and parents were often expected to carry out instructional objectives with their children at home. This service delivery model did not fully take into account the realities of the family setting, and parents were often overwhelmed by the expectations of service providers. Today parents and professionals work in partnership to provide the best services for the family. Families and service providers have joined together to bring about an awareness of the importance of early childhood in the field of special education. These efforts have included the creation of the Division for Early Childhood (DEC), a division of the Council for Exceptional Children (CEC), in 1973.

One of the most important steps by the federal government in support of children with disabilities was the passage of the Education for All Handicapped Children Act of 1975 (PL 94-142), now known as the Individuals with Disabilities Education Act. This law mandated free, appropriate public education for all school-age children with disabilities. Incentives were provided for preschool-aged children that formed the basis for the comprehensive services for this group that came in the 1980s and 1990s.

In the 1980s, service providers acknowledged that the family, and particularly the caregivers, were the most influential people in a child's life, while service providers may be transient in the child's life. Thus in 1986, through the grassroots efforts of families and service providers, PL 99-457 amended PL 94-142. This law established early intervention services for preschool children age 3 to 5 years and promised federal incentives for states to establish comprehensive, coordinated services for young children from birth to age three. In 1990, PL 101-476 reauthorized the federal law and changed its name to the Individuals with Disabilities Education Act (IDEA), extending the original intent of PL 94-142. A year later, in 1991, PL 102-119 was added as an amendment to IDEA. This law specified services that were to be made available to infants, toddlers, and their families. It also strengthened the role of the family in the education of young children.

All states receiving federal funds are required to develop and implement comprehensive, interagency plans for service delivery to infants, toddlers with disabilities, and their families. Under this agreement, the governor of the state names the lead agency that administers and monitors the early intervention system with the coooperation of the State Interagency Coordinating Council (SICC). The SICC is composed of parents, service providers, and members of various agencies (including those that deal with early intervention, preschool, health insurance, Head Start, and child care, as well as personnel education and state legislature) involved in services for young children with disabilities. Some states may include a representative from the Bureau of Indian Affairs or tribal council. There are also community ICCs at the local level.

Each state is also required to provide a central directory and a comprehensive child-find system to locate and refer children with disabilities (Brunim, 1990). The plan must include timelines and provision for participation by primary referral sources. Many states have implemented a central referral system that utilizes a single point of entry for accessing services. This central directory includes information on services and resources, including research and demonstration projects being conducted in the state. States are also required to have a comprehensive system of personnel development, to ensure an assessment process, and to oversee the Individualized Family Service Plan (IFSP) meeting, which documents the working relationship between families and service providers.

In the early stages of developing the IFSP, the National Early Childhood Technical Assistance System (NECTAS) and the Association for the Care of Children's Health (ACCH) developed guidelines that set out the underlying principles of the IFSP, principles which remain as pertinent today as they were during the initial development of federal policy:

PRINCIPLES UNDERLYING THE IFSP PROCESS

- Infants and toddlers are uniquely dependent on their families for their survival and care.
- States and programs should define "family" to reflect the diversity of family patterns and structures.
- Each family has its own structure, roles, values, beliefs, and coping styles.
- Respect for family autonomy, independence, and decision-making means that families should participate in determining not only the level and nature of services but also the duration and intensity of involvement in early intervention.
- Families and professionals participate as partners in designing, implementing, and evaluating the success of the early intervention program.
- Early intervention services should be flexible, accessible, and responsive to family's identified issues and concerns.
- Early intervention services should be provided according to the normalization principle—that is, families should have access to services provided in a reasonable way and in natural environments. Environments should promote the inclusion of both the child and family within the community.
- Cultural differences are recognized as strengths, not concerns, and choices that reflect a family's beliefs, priorities, and concerns should be respected.
- No one agency or discipline can meet the needs of families with diverse and complex concerns. A team approach that includes the efforts of family members is necessary to plan and implement the IFSP process.

Adapted from M. J. McGonigel, R. K. Kaufmann, and B. H. Johnson (Eds.), 1991, *Guidelines and Recommended Practices for the Individualized Family Service Plan,* 2nd ed., Bethesda: Association for the Care of Children's Health.

In 1990, the Individuals with Disabilities Education Act (IDEA) (PL 101-476) replaced the earlier Education for the Handicapped Act (EHA) of 1986. In 1991 amendments to IDEA were passed including, PL 102-119, Part H, legislation. The new law included provisions for a seamless transition to service delivery for preschool-age children; it also strengthened the role of families. The IFSP process, which included assessment of family resources, priorities, and concerns, was to be family-directed.

In 1997, Congress reauthorized IDEA and added some changes to the original legislation. The reauthorization created IDEA with four parts: Part A, General Provisions; Part B, Assistance for Education of All Children with Disabilities, Part C, Infants and Toddlers with Disabilities; and Part D, National Activities to Improve Education of Children with Disabilities. It is not within the scope of this book to cover all of the changes to IDEA; however, the changes affecting infants and toddlers and their families are important considerations. The Internet Web site (www. ideapractices.org, maintained by the federally funded IDEA Partnership project) contains the full text as well as summaries of the law.

Under Part A, General Provisions: option for use of "developmental delay" at state and local discretion was added to the definition of disability for children between three and nine years old. In addition, the new legislation added "orientation and mobility services" to the definition of "related services."

Part C (formerly known as Part H) states the purpose of federally funded early intervention programs, including:

- Maintain and implement a statewide, comprehensive, coordinated, multidisciplinary, interagency system of early intervention services for infants and toddlers with disabilities and their families;
- Facilitate the coordination of payment for early intervention services from Federal, State, local, and private sources (including public and private insurance coverage);
- Enhance the States' capacity to provide quality early intervention services and expand and improve existing early intervention services being provided to infants and toddlers with disabilities and their families; and
- Enhance the capacity of State and local agencies and service providers to identify, evaluate, and meet the needs of historically underrepresented populations, particularly minority, low-income, inner-city, and rural populations.

Early Intervention Program (1999), § 303.1

States are also encouraged to expand opportunities for children under the age of three who would be at risk of having substantial developmental delay if they did not receive early intervention services. States that do not provide services for at-risk infants and toddlers may now use funds to strengthen this statewide system by establishing or strengthening ties with community-based programs and agencies to help identify and evaluate infants and toddlers at risk (Early Intervention Program, 1999, § 303.3).

Under the new law, a transition plan arranged by the designated lead agency will ensure a smooth transition for children receiving early intervention services. A description of how the families will be included in the transition plan is also required.

State eligibility has been revised to allow states that have adopted a policy for appropriate early intervention services for all eligible children and their families to apply for federal funds. In this area, a major change has been made to allow states to establish policies and procedures to ensure that early intervention services are provided in a child's natural environments, whenever possible. According to the law, "natural environments means settings that are natural or normal for the child's age peers who have no disabilities" (Early Intervention Program, 1999, § 303.18). Services provided in a setting other than a natural environment occur only when early intervention cannot be achieved satisfactorily in a natural environment. In addition, justification must be indicated in the IFSP if early intervention services will not be provided in a natural environment.

In a position statement, the DEC (1998) endorsed the natural environments policy.

DEC supports the rights of all children, regardless of their diverse abilities, to participate actively in natural environments within their community. A natural environment is one in which the child would spend time if he or she did not have special needs. Family-centered and community-based care means that service providers not provide support for children, but they provide support to families and those in the community as well. Service providers must be able to facilitate parent-to-parent connections that link young children and their families to community-based natural supports such as babysitters, play groups and libraries. Instead of providing direct supports and services only to young children and their families, service providers must also serve as consultants, advocates, facilitators, and team members with community providers.

Changes to service delivery under Part C of IDEA may not be easy to implement at the local level. For example, fiscal restraints may prevent some service providers from changing their present direct-service delivery system. As one occupational therapist working in a center-based program for children with disabilities said, "We are not reimbursed for travel time to children's homes or their community." Another service provider questioned the definition of natural environments. In the inner city, community settings such as parks and fast food restaurants may not be safe places for families.

ENTERING THE SYSTEM

According to federal statute, infants and toddlers from birth to age 2, inclusive, are eligible for early intervention services if they are experiencing developmental delays. Service providers must document eligibility through the use of appropriate diagnostic instruments and procedures in one or more developmental areas: cognitive, physical, communication, social and emotional, or adaptive behavior. The child is also eligible if he or she has a diagnosed physical or mental condition that has a high probability of resulting in developmental delay. Infants and toddlers who are at risk of having substantial developmental delay may receive services at the state's discretion (Early Intervention Program, 1999, § 303.16). See Chapter 5 for a complete description of eligibility requirements.

All states must have criteria for entry into early intervention systems. Because various agencies work together in identifying and referring children with disabilities, services begin soon after diagnosis. Although the waiting period has decreased for many families who did not know how to access the early intervention system. For families who have just learned about a diagnosis, or are bringing a newborn home from an extended hospital stay, immediate service delivery can be intrusive. All new families need privacy to adjust to their new schedule and lifestyle, and this is certainly true when a child has a disability. The law is flexible in allowing a family time to adjust. For example, with parental consent, the team may provide services prior to completion of the assessment.

The age range of children entitled to services under Part C includes ages birth to three years (the entire second year is included). Many programs serving infants and toddlers provide home-based intervention until age three, when the child is transitioned to center-based services. With an increase in out-of-home child care for children under the age of three, service providers may see children both in the home and in other settings. Therefore, service providers should be trained to work successfully in a variety of environments (see Chapter 6).

The hallmark of Part C legislation is the Individualized Family Service Plan (IFSP). The key elements of the plan include:

- A statement of the child's present developmental status (based on appropriate assessment of the developmental domains: cognitive, communication, social/emotional, and adaptive)
- A statement of family's resources, priorities, and concerns related to enhancing the development of the child
- A statement of major outcomes expected to be achieved for the child and family (including criteria, procedures, and timelines used to determine the degree of progress toward those outcomes)
- A list of specific early intervention services and supports needed, and plan for service coordination (including frequency, intensity, and method of service delivery)
- A statement of the natural environments in which services will be provided (including justification, if necessary, to the extent that services will not be provided in the natural environment)
- The projected dates for service initiation and the anticipated duration of services
- The name of a qualified, appropriate service coordinator who will be responsible for coordinating services and implementing the plan
- Transition plans to support the child and family as they move on to preschool or other appropriate services
- The provisions for ongoing review, evaluation, and revision of the plan

Early Intervention Program (1999), § 303.344

PARTNERSHIPS WITH FAMILIES

The IFSP was developed for families to work in partnership with service providers in implementing early intervention services. An assumption underlining the plan is that service providers must understand the family from a systems perspective. Relationships within a family are driven by interacting subsystems (Minuchin, 1988; Turnbull & Turnbull, 1990). Different members within the family make up several subsystems that are mutually influential. For example, the marital subsystem is composed of the interaction of two primary caregivers (traditionally the parents). Other subsystems include the parent/child, sibling, and extended family.

Understanding the influence of these interacting subsystems will help service providers work with families in a more effective way. All families follow rules of interaction that are embedded in the individual cultural and ideological beliefs of the family (Blasco & Pearson, 1995). It is important to acknowledge family rules and boundaries established to delineate membership within a subsystem. Boundaries may either keep service providers outside of family interaction or let agencies into the inner core of the family. Families may respond differently to service providers at different times in their history. For example, when a family is in crisis, boundaries may be confused, inconsistent, or nonexistent (Minuchin, 1988). Thus, a service provider may be closed out of the family at a time when services could be most helpful. This scenario can be very frustrating to a service provider who feels he or she is doing everything possible to engage the family. Acknowledgment of the family's wishes and a willingness to follow the family's lead will help to establish the trust necessary for a continued working relationship.

The emotional bond that holds the family together is called *family cohesion* (Olson et al., 1989). Family cohesion occurs along a continuum of behavior ranging from enmeshment to disengagement. Healthy families tend to fall in the middle of the continuum. Enmeshment occurs when the boundaries between subsystems become confused or weak. Turnbull and Turnbull (1990) gave the example of the parent of a child with a disability who has devoted all of his or her time and energy to that child, at the expense of other family members. A family who is disengaged may forget about a home visit or miss several appointments with service providers.

Family adaptability refers to the ability of the family to change its power structure, role relationships, and rules in response to events that occur over a lifetime (Olson et al., 1989). Like cohesion, adaptability exists along a behavioral continuum, from rigidity to chaos. Families characterized as rigid may have too many rules that are not adaptable to a specific situation. Families that are chaotic may have few or inconsistent rules. Inconsistent or nonexistent rules can be very confusing for young children who developmentally are comforted by parental expectations and routines. Consider Vignette 1.1, from an inner-city child care center.

VIGNETTE 1.1 DAILY ROUTINES

Debbie is a child care worker at an inner-city child care center. In the morning the children enter the room and are greeted by the adults, who place themselves strategically within the room. Marietta is greeting children and parents at the door. Several parents arrive as a result of a court order to participate in parenting classes. Many of the children with disabilities arrive by bus.

Several of the children have histories of living in violent environments. Three of the children were exposed prenatally to cocaine, and two children have diagnosed attachment disorders. One child has fetal alcohol syndrome. Debbie and Marietta realize that routines and predictability are key ingredients for these children and for their families. After a brief free-play session, they ask children and parents who are present to join them in some singing. After a few get-together songs, Debbie goes over the morning schedule and reminds everyone of the events for that day, including daily routines. One of the parents, Tanya, asks, "It is a nice day, why don't they just stay outside on the playground all morning?" Debbie tries to explain that they want to follow the plan so the children know what to expect every day. Tanya replies, "At home, we just do what feels good. If they don't like what we're doing and fuss, I whoop them good and they come around." There is an embarrassed silence as Debbie and Marietta look at each other. Finally, one of the other parents, Akira, says, "They don't understand why you hit them if they don't know what they are supposed to do."

In Vignette 1.1, Tanya has difficulty understanding the need for routines. Tanya herself was an abused child, and her parents gave inconsistent messages regarding discipline. Akira's comment was well timed and probably helpful because it came from another parent, who has also experienced difficulty with parenting.

Flexibility is characteristic of families who can adapt to new situations, stresses, and demands appropriately (Minuchin, 1988). Families that have established open communication are more likely to engage in decision-making and conflict resolution with service providers. Positive communication skills such as reflective listening, clarification, and supportive comments help families and service providers engage in meaningful dialogue. Negative communication skills such as criticism, scolding, and judging are likely to disrupt or delay successful dialogue.

It is important to remember that a family systems approach, while helpful in providing a framework for understanding families, also requires a team effort in clinically describing a family and their behavior. Service providers should rely on the expertise of mental health and social service professionals when working with families. It is also important to acknowledge that all families may experience extreme behavior at different times in their development. However, many families eventually achieve a healthy balance. When the family is unable to find a balance, professionals in family therapy need to guide the intervention.

Supporting Families in Early Intervention

Figure 1.1 demonstrates how formal and informal support can be available to the family through service provision (Turnbull & Turnbull, 1990). The concentric lines at times may be either open or closed, depending on how the family is functioning at that particular time in their life cycle.

Life cycle refers to the family's developmental trajectory. Every family goes through a series of transitions that produce stress. For example, the birth of a child, though considered a joyous occasion, produces stress in the form of demands for new routines, challenges, and changes in living habits. The birth of a child with a disability may exacerbate such stress and leave the family feeling out of control.

Family Response to Disability

In the past, service providers often made judgments about families based on research conducted in the medical field. Drotar et al. (1975) published a study based on a questionnaire assessing parental perceptions, feelings, and attachment

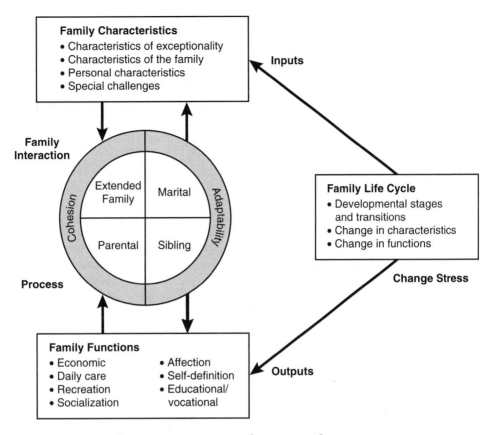

FIGURE 1.1   Family Systems Conceptual Framework

Source: From *Working with Families with Disabled Members: A Family Systems Approach*, by A. P. Turnbull, J. A. Summers, and M. J. Brotherson, 1984, Lawrence: University of Kansas, p. 60. Adapted by permission.

to their child with a disability. They developed a linear model that showed parents following a progression of feelings starting with shock and filtering through denial and anger until the parent comes to a point of reorganization, when parents are ready to deal with the responsibilities of their child.

In the 1980s many of these theories were disputed by researchers who stated that this kind of categorizing of feelings does families a disservice (Blacher, 1984). Families will respond differently to crises based on individual resources and support and previous coping strategies for dealing with difficult situations (Farran, Metzger, & Sparling, 1986). For example, a family can draw from religious or ideological beliefs to develop acceptance and love. Other families may receive support and guidance from another family member or friend who also has a child with a disability. The social and political influence of our society toward persons with disabilities will also affect a family's reaction. The more information is available to families, the better they can make the decisions necessary to move forward. Bailey and Blasco (1990) identified the need for information as one of the most important services that providers can give to families.

The Guzman family expressed their need for information early on as a way of dealing with the diagnosis of Cornelia deLange syndrome in their daughter, Alex. At the time of Alex's birth, Lori had a five-year-old son, Shawn, from a previous marriage. George, her husband, missed Alex's birth but arrived shortly after and was told "the news," as vignette 1.2 reveals.

VIGNETTE 1.2   INITIAL DIAGNOSIS

I knew right away something was wrong. They wouldn't let me see Alex and they kept asking me when would my husband arrive. The doctor finally came in and said he had to tell me some bad news about my child. They still needed to do some tests but they thought she had a syndrome of some type. Within a few days, they confirmed that she had Cornelia deLange syndrome. The medical team spent hours explaining the syndrome and its characteristics to us. I don't remember anything they said. They told me she would be severely retarded, possibly deaf and blind. Only one characteristic stood out in my mind that day. The physician said her hair would not grow beyond her ears. I remember thinking what a ridiculous thing to say to a parent. Years later when Alex had her school picture taken with hair well beyond her shoulders, I thought of sending a copy of that picture to the physician.

A concept that has recently resurfaced in the literature is that of *chronic sorrow,* a condition first described by Solnit and Stark (1961). Many families of children with disabilities describe their emotional state as a roller coaster ride. There are highs and lows, yet families never lose the sense of sadness that their child has a disability that will affect their lives forever. Events may reignite the sense of sadness, which can lead to depression and despair. In the literature, researchers pointed out that milestones, such as the beginning of school or the child's first birthday, can inspire chronic sorrow (Turnbull & Turnbull, 1990). Again, it is important to realize that each family is unique and, depending on cultural differences and beliefs, will vary in their responses to all aspects of raising a child with a disability.

During initial diagnosis of a child's disability, service providers can help families by listening to their concerns and issues. Providing an empathetic ear will allow families the time to sort through the multiple feelings and sense of confusion that accompany any time of change.

UNDERSTANDING THE IFSP PROCESS FOR ONE FAMILY

When Alex Guzmán was born with a disability in 1988, she was eligible for early intervention services at home. At that time, the IFSP process was relatively new in her state. At first, Lori and George Guzmán were frustrated by the thought of completing yet another long, complicated form. They had already completed an Individualized Education Plan (IEP), an Individualized Support Plan (ISP), and a nursing care plan. The early intervention team moved quickly, however, to involve the family in the IFSP process. Lori and George learned that the IFSP could combine all of the best aspects of the former care plans, the positive aspects of Alex's abilities, and the family's concerns, priorities, and resources as they related to Alex.

According to Lori,

> The IFSP process allows the family to identify what it needs to support the child, and to help the child achieve his or her outcomes. The family can identify its concerns and assign each a priority. Our family felt that getting more information about our child's syndrome was more important than getting an audiology report. (Guzmán & Guzmán, 1992, p. 1)

Figure 1.2 shows the part of the plan as written by the mother, Lori; the father, George; and brother, Shawn.

In many families, individuals have different opinions of and concerns for the child with disabilities. For example, George was more concerned about receiving information on Cornelia deLange syndrome and medical provisions for his daughter. While Lori too was eager for more information on medical procedures, she also needed help balancing her work schedule with the new demands of caring for Alex, and wanted to see Alex gain weight and to learn how to communicate with her. Since the Guzmáns are a dual-income family, Lori was worried about the financial costs of caring for Alex and the potential loss of her income. She was also concerned about Shawn and his needs for care and attention. Shawn wanted to see his sister become more like other children. Finally, Lori mentioned that there was some concern for the grandparents, who spoke Spanish and had difficulty understanding all the medical issues.

Bailey, Blasco, and Simeonsson (1992) found significant differences in the concerns expressed by mothers and fathers regarding social and family support and child care. All family members should have the opportunity to express their feelings and understanding during the IFSP process. From a family systems perspective, this approach will help ensure that services are understood and that all family members who wish to be included are participating to the fullest extent in the intervention plan.

Another important component of the IFSP is the flexibility in defining both child and family outcomes. For example, Lori was quite concerned with the loss of a connection with her neighbors as a result of the time and energy needed to care for Alex.

> The family was so involved with the medical procedures and the efforts of simply keeping our child alive that we missed every neighborhood picnic and gathering during the first year-and-a half of Alex's life. We became completely detached from our neighbors and friends, not by choice, but by circumstance. The IFSP not only allows for inclusion of neighbors and friends on the IFSP team, but also allows for them to be included in carrying out the actual plan. (Guzmán & Guzmán, 1992, p. 1)

Child's Name _____ *Alexandra Guzmán*

5-1-92
by Lori (mother)

Family Considerations for the Individual Family Service Plan

1. Please describe how you see your child (what you like most, any concerns or needs).

   Likes: Long eyelashes, dark eyes, dark hair – her Mexican heritage shows.
   Concerns: apparent inability to gain weight; bouts of apnea + breathing difficulties;
   the diagnosis of severe mental retardation; will she ever walk?

2. What type of help would you want for your child and family in the months or year ahead?

   How to get mom back to work; Alex to gain weight – more instruction on how to
   care for her medically; how to get away; how to help brother feel okay; how to
   change retardation level from severe to mild; how to help pay for medical bills;
   how do we communicate with her.

3. Which of the following do you or other family members feel are important concerns or areas about which you would like more information?

   for your child

   - ✓ getting around
   - ✓ communicating
   - ✓ learning
   - ✓ feeding, nutrition
   - ___ having fun with other children
   - ___ challenging behaviors or emotions
   - ✓ equipment or supplies
   - ✓ health or dental care
   - ✓ pain or discomfort
   - ✓ vision or hearing
   - ___ other

   for your family . . .

   - ___ meeting other families whose child has similar needs
   - ___ finding or working with doctors or other specialists
   - ___ coordinating, making appointments, dealing with agencies
   - ✓ coordinating your child's medical care
   - ___ finding out more about how different services work or how they could work better for you
   - ✓ planning or expectations for the future
   - ✓ more information about what resources might be available
   - ___ transportation

   notes:

   - ___ child care
   - ✓ finding a support group
   - ✓ finding or working with people who can help you in your home or care for your child so you can have a break
   - ___ housing, clothing, jobs, food, telephone
   - ✓ information or ideas for brothers, sisters, friends, relatives, others
   - ✓ information about the disability or diagnosis
   - ___ money for extra costs of child's special needs
   - ___ help with insurance
   - ___ recreation
   - ✓ other – *talking to another parent*

4. What else do you think would be helpful for others to know about your child?

   We are tired of being protected from the truth about our daughter's diagnosis + needs.

5. . . . about your family? *Grandparents speak Spanish; difficulty understanding her needs.*

FIGURE 1.2   Sample Individual Family Service Plan

Family Considerations for the Individual Family Service Plan

5-1-92
by George (father)

1. Please describe how you see your child (what you like most, any concerns or needs).

   Little, Fighter

2. What type of help would you want for your child and family in the months or year ahead?

   Info on syndrome, what medical options are out there

3. Which of the following do you or other family members feel are important concerns or areas about which you would like more information?

   notes:

   for your child
   - ✓ getting around
   - ✓ communicating
   - ✓ learning
   - ✓ feeding, nutrition
   - ___ having fun with other children
   - ___ challenging behaviors or emotions
   - ✓ equipment or supplies
   - ✓ health or dental care
   - ✓ pain or discomfort
   - ✓ vision or hearing
   - ___ other

   for your family . . .
   - ___ meeting other families whose child has similar needs
   - ___ finding or working with doctors or other specialists
   - ___ coordinating, making appointments, dealing with agencies
   - ___ coordinating your child's medical care
   - ___ finding out more about how different services work or how they could work better for you
   - ✓ planning or expectations for the future
   - ___ more information about what resources might be available
   - ___ transportation

   - ___ child care
   - ✓ finding a support group
   - ✓ finding or working with people who can help you in your home or care for your child so you can have a break
   - ___ housing, clothing, jobs, food, telephone
   - ___ information or ideas for brothers, sisters, friends, relatives, others
   - ✓ information about the disability or diagnosis
   - ___ money for extra costs of child's special needs
   - ✓ help with insurance
   - ✓ recreation
   - ___ other

4. What else do you think would be helpful for others to know about your child?

5. . . . about your family?

FIGURE 1.2 Continued

15

Family Considerations for the Individual Family Service Plan

by Shawn (brother)
5-1-92
age 8

1. Please describe how you see your child (what you like most, any concerns or needs).

sister

Small and soft

2. What type of help would you want for your child and family in the months or year ahead?

sister

Get her to go out side - take her for walks or to be able to do things other kids could do. better of things other kids could do.

3. Which of the following do you or other family members feel are important concerns or areas about which you would like more information?

for your child

___ getting around
___ communicating
✓ learning
✓ feeding, nutrition
✓ having fun with other children
___ challenging behaviors or emotions
___ equipment or supplies
✓ health or dental care
✓ pain or discomfort
✓ vision or hearing
___ other

for your family . . .

___ meeting other families whose child has similar needs
✓ finding or working with doctors or other specialists
✓ coordinating, making appointments, dealing with agencies
___ coordinating your child's medical care
___ finding out more about how different services work or how they could work better for you
___ planning or expectations for the future
✓ more information about what resources might be available
✓ transportation

notes:

✓ child care
✓ finding a support group
✓ finding or working with people who can help you in your home or care for your child so you can have a break
___ housing, clothing, jobs, food, telephone
___ information or ideas for brothers, sisters, friends, relatives, others
✓ information about the disability or diagnosis
___ money for extra costs of child's special needs
___ help with insurance
___ recreation
___ other

4. What else do you think would be helpful for others to know about your child?

5. . . . about your family?

FIGURE 1.2   Continued

16

IFSP Team Membership Selection - possibilities to consider for team members which will be helpful or supportive to child and family outcomes/issues/tasks

Family/Community:
- (•) parents
- other family members, relatives, friends
- community, civic, disability or parent groups
- respite, child care providers
- advocates
- legal representation
- ministry, other support source
- other: *another parent*

Social Services:
- (–) developmental disabilities case worker
- income maintenance/economic assistance
- mental health
- child welfare
- social worker
- other private providers

Health Care:
- primary physician
- other physician
- private home health care
- primary nurse

   — = considered
   O = invited

* must attend to meet IEP requirements

Health Care continued
- other hospital staff
- (–) public health nursing
- community health services
- habilitation providers (private therapy)
- Services for Children with Handicaps
- mental health providers
- personal care attendants
- other:

Education
- (•) administrator or designee
- (–) Early Childhood Special Education
- school nurse
- Early Childhood Family Education
- Head Start
- Community Education
- early childhood programs (e.g., nursery school, child care)
- kindergarten-regular/special educators, related services
- occupational therapy
- physical therapy
- speech therapy
- other:

SCHEDULING IFSP MEETING

Settings and times convenient to family to ensure that they will be able to attend.

M or T   late afternoon (after 3:00)
F   any time/ prefer only 5-6 people

at parents' home — 1½ - 2 hrs. length

* Tues June 9   3 - 5 p.m.

Fill in details of team members on next page.

Page 3

Agenda for the IFSP meeting. (After reviewing the Family Considerations (page 2).) The family and Facilitator create an agenda for the IFSP team meeting. (List the topics, questions and information to share; decide what sequence to follow and how much time will be needed.)

1. Introductions – how we got acquainted
2. Info about Alex – pictures (page 5)
3. Family issues (page 2)
4. Review page 6 – update, additions
5. Specify who will work on outcomes
6. Decide about next meeting – (where, when) and ongoing communication
7. Assign service coordinator

things to bring
nametags
flip chart
form
photos

FIGURE 1.2 Continued

Summary of Child's Present Levels of Performance (To be completed by the IFSP Team. Draw from description of the child, additional assessments and observations, for each category. Include needs and functioning in context of daily routine settings. Address all areas listed.)

1. Current health and medical status	2. Basic senses including hearing and vision	3. Communication: speech and language development
4. Social/emotional/behavioral development	5. Physical/motoric development 6. Cognitive development	7. Self-help skills 8. Academic Performance (when appropriate)

Present Levels of Performance	Child's Needs
Alex is awake a lot. She likes to swing and play with her hands in front of her face.∧ She likes music on the tape recorder by her head.∧ She's usually hot – don't use blankets much. She tolerates holding but cries if you hold her too tight. Her cry has a low growling sound.	
Alex's arms appear shorter than they should be; hands and fingers are extremely small. Her arms are bent up and her neck and legs seem stiff.	
Alex has had trouble breathing – gagging or apnea spells occur 1-2 x/day. When mucus collects and suctioned out Alex becomes frantic and cries; sometimes she turns blue because her heart has slowed down or stopped.	to breathe steadily and independently
Alex is fed through a gastrostomy tube; she has trouble with sucking and swallowing. Low birth weight, slow weight gain.	to gain weight to drink from a bottle/eat by mouth

FIGURE 1.2   Continued

Initial Team List of IFSP Outcomes/Tasks/Issues

(An outcome is a statement of the changes family members want to see for their child, or for themselves, related to their ability to enhance their child's development.)

Priority #	Outcome/Issue/Task	People who can help with this outcome (to assess, plan, commit resources, and/or carry out the plan).	Additional Assessment Needed* INITIAL	FURTHER	NO
7 in process	extended family fears and concerns (cultural) support for older brother	facilitator — local church — parents, cultural resources, sibling support group — ARC Hennepin			✓
2 done by day 30	more info about CdL syndrome – what will future bring?	MDH literature search by PHN, another parent – Pilot Parent or CdL Syndrome Foundation			✓
(4) checked day care - no answers no application pending MA·SS	help in home to care for Alex - possibly day care or respite options	Soc. Serv. for respite possibilities, PHN for MA options, home care or respite options	✓ ✓		
3 CPR done by day 30	training on medical procedures etc. for family including grandparents and friends	PHN, hospital staff, programs e.g. CPR, parents			
6 school assess. cmpltd. by day 30	communication - hearing	school staff, audiologist, parents	✓		
(5) school assess. cmpltd. by day 30 ROM	minimize level and effect of mental retardation; reduce contractures at elbows; improve hip range of motion	school staff, hospital OT/PT, parents	✓		✓

*Attach assessment permits as needed

Page 6

FIGURE 1.2 Continued

Initial Team List of IFSP Outcomes/Tasks/Issues

(An outcome is a statement of the changes family members want to see for their child, or for themselves, related to their ability to enhance their child's development.)

Priority #	Outcome/Issue/Task	People who can help with this outcome (to assess, plan, commit resources, and/or carry out the plan).	Additional Assessment Needed? INITIAL	FURTHER	NO
⑧ MA pending	help with medical bills	Soc. Services/Employment + Economic Assistance PHN	✓		
① in process— ongoing	basic health concerns — apnea, breathing weight gain	doctor parents PHN			✓

*Attach assessment permits as needed

FIGURE 1.2   Continued

Although the plan requires more documentation of child and family strengths and concerns than its predecessors, it does not have to be a labor-intensive process. Documents that only add more paperwork discourage both families as well as service providers. In fact, many states are working on flexible documentation that can be completed in a variety of settings, including a Neonatal Intensive Care Unit (NICU). Many have computerized the IFSP to make recording more efficient and less time-consuming.

SERVICE COORDINATION

One of the most important provisions of Part C of the IDEA is the inclusion of a service coordinator to help streamline early intervention services. Services are provided to infants and toddlers and their families by different professionals working together as a team. In Chapter 9, the varied approaches to teaming are discussed. The team is typically composed of parents and qualified personnel, including early childhood special education teacher, early childhood teacher or child care provider, speech and language clinician, occupational therapist, physical therapist, nurse or public health nurse, nutritionist, physician, social worker, audiologist, and psychologist. The role of the service coordinator is to coordinate and integrate the multiple agencies serving individual families. According to federal law, the service coordinator is responsible for seven main activities: coordinate evaluations and assessments; facilitate the development, implementation, and evaluation of the IFSP; assist families in the identification of service providers; coordinate and monitor the delivery of services; coordinate medical and health care; and facilitate the transition plan to preschool services.

Service coordination, although a new term, has been in existence in many fields allied with education services. For example, social workers are often assigned to a family as case managers (Bailey, 1989). This model of intervention focused on the family's problems. In other words, the family was viewed as a client and services addressed the "dysfunctional" aspect of the family. From a family systems perspective, social workers are assigned to families who are clinically in need of intervention. According to this model, families need help before they can be self-reliant.

Following a family empowerment model, Dunst and Trivette (1989) suggested that parents and professionals work together to secure and maximize services. These authors emphasized the importance of promoting the competencies of the family. There are basic strategies for working with families in partnerships, including:

- Working with the family from a systems perspective
- Helping to identify family issues and concerns
- Using reflective listening skills
- Engaging in constructive conflict and negotiating needs
- Locating and referring to community, state, and national resources

With the IDEA, the term service coordination replaced case management. The shift to service coordination reflects a change not only in terminology but also in attitude. Families are no long viewed as "cases" to be "managed" by experts. Rather, service coordination is more reflective of the involvement of families as partners in their child's intervention program (Hausslein, Kaufmann, & Hurth, 1992). Indeed, in some situations, families drive the process of making services work for their child.

In many states, the position of the service coordinator is still evolving. According to federal standards, service coordinators must have an understanding of eligibility requirements for infants and toddlers, Part C regulations, and early intervention services in their state. It is up to the state, and in many cases local agencies, to define the role of service provider within their community. Thus the lead agency within a state may view service coordination differently in different locations. For example, if the lead agency is education, some school districts may assign a service coordinator to a family once that family enters the early intervention system. Other school districts allow the families to chose from a menu of options for service coordination. That may include a service coordinator who is a parent, someone not connected with any of the agencies, or a familiar team member.

The use of parents as service coordinators can help ease the family's entry into a sometimes difficult system (Glisczinski, 1995). According to one parent coordinator:

> A seasoned early intervention parent can point new parents in the right direction—they know the ins and outs of paperwork and can provide helpful hints for accessing "the system" and working through loopholes. They know, for example, that the social worker with the brown glasses in the second room on the left is far more accommodating than the other social worker in the same room without glasses. (p. 40)

Whatever the particular job description, it is imperative that a service coordinator have excellent "people" skills as well as expertise in early intervention. That is, the service coordinator must be able to keep the lines of communication open between various agencies and the family. The coordinator may act as a troubleshooter for the family, because he or she is the person in whom the family have placed the most trust and belief. A good service coordinator is an empathetic listener who can also move families and agencies toward mutual agreement.

Dinnebeil and Rule (1994) surveyed families and service coordinators. They found that, according to parents, the important characteristics of service providers include strong skills in rapport building and in gathering and synthesizing resources, as well as a positive, concerned attitude. Finally, the service coordinator helps the family transition from the birth-to-three program to the preschool program. This transition may include stressful separation issues for all involved. Families not only experience anxiety for their child, who may be entering a center-based program for the first time, but also must prepare themselves for dealing with a new team and, in many situations, a new setting. Transition strategies are described in Chapter 7.

THEORETICAL APPROACHES

The Medical Model

Services to young children and their families have been influenced by the theoretical approaches of different delivery systems. For example, the diagnosis of a disability for children under the age of three often occurs within a medical setting. The *medical model* of service delivery is frequently characterized as a difficult system for families to negotiate. Health care personnel assume the role of the expert whose main purpose is to cure or fix the problem, but families have provided abundant stories about insensitive doctors and other professionals in these settings. Medical training has not provided trainees with the skills necessary to implement family-centered care. As one physician stated:

> Medical students' success is measured almost exclusively on how they perform on standardized tests of knowledge. Deductive reasoning and problem-solving is not always taught formally. Students trained in this particular scientific/data paradigm approach a child or a parent using the perspectives they were taught: collect data and use it to make a diagnosis, then recall the accepted therapeutic interventions and apply them. (Sharp & Lohr, p. 75)

Fortunately, many medical training programs have now added family-centered care as part of their training curriculum. The American Academy of Pediatrics has issued guidelines for physicians participating in the Individualized Family Service Plan. Today, many health care workers also participate on the statewide Interagency Coordinating Council (ICC).

The Developmental Perspective

The training received by service providers in both education and the allied health professions in early intervention is based on theories of the stages of development. Arnold Gesell, a psychologist in the early part of the twentieth century, linked the growth of physical and cognitive abilities to the stages in a linear model of development (Gesell & Amatruda, 1941).

Piaget (1962) followed with a model that also showed children gaining increasingly complex cognitive concepts in stages. In the early years, those stages are the sensorimotor stage (birth to 18 months) and the preoperational stage (1½ to 4½ years). Piaget believed that the infant learned through exploration and play. His work formed the basis for much of the research on the sensorimotor period.

The developmental perspective is reflected in recommended practices in early childhood today. Children are viewed as active learners who gather knowledge from physical, social, and cultural experiences to construct their understanding of the world around them (NAEYC, 1996).

Most of the curriculum that has been subsequently developed for infants and toddlers applies developmental milestones in the development of activities for young children. These milestones are further discussed in Chapters 3 and 4. Although milestones are very useful for describing typical development and form the basis for understanding atypical development, they should not be rigidly applied to instruction for every infant and toddler. In Vignette 1.3, Michelle teaches her service providers a lesson along these lines.

VIGNETTE 1.3   LEARNING FROM MICHELLE
Michelle was a 15-month-old with biliary atresia. Michelle had learned to sit at the age of 12 months and showed an interest in standing at 15 months. Following a developmental milestone guide, the occupational therapist and the teacher thought it would be a good idea to help Michelle learn to crawl. However, whenever Michelle was placed in a crawl position she would cry out in pain and agitation. One day, Michelle was playing on a mat when she saw a toy of interest on a low shelf. The teacher observed Michelle's attempts to pull herself to a stand (a higher skill on the milestone chart). In the next team meeting, the teacher and the occupational therapist realized that due to her illness, Michelle was never likely to crawl, but she could pull herself up to stand and cruise. Within a month, Michelle was standing at the low shelf and cruising to retrieve toys placed slightly out of reach.

The Behavioral Perspective

Special educators are most familiar with the behavioral approach, largely through the work of B. F. Skinner (1904–90) on operant conditioning, which continues to be used today. According to this approach, the service provider examines the antecedent events and the consequences related to a behavior, and then applies direct instruction and reinforcement to change the behavior (Zirpoli & Melloy, 2001).

The different approaches to early childhood are reflected by comparing the orientation of professionals who work in regular and special early childhood education. For example, service providers working with children in early childhood centers provide services that are typically more child-oriented and follow the child's lead. On the other hand, children in early childhood special education may experience a more structured approach to instruction based on behavior modification.

For infants and toddlers, these diverse practices may be less of an issue than for older preschool-age children, particularly in segregated, center-based programs. However, it is important to realize that service providers may have philosophical differences in both training and practice.

The Ecological Perspective

Greenspan and Meisels (1995) have provided the following explanation of the theoretical basis of the ecological perspective of development:

Related to the interactivity among areas of development is the fact that both biological and environmental influences operate to support, facilitate, or impede the
development of infants and young children. (p. 2)

Bronfenbrenner (1979) introduced an ecological model for understanding
the influences that shape human development. He identified four systems that
interact to affect the family both positively and negatively: the microsystem, the
mesosystem, the exosystem, and the macrosystem. The *microsystem* consists of the
child's immediate environment. For the young child, this would include people,
objects, and events in his or her natural environment, including family members,
peers, neighbors, etc. The microsystem lends support to the child in meeting his or
her physical, cognitive, and emotional needs. Consider the story of Mariam
Wright Edelman in the following vignette:

VIGNETTE 1.4   COMMUNITY SUPPORT
I went everywhere with my parents and was under the watchful eye
of members of the congregation and community who were my
extended parents. They kept me when my parents went out of town,
they reported on and chided me when I strayed from the straight and
narrow of community expectations, and they basked in and supported
my achievements when I did well. (Edelman, 1992, p. 4)

For Edelman, her family and her community provided the safety net she
needed to develop as a child. Think of all the children who have no safety net;
these may include many children with developmental disabilities.

When the microsystem is unable to meet the needs of the child, for whatever
reason, it becomes a source of developmental risk. Researchers have identified
several factors that put a young child at risk developmentally, including caregiver
mental health, attitude and anxiety, education and occupation, and reduced family support (Sameroff & Fiese, 1990; Sameroff & Seifer; Werner & Smith, 1989).
For example, consider the recent research that indicates children prenatally
exposed to substance abuse are additionally at risk due to ongoing environmental
factors such as continued substance abuse, domestic violence, and poverty (Griffith, Azuma, & Chasnoff, 1994).

The *mesosystem* is composed of the interactions between various microsystems, for example, the interactions between the home and child care setting,
or the home and community settings. Interactions that are positive and supportive, such as frequent, supportive contact between the family and service
providers, will help the child grow in all developmental areas. Interactions that
are negative or confusing for the family will have a negative impact on the infant
or toddler.

The *exosystem*—settings that indirectly influence the child—can have a positive or negative impact on the child's microsystems and mesosystems (Zirpoli,
1995). For example, when a parent's workplace provides on-site child care that is
a nurturing environment and meets the family needs, the child will also experience a positive sense of well-being that fosters growth and development.

Finally, the *macrosystem* is represented by the ideological and institutional beliefs of a particular society. Today our society increasingly values and supports persons with disabilities. It is now more common to see such individuals in all aspects of modern life (e.g., in the media, in advertisements, etc.). Not long ago, our society did not value persons who were different from the mainstream. Many with a disability or mental illness were institutionalized and not seen in the public arena. The macrosystem influences all of the other interaction systems, and can change as society and values change.

SUMMARY

This chapter introduced the field of early intervention for infants and toddlers. Over the last two decades, federal and state legislation has ensured quality early intervention services, as the emphasis on the role of the family and service coordination has led to many changes in service delivery. The interagency collaboration in birth-to-three services has made this field unique in its approach to comprehensive family-centered care.

An understanding of the family from a systems perspective will enable service providers to approach families as partners in the education and development of their young children. Flexibility is the key in working with families who are experiencing stress. It is also an attribute of families who can adapt to new stresses and demands in an appropriate way. Open communication with families will allow professionals to understand the family dynamics and individual differences that are part of each family. Families who are supported are more likely to respond to intervention services in a meaningful way.

Families experiencing a new diagnosis or the birth of a child with a disability respond differently to the situation. Some rely on prior coping strategies for dealing with a crisis. Some pull together; others fall apart. Families also vary in their initial response to services from the early intervention team. It may be helpful to give families more time before introducing services, but this should be a family decision. Eligibility requirements vary in each state, although general guidelines are required through federal legislation.

The IFSP is the hallmark of recent legislation in early intervention. This document is family-centered and includes information given by the family on what they perceive to be the priorities for services. The IFSP must include a statement by the family that addresses what they see as strengths and concerns relating to the development of the child. However, it may be that families do not wish to complete this statement, and they should have the opportunity to refuse to do so. Due to prior negative experiences with authorities or other service providers, some families may need time before a sense of trust is established. A service coordinator can help the family organize the many different services and agencies that will play a role in their lives. Characteristics of helpful service coordinators include the ability to build rapport, gather information, and maintain a positive proactive attitude. Service coordinators provide the link between the early intervention program, other agencies, and the transition to early childhood classrooms.

An important consideration in times of budget cuts and shrinking resources is whether early intervention is effective. The field of early intervention remains divided on whether early intervention is effective for all children. Much of the current legislation was passed without a substantial research basis. One issue in the research is whether it makes sense to look beyond statistical analysis for evidence of positive effects. More and more researchers are using qualitative analysis, including interviews and observations, to address questions of efficacy in early intervention.

When providing early intervention services, we should be aware of the influence of environmental benefits and constraints on the child and family. Bronfenbrenner's (1979) model enables us to view the child and family within the framework of both internal and external influences.

REFERENCES

Bailey, D. B. (1989). Case management in early intervention. *Journal of Early Intervention, 13,* 120–134.

Bailey, D. B., & Blasco, P. M. (1990). Parents' perspectives on a written survey of family needs. *Journal of Early Intervention, 14,* 196–203.

Bailey, D. B., Blasco, P. M., & Simeonsson, R. (1992). Needs expressed by mothers and fathers of young children with disabilities. *American Journal on Mental Retardation, 97,* 1–10.

Blacher, J. (1984). Sequential stages of adjustment to the birth of a child with handicaps/Fact or artifact? *Mental Retardation, 22,* 55–68.

Blasco, P. M., & Pearson, J. (1995). Working with families. In T. J. Zirpoli (Ed.), *Understanding and affecting the behavior of young children* (pp. 219–241). Englewood Cliffs, N.J.: Merrill.

Bronfenbrenner, U. (1979). *The ecology of human development.* Cambridge, Mass.: Harvard University Press.

Brunim, I. A. (1990). *Strengthening the roles of families in states' early intervention systems: Policy guide to procedural safeguards for infants, toddlers, and their families.* Washington, D.C.: Mental Health Law Project, and Reston, Va.: Division for Early Childhood of the Council for Exceptional Children.

Dinnebeil, L. A., & Rule, S. (1994). Variables that influence collaboration between parents and service coordinators. *Journal of Early Intervention, 18,* 349–361.

Division for Early Childhood, Council for Exceptional Children. (1998). *Position statement on services for children birth to age eight with special needs.* Denver, Colo.: Author.

Drotar, D., Baskiewicz, A., Irvin, N., Kennell, J., & Klaus, M. (1975). The adaptation of parents to the birth of an infant with a congenital malformation: A hypothetical model. *Pediatrics, 56,* 710–716.

Dunst, C. J., & Trivette, C. M. (1989). An enabling and empowerment perspective of case management. *Topics in Early Childhood Special Education, 8,* 87–102.

Early Intervention Program for Infants and Toddlers with Disabilities, 34 C.F.R. 303 (1999, July 1).

Edelman, M. W. (1992). *The measure of our success: A letter to my children and yours.* Boston, Mass.: Beacon Press.

Essa, E. (1999). *Introduction to early childhood education* (3rd ed.). Albany, N.Y.: Delmar.

Farran, D. C., Metzger, J., & Sparling, J. (1986). Immediate and continuing adaptations in parents of handicapping children. In J. Gallagher & P. Vietze (Eds.), *Families of handicapped persons* (pp. 143–163). Baltimore: Paul H. Brookes.

Gesell, A., & Amatruda, C. (1941). *Developmental diagnosis.* New York: Harper.

Glisczinski, C. P. (1995). *Family-focused early intervention: One family's experience.* Unpublished master's thesis. St. Paul, Minn.: University of St. Thomas.

Greenspan, S. I., & Meisels, S. (1995). Toward a new vision for the developmental assessment of infants and young children. *Zero to Three, 14,* 1–8.

Griffith, D. R., Azuma, S. D., & Chasnoff, I. J. (1994). Three-year outcome of children exposed prenatally to drugs. *Journal of the American Academy of Child and Adolescent Psychiatry, 33,* 20–27.

Guzmán, G., and Guzmán, L. (1992, June). Reflecting on the strengths of the IFSP. *Arc Light: A publication of the Association for Retarded Citizens* (pp. 1–3).

Hausslein, E., Kaufmann, R., and Hurth, J. (1992, February). From case management to service coordination: Families, policymaking, and Part H. *Zero to three, 3,* 10–13.

Head Start Bureau. (1999, November 19). *1999 Head Start fact sheet* [On-Line]. Available: http://www2.acf.dhhs.gov/programs/hsb/research/99_hsfs.htm

Lynch, E. W., and Hanson, M. J. (Eds.). (1992). *Developing cross-cultural competence: A guide for working with young children and their families.* Baltimore: Paul H. Brookes.

McGonigel, M. J. (1991). Philosophy and conceptual framework. In M. J. McGonigel, R. K. Kaufmann, & B. H. Johnson (Eds.), *Guidelines and recommended practices for the individualized family service plan* (pp. 7–14). Bethesda: Association for the Care of Children's Health.

Minuchin, P. (1988). Relationships within the family: A systems perspective. In R. A. Hinde & J. Stevenson-Hinde (Eds.), *Relationships within the families* (2nd ed., pp. 7–26). New York: Oxford University Press.

NAEYC (1996). *Position statement on developmentally appropriate practice in early childhood programs serving children from birth through age 8.* Washington, D.C.: Author.

National Head Start Association. (1999). *Head Start* [On-line]. Available: www.nhsa.org.

Olson, D. H., McCubbin, H. I., Barnes, H., Larsen, A., Muxem, M., & Wilson, M. (1989). *Families: What makes them work* (2nd ed.). Los Angeles: Sage.

Peterson, N. L. (1987). *Early intervention for handicapped and at-risk children.* Denver: Love.

Piaget, J. (1962). *Play, dreams, and imitation in childhood.* New York: Norton.

Rosenblith, J. F. (1992). *In the beginning: Development from conception to age two* (2nd ed.). Newbury Park, Calif.: Sage.

Sameroff, A. J., & Fiese, B. H. (1990). Transactional regulation and early intervention. In S. J. Meisels & J. P. Shonkoff (Eds.), *Handbook of early childhood intervention* (pp. 119–149). New Rochelle, N.Y.: Cambridge University Press.

Sameroff, A. J., & Seifer, R. (1990). Early contributors to developmental risks. In J. Roth, A. S. Masten, D. Cicchetti, K. H. Nuechterlein, & Weintaub, S. (Eds.), *Risk and protective factors in the development of psychopathology* (pp. 52–60). New York: Cambridge University Press.

Schweinhart, L. J., & Weikert, D. P. (1981). Effects of the Perry Preschool Program on youths through age 15. *Journal of the Division for Early Childhood, 4,* 29–39.

Shackelford, J. (1998). *State and jurisdictional eligibility definitions for infants and toddlers with disabilities under IDEA.* Chapel Hill, N.C.: NECTAS.

Sharp, M. C., & Lohr, J. A. (1994). The nature of teaching hospitals. In S. L. Hostler (Ed.), *Family-centered care: An approach to implementation* (pp. 71–88). Charlottesville: University of Virginia, Kluge Children's Rehabilitation Center.

Solnit, A., & Stark, M. (1961). Mourning and the birth of a defective child. *The Psychoanalytic Study of the Child, 16,* 523–537.

Turnbull, A. P., Summers, J. A., & Brotherson, M. J. (1984). *Working with families with disabled members: A family systems approach.* Lawrence, Kans.: University of Kansas.

Turnbull, A. P., & Turnbull, H. R. (1990). *Families, professionals, and exceptionality: A special partnership* (2nd ed.). Columbus, Ohio: Merrill.

Werner, E. E., & Smith, R. S. (1989). *Vulnerable but invincible: A longitudinal study of resilient children and youth.* New York: Adams, Bannister, & Cox.

Zigler, E., & Muenchow, S. (1992). *Head Start: The inside story of America's most successful educational experiment.* New York: Basic Books.

Zirpoli, T. J. (1995). Framework for understanding and affecting behavior. In T. J Zirpoli (ed.), *Understanding and affecting the behavior of young children* (pp. 2–33). Englewood Cliffs, N.J.: Merrill.

Zirpoli, T. J. & Melloy, K. J. (2001). *Behavior managment: Applications for teachers* (3rd ed.). Upper Saddle River, N.J.: Merrill.

CHAPTER TWO

THE PRENATAL PERIOD: BEGINNING THE JOURNEY

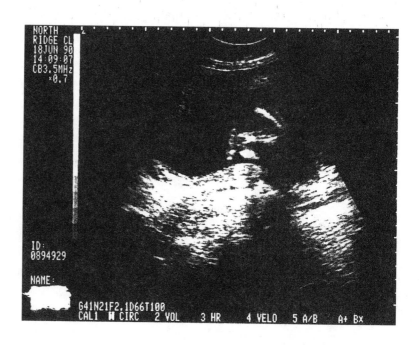

OBJECTIVES

- To understand the process of conception and development during the prenatal period
- To discuss the importance of prenatal development in terms of behavioral state and future development
- To understand the influence of the prenatal environment and the consequences for future development
- To understand the role of parents/caregivers during pregnancy
- To understand the process of prenatal diagnosis and the implications for families expecting a child with disabilities
- To explore the advent of gene therapy and implications of genetic engineering in the twenty-first century
- To discuss intervention strategies during the prenatal period, including planning for a difficult birth and dealing with grief and loss
- To understand ethical issues involving prenatal diagnosis

THE PRENATAL PERIOD

In recent years, there has been a growing interest in the impact of the fetal environment on later development (Graves, 1989). The hypothesis that fetuses prepare themselves for the next environment is not new. However, the increasing number of research articles demonstrating the competence of the newborn has refueled the issue in the last decade. During prebirth growth and development, first the embryo and then the fetus begins a process of growth and development analogous to life after birth.

In an attempt to understand this process, O'Leary (1992) related the prenatal experience to the neurological stages of development across the lifespan, as originally described by Gesell, which can be applicable to behavior. Beginning with conception, the fetus's development follows an orderly progression, with each stage achieving a new level of maturation. The end product of this process (the baby) is the result of the continuing reciprocity between the influences of nature (genetic endowment) and nurture (the prenatal environment).

During the prenatal period, the fetus moves through six stages of equilibrium and disequilibrium. The *smooth stage* prepares the intrauterine environment for conception as well as the birth. The *break-up stage* is characterized by the formation of all body cells in the fetus. At this point, the mother is undergoing tremendous psychological and physical changes. In the *sorting-out stage*, the fetus begins to move through flexion and extension and to explore the uterine environment. For example, by 20 weeks the fetus can hear sounds transmitted through the uterus and recognizes auditory stimuli. The mother is thinking about changes in her lifestyle. She might consider changes in her work, social life, and home life. The fetus settling into a mutually reciprocal relationship with the

TABLE 2.1   Developmental Cycles of Parenting During "Normal" Pregnancy

PHASES OF CYCLE	SMOOTH CONCEPTION	BREAK-UP BLASTOCYTE–12 WEEKS	SORTING OUT 12–24 WEEKS
Caplan's psychological tasks		Acceptance of Pregnancy Emotional affiliation with baby	
Fetal physiology	Conception	All organ systems forming & differentiate Most vulnerable to adversity	Rapid growth Placental functions in relationship with mother
Fetal behavior baby	Potential	**Energy:** Baby forming into who she is; reflex actions more differentiated **Mouth:** Opens; jaws snap rapidly **Fingers:** Close incompletely **Body:** Generalized movement **Extremity:** Isolated arm or leg movement **Eyes:** Move	Grasp with hands Sucks and swallows Coordinated hand to mouth movements Reacts to sounds Limb movements both reciprocal & symmetric Breathes
Maternal physiology	Ovulation & conception	Implantation HCG rises Progesterone, estrogen rise Breast size increases Fatigue	Quickening Placenta functions Becomes used to pregnancy Looks pregnant Fewer disruptive symptoms
Behavior and psychosocial partner and family	Calm, satisfied, & in harmony with body & environment Uncertain, variable	Oppositional At odds with self and environment Emotional roller coaster Ambivalence Own family background resurfaces	Temporary What fits? Seeking out other people & support Discover & explore Problem solving Time of questioning Mother sorts uterine contractions from baby movements Prepare financially Dream Prenatal Testing

From "The Parenting Process in the Prenatal Period: A Developmental Theory" by J. O'Leary, 1992, *Pre & Perinatal Psychology*, 7(2), 113–123. Reprinted by permission.

INWARDIZING 24–32 WEEKS	EXPANSION 32 WEEKS LABOR/BIRTH	"NEUROTIC" FITTING TOGETHER PP–4 WEEKS
	Perception of baby as separate individual	
Baby assumes fetal position Growth spurt Fetal heart rate (FHR) reacts to activity	Lungs mature Settles into mother's pelvis	Transition from fetal circulation to extrauterine life re: resp, HR, temp
Movements strong Pattern of movement Grasp nearly sufficient to support baby	Consciousness more closely defined after 38 weeks Sleep/awake cycles; awake longer Stretch & extend limbs with contractions Hearing more acute Much more aware of intrauterine life Competence increases	Copes with gravity; still flexed and mobile Shuts down if unfamiliar sounds Needs soft light Slow pace to see & hear together Movements more purposeful & less reflexive
Abdominal size & weight increase Notices fetal movements, uterine contractions	Uterine contractions, blood volume increase Cervical ripening Labor and birth	Involution Lochia Lactation Maternal hormones decrease
Restriction of view Work with parts to create new whole Introspective Concentrates energy on child within Can feel left out May distance self Seek help to affiliate with baby Fewer people around, not future oriented	New energy burst "Nesting" Prepares for birth, ready for birth class, ready to release baby to outside Seeks safe place & people to birth with	Emotional Sleep deprived Identity change: "Mom" & "Dad", not couple Let baby lead into roles

intrauterine environment characterizes the *inwardizing stage*. The fetus continues to gain weight and moves down toward the pelvis. The parent(s) start childbirth classes, and may decrease their social and work activities. During the *expansion stage*, the fetus becomes more active by stretching and expanding its body and, in turn, helps the uterus prepare for the impending birth, when the baby pushes and expands as she moves through the birth canal. (The mother who has a cesarean section experiences the expansion stage prior to the actual birth.) Finally, in the "neurotic," or fitting-together stage, the baby learns to adapt to external stimuli through six stages of consciousness. She is ready to eat, having practiced sucking and, in many cases, swallowing in utero. She learns to adjust to seeing and hearing in this new environment. The mother experiences the emotional impact of the baby who seeks out her parents with her eyes and knows their voices.

As this framework demonstrates, the baby takes the lead in the interactive ballet at the beginning of life. The pattern appears to be the same for all fetuses, regardless of later disability or medical complication (O'Leary, 1992). Although all families also experience these stages, one must consider individual differences and recognize that different families respond differently to similar events.

THE BEGINNING OF THE BIRTH PROCESS

From the very beginning, as a fertilized egg forms into a human being, the sequenced steps that occur are important for understanding the many disabilities that are possible as well as preventable. Basic to understanding conception is the fact that the male sperm contains 23 chromosomes that combine with the 23 chromosomes from the female. Therefore, the fertilized egg contains 46 chromosomes. Except for the sex chromosomes (X and Y), all other chromosomes are paired. The single-cell egg undergoes a process of successive cell divisions, and certain mishaps may occur when the cell divides. For example, if there is an extra number 21 chromosome, the child will have Down syndrome. With a procedure known as karyotyping, scientists are able to determine when cell division has been problematic by observing under a microscope the characteristics of chromosomes in terms of size, shape, and banding pattern (Batshaw, 1997).

INFLUENCES OF THE PRENATAL ENVIRONMENT ON DEVELOPMENT: TERATOGENS

Teratogens are agents such as infections, drugs, radiation, environmental pollutants, and chronic illness in the mother that lead to disruptions in fetal development (Graham & Morgan, 1997). Table 2.2 lists a number of teratogenic agents. The degree to which the fetus is affected depends on the timing and intensity of

TABLE 2.2   Teratogenic Agents

TERATOGEN	EXAMPLES
Drugs	Thalidomide, valproic acid, phenytoin
Environmental chemicals	Mercury
Radiation	X rays
Viruses	Rubella
Mechanical pressure	Amniotic band syndrome
Immobility (i.e., paralysis from a variety of causes)	Arthrogryposis multiplex congenita
Intrauterine environmental factors	Maternal phenylketonuria (PKU) Maternal diabetes Maternal fever

Courtesy of Peter A. Blasco, Oregon Health Sciences University, Portland.

contact. Since most of the human organs are formed between 10 and 60 days post-conception, this is generally the most vulnerable time for the fetus (Batshaw, 1997). In addition, teratogens are one of the leading causes for developmental disabilities, particularly mental retardation, hearing loss, and vision loss (Graham & Morgan, 1997; Roizen & Johnson, 1996).

Infectious Diseases

While parents may devote time and resources to providing a prenatal environment conducive to optimal growth and development, no one can be absolutely certain that the fetus is safe from viral infection. Viral diseases usually affect approximately 5 percent of pregnant women (Rosenblith, 1992). A woman can contract a disease while she is pregnant or become pregnant when she is already infected. In the past, the most common congenital infections of the fetus and the newborn were known as the "TORCHS": *TO*xoplasmosis, *R*ubella, *C*ytomegalovirus, *H*erpes, and *S*yphilis. The number of disorders has expanded, as outlined below, but this acronym is often used by health care workers as an abbreviation for any or all congenital infections. (See Table 2.3.)

Toxoplasmosis.   *Toxoplasma gondii* is a fairly common parasite that can produce the disease known as toxoplasmosis, which is asymptomatic in adults but is devastating to a developing fetus (Batshaw, 1997). The disease can be transmitted to the adult through eating raw eggs or meat and by unprotected exposure to cat or horse feces (Roizen & Johnson, 1996). Pregnant women may thus want to find a volunteer to change the kitty litter or purchase a self-cleaning litterbox. If the fetus

TABLE 2.3   Congenital Infections

INFECTIOUS DISEASE SYNDROME	CAUSATIVE AGENT	DURATION OF ACTIVE INFECTION	INFECTIVITY RISK TO:	
			Children	*Personnel*
Congenital Toxoplasmosis	Toxoplasma gondii	Ceases with treatment	– (never excretes oocysts) –	
Congenital Rubella Syndrome	Rubella virus	Months postnatal	+	– (should be vaccinated)
Cystomegalic Inclusion Disease	Cytomegalo-virus	? Up to 7 years	+	+/– (See text)
Neonatal Herpes Types 1 and 2	Herpes simplex virus	Indefinite, mostly latent	+ when active lesions present	+/– (requires impossibly intimate contact for type 1 virus)
Congenital Syphilis	Treponema pallidum	Ceases with treatment	+ until treated	+ until treated but requires intimate contact
Varicella Embryopathy	Varicella zoster virus	Lifelong, mostly latent	+	– (should be immune)
HIV Embryopathy	HIV	Lifelong	+/– (requires intimate contact)	

+, high infection risk; –, no infection risk.

becomes infected during the first trimester, the resulting complications are more severe than if the infection occurs in the third trimester.

At birth, there is no obvious sign of the disease in 90 percent of the infants infected with toxoplasmosis. In addition, according to Freij and Sever (as cited in Roizen & Johnson, 1996), a thorough examination yields positive results in only one-third of the infected infants. For those infants who are symptomatic, signs of toxoplasmosis include hydrocephalus, microcephaly, microphthalmia, visual impairment, and central nervous system damage (Roizen & Johnson). Other systemic conditions can include anemia, fever, liver damage, and respiratory distress.

According to Roizen and Johnson, without prenatal or postnatal treatment, 90 percent of those infants who manifested systemic or neurological signs of toxoplasmosis by the first year of life will have residual auditory, cognitive, and/or motor impairments. Treatment prenatally is very promising although controversial. In one study, 35 pregnant women were screened and suspected to be carrying the infection. One woman decided to have an abortion. The fetuses were treated in utero with antibotics (given via the mother) and followed after birth by the medical team. Only one child had symptoms by two months of age (Ghidini, Sirtori, Spelta, & Vergani, 1991); all the other children had typical development.

Rubella.   Rubella, also known as German measles, is an infection that is capable of penetrating the placenta. In the 1960s investigators discovered that when the mother contracted rubella in the first trimester, 15–25 percent of all fetuses would have congenital deafness (Rosenblith, 1992). The time of infection is important in terms of the consequences for the fetus. If the mother contracts rubella within the first 60 days of pregnancy, the fetus is likely to develop cataracts; if she contacts it during the first 11 weeks, heart defects and deafness are likely. In the second trimester, deafness and retina involvement can also occur, but only 10 percent of fetuses are affected (Rosenblith, 1992). Today, most women are vaccinated against rubella; however, a disproportionate number of women from multicultural backgrounds may be at increased risk (Kaplin, Cochi, Edmonds, Zell, & Prelud, 1990).

Cytomegalovirus (CMV).   Cytomegalovirus (CMV) is the most common cause of congenital infection in this country (Grose and Weiner, 1990). Most infected women are unaware that they have the virus. It typically affects the mother's cervix, breasts, and urinary tract (Rosenblith, 1992). The infant most commonly contracts the virus when passing through the birth canal. The leading cause of mental impairment and congenital deafness, CMV resulting in permanent disability occurs in 1 in 5,000 to 1 in 20,000 births (Batshaw, 1997).

Herpes Simplex Virus (HSV).   Herpes simplex virus (HSV) is another infection that is most commonly (85 percent) contracted as the baby moves through the birth canal, although in some cases it is acquired after birth (10 percent) or in utero (5 percent) (Connelly & Stanberry, 1995). Growth delay, skin lesions, retinal abnormalities, and microcephaly are considered warning signs for HSV (Graham & Morgan, 1997). In addition, Roizen and Johnson (1996) believe seizures and fever may be indicative of HSV in infancy. With early detection and treatment, the infant will survive. Unfortunately, of those infants who do survive, half will develop microcephaly, cerebral palsy, seizures, deafness, and blindness.

Recognition of maternal HSV infection prior to delivery is the key to early identification of the at-risk infant and prevention of perinatal (at birth) transmission of the infection. If the medical team suspects maternal HSV, the baby can be delivered via caesarean section in order to avoid exposure to the virus (Roizen & Johnson, 1996).

Varicella Zoster.   The varicella zoster virus is the causative agent of chicken pox. It can persist silently in the host (known as a latent infection) for decades and then reappear as a localized eruption referred to as shingles. Very rarely, the fetus of a woman with active varicella or active zoster can become infected with resultant congenital deformities, usually of the limbs. This is known as the fetal varicella syndrome (Alkalay, Pomerance, & Rimoin, 1987).

Human Immunodeficiency Virus (HIV).   The human immunodeficiency virus (HIV) causes a devastating, progressive, and almost always fatal illness. Until very recently, a pregnant woman with the HIV infection had a 20 percent chance of transmitting the infection to her newborn (Newell & Peckman, 1993; Peckham and Gibb, 1995). In the past five years treatment of the mother with newly developed antiretroviral drugs (Conner et al., 1994) and additional strategies to shield the baby during and after delivery (Rogers & Shaffer, 1999) have decreased the risk of transmission to 5 percent or less. The odds are worse, however, for babies born in underdeveloped countries.

Syphilis.   The agent that causes syphilis (known as a spirochete) can cross the placenta and is likely to infect the fetus in the later stage of pregnancy, after 16 to 18 weeks. It causes injury to many organs and can produce permanent damage. For example, lesions on the cornea can produce scarring and blindness. The infant born with syphilis is likely to be small for gestational age and have chronic liver problems, peritonitis (inflammation of the lining of the abdomen), anemia, and damage to the nervous system (Rosenblith, 1992). For children over two, late indicators of congenital syphilis include Hutchinson teeth (peg-shaped) and blurred vision (Roizen & Johnson, 1996).

If an infected mother is identified during pregnancy, congenital syphilis can be prevented with prenatal antibiotic treatment. However, as with rubella, women from low socioeconomic groups may not receive proper prenatal care, and are at a higher risk for the infection (Roizen & Johnson, 1996).

Radiation

One reason we know that radiation will cause birth defects is that women who had survived the nuclear bombing of Hiroshima and Nagasaki gave birth to children with multiple congenital abnormalities. Again, as with any teratogen, the amount of radiation exposure received during pregnancy makes a significant impact on the degree of disability. Women who were within one and one-quarter miles of the bombing had infants with microcephaly, but those who were outside a two-mile radius had apparently healthy infants, although years later, some developed leukemia (Graham & Morgan, 1997).

At present, scientists are not certain how much radiation is damaging to the fetus. The major concern, of course, is exposure to medically diagnostic X rays. Studies suggest that pregnant women can obtain a routine medical X ray (less than 5 rads) without harming the fetus (Graham & Morgan, 1997). The timing as well as the amount of radiation will determine the fetal effect. During the first month postconception, the embryo will either die as a result of exposure or survive to be a healthy infant. During the second and third months of pregnancy, when the fetus is very sensitive to teratogens, growth retardation is likely to occur. During the fourth and fifth months, the fetus is less sensitive but may still develop microcephaly and eye abnormalities (Graham & Morgan, 1997).

Exposure to radiation has led to concerns among expectant families as well as physicians about other medical procedures and about environmental radiation.

Ultrasound, sound waves that produce a moving image of the fetus, is often used during pregnancy and has proved to be essentially risk free (Blasco, Blasco, and Zirpoli, 1994). Today, most expectant parents carry an ultrasound picture of their future baby or babies to show to friends and family. Similarly, exposure to microwave ovens, radar, radio waves, and emissions from computer screens is apparently harmless (Graham & Morgan, 1997).

Medication and Chronic Illness

One of the most well-known examples of how medication used during pregnancy can affect a fetus occurred with the drug thalidomide, which was prescribed to pregnant women in Europe in the late 1950s and early 1960s to control nausea. Once again, the timing of the exposure resulted in different outcomes. If the mother took the drug between 21 and 35 days postconception, the infant was born with shortened or missing arms. If the drug was taken between days 21 and 30, the infant was born with shortened or missing legs as well as arms. If the mother took the drug more than 35 days postconception, the infant was born healthy (Graham & Morgan, 1997).

Other maternal medications that can affect the fetus include anticonvulsant drugs. For example, women who are on medication for seizure control may risk having children with fetal malformations, particularly cleft lip and palate. Not all women using antiepileptic drugs have children with congenital malformations (only 10–20 percent of children are affected). Women should work with their primary health care provider to determine whether a low dose of the medication is appropriate. Discontinuing medication during pregnancy could put both the mother and child at risk for convulsions (Graham and Morgan, 1997). When treating expectant mothers who require such medication, the medical team must balance the need to control her seizures with the necessity of minimizing possible harm to the fetus (Yerby, 1994).

Vignette 2.1 presents two cases of teratogenic syndromes, one due to a virus and the other to a drug effect.

VIGNETTE 2.1   PRENATAL EVENTS
Alicia was born at 38 weeks gestation to a primigravida woman (her first pregnancy) who had a mild illness in the second month of the pregnancy.

Alicia's mother had developed a rash, low-grade fever, malaise, and some joint aches, lasting 9–10 days. At birth the baby weighed 4 pounds, 3 ounces, and had a small head and a congenital heart defect. Later, it was determined she was deaf, and she had cataracts as well as retinal abnormalities. Developmentally, she made very slow progress and eventually was diagnosed with cerebral palsy, mental retardation, deafness, and visual impairment.

Peter is a three-year-old born at full term to a woman with epilepsy who took the anticonvulsant drug phenytoin (Dilantin) throughout her pregnancy. Peter is proportionally small and has coarse, dark hair. He also has a number of musculoskeletal anomalies, most notably, small fingers with dysplastic nails. Developmentally, he has been consistently delayed to a mild degree with developmental quotients (DQs) in the 60–70 range.

Alicia shows a classic clinical picture of the congenital rubella syndrome, and this diagnosis was confirmed by a blood test that revealed high levels of antibody to the rubella virus. Her mother's illness was typical of German measles; either she had never been vaccinated or had been a vaccine failure. Peter's mother, on the other hand, was required to stay on medication during her pregnancy because of the severe nature of her seizures, although she knew her baby had about a 10 percent risk of acquiring the fetal hydantoin syndrome, which he did develop.

The number of teratogenic syndromes and their clinical manifestations are myriad. The early interventionist, when working with a child with a known syndrome diagnosis, should consult the literature for specific information. The single best resource is *Smith's Recognizable Patterns of Human Malformation* (Jones, 1996). Another superb resource for professionals, and especially for parents, are diagnosis-specific parent support groups, which can be accessed through *Exceptional Parent* magazine.

EMBRYOLOGY AND STRUCTURAL ABNORMALITIES

As discussed earlier, embryology is the study of the formation and development of the embryo, when spectacular changes take place as the single-celled being (known as a zygote) matures until ready for birth. Along the way, damaging events occur that, depending on their timing and nature, can lead to wide-ranging and severe or quite focal and mild structural abnormalities, referred to as malformations, disruptions, and deformations.

Dysmorphology

Physical features that do not conform to standard norms for physical development are referred to as dysmorphisms or anomalies. The condition known as Down syndrome, for example, is associated with multiple dysmorphic features. (In fact, 29 signs have been recognized in the disorder and were the sole basis for diagnosis before chromosome analysis became available (see Jackson, North, & Thomas, 1976). Major malformations are defined as those that require modification, in terms of either ongoing care, or specific surgical or medical intervention, and that will likely alter the child's and family's life in significant ways. Major malformations occur in 2 percent of all newborn infants (Jones, 1996). Usually, they are isolated, such as a hole between the ventricles of the heart (ventricular septal defect).

In contrast, minor anomalies or malformations are morphologic features that are unusual but of no serious medical or cosmetic consequence (Jones, 1996). They are much more common, a single one occurring in 13–27 percent of all individuals. Rarely are they of any functional consequence. Very few children will have more than one minor malformation (1.5 percent), and as the number of minor anomalies increases to three or beyond, the likelihood of associated major anomalies becomes extremely high. The analysis of dysmorphic features falls to the specialties known as genetics and dysmorphology. These categories are discussed in detail in Chapter 8.

Syndromes

When a collection of malformations, major and minor, appear repeatedly together, the particular pattern is referred to as a syndrome. Examples would include Down syndrome, the congenital rubella syndrome noted above, and so on. Syndromes are considered to have a single, specific cause. Numerous specific syndromes have been identified. Many, but not all, have been named and each year new ones are added to the list.

Cellular and Molecular Genetics

In contrast to teratogens, which produce damage in what otherwise would have been a normal structure, some structural anomalies evolve naturally as a consequence of missing, altered, or even excessive genetic material in our cells. Thus, abnormal genes provide the code for the features of a given disorder. The best-known "inherited" genetic syndromes are those associated with extensive chromosome abnormalities: Down syndrome (chromosome 21 trisomy), Turner syndrome (X chromosome monosomy), and cri du chat syndrome (chromosome 5 partial deletion). Large numbers of genes are involved in these disorders.

Single-gene disorders involve only a tiny, localized portion of a chromosome and are generally inherited according to certain principles, known as Mendel's laws. Most disorders are either recessive or dominant in terms of their inheritance pattern. Since 44 of our 46 chromosomes are paired (the X and Y chromosomes that determine sex are a mismatch), each gene is represented twice in a normal cell—once on a maternally derived chromosome and once on the complementary paternally derived chromosome. If a defective gene is transmitted in a recessive fashion, it is merely silent, with the gene from the other parent supplying adequate amounts of whatever protein is needed. Recessive genes generally code for enzymes, and only one gene will produce enough enzyme for the cellular machinery to work. For the occurrence of the disorder, *both* recessive genes, that is, one from each parent, must be defective. In contrast, dominant genes usually code for a structural protein. In that case, some proportion of the body cell structure will contain protein derived from the defective gene, and, therefore, those areas will be weakened or disrupted. This is likely to have clinical consequences, sometimes severe, sometimes mild. Examples of dominatingly inherited disorders would include the Marfan syndrome, achondroplasia, and neurofibromatosis.

VIGNETTE 2.2   GENETIC TRAITS

At the turn of the twentieth century, the ruling family of Russia were the Romanovs, headed by Tsar Nicholas II and Tsarina Alexandra. Alexandra's grandmother was Queen Victoria of England, who carried the gene for hemophilia. Alexandra was one of eight children born to Victoria; her older sister was also a carrier, and one brother had the disease. Nicholas and Alexandra produced five children: four girls and one boy, Alexis, who is perhaps the most famous hemophiliac in history. It was Alexis's disease that brought his mother under the spell of the unscrupulous Rasputin, to whom she turned for spiritual guidance. His influence on Alexandra and the rest of the royal family was one of the key factors leading to the Russian Revolution and the end of the Russian monarchy in the early 1900s.

Genes located on the X chromosome constitute a special situation. Since males only have one X chromosome, a "recessive" gene abnormality on that chromosome would actually be expressed in males, because they, unlike women, have no second X to supply a functional gene. These disorders are referred to as X-linked (or sex-linked) conditions (see Vignette 2.2). The defective gene must come from the mother (who supplies the X for her sons, with the Y coming from the father). The mother, as a rule, is a silent carrier of X-linked recessive conditions. Since she has two X chromosomes, one normal and one with the gene that is defective, each male offspring has a 50-50 chance of having the disorder, whereas each female offspring has a 50-50 chance of being a carrier. Dominant X-linked conditions are generally fatal in males, with death occurring during gestation or very soon after birth. Females with dominant X-linked conditions may express them to a mild degree (and, therefore, be able to reproduce) or to a severe degree.

Many genetic phenomena, however, are not explained by Mendelian inheritance. These mechanisms of non-Mendelian genetic inheritance—mosaicism, uniparental disomy, genomic imprinting, and others—get quite complicated. Blizzard (1993) and Austin and Hall (1992) provide concise reviews of genetic textbooks. In many diseases (e.g., pyloric stenosis, diabetes mellitus) and some syndromes and birth defects (e.g., spina bifida, cleft palate), genes play a partial role in concert with other noninherited (i.e., environmental) factors. This situation is commonly referred to as multifactorial inheritance.

Prenatal diagnosis, which is discussed in greater depth later in the chapter, takes advantage of the known genetic facts about a given situation and applies them to the unborn fetus in an effort to predict abnormalities. Recent developments in the use of prenatal diagnosis have the potential to affect the incidence of certain genetic disorders, the psychological well-being of future parents, and the social and moral standards of society.

THE FUNCTIONING FETUS

The sequence of events that occur once the embryo is formed continues to have implications for the fetus. Although we expect a pregnancy to follow a certain developmental progression, few viewed the fetus as an active partner in that progression. Examining the role of the fetus as a functioning, sensory organism is a new critical frontier in early development. One week after conception, the fertilized egg attaches itself to the uterine wall in a process known as implantation (Batshaw, 1997). The uterine wall provides nutritional support for the developing embryo (Rosenblith, 1992). By three weeks, a primitive placenta develops and increases the flow of nutrition to the embryo. At three weeks to one month, the embryo begins to develop a nervous system when the outermost layer of cells, the primitive neurectoderm, folds over on itself to form the neural tube. A defect in this process may result in an opening in the spine. Myelomeningocele occurs when the spinal column and surrounding membranes form a pouch extending from the opening in the spine (Wolraich, 1992). The medical and educational implications of this condition and related conditions will be discussed in Chapter 8.

Around the fifth week, the heart begins to form and limb buds are formed. At eight to ten weeks, the six pharyngeal arches in the facial structure will join to form the lips, palate, and mandible. If these arches do not completely fuse, the child will have cleft lip and/or cleft palate. By the second month, the embryo begins to look like a human being. The term *fetus* is now used to describe the growing baby. The heart is beating and blood is circulating through the body and muscles. This is a period of rapid brain growth. Between three and six months the fetus continues to grow and develop. By week 35 of pregnancy, the fetus can tell the difference between dark and light. At this stage, 50 percent of fetuses have mature lungs. During weeks 35 and 36, the fetus is busy gaining weight. The eyes are open, and the irises are a deep blue. The fingernails reach to the ends of the fingers. The baby will attempt to descend into the pelvis area and fit its head snugly into the birth channel. From weeks 37 to 40, the baby continues to put on weight, sometimes up to an ounce a day. The fingernails have surpassed the fingertips and will need to be cut after delivery. Figure 2.1 provides an overview of fetal growth from conception to birth.

Fetal Movement

? Cause for concern is no or minimal movement?

Most pregnant women will experience the first fetal movement, called quickening, by the sixteenth week of gestation. However, the fetus is able to show reflexive movement between 10 and 11 weeks gestation. For example, a fetus will respond to a touch stimulus in the palm of the hand; these early reflexive movements continue into postnatal life. By 15–16 weeks, the fetus will respond orally to stimulation similar to the postnatal sucking reflex. The fetus will move and change position frequently between 10 and 15 weeks. By the fifth month of pregnancy, almost all mothers will feel the movement of the fetus regularly. Over the

AGE weeks	LENGTH cm.		WT. gm.	GROSS APPEARANCE	CNS	EYE, EAR	FACE, MOUTH	CARDIO-VASCULAR	LUNG
	C-R	Tot.							
7½	2.8				Cerebral hemisphere Infundibulum, Rathke's	Lens nearing final shape	Palatal swellings Dental lamina, Epithel.	Pulmonary vein into left atrium	
8	3.7				Primitive cereb. cortex Olfactory lobes Dura and pia mater	Eyelid Ear canals	Nares plugged Rathke's pouch detach. Sublingual gland	A-V bundle Sinus venosus absorbed into right auricle	Pleuroperitoneal canals close Bronchioles
10	6.0				Spinal cord histology Cerebellum	Iris Ciliary body Eyelids fuse Lacrimal glands Spiral gland different	Lips, nasal cartilage Palate		Laryngeal cavity reopened
12	8.8				Cord-cervical & lumbar enlarged, Cauda equina	Retina layered Eye axis forward Scala tympani	Tonsillar crypts Cheeks Dental papilla	Accessory coats, blood vessels	Elastic fibers
16	14				Corpora quadrigemina Cerebellum prominent Myelination begins	Scala vestibuli Cochlear duct	Palate complete Enamel and dentine	Cardiac muscle condensed	Segmentation of bronchii complete
20						Inner ear ossified	Ossification of nose		Decrease in mesenchyme Capillaries penetrate linings of tubules
24		32	800		Typical layers in cerebral cortex Cauda equina at first sacral level		Nares reopen Calcification of tooth primordia		Change from cuboidal to flattened epithelium Alveoli
28		38.5	1100		Cerebral fissures and convolutions	Eyelids reopen Retinal layers complete Perceive light			Vascular components adequate for respiration
32		43.5	1600	Accumulation of fat		Auricular cartilage	Taste sense		Number of alveoli still incomplete
36		47.5	2600						
38		50	3200		Cauda equina, at L-3 Myelination within brain	Lacrimal duct canalized	Rudimentary frontal maxillary sinuses	Closure of: foramen ovale ductus arteriosus umbilical vessels ductus venosus	
First postnatal year +					Continuing organization of axonal networks Cerebrocortical function, motor coordination Myelination continues until 2-3 years	Iris pigmented, 5 months Mastoid air cells Coordinate vision, 3-5 months Maximal vision by 5 years	Salivary gland ducts become canalized Teeth begin to erupt 5-7 months Relatively rapid growth of mandible and nose	Relative hypertrophy left ventricle	Continue adding new alveoli

FIGURE 2.1   Fetal Development

From *Recognizable Patterns of Human Malformation,* 3rd ed., by D. W. Smith & K. L. Jones, 1982, Philadelphia: W. B. Saunders, inside front cover. Reprinted by permission.

course of the next four months, family members and others may be encouraged to feel for the baby.

Although fetal movement patterns vary from individual to individual, all fetuses demonstrate movement throughout the latter stages of pregnancy (Loman, 1994). Researchers who have studied fetal movements describe the rhythms and flow of movement as outlined below:

Tension-flow Rhythms. Patterns of tension that may be frequent or infrequent and serve to satisfy the baby's needs. Several of the behaviors observed at birth and during the first year of life, including sucking, biting, twisting, straining, and swaying have roots in prenatal movement (Loman, 1994).

Tension-flow Attributes. Attributes that are related to an individual's temperament, characteristics of arousal, and the ability to calm oneself, which Sossin and Loman (1992, p. 21) have described as qualities of intensity (see Table 2.4).

The quality of parental recognition of and attunement to fetal movement may be a predictor of the later parent-infant attachment. Expectant parents can learn to understand the flow of fetal movement. In one parenting class, mothers drew visual representations of their fetuses' movement on paper. In Vignette 2.3, one mother of twins describes her experience with tuning into her babies.

> **VIGETTE 2.3 WHERE ARE YOU?**
> I saw so many ultrasounds that I knew exactly where both twins were and who had all the room. Andrew, my son, was head down, snugly heading for the birth canal, and his movements were usually long and slow. Caitlin, my daughter, was squished on the left side, and her movements were rapid, quick, and short in duration. When I

TABLE 2.4   Attributes of Tension Flow

1. **Even-flow:** Tension in the fetus is regulated at the same level, suggesting rest, steadiness, and an even temperament.
2. **Flow-adjustment:** Tension in the fetus will adjust to new situations, suggesting an accommodating temperament.
3. **High intensity:** Tension in the fetus becomes extreme, suggesting intense feelings such as joy or anger; indicative of an excitable temperament.
4. **Low intensity:** Tension stays at a moderate level, suggesting low-key behavior and a mild temperament.
5. **Abrupt:** Tension varies rapidly, suggesting impulsivity, impatience, and alertness.
6. **Gradual:** Tension varies but at a slow pace, suggesting patience and endurance.

Adapted from "Attuning to the Fetus and the Young Child: Approaches from Dance Movement Therapy" by S. Loman, 1994, *Zero to Three, 15,* 21.

was placed on bed rest, the nurse would tell me to lie on my left side. Although I knew my position would not affect the babies, I felt like Caitlin was being squished and pushed by her brother. My suspicions were confirmed when they were born; Caitlin weighed one and a half pounds less than her brother did. My obstetrician imitated her arrival into the world by mimicking, "I am here, and I am sick and tired of not having any room and less food, and now you're all going to pay for this!" Caitlin had to stay in the hospital an extra three weeks, as she was born at 3 pounds, 9 ounces. She seemed to be gaining weight steadily and quickly became a favorite with the Newborn nurses. One morning we received a call from the resident on duty. He was very concerned that Caitlin had necrotizing enterocolitis (NEC), a condition that severely damages the small intestine. They would do some tests, but would have to stop all feedings for Caitlin. I arrived to visit her with her brother in his infant seat. She had been screaming all morning and her face was close to purple. She had lost the full cheeks she had gained in the last few days and I was very frightened for her health. I was not allowed to feed her, so I sat and rocked her. She continued to cry and look at me as if to say, "How could you do this to me?" That night, the test showed that she was okay and she could continue to eat again. She has been a feisty, spirited child ever since!

Many parents express knowledge of their baby's environment prior to birth. The enhanced and regular use of ultrasound and other medical technologies has led to an increased parental awareness of the prenatal environment. More and more parents use yoga, music, and sensory inputs in hopes of enhancing later child development. To date, there is no scientific evidence of a link between these methods and later development. However, we know that a prenatal environment free of stress and toxic agents (e.g., drugs, alcohol) is essential for a healthy outcome.

Early Sensory Behaviors

While it may be premature to record with certainty the existence of fetal emotional expression (e.g., crying, facial expressions), early sensory behaviors of the fetus may be indicative of the prenatal roots of ego functions that emerge later in the developed child (Graves, 1989). Facial expressions of happiness, sadness, anger, and disgust are observable very early in life. This has led researchers to believe that they have a strong biological connection to the fetal origins of neural structure (Campos, Barrett, Lamb, Goldsmith, & Stenberg, 1983; Izard & Malatesta, 1987). Research continues to expand our knowledge of fetal neurobehavioral development with the hopes of gaining knowledge of later behavioral development (DiPietro, Hodgson, Costigan, & Hilton, 1996). Whatever the outcome, we know that the newborn enters the world prepared for social contact (Lally et al., 1997).

Maternal and Paternal Contributions

The fetus's nine months of growth is also a time of anxious anticipation and growth for the parents. As mentioned in Chapter 1, society influences the role parents assume as they prepare for the birth of a child. Years ago, most fathers did not actively assist the mother through childbirth. Women often delivered under anesthesia and were pleased to wake up and find the perfect baby waiting for them. Fathers paced in the hospital corridors and passed out cigars with blue or pink bands to announce the birth. All of that changed in the 1970s for the majority of families experiencing childbirth. The revolution toward mutual partnering in childbirth had controversial beginnings, however. In 1976, Klaus and Kennell developed the theory that there is a "critical period" during which the newborn and the mother must bond in order to ensure a healthy developmental future for the baby. Basing their information on a study of mothers and their babies immediately after birth, they claimed that mothers who had more contact time with their infants demonstrated better "mothering skills" than mothers who had less time with their infants. But several researchers disputed these findings, and in 1982 the authors amended their position to extend bonding experiences to fathers and to mothers whose infants were unavailable immediately after birth (e.g., infants in a special care unit) (Klaus & Kennell, 1982).

Despite the controversy over their findings, the researchers' work was very fruitful in that they precipitated an enormous increase in opportunities for parental access to their newborns. Updated birthing rooms, equipped to produce a relaxed environment, replaced sterile maternity units. Families were given the opportunity to be together and to participate in the birth process (Blasco & Pearson, 1995). Unfortunately, with the increase in managed health care and the decrease in the amount of time families can stay in the hospital after the birth of a child, some of these practices may become a thing of the past.

In order to prepare for the event, many parents attend childbirthing classes that help them to understand the changes in both the mother and baby over the nine months of pregnancy. These classes vary in methodology, but generally teach parents breathing exercises and what to do and expect during the delivery. For parents who are anticipating the birth of a child with a disability, these classes may be emotionally difficult, since they are geared toward a typical birth. Also, parents who have had a child with a disability and are expecting the birth of another child may need extra support at this time.

PRENATAL DIAGNOSIS

Years ago, parents were unaware that their child had a disability until birth or during the early childhood years. Now, expectant parents can be largely assured that their developing baby does not have a genetic disorder during the early months of pregnancy (Blasco, Blasco, & Zirpoli, 1994). And if a disability does exist, the ability to have a prenatal diagnosis may give expectant parents more time to seek information and services relating to their child's impairment prior to birth.

Families have a choice of continuing ending the pregnancy after prenatal diagnosis. Whatever the family's decision, service providers should be aware that they need continuing support. If the family decides to end the pregnancy, they may experience feelings similar to those families who suffer the loss of a child. If the parents decide to continue the pregnancy, they will need assistance in preparing for the birth and in locating appropriate community services (Blasco et al., 1994). Because the termination of a pregnancy is considered a medical risk, families may be hurried by the medical team to arrive at a decision in a few days. This kind of pressure can increase stress for all family members. Pauker and Pauker (1994) advocated the use of a decision tree to help families evaluate risks and attitudes toward miscarriage, elective termination, and the birth of a child with a known disability.

Diagnostic Screening

Diagnostic procedures have been refined over the last decade. Yet despite this improvement, expectant couples receive a diagnosis only of the disability, not of its severity. For example, a couple may be told that their expected child will have Down syndrome; however, the extent of the disability, including mental impairment, is not known at the time of the diagnosis. In addition, many known disabilities have several secondary disabilities related to the original disorder (Batshaw, 1997). The extent to which related disabilities may be involved is mostly unknown at the time of initial diagnosis.

Expectant parents who are viewed medically as a high-risk group are likely to be referred for genetic counseling and subsequent prenatal diagnosis. Issues surrounding the invasiveness of screening for parents has not been addressed in the literature. Some parents may not wish to undergo screening because they are considered high risk. In addition, many families are delaying childbirth for personal, financial, and professional reasons. Women over 35 are routinely offered prenatal diagnosis, usually amniocentesis, because of the increased risk for genetic defects in the fetus with increasing maternal age (Haddow, Polomaki, & Knight, 1992). However, many women and their partners are electing to have their first child in their forties and do so without complications. As a result, more and more physicians are questioning the age of 35 as a "magic number" for routine screening (Pauker & Pauker, 1994). In other words, some physicians do not believe maternal age should be the only criterion for prenatal testing.

Prenatal Screening Techniques

Several types of prenatal screening measures are now used on a routine basis. Amniocentesis, usually performed between 14 and 17 weeks of gestation, is probably the most widely known test. The technique involves the insertion of a needle through the abdominal wall into the amniotic fluid surrounding the fetus. Ultrasound is always used during amniocentesis to guide the needle into the uterus. The fluid can be used for specific biochemical tests, and the viable cells floating in it are cultured for chromosomal and DNA studies. Results are available in a few days to a few weeks, depending on the test being done (Batshaw, 1997).

Over 250 genetic disorders can be identified by analyzing amniotic fluid. The risk of miscarriage following this procedure is 0.5 percent, which is the same rate for fetal loss at the same point in gestation (Blasco et al., 1994). Other risks include fetal damage from needle puncture, leakage of amniotic fluid, maternal infection, and premature labor, but these complications are extremely rare.

Chorionic villus sampling (CVS) is a procedure performed between 9 and 11 weeks of gestation. Many families prefer CVS to amniocentesis because it is done earlier in the pregnancy and results are available within a few days. During this procedure, a catheter is inserted through the vagina and threaded into the uterus to the developing placenta using ultrasound guidance. A small sample of placental tissue is removed and placed into culture. Since the cells do not have to grow in a culture for several weeks, preliminary results are usually available in 48 to 72 hours (Blasco et al., 1994). The risk of miscarriage directly related to the CVS procedure (i.e., over and above the expected spontaneous loss rate) has been estimated to be 1 percent or less (Rhoads et al., 1989).

A new avenue for obtaining fetal cells is through the maternal blood (Bianchi, 1995). At present, it is still difficult to distinguish between fetal cells and maternal cells in a blood sample, but as fetal cell isolation techniques are advanced and perfected, the fetal genome will be easily detected (Bianchi, 1995). Fetal cell isolation has advantages over the commonly used procedures because of reduced risk and cost. As more and more women and families are requesting prenatal diagnosis regardless of their risk category, science attempts to keep pace.

Maternal serum alpha fetoprotein (AFP) is a screening test that may be completed prior to amniocentesis, between 16 and 18 weeks gestation. In fact, many physicians are recommending the use of this simple blood test over more invasive procedures if the mother is not high risk (Haddow et al., 1992; Bianchi, 1995). AFP can be measured in the maternal serum or in the amniotic fluid. High levels of AFP in the maternal serum suggest the possibility of a neural tube defect. Approximately 85 percent of such defects and some abdominal wall defects can be found with this simple blood test (Schnatterly, Hogge, and Felder, 1990). A low serum AFP level may be indicative of Down syndrome (Schoenfeld-DiMaio et al., 1987; Hershey, Crandall, & Perdue, 1986) and trisomy 18 (Simpson et al., 1986). Further diagnostic testing is almost always recommended when a positive result is found, because fewer than 10 percent of women with an abnormal serum AFP level are carrying a fetus with a disability (Batshaw, 1997). For example, a high serum AFP level may simply indicate that the mother is carrying twins.

Because AFP levels rise between 13 and 32 weeks, the precise period of gestation must be determined to interpret the results correctly. An over- or underestimated gestation will provide false comparison levels and potentially incorrect findings. The importance of adjusting AFP levels based on maternal weight in order to assign accurate risk status has been emphasized as well (Macri, Kasturi, Krantz, & Koch, 1986). Newer maternal serum markers for chromosome abnormalities are currently being developed and offer promise for much greater diagnostic sensitivity and specificity when combined with maternal serum AFP (Haddow, Palomaki, & Knight, 1992; Bianchi, 1995).

Ultrasound is a commonly known screening technique that can be used as early as two to three weeks conceptional age to identify a successful pregnancy. This procedure transposes reflected sound waves into images of the fetus on a computerlike screen. It is considered to be relatively risk free to both the mother and the fetus. In high-risk cases, it is not uncommon for women to have multiple ultrasound examinations during the course of a pregnancy.

Ultrasound is used for its own diagnostic value and also as a tool in other prenatal procedures. For example, it can be used to measure the length of the fetal femur, which is an excellent indicator of gestational age (Abramowicz, Jaffe, & Warsof, 1989). Ultrasound is used to guide needle insertion during amniocentesis as well as during intrauterine transfusion into an umbilical vessel (Charrow, 1985). It can successfully guide instruments during fetal surgery as well. Ultrasound is also used to identify tubal pregnancy, twins, some disabilities, and gender of the fetus.

Parents who do not want to undergo an invasive procedure that carries some risk, such as CVS or amniocentesis, can have an ultrasound examination between 18 and 22 weeks to confirm obvious structural abnormalities such as microcephaly, hydrocephalus, anencephaly, limb deformity, and spina bifida. Thorp and Bowes (1989) reported that ultrasound examination detected 90 percent of open neural tube defects among a group of parents who would not consider abortion. Another advantage of this procedure is that feedback is instantaneous. Ultrasound has also been used to detect more subtle malformations of internal organs such as cardiac abnormalities, fetal tumors, and fetal hernia (Campbell & Pearce, 1983).

Another technology available for prenatal diagnosis is DNA analysis. For example, developments in gene cloning and gene mapping have resulted in new tests for carrier detection of Mendelian, or monogenic (single-gene) defects (Ostrer, 1989). The first important contribution of prenatal DNA analysis came with the clarification of the gene that causes sickle cell disease (Chueh & Golbus, 1990). Other disorders that can be detected through DNA analysis include cystic fibrosis, Duchenne and Becker muscular dystrophy, myotomic dystrophy, Huntington disease, phenylketonuria (PKU), and Tay-Sachs disease, with the list expanding at a rapid rate. Within the next 15 years, molecular genetic techniques will likely be available for detecting most monogenic disorders (D'Alton & De-Cherney, 1993).

Commercial and university-based laboratories offer diagnosis using DNA techniques. Prior to the test, genetic counseling is advised so that a complete pedigree can identify family members who are at risk. Genomic DNA from any tissue is suitable for analysis. Parents are often requested to provide whole-blood samples (in which case the white cells are utilized) from themselves and their children. A disadvantage of this procedure is that it often requires analysis from multiple individuals to obtain a result. In addition, mothers need to undergo CVS or amniocentesis to provide a sample of cells from the fetus. Research directed at separating fetal cells circulating in the maternal bloodstream may eventually make it possible to substitute a simple maternal venipuncture for the much more invasive procedures (Simpson & Elias, 1993). This will enhance the availability and timeliness of sampling, since special on-site expertise and technology will no longer be necessary.

In Table 2.5, the most common types of prenatal diagnosis are summarized.

Preimplantation Sampling

The latest technique in prenatal screening involves sampling cells from early embryos prior to uterine implantation. With the establishment of in vitro fertilization as a routine technique, it has been demonstrated that it is possible to extract several cells from the developing embryo at the blastomere stage (where no cell differentiation has yet taken place). Rapid DNA amplification and the newest diagnostic techniques can then be applied to these few cells (literally one or two) (Simpson & Carson, 1992). Once the status of several embryos has been determined, the normal ones can be selected for introduction into the mother's uterus in time for implantation. Handyside, Lesko, Tarin, Winston, and Hughes (1992) have reported the successful application of this technique in a family in which both parents were carriers of the gene deletion for cystic fibrosis.

TABLE 2.5   Common Prenatal Screening and Diagnostic Procedures

PROCEDURE	TIMING	RESULTS	RISK	PURPOSE
Ultrasound	Anytime	Immediate	None	Observe fetal structure and growth, placenta and cord
Chorionic villus sampling (CVS)	9–11 weeks	2–3 days	<1%	Chorionic cell analysis
Amniocentesis	14–18 weeks	Fluid 2–3 days Cells 3–4 days	<1%	Amniotic fluid and fetal cell analysis
Maternal serum alpha fetoprotein (AFP)	16–18 weeks	2–3 days	None	Identify possible deformities and chromosome aberrations
DNA analysis (completed after CVS or amniocentesis)	9–18 weeks	Variable*	None	Identify specific genetic disorders
Maternal fetal circulating cells	Anytime	3–4 days	None	Fetal cell analysis (experimental; difficult to separate maternal from fetal cells)

*Results depend on number of family members involved and type of disease

Adapted from "Prenatal Diagnosis: Current Procedures and Implications for Early Interventionists Working with Families" by P. M. Blasco, P. A. Blasco, & T. J. Zirpoli, 1994, *Infants and Young Children, 7*(2), 33–42.

PRENATAL INTERVENTION

One advantage of early detection is the possibility of intervention directed at the developing fetus. The field of fetal surgery is not new but has continued to grow as more sophisticated equipment and techniques become available. The advantages of fetal rather than newborn surgery include: (1) early correction of a defect that could result in death, (2) lower rejection rate of early allogenic grafts by the immature immune system, and (3) quicker postoperative healing in the uterine environment. Procedures currently in use largely focus on life-threatening problems and include fetal blood sampling and transfusion, intrauterine shunting for hydrocephalus, repair of lung and diaphragm anomalies, and correction of urinary tract obstruction (Lorenz, Adzick, & Harrison, 1993; Estes, MacGillivray, Hedrick, Adzick, & Harrison, 1992).

One example of such surgery is the correction of fetal hydrocephalus. During surgery, ultrasound is used to insert a plastic shunt catheter into the fetal skull. The shunt is left in place, with the distal end in the mother's amniotic fluid. During birth, a cesarean section is carried out to avoid compression of the fetal head and bacterial infection of the shunt (Bland, Nelson, Meis, Weaver, & Abramson, 1983). At a later date, the original catheter is replaced with a ventriculoperitoneal shunt. Intrauterine shunting, however, has been somewhat disappointing in terms of outcome. For example, many professionals are concerned with the poor prognosis of patients regardless of treatment (Glick, Harrison, Nakayama et al., 1984; Drugan et al., 1989). The poor prognosis is likely related to other associated anomalies. Those babies who do have isolated progressive hydrocephalus will have varying needs for postnatal shunting (Evans, Drugan, Manning, & Harrison, 1989).

Open fetal surgery is still experimental and performed at only a few research centers. With technical advances employing fetoscopic techniques, open uterine surgery, which is riskier, can be avoided and earlier intervention for nonlife-threatening malformations can be considered (Estes et al., 1992). In a recent situation, a baby was diagnosed with an open heart defect in utero. An infant heart donor was found, and within several hours, the baby with the heart defect was delivered and then received the heart transplant.

Until now, more than 90 percent of children with spina bifida required a shunt to drain fluid off the brain. Fetal surgery for spina bifida is intended to decrease the disabilities associated with the condition. Researchers have found that the procedure apparently affects the way the brain develops in utero, allowing specific malformations of the brain, typically associated with spina bifida, to correct themselves (Adzick, Sutton, Crombleholme, & Flake, 1998). Promising research indicates that among infants who have had fetal surgery for spina bifida the need for a shunt is reduced by 33 to 50 percent (Bruner, Richards, Tulipan, & Arney, in press). As with any new procedure, fetal surgery for spina bifida is not risk free for either the mother or fetus. There are also ethical considerations, which will be discussed later in the chapter.

Drug Interventions

Other prenatal interventions that are effective include treating HIV-positive pregnant women with the drug azidothymidine (AZT), which can inhibit the replication of HIV and prohibits the lengthening of the viral DNA (Mueller & Pizzo, 1992). Although this treatment has reduced the likelihood of viral transmission to the developing fetus, it remains controversial for two reasons: (1) no one knows at what point during gestation transmission occurs; (2) only one out of three infants actually develops the infection (Mueller & Pizzo, 1992).

Gene Therapy

The most hopeful and potentially ameliorative technique for the prevention of developmental disabilities is gene therapy. At the same time, the implications of this treatment and the ethical and moral dilemmas surrounding it will be debated over the next few decades. Physicians now have the techniques for removing a defective gene and replacing it with a normal one, thus decreasing morbidity and mortality (de la Cruz & Friedmann, 1995).

In 1990, the first gene therapy experiment was federally approved and begun on a four-year-old girl with adenosine deaminase deficiency (ADA), which caused her to have a poor immune system that led to numerous potentially fatal illnesses and infections. As one can imagine, her life was far from typical for a four-year-old child. A safe, modified viral vector was used to carry a normal copy of the ADA gene (Fletcher, 1995). After the gene therapy, her immune system began to improve steadily.

Scientists still have a long way to go in understanding the potential benefits as well as the drawbacks of gene therapy. Currently, only single-gene disorders that cause severe mental disabilities are likely to have treatment with such means (Moser, 1995). These individuals account for less than 20 percent of persons with mental disabilities. In terms of the general population, only 0.3 to 0.6 percent of the population have single-gene disorders, such as Down syndrome or fragile-X syndrome (Moser, 1995).

Gene therapy raises many ethical and moral questions that have not been addressed by our society. As by Fletcher (1995) stated, "Experimental gene therapy for mental retardation will require heightened ethical sensitivity because it will be done with young children and infants, who are among the most vulnerable research subjects"(p. 8). Most hospitals have ethical review boards that are active in helping both physicians and families make such decisions.

WORKING WITH FAMILIES
DURING PRENATAL DIAGNOSIS

Given the increase in the use of prenatal screening and technology in diagnosing and treating abnormalities prior to birth, families are faced with situations that never arose 10 years ago. Research shows that not all prospective parents receive all the information necessary to make informed decisions regarding a pregnancy (Heidrich & Cranley, 1989). In fact, couples or family members may be advised "not to waste time" with the fetus and they may instead be presented with a "therapeutic abortion" as the only option (Hassed et al., 1993). Some families consider themselves only "temporarily pregnant" as they wait for the results of prenatal diagnosis.

To date, prenatal testing is not included under services provided through the Individual with Disabilities Education Act (IDEA). Many families from improverished backgrounds do not seek prenatal care (including prenatal diagnosis) and in fact may be more at risk for prenatal problems such as poor nutrition and use of substances. These families tend to underutilize prenatal services (Arcia & Gallagher, 1993).

Prospective parents who do undergo prenatal diagnosis are learning to add their voice to the decision-making process, even when the diagnosis is terminal. In one study in which a lethal condition was diagnosed prenatally, 43 families (33 percent) elected to continue rather than terminate the pregnancy (Kaplan, 1993). In Vignette 2.4, one parent discusses her feelings regarding the choice to give birth to her son.

> **VIGNETTE 2.4   THE BIRTH OF A CHILD WITH A TERMINAL DIAGNOSIS**
> I remember being scared for my baby. I knew his short life would
> come to an end soon. My labor was long because of my baby's syn-
> drome. I didn't know what was happening or how to work with the
> contractions. At the time, I acted like a parent soothing my little baby.
> I remember being shocked at his appearance and panicked when he
> tried to take a breath. Those few moments with my son were worth
> all of the pain and sorrow I had felt in the previous months.

In terms of decision making during pregnancy, most families are given some support from the medical team, but, despite being well informed by physicians and genetic counselors, families may be missing important information that can be supplied only at birth. For example, when parents are told that they are carrying a child with Down syndrome, they have little or no information regarding the number or severity of defects. As with most disabilities, the range of severity is great. One child with Down syndrome may have mild mental impairments, while another may have several severe mental and/or multiple medical concerns.

In the case of a life-threatening situation, families cannot make these decisions alone. Ethical review boards, which make recommendations regarding institutional policies and national guidelines, may offer families help with the decision-making process but, at times, may advise against the parent's wishes. The committees act in an advisory capacity to help families weigh the benefits and concerns of treatment. When physicians, families, and consultants cannot agree upon a course of action, legal services are used to settle the situation. In Table 2.6, landmark cases in this area are outlined according to the ethical dilemma and the legal outcome.

TABLE 2.6   Legal Decisions Regarding Ethical Dilemmas of Newborns

CASE	YEAR	CONDITION	OUTCOME
Baby Houle	1974	Congenital malformations, including no left eye and suspected brain damage. Parents refused to consent for surgery.	Judge ordered surgery to protect the newborn from "neglect."
Baby Doe	1982	Down syndrome and correctable gastrointestinal malformation. Parents refused to consent for surgery.	Parents' right of refusal upheld by Indiana Supreme Court. Department of Health and Human Services issued new regulations known as "Baby Doe Directives."*
Baby Jane Doe	1983	Myelomeningocele, microcephaly, and hydrocephalus. Parents wanted conservative treatment but not surgery.	Ruled that these decisions should be made in private by parents and medical team, without government interference.
Baby K	1992	Anencephaly. Mother wanted the child treated; physicians wanted to discontinue life support.	Judge ruled in favor of mother. Hospital took the case to an appeals court, where similar decision was rendered.

*These directives required hospitals to place notices stating that failure to provide nutrition or medically beneficial treatment to an infant because of a disability was a violation of the federal Rehabilitation Act of 1973.

In 1984, Congress passed amendments to the Child Abuse and Neglect Prevention and Treatment Act (PL 98-457), establishing that withholding medically indicated treatment from a newborn or infant was a form of child abuse and neglect (Hastings Center Report, 1987). This legislation required states to comply with a set of regulations to handle cases of medical neglect, which was defined as withholding medically indicated treatment from disabled infants with life-threatening conditions. Treatment of life-threatening conditions includes appropriate nutrition, hydration, and medication. Treatment does not have to be administered if the following conditions apply:

1. The infant is irreversibly comatose;
2. Such treatment would merely prolong dying, or not result in ameliorating or correcting all of the infant's life-threatening conditions, or otherwise be futile in terms of the survival of the infant; or
3. Such treatment would be futile in terms of the survival of the infant and the treatment itself under such circumstances would be inhumane (PL 98-457, Section 121[3], cited in Hastings Center Report, 1987, p. 9).

PRINCIPLES OF ETHICS IN PRENATAL DIAGNOSIS

> *Ethics is not the only way to look at what is right and wrong. We*
> *understand ethics as a way to understand a situation that provides*
> *common ground for people who have different cultural backgrounds,*
> *different religious beliefs, and different personal experiences. Because*
> *health care is the shared effort of many people, it is helpful to have*
> *at least some way of understanding a situation that provides a system*
> *of looking at things which doesn't depend on individual, religious, or*
> *cultural group beliefs, but at the same time makes room for those beliefs.*
>
> —Brunnquell, 1993

Beauchamp and Childress (1989) outlined four principles used by most hospital review committees and apply to questions of ethics. These include:

1. *Respect for autonomy*: Each person should decide what is best for himself or herself. Individuals should have an opportunity to give "informed consent." In order to do this, one must have complete, unbiased information about a situation.
2. *Nonmaleficence*: The first premise in health care is to "do no harm." There are, however, times when some amount of harm may be inflicted in order to reap larger benefits, such as saving life. It stands to reason that different individuals will disagree on what measures constitute harm. Therefore, it is an important role of review committees to help make decisions regarding these controversies.
3. *Beneficence*: This principle supports the benefits of medical intervention. What constitutes a benefit is controversial. From a family systems perspective, one must look at the multiple effects of benefits. Who decides the definition of benefit? Is the recipient of the benefit the infant, the family, or society as a whole (Brunnquell, 1993)? All benefits have some drawbacks that must be addressed by the committee.
4. *Justice*: To ensure that everyone has been heard in ethical dilemmas, fairness to the various individuals should be evaluated. For example, one has to examine what is beneficial not only for the expectant family but also for society at large. This principle supports investigating the allocation of resources within our society. When expectant parents of a child with anencephaly decide to harvest their child's organs for the future of science, an ethical review committee must decide if this is really being done for the good of the community (see Vignette 2.5).

VIGNETTE 2.5   BABY GABRIELLE

Controversial issues were raised when an infant known to have anencephaly (a condition where most of the brain is missing) was kept alive on a respirator so her heart could be transplanted into another infant. One hospital, the Loma Linda Medical Center, advertised plans to accept babies born with anencephaly so that the organs could be harvested for transplant. Many parents who knew their babies would be born with anencephaly willingly offered their children because they wanted something good to come of their pregnancy and their child.

Ethicists, including Arthur Caplan, former Chair of the Bioethics Program at the University of Minnesota (1988), expressed concerns about infants' being placed on life support for the sole reason of harvesting their organs. Ethical questions include the length of time an infant is placed on a respirator and the use of technology to prolong an unsustainable life simply for the viable organs (Blakeslee, 1987). Such dilemmas will continue to be a concern during the twenty-first century.

SUMMARY

Years ago, society believed that infants entered the world as helpless individuals with no personality or abilities. Today, we know that they begin their development long before they enter the world. We are also learning more and more about the impact of the prenatal environment on later infant development.

O'Leary (1992) related the prenatal experience to Gesell's neurological stages of development. Beginning with conception, development follows an orderly progression, with each stage achieving a new level of maturation. Most pregnant women experience the first fetal movement, called quickening, by the sixteenth week of gestation. The quality of parental recognition of and parental attunement to fetal movement may be a precursor of later parent-infant attachment. Expectant parents may learn to understand the flow of fetal movement.

Early sensory behaviors of the fetus may be indicative of the prenatal roots of the egocentric phase that emerges later in the child. In vitro, facial movements such as opening and closing of the lips, thumb sucking, wrinkling of the brow and forehead, and turning of the head have all been observed. Therefore, we know that infants, after nine months in utero, enter the world preprogrammed to interact with and have an impact on the environment.

The prenatal period is the current frontier in research into developmental disabilities. For example, scientists recently discovered the gene for fragile X, one of the major causes of mental retardation. Prenatal diagnosis allows expectant families to know whether their unborn child is developing typically or if he or she will have a disability. Understanding the impact of prenatal diagnosis on families of children with disabilities is essential for service providers today. Often these families are viewed by medical personnel as being "at risk" and are thus targeted for prenatal diagnosis.

Preventing developmental disabilities is another result of prenatal diagnosis. Teratogens, including infections, radiation, and chronic illness in the mother, can affect the fetus, depending on the timing and intensity of exposure. Mothers who are aware of these risks can take precautions that may prevent future developmental disabilities in their child.

Finally, as science and technology become increasingly sophisticated, the ethical and moral dilemmas raised by gene therapy and genetic planning will increase. It is estimated that the number of genetic tests being administered will increase significantly over the next 10 years (Rennie, 1994). As a result, questions will be raised regarding family privacy and decision-making in high-risk populations. Will genetic testing cause expectant couples to lose jobs or insurance benefits? Will parents who decide to continue a pregnancy, despite the high probability of a genetic defect, be ostracized by society? These are just a few of the questions our society will need to address in the near future.

REFERENCES

Abramowicz, J. S., Jaffe, R., & Warsof, S. L. (1989). Ultrasonographic measurement of fetal femur length in growth disturbances. *American Journal of Obstetrics and Gynecology, 161,* 1137–39.

Adzick, N. S., Sutton, L. N., Crombleholme, T. M., & Flake, A. W. (1998). Successful fetal surgery for spina bifida. *Lancet, 352*(9141), 1675–1676.

Alkalay, A. L., Pomerance, J. J., & Rimoin, D. L. (1987). Fetal varicella syndrome. *Journal of Pediatrics, 3,* 320–323.

Arcia, E., & Gallagher, J. J. (1993). Who are the underserved by early intervention? Can we tell? *Infant-Toddler Intervention, 3,* 93–100.

Austin, K. D., & Hall, J. G. (1992). Nontraditional inheritance. *Pediatric Clinics of North America, 39,* 335–348.

Batshaw, M. L. (1997). *Children with disabilities* (4th ed.). Baltimore: Paul H. Brookes.

Beauchamp, T., & Childress, J. (1989). *Principles of biomedical ethics* (3rd ed.). New York: Oxford University Press.

Bianchi, D. W. (1995). Prenatal diagnosis by analysis of fetal cells in maternal blood. *Journal of Pediatrics, 127,* 847–856.

Blakeslee, S. (1987, December 14). New attention focused on infant organ donors. *New York Times,* p. 18.

Bland, R. S., Nelson, L. H., Meis, P. J., Weaver, R. L., & Abramson, J. S. (1983). Gonococcal ventriculitis associated with ventriculoamniotic shunt placement. *American Journal of Obstetrics and Gynecology, 147,* 781–784.

Blasco, P. M., Blasco, P. A., & Zirpoli, T. J. (1994). Prenatal diagnosis: Current procedures and implications for early interventionists working with families. *Infants and Young Children, 7*(2), 33–42.

Blasco, P. M., & Pearson, J. A. (1995). Working with families. In T. J. Zirpoli (Ed.), *Understanding and affecting the behavior of young children* (pp. 218–241). Englewood Cliffs, N.J.: Merrill.

Blizzard, R. M. (1993). Genetics and growth: New understanding. *Pediatric Rounds, 2* (2), 1–4.

Boyer, P. J., Dillon, M., Navaic, M., Deveikis, A., Keller, M., O'Rourke, S., & Bryson, Y. J. (1994). Factors predictive of maternal-fetal transmission of HIV-1: Preliminary analysis of zidovudine given during pregnancy and/or delivery. *Journal of the American Medical Association, 271,* 1925–1930.

Bruner, J. P., Richards, W. O., Tulipan, N. B., & Arney, T. L. (in press). Endoscopic coverage of fetal myelomeningocele in utero. *American Journal of Obstetrics & Gynecology.*

Brunnquell, D. (1993). *Ethical principals and analysis: A brief guide.* Unpublished manuscript, Minneapolis Children's Medical Center.

Campbell S., & Pearce, J. M. (1983). Ultrasound visualization of congenital malformations. *British Medical Bulletin, 39,* 322–331.

Campos, J. J., Barrett, K. C., Lamb, M. E., Goldsmith, H. H., & Stenberg, C. (1983). Socio-emotional development. In M. M. Haith and J. J. Campos (Eds.), *Infancy and developmental psychobiology* (4th ed., pp. 784–857). New York: Wiley.

Charrow, J. (1985). Prenatal diagnosis and management of endocrine and metabolic disorders. *Special Topics in Endocrinology Metabolism, 7,* 131–174.

Chueh J., & Golbus, M. S. (1990). Antenatal diagnosis by DNA analysis. *Contemporary Obstetrics/Gynecology, 35,* 1–96.

Connelly, B. L., & Stanberry, L. R. (1995). Herpes simplex virus infections in children. *Current Opinion in Pediatrics, 7,* 19–23.

Connor, E. M., Sperling, R. S., Gelber, R., Kiselev, P., Scott, G., O'Sullivan, M. J., VanDyke, R., Rey, M., Shearer, W., & Jacobson, R. L. (1994). Reduction of maternal-infant transmission of human immunodeficiency virus type 1 with zidovudine treatment. *New England Journal of Medicine, 331,* 1173–1180.

D'Alton, M. E, & DeCherney, A. H. (1993). Prenatal diagnosis. *New England Journal of Medicine, 328(2),* 114–120.

de la Cruz, F., & Friedmann, T. (1995). Editorial: Prospects for human gene therapy in mental retardation and developmental disabilities. *Mental Retardation and Developmental Disabilities Research Review, 1,* 2–3.

DiPietro, J. A., Hodgson, D. M., Costigan, K. A., & Hilton, S. C. (1996). Fetal neurobehavioral development, *Child Development, 67,* 2553–2567.

Drugan, A., Krause, B., Canady, A., Zador, I. E., Sacks, A. J., & Evans, M. I. (1989) The natural history of prenatally diagnosed cerebral ventriculomegaly. *Journal of the American Medical Association, 261,* 1785–1788.

Estes, J. M., MacGillivray, T. E., Hedrick, M. H., Adzick, N. S., & Harrison, M. R. (1992). Feto-scopic surgery for the treatment of congenital anomalies. *Journal of Pediatric Surgery, 27,* 950–954.

Evans, M. I., Drugan, A., Manning, F. A., & Harrison, M. R. (1989). Fetal surgery in the 1990's. *American Journal of Disabled Children, 143,* 1431–1436.

Fletcher, J. C. (1995). Gene therapy in mental retardation: Ethical considerations. *Mental Retardation and Developmental Disabilities Research Review, 1,* 7–13.

Gesell, A., & Amatruda, C. (1941). *Developmental diagnosis.* New York: Harper.

Ghidini, A., Sirtori, M., Spelta, A., & Vergani, P. (1991). Results of a preventive program for congenital toxoplasmosis. *Journal of Reproductive Medicine, 36*(4), 270–273.

Glick, P. L., Harrison, M. R, Nakayama, D. K., et al. (1984) Management of ventriculomegaly in the fetus. *Journal of Pediatrics, 105,* 97–105.

Graham, E. M., & Morgan, M. A. (1997). Growth before birth. In M. L. Batshaw (Ed.), *Children with disabilities* (4th Edition, pp. 53–69). Baltimore: Paul H. Brookes.

Graves, P. L. (1989). The functioning fetus. In S. I. Greenspan & G. H. Pollack (Eds), *The course of life. Volume 1: Infancy* (pp. 433–464). Madison, Wisc.: International University Press.

Grose, C., & Weiner, C. P. (1990). Prenatal diagnosis of congenital cytomegalovirus infection: Two decades later. *American Journal of Obstetrics & Gynecology, 163,* 447–450.

Haddow, J. E., Palomaki, G. E., Knight, G. J. (1992). Prenatal screening for Down syndrome with use of maternal serum markers. *New England Journal of Medicine, 327,* 588–593.

Handyside, A. H., Lesko, J. G., Tarin, J. J., Winston, R. M. L., & Hughes, M. R. (1992). Birth of a normal girl after in vitro fertilization and preimplantation testing for cystic fibrosis. *New England Journal of Medicine, 327,* 905–909.

Harrison, M. R., Adzick, N. S., Longaker, M. T., et al. (1990). Successful repair in utero of a fetal diaphragmatic hernia after removal of herniated viscera from the left thorax. *New England Journal of Medicine, 332,* 1582–1584.

Hassed, S. J., Miller, C. H., Pope, S. K., Murphy, P., Quirk, J. G., & Curnmiff, C. (1993). Perinatal lethal conditions: The effects of diagnosis on decision making. *Obstetrics & Gynecology, 82,* 37–42.

Hastings Center Report. (1987, December). *Imperiled infants.* New York: Author.

Heidrich, S. M., & Cranley, M. S. (1989). Effect of fetal movement, ultrasound scans, and amniocentesis on maternal-fetal attachment. *Nursing Research, 38*(2), 81–84.

Hershey, D. W., Crandall, B. F., & Perdue, S. (1986). Combining maternal age and serum alphafetoprotein to predict the risk of Down syndrome. *Obstetrics and Gynecology, 68 (2),* 177–180.

Iosub, S., Bamji, M., Stone, R. K., Gromisch, D. S., & Wasserman, E. (1987). More on human immunodeficiency virus embryopathy. *Pediatrics, 80,* 512–516.

Izard, C. E., and Malatesta, C. Z. (1987). Perspectives on emotional development: Differential emotions theory of early emotional development. In J. D. Osofsky (Ed.), *Handbook of infant development* (2nd ed., pp. 494–554). New York: Wiley.

Jackson, J. F., North, E. R., and Thomas, J. G. (1976). Clinical diagnosis of Down syndrome. *Clinical Genetics, 9,* 483–487.

Jones, K. L. (1996). *Smith's recognizable patterns of human malformation* (5th ed.). Philadelphia: W. B. Saunders.

Kaplan, D. (1993). Prenatal screening and its impact on persons with disabilities. *Clinical Obstetrics & Gynecology, 36*(3), 605–612.

Kaplan, K. M., Cochi, S. L., Edmonds, L. D., Zell, E. R., & Prelud, S. R. (1990). A profile of mothers giving birth to infants with congenital rubella syndrome: An assessment of risk factors. *American Journal of Diseases of Children, 144,* 118–123.

Klaus, M., & Kennell, J. (1976). *Maternal-infant bonding: The impact of early separation or loss on family development.* St. Louis: Mosby.

Klaus, M., & Kennell, J. (1982). *Parent-infant bonding.* St. Louis: Mosby.

Klein, S. D. (1993). The challenge of communicating with parents. *Journal of Developmental and Behavioral Pediatrics, 14,* 184–191.

Lally, R., Griffin, A., Fenichel, E., Segal, M., Szanton, E., & Weissbourd, B. (1997). Developmentally appropriate practice for infants and toddlers. In S. Bredekamp & C. Copple (Eds.), *Developmentally appropriate practice in early childhood programs serving children birth through age 8* (pp. 55–94). Washington, D.C.: NAEYC.

Loman, S. (1994). Attuning to the fetus and the young child: Approaches from dance movement therapy. *Zero to Three, 15,* 20–26.

Lorenz, H. P., Adzick, N. S., & Harrison, M. R. (1993). Open human fetal surgery. *Advances in surgery, 26,* 259–273.

Macri, J. N., Kasturi,R. V., Krantz, D. A., & Koch, K. E. (1986). Maternal serum alpha-fetoprotein screening, maternal weight, and detection efficiency. *American Journal of Obstetrics & Gynecology, 155,* 758–760.

Moser, H. W. (1995). A role for gene therapy in mental retardation. *Mental Retardation and Developmental Disabilities Research Review, 1,* 4–6.

Mueller, B. U., & Pizzo, P. A. (1992). Medical treatment of children with HIV infection. In A. C. Crocker, H. J. Cohen, & T. A. Kastner (Eds.), *HIV infection and developmental disabilities: A resource for service providers* (pp. 63–73). Baltimore: Paul H. Brookes.

Newell, M. L., & Peckham, C. (1993). Risk factors for vertical transmission of HIV-1 and early markers of HIV-1 infection in children. *AIDS, 7,* Supp: S91–S97.

NICHD National Registry for Amniocentesis Study Group. (1976). Midtrimester amniocentesis for prenatal diagnosis: Safety and accuracy. *Journal of the American Medical Association, 236,* 1471–1476.

Nilsson, L. (1977). *A child is born.* New York: Dell.

O'Leary, J. (1992). The parenting process in the prenatal period: A developmental theory. *Pre- and Perinatal Psychology Journal, 7,* 113–123.

O'Leary, J., & Torwick, C. (1993) Parenting during pregnancy: The infant as the vehicle for intervention in high risk pregnancy. *International Journal of Prenatal Perinatal Psychological Medicine, 5(3),* 303–310.

Ostrer, H. (1989) Prenatal diagnosis of genetic disorders by DNA analysis. *Pediatric Annals, 18*(11), 701–713.

Pauker, S. P., & Pauker, S. G. (1994). Prenatal diagnosis: Why is 35 a magic number? *New England Journal of Medicine, 330,* 1151–1152.

Peckham, C., & Gibb, D. (1995). Mother-to-child transmission of the human immunodeficiency virus. *New England Journal of Medicine, 333,* 298–302.

Rennie, J. (June 1994). Grading the gene tests. *Scientific American, 270,* 88–97.

Rhoads, G. G., Jackson, L. G., Schlesselman, S. E., de la Cruz, F. F., Desnick, R. J., Golbus, M. S., Ledbetter, D. H., Lubs, H. A., Mahoney, M. J., & Pergament, E. (1989). The safety and efficacy of chorionic villus sampling for early prenatal diagnosis of cytogenetic abnormalities. *New England Journal of Medicine, 320,* 609–617.

Rogers, M. F., & Shaffer, N. (1999). Reducing the risk of maternal-infant transmission of HIV by attacking the virus. *New England Journal of Medicine, 341,* 441–442.

Roizen, N. J., & Johnson, D. (1996). Congenital infections. In A. J. Capute & P. J. Accardo (Eds.), *Developmental disabilities in infancy and childhood* (pp. 175–193). Baltimore: Paul H. Brookes.

Rosenblith, J. F. (1992). *In the beginning: Development from conception to age two.* Newbury Park, Calif.: Sage.

Schnatterly P., Hogge, W. A., & Felder, R. (1990). *AFP (Alpha fetoprotein): A helpful test in pregnancy.* Charlottesville: University of Virginia Press.

Schoenfeld-DiMaio, M., Baumgarten, A., Greenstein, R. M., Saal, H. M., & Mahoney, M. J. (1987). Screening for fetal Down syndrome in pregnancy by measuring maternal serum alpha-fetoprotein levels. *New England Journal of Medicine, 316,* 342–346.

Simpson, J. L., Baum, L. D., Marder, R., Elias, S., Ober, C., & Martin, A. O. (1986). Maternal serum alpha-fetoprotein screening: Low and high values for detection of genetic abnormalities. *American Journal of Obstetrics & Gynecology, 155,* 593–597.

Simpson, J. L., & Carson, S. A. (1992). Preimplantation genetic diagnosis. *New England Journal of Medicine, 32,* 951–953.

Simpson, J. L., and Elias, S. (1993). Isolating fetal cells from maternal blood: Advances in prenatal diagnosis through molecular technology. *Journal of the American Medical Association, 270*(19), 2357–2361.

Sossin, K., & Loman, S. (1992). Clinical applications of the Kestenberg Movement Profile. In S. Loman & R. Brandt (Eds.), *The body mind connection in human movement analysis.* Keene, N.H.: Antioch New England Graduate School.

Thorp, J. M., & Bowes, W. A. (1989). Prenatal diagnosis for couples who would not consider abortion. *American Journal of Obstetrics & Gynecology, 74,* 828–829.

Yerby, M. S. (1994). Pregnancy, teratogenesis, and epilepsy. *Neurologic Clinics, 12*(4), 749–771.

Wolraich, M. (1992). Myelomeningocele. In J. Blackman (Ed.), *Medical aspects of developmental disabilities in children birth to three* (pp. 159–165). Rockville, Md.: Aspen.

CHAPTER THREE

LIVING IN OUR WORLD: THE FIRST YEAR

WITH JOLENE PEARSON

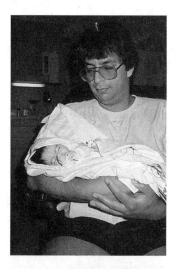

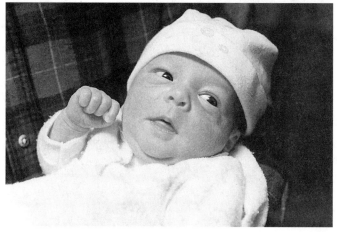

- To provide an overview of the infant's development in terms of competencies and skill acquisition during first year of life
- To give an appreciation and understanding of the individual infant's developmental style and temperament
- To provide an understanding of the evolution of the study of infant development and the role of parenting
- To provide insight into the complexities of the parent-infant relationship
- To provide insight into the concerns and questions parents typically express during the first year of their child's life
- To explore the implications of prematurity on the child's and family's development
- To explore the implications of multiple births on the child's and family's development
- To explore the implications of disabilities on the child's and family's development
- To define and discuss ethical issues and their effects on infants and families

GETTING ACQUAINTED: THE NEWBORN

In the previous chapter, we explored the concepts of development and parenting in the prenatal period. In this chapter, our focus is on life after birth through the first year. The first year of life presents many rewards and challenges for the infant and the family. It is during the first year that many families will find out that something is not quite right with their baby. Some families will be told immediately that their child has a syndrome or medical condition, if they had not learned this prenatally. This was the situation for the Guzman family, introduced in Chapter 1. In this chapter, we look at specific disabilities that are identified during the prenatal, perinatal, and neonatal periods. However, in order to understand the development of infants and toddlers with disabilities, service providers also need a firm understanding of typical development in infants and toddlers.

Starting from the Beginning

The birth process and physical immaturity explain why newborns do not look the way their parents had anticipated. For example, almost all babies arrive having some molding or distortion of their head shape from the birth itself. Such molding is normal, and most infants' heads return to their naturally round shapes within 24–48 hours. Babies born by cesarean section or breech deliveries generally do not have skull molding. In the case of prolonged or difficult labor, infants may also arrive with a *caput succedaneum*, a swelling of the scalp caused by the pressure of the baby's head on the dilating cervix (Tappero & Honeyfield, 1993). This gradually disappears in the first 12 to 24 hours. Another common mark is a *cephalhematoma*, a bruise caused by blood vessels breaking. These bruises can be quite large and are almost always the result of a difficult labor. No treatment is required, but the bruises should be monitored for swelling and evidence of healing. This condition can take up to six months to resolve (Tappero & Honeyfield, 1993).

Physical Growth and Development

Birthweight helps set the stage for growth and development. Recording and following an infant's growth pattern provides a baseline for understanding both prenatal and future development. For example, if the mother had eclampsia (toxemia of pregnancy), the infant may be small for gestational age or premature (Forouzan, Morgan, & Batshaw, 1997). The average weight of a full-term baby (38–40 weeks of gestation) is 7 pounds, 3 ounces. There is, however, wide variation due to many factors, including genetic predisposition and nutrition during pregnancy.

It is important to differentiate between premature infants and those who have *low birth weight* (LBW), which is defined as less than 5 pounds, 8 ounces, or 2,500 grams. *Very low birthweight* is defined as less than 1,500 grams (Allen, 1996). Another important parameter is *small for gestational age* (SGA), which occurs when infants have suffered *intrauterine growth retardation* (IUGR). Tests are widely used by the medical team to determine the gestational age of an infant at birth (Dubowitz, Dubowitz, & Goldberg, 1970; Dubowitz, 1995). It is possible for an infant to be both premature and small for gestational age, or premature and large for gestational age.

The Apgar Scoring System

Within the first minutes of life the status of the new baby is quickly evaluated to determine if any intervention is needed. This is routinely done using a screening tool, developed by Virginia Apgar in 1953, and used in hospitals throughout the United States and in many other parts of the world. Administration involves rating each of five traits, at 1 minute after birth and again at 5 or 10 minutes, with a score of 0 if the trait is absent, 1 if the trait is observable, and 2 if the trait has an optimal condition (see Table 3.1).

It is rare for an infant to have a score of 10, yet parents are sometimes concerned if their infant's rating is not optimal. A low Apgar score is a red flag that the infant is in immediate distress and warrants close monitoring and possible further investigation. The rating does not indicate that the child will have a developmental disability. Apgar scores have been found to have varying degrees of correlation to other studies of fetal heart rate, intelligence, neonatal mortality, and maternal medication during childbirth (Self & Horowitz, 1979).

Again, it is important to note that in and of itself the Apgar score is not predictive, although it serves as a useful descriptor of how an infant began life outside of the uterus. Apgar scores are routinely noted in the birth history and become part of the child's pediatric health history.

TABLE 3.1   Apgar Screening Tool

	SCORES		
	0	*1*	*2*
Heart rate	Absent	<100	>100
Breathing	Absent	Irregular	Normal Crying
Muscle tone	Limp	Some Flexion	Active Movement
Gag Reflex	No response	Grimace	Sneeze; Cough
Color	Blue	Pink with blue Extremities	Pink all over

From "A Proposal for a New Method of Evaluation of the Newborn Infant" by V. Apgar, 1953, *Current Research in Anesthesia and Analgesia, 32,* 260–265.

THE NEONATAL PERIOD

Transition from Womb to the World

As discussed in the previous chapter, the neonate enters the world able to feel, hear, see, smell, and move. However, adapting to the external environment brings new ways to experience life. In the uterus, movement was limited by the boundaries of the uterine walls. The fetus assumed a flexed position with hands close by the face in easy reach for sucking. In contrast, birth means the loss of those comfortable boundaries, and when the infant moves he often sets off startles and tremors that surprise him.

Additionally, after birth, infants are placed in extended rather than flexed positions, and for the first time, they must learn to adapt. Lying on their backs, exposed and vulnerable, is new to them and initially causes them stress. Sound is no longer filtered through the uterine wall, and infants must adjust to the varied sounds in this new world. They have visual capabilities at 34 weeks and can see from the moment of birth. But the typical bright overhead lighting found in hospitals makes it difficult for infants to demonstrate their developed visual capacities. Lowering the lights often supports a quiet, alert state where babies can lock onto and follow parents with their eyes. This is but one of the amazing capabilities of the human newborn. Vignette 3.1 provides one mother's view of what occurred after the birth of her twins.

VIGNETTE 3.1   WELCOME TO OUR WORLD

The birth of twins continues to be somewhat more risky than that of singletons. I had made up my mind that I wouldn't go kicking and screaming into the operating room if the doctor felt a cesarean (C-section) was necessary. I was already diagnosed with preeclampsia and respected my doctor's opinion.

Still, I was given the opportunity to try for a vaginal delivery. My husband and I were working hard on breathing through the contractions, when the nurse frowned and left the room. I knew immediately that something was wrong. My doctor came into the room to tell us the problem. I would have to have a C-section; my son was not breathing right and she didn't want to take a risk. She did tell us there would be time for an epidural (spinal anesthesia) so I could be awake during the birth.

I waited with anticipation as my son was pulled from my womb. The doctor held him up for me to see before passing him to a nurse. My daughter was next, less than one minute after my son, but this time, the doctor did not hold her up for me to see. She was handed over to the neonatologist standing by. By this time, my husband had our son in his arms and was holding him toward me. I couldn't touch him because I had an electrode taped to my finger, but I reached for him anyway. He look like a content, relaxed baby with his eyes closed and snug in my husband's arms. I was reassured by his calm presence.

Then the neonatologist brought my daughter over. She weighed 3 pounds, 4 ounces, and had been small for gestation age, had an ineffective placenta, and was born two weeks early. The doctor held her while he told me she was doing fine. She stared at me as if to say, "I haven't figured this out yet but I'm sure you had something to do with it." It was an expression I never forgot, despite the fact that the delivery led to full-blown eclampsia and I became extremely ill. It was three more days before I saw my twins again. I thought then that my daughter would be a spirited, intelligent child and today, at age five, she has shown that I was right. My son remains a calm, sensitive child who often helps his sister channel her extra energy.

Understanding the complexities and subtleties of newborn behavior and development has been the lifelong work of pediatrician and researcher T. Berry Brazelton. Brazelton, along with his colleagues, developed a systematized way to evaluate newborns both to understand the individual behavior of particular infants and to compare groups of infants for research purposes. This tool, the Neonatal Behavorial Assessment Scale (NBAS) (Brazelton & Nugent 1995), was first published in 1974 and revised in 1984 and again in 1995. The NBAS offers several important concepts that give us insight not only into the infant but also into the developing relationship between the infant and the parents. The NBAS as an assessment tool will be discussed in Chapter 6.

During the neonatal evaluation of newborns, their states of consciousness (Table 3.2) must be taken into consideration in order to interpret their responses (Brazelton, 1992).

Important Signals

Newborns are quite competent in developing a series of signals to help adults become aware of their emotional needs and desires. When a newborn has become overstim-

TABLE 3.2   Behavioral States

Deep sleep: The infant engages in regular breathing and is capable of shutting out the world around him. The infant's eyes are closed, and he is motionless, with his arms and legs curled up in a flexed position, except for startled or jerky movements at regular intervals.

Light, or REM (rapid eye movement), sleep: The infant's breathing is irregular. In this state, he might startle once or twice and is more susceptible to the outside world. If he is aroused, he may become drowsy or struggle to get back into a deep sleep. Eye movements are observed under closed lids.

Drowsy, or semi-alert. Eyes may be open or closed. He may become active if aroused, but the degree of activity will vary.

Quiet alert state: The infant adapts to his surrounding. If he is excited by an object or person, he will breathe deeply. His movements seem organized and he can follow an adult's face or an object such as a rattle. He can also gaze intently at a person or object.

Fussy, wide-awake state: The infant's eyes are open, and he engages in considerable motor activity. He is not able to control himself.

Fussy, crying state: The infant's breathing is again irregular. His movements become jerky, and he will thrash about, trying to reorganize or gain control of himself. This is a difficult state for parents to accept and understand as part of development. The parents will often attempt to calm the baby down. When the baby does not respond to calming, the parents may feel ineffective too.

Reprinted from Understanding the Emotional and Behavioral Development of Young Children: Birth to 3 Years by P. M. Blasco, 1995, in T. J. Zirpoli (Ed.), *Understanding and Affecting the Behavior of Young Children,* Englewood Cliffs, N.J., Merrill, p. 42.

ulated, for example, she may close her eyes, sneeze, or turn her head away from the stimuli. Brazelton (1992) suggested that spit-ups and bowel movements may be a sign of stress from overstimulation. The caregiver should interpret this behavior as a red flag if it seems the newborn has been subjected to overwhelming stimulus.

Newborns are also adept at calming themselves after a stressful event by placing a thumb or fist in their mouths, or by pulling all of their limbs into a flexed position. In this way, the newborn takes control over her environment. Her ability to experience the environment through her senses and to begin to regulate that environment is the foundation of emotional development (Greenspan & Thorndike-Greenspan, 1985).

Table 3.3 describes some key points in the arrival of a newborn. Although the families discussed are typical of most, the responses of newborns vary widely according to individual resources, cultural differences, and sources of support.

MOTOR DEVELOPMENT

As the infant is learning to engage the caregiver, she is also busy learning to engage the world around her. She learns that by kicking and waving her arms, the mobile

TABLE 3.3   Full-Term Babies and Their Families

- Parents have gone through a full forty-week pregnancy and hopefully are psychologically ready to have their baby. This may also include practical preparations, such as completing birthing classes, preparing the nursery, and gathering clothing for the baby. This process is often referred to as *nesting*. Mothers-to-be, who early in the pregnancy were concerned about the physical process and discomforts of birth, are now "ready to get this baby out!"
- The infant is ready to be born and comes into the world prepared to stabilize herself physiologically. The baby possesses all the wonderful beginning capabilities that allow her to take in the world and communicate.
- Parents have a surge of emotion, a combination of relief, that they had a healthy baby and safe delivery, and amazement at their accomplishment. Predominant feelings are of success, achievement, and fulfilled expectations.
- Parents leave the hospital with their baby and thus begin the great adventure of learning to read their baby's cues, satisfying her nutritional needs, and providing all of the normal caregiving their baby needs. Parents and infants are nearly inseparable in these early days. Although new parents may not feel confident immediately, their confidence grows quickly through the opportunities they have to interact with one another and be successful.

over her crib will tinkle and even turn. Movements become increasingly sophisticated compared to the primitive reflexes she demonstrated as a newborn. The infant learns to grasp objects with the entire hand and bring objects into midline for further visual inspection. The infant will turn her head to sounds and hold it steady for brief periods. If the infant is placed on a mat facedown, she will turn from side to side and lift her head for brief periods.

Primitive Reflexes

In the past 20 years, neurodevelopmentalists have begun to establish the precise clinical importance of persistent primitive reflexes, delay in postural reaction evolution, and the more subtle qualitative and quantitative aspects of each. Capute, Accardo, and Vining (1978) emphasized the distinction between primitive reflexes and postural reactions. While both represent patterns of movement, primitive reflexes are true reflexes in the sense that they are highly stereotyped and are elicited by specific sensory stimuli (Blasco, 1994). The neurological connections necessary are located at a subcortical level in the brain stem (Capute, Shapiro, & Accardo, 1982). The maturation of cortical connections appears to override the brain stem primitive reflex generators to alter their intensity and eventually leads to their "disappearance" (some prefer the term *integration*) with age.

Primitive reflexes begin to make their appearance prior to term in the normal fetus, as early as 25 weeks of gestation, and they remain visibly evident through the first three to six months of life (Allen & Capute, 1986) (see Figure 3.1). In children who are developing typically, almost all primitive reflexes have visibly disappeared after six months. The symmetric toxic neck reflex (STNR) and the Galant reflex (primitive trunk incurvation from paraspinal pressure) remain the only exceptions. The Galant reflex persists the longest, and is visibly present in 50 percent of infants between 12 and 18 months of age (Blasco, 1994). The STNR has a history of subtlety in the newborn and becomes apparent in only a fraction of babies after term birth, but then disappears (Blasco, 1994).

When cortical integration is jeopardized prenatally or neonatally, primitive reflex responses persist beyond the usual age of disappearance and are visibly exaggerated. In the situation of later acquired brain injury, these reflexes often reappear (Haley, Baryza, Troy, Geckler, & Schoenberg, 1991). For example, a three-year-old who receives a head injury as a result of a car accident will often demonstrate these reflexes in the early stages of recovery. A posture is considered obligatory when the child becomes fixed or stuck in the primitive reflex posture, or in other words, "obligated" to remain there until the stimulus is removed (Blasco, 1994).

Postural reactions, unlike primitive reflexes, typically are not present in the newborn. They begin to make their functional appearance with lateral head-righting at two to three months of age in the full-term infant. Postural mechanisms are not true reflexes, because they are based on multiple, interacting, input modalities that require cortical integrity (Blasco, 1994). In the infant with brain damage, postural mechanisms appear later than usual, if at all, and are less effective. These mechanisms serve a functional purpose in the typically developing infant, as the names of their descriptive subgroups indicate: righting, protection, and equilibrium leading to the evolution of motor-skill development.

For children with physical disabilities such as cerebral palsy, the disappearance of primitive reflexes and the evolution of postural reactions form the basis for locomotor prognosis. Cerebral palsy is defined as a nonprogressive disorder of movement caused by a single or multiple lesions of the brain that affect motor development. Persistence of obligatory primitive reflexes beyond 12 months of age carries an unfavorable prognosis for eventual walking (Blasco, 1994). Table 3.4 lists typical gross and fine motor skills from birth through three years.

In the absence of early intervention, infants and young children with motor impairments will retain primitive reflexes and develop atypical movement patterns, which may lead to muscle tightness, joint contractures, and musculoskeletal deformities (Harris, 1997). See Chapter 4 for a detailed description of interventions for infants and toddlers with motor impairments.

INFANTS BORN PREMATURELY

Deciding if an infant is premature has to do with gestational age—or the amount of time the baby spent in the womb. A full-term baby develops in utero for 38–42 weeks. If born before 38 weeks, infants do not necessarily display the same

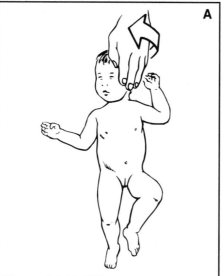

The sensory limb of the ATNR probably involves cervical proprioceptors. With either active or passive head turning to the side, the baby *reflexively* extends the fingers, arm, and leg on the face side and flexes the extremities on the occiput side. There is also some mild paraspinous muscle tightening on the occiput side, often producing subtle trunk curvature.

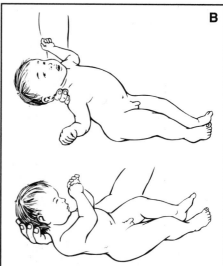

In the supine position, the baby's head is mildly extended (about 45 degrees) by gentle support under the shoulders. This yields relative extension of the legs and retraction of the shoulders, producing the upper extremity "surrender posture". With active or passive neck flexion (ideally to 45 degrees above the plane of the body) the arms come forward to the midline and the legs flex.

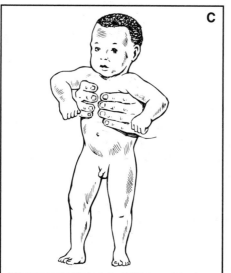

With support around the trunk, the child is suspended and lowered to pat the feet gently on a flat surface. This stimulus produces reflex extension at the hips, knees, and ankles so the baby stands straight. Often children may go up on their toes initially, but should come down flat within 20 to 30 seconds before sagging back down toward a sitting position.

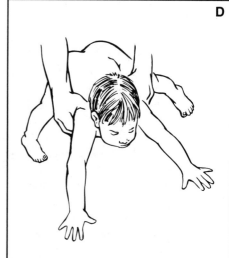

The examiner has suspended the child horizontally by the waist and lowered him face down toward a flat surface. The arms extend in front, slightly abducted at the shoulders, and the fingers spread as if to break a fall.

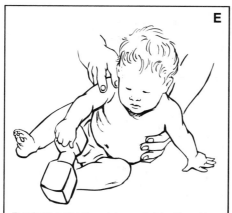

The infant is comfortably seated, supported about the waist (if necessary) and distracted by a toy or parent. The examiner gently tilts the child to one side, noting deviation of the head back toward the midline (head-righting), lateral extension of one arm toward the side of the fall (protection), and upward counter movements of the arm and leg (equilibrium reactions).

FIGURE 3.1   Primitive Reflexes and Postural Reactions. A, Asymmetric tonic neck reflex. **B,** Tonic labyrinthine reflex. **C,** Positive support reflex. **D,** Normal parachute reaction. **E,** Postural mechanisms.

Source: From "Normal and Abnormal Motor Development" by P. A. Blasco, 1992, *Pediatric Rounds, 1*(2), 4–5.

behavioral competencies and skills as their full-term peers. The earlier the baby is born, the more important it is to understand the behavior and organization of the premature infant. Als (1982) has proposed a framework for understanding the premature infant, known as the synactive theory of development, based on the infant's reactivity and threshold for disorganization and stress in response to environmental stimuli. An important issue here is the ability of the infant born prematurely to self-regulate to maintain or regain a balanced state (Rosenblith, 1992). The tool used to document this process is the Assessment for Preterm Infant Behavior (APIB) (Als, Lester, Tronick, & Brazelton, 1982). The work of Als and her colleagues has led to changes in the developmental care of premature and high-risk infants (Als & Gilkerson, 1995).

It is important to understand the keen differences between the experiences of giving birth to a full-term infant and one who is premature or high-risk. All families wish for a healthy, term delivery. Even when parents anticipate an early baby, they are not planning for the complications and sometimes the uncertain

TABLE 3.4   Gross and Fine Motor Development

GROSS MOTOR DEVELOPMENT		FINE MOTOR DEVELOPMENT	
Gross Motor Milestone	*Age*	*Motor Milestone*	*Age*
PRONE POSITION		Retain ring	1 month
(ON STOMACH)		Hand unfisted	3–4 months
Head up	1 month	Reach	3–4 months
Chest up	2 months	Hands to midline	3–4 months
Up on elbows	3 months	Transfer	5 months
Up on hands	4 months	Take one-inch cube	5–6 months
		Take pellet (crude grasp)	6–7 months
ROLL		Immature pincer	7–8 months
Front to back	3–5 months	Mature pincer	10 months
Back to front	3–5 months	Release	12 months
SIT			
With support	5 months		
Without support	7 months		
Come to sit	8 months		
Pull to stand	8–9 months		
Cruise	9–10 months		
WALK			
With 2 hands held	10 months		
With 1 hand held	11 months		
Walk alone	12 months		
Run (stiff-legged)	15 months		
Walk up stairs (with rail)	21 months		
Jump in place	24 months		
Pedal tricycle	30 months		
Walk down stairs, alternating feet	3 years		

Adapted from "Normal and Abnormal Motor Development" by P. A. Blasco, 1992, *Pediatric Rounds, 1*(2), 1, 3.

future facing their child. Table 3.5 discusses some of the experiences of parents of infants who are premature.

There have been remarkable advancements in techniques for caring for infants born prematurely, including the use of surfactants, which has led to the survival of infants born at 23 to 24 weeks of gestation (Allen, Donohue, & Dusman, 1993). Although some of these infants live healthy, typical lives, others will have chronic medical conditions. Because the medical technological advances have come so rapidly and because these very early-born infants are newcomers to researchers, it is not possible to make generalized statements about their develop-

TABLE 3.5   Infants Who Are Premature and Their Families

- Parents have not gone through a full, 40-week pregnancy. At the point they deliver, they may not be able to focus on the baby; their focus may be, rather, the loss of the pregnancy and/or guilt and confusion as to why the baby came early.
- Parents will need time and support to process the feelings of loss and at the same time develop a relationship with their baby. Attachment takes time and experience with the baby, just as it does with a full-term experience.
- The baby enters the world before she is ready and may need intensive medical care to survive. During this time she is less alert and available for interaction with parents. Because of the early arrival and subsequent medical complications, it may be weeks before parents are able to hold the infant. Interactions are limited and the infant's responses may be more indicative of stress than pleasure. It can be a frustrating time for the new parents, as the staff have more access to the infant than the parents.
- Parents may have surges of emotion that include shock, anger, and grief. Depression is not uncommon at this time. Parents often have a sense of the loss of a dream. Friends and family may be hesitant to offer congratulations because of the uncertain future. This can add to the parents' sense of loss.
- Parents may not leave the hospital with their baby, which mothers have said was the most difficult part of the experience. After carrying the baby for nine months, the parents are left with a sense of emptiness and lack of reciprocity with the baby they were getting to know through kicks and movements. Experiences in the NICU that can help families reunite with the infant are very important.
- Parents often feel at a disadvantage in understanding treatment alternatives or differences of opinion among physicians. They may feel they are being given "half-truths" or vague statements.
- Parents may feel excluded from the decision-making process due to the life-threatening nature of their newborn's situation.

Adapted from *Premature Babies: A Different Beginning* by W. A. H. Sammons and J. M. Lewis, 1985, St. Louis: Mosby; and "Ethical Issues in Family-Centered Neonatal Care" by H. Harrison, 1998, in A. H. Widerstrom, B. A. Mowder, and S. R. Sandall (Eds.), *Infant Development and Risk*, 2nd ed., 1998, Baltimore: Paul H. Brookes, pp. 175–196.

mental potential. For parents this can be frustrating, as they are on a unique journey with their child (Klaus, 1993). Vignette 3.2 describes one family's experience when their baby was born prematurely.

VIGNETTE 3.2   PREMATURITY: A DIFFERENT BEGINNING
Sara was born at 24 weeks of gestation. A year before her birth, her parents, Katherine and Michael, had a miscarriage at 20 weeks. Therefore, Sara's birth was seen as a miracle. But her survival also meant weeks and months of medical treatment and anxiety for the family.

Katherine was alert to the signs of premature labor. When she began to suspect that once again she was in early labor, she went immediately to the doctor's office. She was admitted to the hospital and placed on medication (magnesium sulfate) to arrest the labor. In addition, injections of betamethasone were administered to speed the maturity of the fetal lungs in the event that the baby was early. After two days, Katherine's water broke. Because she had a slight fever, it was suspected she might have an infection and all medication was stopped. Within six hours, baby Sara was born, weighing 1 pound, 3 ounces. In the delivery room a neonatal team was in place and ready to treat the baby. They were able to stabilize her for transport to the Neonatal Intensive Care Unit. The neonatal team had spoken with parents prior to the delivery and explained that Sara's chances were about 50-50. Michael and Katherine said that they would like all measures taken to keep their baby alive.

After the birth, Katherine caught a glimpse of Sara and saw that she had blond hair. Although this is a small detail, it was important for Katherine, as she would not be able to accompany her baby to intensive care. She held in her mind an image of a very tiny baby with a head of blond hair. Michael, although confused about whether to stay to support his wife, accompanied the baby to the intensive care unit. This was not at all how the parents envisioned the circumstances around birth. It seemed that the joy of the birth was greatly overshadowed by the fear they felt upon seeing their tiny, fragile daughter intubated and whisked off to newborn intensive care.

The next three months were an emotional roller coaster for the family. While they were able to touch Sara through the portholes of the isolette, it would be three and a half weeks before they were able to hold her for even a few minutes. At that point, the family struggled to understand all of the medical terminology and highly technical equipment. They felt there was little they could actually do to help Sara. They came each day and sat near her isolette. The nurses gave them information and whenever possible showed them how to administer some of Sara's care. Changing a diaper was never such a challenging or triumphant event! Sara initially did well, but at two weeks of age became ill with an infection. There were a number of times during this period when they thought she might not live through the night. Once this was resolved, Sara gradually was weaned off the ventilator. The following weeks were tense for the family. Sara's immature nervous system was susceptible, and she often exhibited apnea (forgetting to breathe) and bradycardia (slowed heart rate). It was especially terrifying when she had an apnea spell while Katherine was holding her.

After the third month of hospitalization, the parents were able to use "kangaroo care" with Sara. This is a way of holding the baby on the parent's chest with as much skin-to-skin contact as possible. In this position, Sara would sleep deeply, never had an apnea or bradycardia spell, and when she was alert seemed more robust and focused. Both the parents looked forward to their kangaroo care sessions with Sara. Katherine, who felt cheated out of her full pregnancy, found kangaroo care a way to feel like she and Sara were together again. It also helped with Sara's breast-feeding, by allowing her to nuzzle the breast.

Finally the day came when Sara would be going home. This brought the parents both joy and concern. They wondered if they would be able to care for their "high-tech" baby at home. While Sara was in the hospital, they had come to rely on the expertise of the nurses, who were always close by and very supportive. Going home meant doing it on their own! With mixed emotions, Katherine and Michael said their farewells and embarked on another milestone in their experience of parenthood: becoming a family at home.

Despite the difficult journey experienced by the family described in Vignette 3.2, once Sara was home, they soon assumed a more typical experience. Sara received early intervention services through home visits from an occupational therapist. She was seen by the medical team in follow-up clinic for two years until they decided she no longer needed services. Today, Sara is a bright, happy child who attends family child care.

Research highlights the changes in both the mortality and morbidity in the population of infants born prematurely. Professionals and parents should use caution when using previous findings to try to see into the future of a particular child. Research, by its very nature, is often somewhat outdated by the time it is published. This is particularly true of longitudinal studies of infants born prematurely (Allen, 1996). Longitudinal studies often do not include many of the earliest-born infants, and older studies do not account for participants who have been the recipients of current therapies and treatments. However, technological advancements and new treatments such as surfactants have greatly improved the potential for such a child's development.

INFANTS AS PARTNERS

As stated, current practices reflect the viewpoint of the infant as an organized, interacting partner as opposed to a passive being. Each newborn enters the world endowed with a personality and characteristics to which parents and caregivers must respond. In that way the infant brings her own special qualities to the developing relationship between parent and child (Worobey & Brazelton, 1990).

When an infant is born with sensory impairments such as visual impairment or deafness, communication must rely on interpretation of different responses (Chen, 1996). According to Chen, parents must adapt their expectations and communicative style in order to identify and respond to their infant's signals. Similarly, when a child has a motor impairment such as cerebral palsy, the parents must adapt their behavior to understand the signals given by the child. For example, the newborn may arch away from the parents rather than cuddle into their arms. This experience can be both frightening and disappointing for the new parents, who have visualized holding their newborn baby during the many months of preparation for birth.

The service provider must be able to work well with the infant to elicit the behaviors in the infant that reflect her best performance (Nugent, 1985; Brazelton & Nugent, 1995). By doing this, service providers can help parents in turn articulate and recognize the individual communicative style of each child, as the experience described in Vignette 3.3 demonstrates.

> **VIGNETTE 3.3   KEITH AND HIS SMILE**
> Many parents view the first smile as one of the most easily remembered and important milestones for their baby. Keith was born with a facial cleft that extended from his eyes to his chin. Both his nose and mouth were misplaced on his face, and Keith would need extensive surgery over the next ten years. Keith was a playful three-month-old but confined to a hospital crib without much opportunity for movement. He was unable to bring his hands to midline, as two splints kept him from pulling at the surgical sutures from his first surgery. The hospital teacher would visit and bring a musical mobile that Keith could bat at and reach without having to flex his arms. When playing together, the teacher noted Keith smiling with his eyes. She exclaimed, "Oh, look at Keith smile." His mother seemed surprised at first, and then laughed and said, "He is smiling. I didn't think he could smile, but look at his eyes."

For many parents of a child with a disability, the day-to-day interaction in the home helps them discover the baby's special cues and interactive patterns. However, in Vignette 3.3, the family was still dealing with the intensity of a hospital setting and a medical future that seemed overwhelming. The opportunity to see her child playing with another adult helped the mother realize that he wanted to play just like other children, despite the obstacles he faced.

Bonding and Attachment

> *Once the birth is over both parents tend to feel that they need time to recover their equilibrium, to think and talk about it and to rest. But the birth resulted in a baby. The presence of that baby usually means no recovery period for either parent. They must somehow struggle straight from giving birth to caring for the baby. There is no time to think about the amazing business of becoming a parent because being one starts straight away.*
> —Leache, 1987, p. 3

As discussed in Chapter 2, Klaus and Kennell (1976) first described the concept of *bonding.* The media focus on the concept resulted in its popularization and perhaps went beyond the bounds of the original studies, which claimed that a few hours of contact between mother and infant in the immediate postpartum period produced a bonding experience that was necessary for the development of a successful mother-infant attachment and a healthier infant (Klaus & Kennell, 1976). The extra early contact that occurs for some families may indeed be important and may be influential in the growth of attachment. It has not been found, however, to be the magic point at which relationships are made or broken. Attachment is a lifelong process that continues even into adulthood.

The positive contributions of the concept of bonding include increased parent participation in labor and delivery as well as after the birth in the form of rooming-in with the baby and demand feeding. The negative influences, however, have been to raise the anxiety of parents who are not able to have the extra physical contact with their infant or infants after birth because the baby or the mother needs special medical care. Their sense of loss and the fear that they will never have a "bonding" experience should be allayed. No study to date has demonstrated that extra contact after birth is necessary for parents and infants to develop a rich and positive attachment.

To address the ongoing need for information and support on the issue of attachment, Abbott Northwestern Hospital, a large perinatal center in Minneapolis, Minnesota, joined with the local Early Childhood Family Education Program to form the New Parent Connection, a group designed to assist parents in the weeks and months following their baby's birth. Table 3.6 presents the Parent Connection philosophical framework.

The purpose of the joint program between the hospital and the local education service is to help all parents understand their new roles. Many families from middle-class backgrounds spend a great deal of time and energy on how-to books on parenting. Families from low-income communities may not have the same opportunity. It is important for community service agencies to understand these families as they try to adjust to their new experiences. Vignette 3.4 describes one family as viewed through the eyes of a service provider.

VIGNETTE 3.4 *COMING TOGETHER*

I was looking forward to participating in the New Parent Connection. I had heard a great deal about this important program and the service it provided for new families. Jolene, the facilitator, had invited several colleagues to observe her class. On this night, she was working with one family. Mom was 19 years old and this was her first baby. She was European-American, and accompanied by the father and her mother. The father was an 18-year-old African American wearing a large earring in one ear. I felt a rush of misgivings as I looked at this new family. How could they afford to take care of this baby? They weren't married and they were too young to have a child. Is Grandma going to raise this child?

Then I watched Jolene go to work. She talked about the baby's alertness. She demonstrated how the baby would turn first to the

TABLE 3.6 The Parent Connection

- With shortened hospital stays, there is little time to recover after childbirth, and parents leave exhausted, having slept little due to the excitement of giving birth. While much information is offered in the hospital, many parents are not able to absorb what is taught, as they are too overwhelmed and have not had much opportunity to interact with their newborn yet. The questions come later when they are at home on their own.
- Many new mothers have arranged leave from work and are committed for a specific number of weeks or months. What seemed like a good plan prior to the birth of the baby makes many mothers (especially) feel a great deal of pressure trying to meet both mothering and work demands. They discover there are many things to learn about their baby. Some parents discover they are uncomfortable putting their child in the care of others. (Some parents find it very difficult even to find child care.)
- Parents are surprised to discover their old routines completely altered by the needs of the new baby. One very common experience is that it is hard to find time to brush your teeth or shower! Many breast-feeding mothers need to make an extra effort to eat well and drink fluids. What was taken for granted before the baby came has now become the focus of regaining a new equilibrium.
- Couples discover their relationship is undergoing transition. Not only must they continue to work together as a couple, but they must integrate this with the baby, who is now a part of their family. This process may be perceived by mothers and fathers differently, and it can become the source of new tension and conflict if not addressed.
- Parents discover they have different ways of doing things, based on values from their family of origin. Old patterns and rituals must be evaluated and at times new ones must be instituted. This is a process that also takes time.
- Infants change so quickly! Our motto is, "Just when you think you've figured your baby out, she will grow and change, moving into new routines and with new needs." Parenting is an ongoing adjustment to the age and developmental stage of the child. This often is surprising to new parents who hoped to find "the way" to handle each situation, such as feeding and sleep.
- Infants are unique individuals. What works for one baby may not work for another. Most new parents receive so much advice that they are overwhelmed with ideas. This advice is usually offered in a way meant to be helpful, but it often challenges the parents' confidence in their process of discovery and competence in taking care of their infant. It is the process of finding out what works for the baby that builds the confidence and skills of new parents.

mother's voice and then to the father's voice. I watched the faces of these young parents as she held their baby and demonstrated all the competencies of this child born less than 24 hours ago. They were concerned, proud parents. The father's eyes sparkled as his new daughter turned to find his voice. I felt a sense of relief; these parents would love and cherish their baby. They knew how to access both informal and formal sources of support. I also learned how easy it is to let our biases interfere with our perceptions when working with families.

Early Stages of Parent-Infant Interaction

Brazelton and Cramer (1990) have developed a theoretical model to help us understand the stages of relationship building (see Table 3.7). They are important indicators of the emotional well-being of the growing and changing relationship between parents and their infants. While Brazelton and Cramer have written

TABLE 3.7   Early Caregiver Interaction

Synchrony: In this phase of attachment, nurturing from adults is critical. The first step is for parents and caregivers to adjust themselves to the baby's rhythms and attend to the baby's needs. Cries for attention are indeed a reflection of real need. As adults meet these needs, the infant comes to know them as reliable and responsive people in their lives. As adults and caregivers, in turn, see that they can help babies become more alert and soothe them when they are irritable, they begin to feel competent as nurturers. This synchrony set the stage for the next step.

Symmetry: As the parent has learned to help the infant remain in control and has begun to learn the language of the infant's behavior, the parent learns ways to draw out the baby's attention. Time is spent in mutual gaze and study of one another.

Contingency: As the growing relationship moves into the next phase, infants are able to vocalize, smile, and cry in response to interaction with their caregivers. Alert babies as young as four to six weeks of age can signal their caregivers to come and play with them. Parents and caregivers learn what "works" in this stage and usually enjoy making the baby smile.

Play: At three to four months of age, infants and caregivers who have mastered synchrony, symmetry, and contingency interactions move into play. In this phase, either the caregiver or infant will begin the interaction. In addition to smiling, infants may coo, look away, increase or decrease motor behavior. Caregivers and infants may imitate and model each other. This is an important milestone for infants as they are learning how to maintain an interaction. For parents/caregivers, we learn to help infants pay attention and respond in a variety of ways.

Autonomy and Flexibility: By about five months of age, infants enjoy these play interactions very much. In this phase parents/caregivers begin to notice the infant is more often initiating the play or stopping it. Infants at this stage often enjoy smiling or cooing at strangers. This stage also occurs at the same point the infant is becoming more developed visually, auditorially, and motorically.

Adapted from *The Earliest Relationship* by T. B. Brazelton and B. G. Cramer, 1990, Reading, Mass.: Addison-Wesley, pp. 121–128.

specifically about parents and infants, it is reasonable to assume that infants with caregivers other than parents may follow a similar progression in establishing a relationship.

ATTACHMENT IN INFANTS

Bowlby (1982) developed a theory of attachment based on both ethology and psychoanalysis that stated that infants' demonstration of need for the proximity of the mother was an adaptive behavior similar to imprinting in birds. Bowlby believed that some mothers were nurturing in their interactions with their children, while others deprived their children of nurturing interactions and responded by withholding care or using negative punishment. His writings influenced many psychologists who studied maternal deprivation and separation. Ainsworth (1969) was influenced by Bowlby and spent some time working with his researchers in the early years of her career. Her initial study of infants in Uganda used direct observation in the natural environment. She noted that the mother provided a secure base from which the infant was free to explore and return for safety. Her name has become synonymous with the concept of the "strange situation," a series of eight types of separation and reunion between mother and child that evaluate the attachment relationship. These episodes classify individual differences according to five interactive categories: proximity seeking, contact maintaining, proximity and interaction avoidance, contact and interaction resistance, and distance interaction. Infants are then categorized according to their behavior as either securely attached, anxious-avoidant, and ambivalent-attached infants.

In her research, Main (cited in Main & Solomon, 1990) noted that some infants did not fit into Ainsworth's categories, and described them as disorganized and/or disoriented. An infant described as disorganized showed a contradiction in movement pattern that related to an inferred contradiction in intention or plan. An infant described as disoriented displayed "a lack of orientation to the immediate environment" (Main & Solomon, 1990, p. 133).

It is equally important to understand the parental contributions to interactive behavior. Achieving synchrony in the parent-infant relationship is one of the first steps in building attachment. Between three and six months, infants demonstrate an understanding of the relationship between themselves and others. They will employ a variety of behaviors, including crying to gain the attention of adults (Zirpoli, 1997). Stroufe (1996) believed that young infants rely on the primary caregiver to help them regulate their emotions. As the infant gets older, he becomes better at expressing his needs. Reciprocally, the adult reinforces appropriate behaviors and redirects others.

An important milestone occurs between seven and eight months, when the infant experiences stranger anxiety. The child may cling and cry for the primary caregiver. This is typical behavior at this age, and parents should not be concerned. As the child grows he should separate more easily from the primary caregiver. Stranger anxiety should not be confused with an attachment disorder, which is a consistent, predictable diagnostic disorder that requires treatment from qualified professionals. Most children will grow out of the stranger anxiety stage. A secure attachment is the foundation from which the infant will grow, separate, and flourish.

Children with disabilities may be at risk in forming secure attachments due to unresolved feelings in the caregiver about the diagnosis. In one study of 91 mothers of children from 15 to 50 months of age, Pianta, Marvin, Britner, and Borowitz (1996) found that approximately half of the mothers were classified as unresolved in terms of their child's diagnosis. For the mothers in the resolved group, cognitive strategies were frequently used to resolve their feelings about the disability.

TEMPERAMENT AND DEVELOPMENT

The first three months of life are a period of tremendous growth and change. Infants learn to communicate with their environment through physical and vocal attempts to engage caregivers. Interpreting the infant's behavior continues to be complex but less stressful as the caregiver learns the infant's signals and routines. For example, although crying may indicate that the infant is experiencing hunger, discomfort, fatigue, or sensory overload, it may also be that the infant simply needs to let off some steam (Brazelton, 1992).

Infants exert a great deal of energy in figuring out their new environment and the caregivers who play an important role in their first three months. One theory regarding infant intelligence has been that there is discontinuity between scores on infants' sensorimotor tests and their later scores on intelligence tests. This theory has been challenged in studies that showed that infants have a visual preference for novel stimuli (Fagan, 1984). For example, researchers have found that infants with Down syndrome showed decreased sensitivity to novel stimuli, which caused them to perseverate in response to the stimulis (Fagan, 1984; Ganiban, Wagner, & Cicchetti, 1990).

In other studies infants showed facial discrimination for the mother over a strange adult (Field, Cohen, Garcia, & Greenberg, 1984; Pascalis et al., 1995). According to Fagan (1984), "The discovery that intelligence is continuous from infancy also has implications for understanding the contribution of genetic endowment and environmental circumstance to intellectual functioning" (p. 5). The question of how much human capability is genetic versus environmentally influenced continues to raise debates among experts and researchers.

Although it is difficult to sort out the nature versus nurture contributions to behavior (Emde et al., 1992), it is evident that infants develop their own way of coping and interacting. Temperament has been defined as individual differences in behavioral style (Thomas & Chess, 1977). Buss and Plomin (1975) defined three distinct characteristics of temperament: emotionality, activity, and sociability. Emotionality relates to the infant's ability to soothe himself or to be soothed once he is upset or irritable. Activity refers to both the tempo and vigor of the infant's behavior. Sociability refers to the infant's response to caregivers and strangers.

One of the first milestones in the early infant's behavioral repertoire is the social smile. Parents will readily tell you the first time their infant smiled and name the recipient of this honor. There are times when a newborn may appear to be smiling due to reflexes. The difference between a reflexive smile and a social smile is that the reflexive smile involves muscles around the mouth and lower face, while the social smile involves both mouth and eye muscles. In Vignette 3.5, a two-and-a-half-year-old infant sends mixed messages to his mother.

VIGNETTE 3.5   THE FIRST THREE MONTHS OF LIFE

Gwen and her son Alexander began attending the New Parents Connection group when Alexander was three weeks of age. Gwen expressed relief that she was not the only mother unsure of herself and "tired day in and day out." Gwen felt her baby was responsive to her, but her husband felt the baby was "unresponsive." In the group, Gwen noted that many of the other babies were smiling and cooing. She thought her husband would be more excited about the baby if he smiled. We asked the other mothers in the group to share when they noticed their babies begin to smile. We used the "expert" opinions of the group members, as it reinforces the notion that they can learn by watching their baby. Gwen learned that it not only would probably be a few more weeks, but that within the group there was quite a bit of variation from one baby to the next. We shared the idea that smiling at and talking to your baby was a way to encourage the baby to smile and talk to you.

In the next months, Gwen became one of the parent "experts" about very young babies. Alexander had "joined the group," as he looked at people who spoke and smiled when spoken to. Gwen came to a session when he was two and a half months old and raised new questions and concerns. Alexander was beginning to stick out his lower lip and whimper if Gwen could not be right in front of him interacting. She was very concerned that he was now spoiled. Her husband agreed that Alexander loved being the center of attention. Gwen was asked to recall how Alexander had begun to smile and coo and how much fun it had been. We asked parents in the group with older babies to describe times when their babies demanded attention. It was clear that there is a time developmentally when babies have learned the fun and enjoyment of interaction with their parents and just can't get enough of it. Parents felt this had been a challenging time for them too and shared the strategies they used to satisfy their baby and still get work done around the house. We shared the importance of the baby's getting to this stage and how it indicated that Alexander was discriminating and attaching to their special relationship. Gwen had not thought of it in that way. As she remembered her previous concern about Alexander's not smiling, she said, "You're right, he really does know us and likes to play!"

In the vignette, the service providers blended information and support to create an empowerment model of parent development. New parents need to enjoy strategies that work for them, based on their best knowledge of the situation. Parents in the group who served as sources of information for other parents increased their own understanding of how much they had learned. Including the whole group allowed for the individuality of both parents and babies to be expressed. It not only helped parents learn an important lesson about parenting their young baby, but also laid the foundation for information gathering and problem-solving all along the way.

During the first three months of life, the infant gradually decreases fussiness and increases alertness. She delights in play involving gentle touch. With increasing awake periods, the infant shows greater interest in the social environment. She will attempt to engage the caregiver in reciprocal play through visual, physical, and vocal engagement. The infant will reach toward a familiar face and respond physically to familiar objects such as a mobile or bottle. By one month, most infants can fixate on a moving object held at 12 inches, and follow the object across 180 degrees both vertically and horizontally. She will study her own hand and use hand movements to swat at objects. Although crying and fussing are the main forms of communication, she will occasionally express other sounds, including vowel sounds in response to social interaction.

Infants learn quickly how to engage their caregivers. Most infants will cuddle when held and prefer the caregiver's voice to that of a stranger. Infants with disabilities may not be able to give these cues to caregivers. For example, infants with cerebral palsy may arch or stiffen when picked up by an adult. This reaction may be interpreted by the adult as a rejection to interactive play. Service providers can help parents interpret their babies' behavior by listening to the parents' concerns, offering suggestions, and modeling appropriate responses.

MASTERY MOTIVATION

The infant shows an increasing interest in objects and persons during the next three months of life. He will actively use his hands to mouth and manipulate objects. He will continue a conversation by "talking" with the adult. Infant talk at this age consists of vowel sounds and raspberries. As he reaches six months, he may make consonant-vowel sounds after imitating an adult. By six months, the infant loves to engage in games such as peekaboo and pat-a-cake. He can sit alone for brief periods of time and roll over. Mobility increases the infant's ability to explore the environment. The innate interest in exploration at this time in the infant's life is referred to as mastery motivation.

Mastery motivation is a theoretical construct that can be related to both cognitive and social competence in the young child (Blasco, 1994). It is most often measured as the child's persistence in challenging goal-directed tasks. White (1959) is credited with applying Piagetian notions of cognitive change to understanding motivational theory. He characterized children's focused attention, exploration, and organizational actions toward the environment as reasonable indicators of their motivation. This behavior is observed in the selected, directed, and persistent attempts of the child to master her environment. Motivation to interact with the environment is one of the earliest processes observed in the infant.

During the first year of life infants learn that they can influence and control their environment through cause and effect. A baby kicking her feet and waving her arms causes the mobile over her head to move slightly. Prior to the beginning of the second year, toddlers are able to complete tasks in order to reach a goal and manipulate objects to create a novel effect.

Mastery During Infancy

The first attempt to study mastery motivation in infancy was made by Yarrow and his colleagues (Yarrow, Morgan, Jennings, Harmon, & Gaiter, 1982; Yarrow et al., 1983; Messer et al., 1986, MacTurk, McCarthy, Vietze, & Yarrow, 1987). In many of these studies an emphasis was placed on the relationship between persistence and cognitive development, and the influence of environmental factors on the development of mastery motivation. Persistence was defined as the percentage of time the child remained engaged in task-oriented behavior. Competence was also assessed by counting the number of times the infant was successful at producing an effect, combining objects, or securing the goal object. Finally, the child's affect during tasks was assessed. This last dimension of mastery was known as mastery pleasure.

Mastery in Play

In addition to its measurement with structured tasks, mastery motivation has also been measured during exploratory play (Belsky & Most, 1981; Belsky, Garduque, & Hrncir, 1984; Jennings, Harmon, Morgan, Gaiter, & Yarrow 1979; Hrncir, Speller, & West, 1985). These researchers believed that infants' exploratory competence is a reasonable indicator of their mastery motivation. Exploration increases the child's knowledge of the environment because the relationship between the infants and their environment is reciprocal in nature (Jennings et al., 1979; Sameroff, 1985).

In response to the child's mastery attempts, the environment provides both feedback and reinforcement, thereby refining the child's acquisition of new skills and leading to more complex manipulations and explorations. Belsky suggested that accurate and meaningful appraisals of children's competence can be made from careful observation of everyday interactions in natural life settings (Jennings et al., 1979; Belsky et al., 1984; Blasco, Bailey, & Burchinal, 1993).

Infants thus have established the ability both to master their environment and to persist at a goal before their second birthday. Many experiences during the period from birth to two years can enhance or inhibit mastery behaviors. Enhancing experiences include being successful at mastery attempts, receiving unobtrusive help to succeed in mastery attempts, having freedom to explore the environment and effect changes, and having a responsive environment early in life.

The Relationship Between Mastery and Environmental Influences

Given the importance of environmental feedback for children's mastery attempts and developmental competencies, parents play a fundamental role in providing experiences that can enhance or undermine mastery motivation. Jennings et al. (1979) found that maternal prohibition in the home was inversely related to infants' persistence and to cognitively mature play. Other studies have focused on the attitudes of parents toward their infants' mastery attempts. Jennings, Connors, Stegman, Sankaranarayan, and Mendelsohn (1985) observed that mothers of children with physical handicaps perceived their children as more dependent on adults than mothers of children without special needs. It follows that parents' attitudes and behaviors may influence the involvement of their children in mastery behavior. In preliminary work, Seifer and Vaughn (1995) also found that the quality of mothers' assistance or the degree to which mothers effectively structured, timed, and formulated their assistance was related to the extent of the child's exploration. Scaffolding, a process by which the parent or caregiver supports the expression of cognitive competence during interaction, has been examined in relation to mastery behavior by a number of researchers (Maslin, Bretherton, & Morgan, 1986; Blasco, Hrncir, & Blasco, 1990). Belsky, Good, and Most (1980) found that family influences on infant exploratory competence appeared to develop best when both parents frequently engaged their toddlers in highly arousing and positively affective social interaction. Studies showed that children whose mothers encouraged autonomy were more likely to be successful at mastery—both nonrisk children (Frodi, Bridges, & Grolnick, 1985) and children with disabilities (Blasco, Hrncir, & Blasco, 1990; Hauser-Cram, 1996).

Children with Disabilities

In a study of exploratory behavior, MacTurk, Hunter, McCarthy, Vietze, and McQuiston (1985) examined the sequences of object manipulations of infants with Down syndrome and of infants developing normally, matched at a mental age of six months. The goal of the study was to discover the distribution of behaviors in both groups during exploratory play in order to identify the similarities and differences in organizational patterns. Although the two groups of children did not vary in the total amount of behavior, they differed widely in the distribution of behavior. MacTurk and his colleagues found that children with Down syndrome had more difficulty discerning social cues (i.e., seeking social reinforcement) than their peers. The infants with Down syndrome who displayed more social responsiveness were more likely to stay on task.

Schwethelm and Mahoney (1986) measured the development of motivation in infants diagnosed with mental disabilities. They utilized the Yarrow paradigm and specifically focused on task persistence as a measure of mastery behavior. The children (ages 12 to 36 months) exhibited persistent behavior with tasks that were in their range of competence and engaged in more exploratory behavior if the tasks were slightly challenging or difficult. The findings indicated that children with mental disabilities were less motivated than their peers to approach and solve challenging tasks. Thus children with mental disabilities may benefit from receiving assistance to succeed in more challenging mastery attempts.

Jennings et al. (1985) studied aspects of mastery motivation in both structured-task and free-play settings among preschoolers with and without physical handicaps. They found that preschoolers with physical handicaps were less likely to engage in mastery tasks than their peers but that they were just as curious. These authors also concluded that the presence of a physical handicap may decrease experiences that facilitate mastery attempts and lead to learned helplessness.

Blasco et al. (1990) examined aspects of mastery behavior in toddlers with cerebral palsy and found that a measure of spontaneous mastery was a better indicator of the child's true developmental abilities than a standardized developmental quotient. In general the research has pursued two fundamentally important questions: (1) what is mastery behavior and how can it be measured? and (2) what factors influence mastery behavior?

Scholars have argued that qualitative differences are observed in the mastery attempts of children with special needs (Jennings et al., 1985; Krakow & Kopp, 1982; MacTurk, Vietze, McCarthy, McQuiston, & Yarrow, 1985; Blasco et al., 1990). For example, a child who is unable to physically manipulate an object may engage his environment through visual attention, vocalization, and/or social interaction.

Another issue in examining mastery motivation in infants and toddlers with disabilities is that developmental age plays a role in the definition of mastery. For example, a one-year-old child with Down syndrome may explore toys the same way as a typical six-month-old. Therefore, pushing a toy to make it turn might be a mastery behavior for this child but not a very challenging task for a typical 12-month-old (Blasco, Bailey, & Burchinal, 1993).

Table 3.8 indicates many of the developmental milestones that are achieved during the first twelve months. It is important to realize that children vary widely in the acquisition of these milestones. In general, the milestones provide a starting point for typical development. For children with disabilities, the type of disability will affect the achievement of milestones. For example, we know that children with Down syndrome often achieve the same milestones as children who are typically developing but at a slower rate. Therefore a one-year-old with Down syndrome may be gaining skills at the six- to eight-month level. A child with autism would have a more scattered profile across domains of development and therefore

TABLE 3.8   Important Milestones: Birth to Twelve Months

BEHAVIOR	AGE OF ONSET RANGE (MONTHS)
Responds positively to feeding and comforting	B–1
Regards person momentarily	B–1
Shows social smile	1.5–3
Quiets with sucking	1.5–3
Shows distress and excitement	1.5–3
Responds with vocal sounds when talked to	1–6
Discriminates mother	1–5
Laughs	3–5
Aware of strange situation	3–6
Discriminates strangers	3–6
Interested in mirror image	5–7
Laughs at games (peekaboo)	5–7
Cooperates in games	5–12
Resists having a toy taken away	5–12
Plays pat-a-cake	5–12
Imitates facial expressions	7–9
Shows stranger anxiety	8–10
Tugs at adult to gain attention	8–12
Offers toy to adult	12–16
Shows affection toward people, pets, or possession	12–17
Enjoys playing with other children	12–17
Engages in tantrums	12–18
Demonstrates mastery pleasure	12–24

would be unlikely to achieve milestones in any consistent pattern (Pat Pulice, personal communication, November 4, 1996).

ALTERNATIVE EXPLORATION

Children explore their environment both mentally and physically. Children with physical and visual disabilities may need to develop alternative methods for exploring their environment. As discussed in Chapter 10, assistive technology is a great equalizer in allowing children with physical limitations to explore and discover through cause and effect.

Alternative methods for children's exploratory behavior motivated physical therapists to question traditional, hierarchical motor theories. For example, the theory that control of movement progressed from proximal to distal control has been challenged as researchers showed through studies of infant reaching that proximal and distal control developed at the same time. These challenges to traditional theory have led to the adoption of a new theory of motor development called dynamic systems theory (Horak, 1991), which conceptualizes the human body as comprising many subsystems that interact to produce coordinated movement (Scalise-Smith & Bailey, 1992).

According to this theory, the infant takes a more active role in solving motor problems rather than simply learning movement patterns. Rather, a motor skill develops out of a need to master the environment. However, the therapist needs to see if the movement solves the motor problem and then help to plan strategies for generalization (Schmidt, 1991). Movement gives the infant an opportunity to explore all aspects of her environment and to learn how her body will support her in acquiring new physical skills such as pulling to stand and walking. For children who are immobile, adaptive equipment and assistive technology help provide the same opportunities their peers enjoy. For example, an infant can activate a single switch to turn a radio on and off. When an infant is positioned properly, he is more likely to show interest in learning activities. Promising practice for the provision of physical therapy includes a transdisciplinary approach to teaching that fully integrates physical therapy within the infant's natural environment (York, Rainforth, & Giangreco, 1990; Eliason, 1995).

FEEDING AND NUTRITION

Infants between the ages of birth and three months are very busy learning how to receive nutrition from an external source, in many cases a bottle. The reflexes of rooting, sucking, swallowing, and gagging are present at birth. Rooting occurs when the infant turns toward the source of food after being stimulated around the corners of the mouth or along the upper and lower lips (Murphy & Caretto, 1999). Sucking is the primary mechanism the infant uses to receive nutrition and plays a role in helping the infant to become calm and later on to explore new materials and objects (Wolf & Glass, 1992). Infants who have difficulty with the sucking reflex may have an anatomic defect (e.g., cleft lip), poor muscular control (e.g., caused by cerebral palsy), or oral pain (e.g., caused by thrush or lesions). Swallowing is a more complex motor sequence that involves the coordination of muscles in the mouth, pharynx, larynx, and esophagus (Wolf & Glass, 1992). Swallowing difficulty may also be due to anatomic or neuromuscular abnormalities. Gastroesophageal reflux occurs when the infant is unable to keep milk in the stomach, and the milk and gastric contents return up the esophagus. This behavior may be symptomatic of failure to thrive, apnea, respiratory disease, or esophageal irritation (Wolf & Glass, 1992).

The gag reflex protects the infant from choking on food or materials dangerous to swallow (Murphy & Caretto, 1999). Prior to four months of age, the infant may gag if given even pureed food. Between four and six months, the infant can handle pureed foods much better. The infant at this age will recognize a bottle and hold her mouth open in anticipation of food. In concert with the exploratory stage, the infant will begin to finger-feed himself and attempt to hold his own bottle. Between 10 and 15 months, the infant will be able to bite soft food and hold a cup to drink liquids. Some infants develop an abnormal bite called the tonic bite reflex, which is manifested by a sudden tense bite with little or no release. The reflex has been observed in infants who experience sensory stimulation around the teeth and gums. The service provider can use a rubber-coated spoon to avoid touching the teeth and gums (Lowman, 1999). After 15 months of age, the infant develops strong lip closure, allowing her to drink and chew with little or no spillage. For most infants and toddlers, eating is a pleasurable experience that awakens the senses and leads to discovery of new tastes and textures. By the age of two, most children can hold their own cup with one hand and drink without spilling.

NEW RESEARCH ON BRAIN DEVELOPMENT

As exciting new advances in neurobiology continue to unfold, greater understanding of the human brain will be a major scientific achievement in the twenty-first century. Researchers and scientists now have imaging tools for viewing the brain from prebirth to adulthood, which have led to a better understanding of the mechanics of memory and learning.

Learning takes place through construction of neural networks. Neurons are the basic functional units of the nervous system. At birth, the brain has its full complement of neurons (close to 100 billion) (Shore, 1997). The weight of the newborn's brain is 25 percent of its adult weight, and by age two, it is 75 percent of its adult weight (Rosenblith, 1992). Sometime between the ages of three and five years, 95 percent of adult brain weight is achieved (Capone, 1996).

The brain is organized developmentally by a series of complex molecular, biochemical, and cellular mechanisms that occur in various regions of the brain (Capone, 1996). These developmental events take place between three and four weeks of gestation and five years of age, emphasizing the importance of the early childhood years. For children with neurodevelopmental disorders, significant research efforts to study the brain and the neurotransmitters that affect behavioral performance may lead to successful treatment and, in some situations, amelioration of a disability. For a complete review of early brain development see Capone (1996) and Shore (1997).

SUMMARY

This chapter examined the first year of life, beginning with the newborn. An important consideration is the role of the newborn in early interaction with caregivers. The infant enters the world endowed with a personality and characteristics to which parents and caregivers must respond. In this way she brings her own special qualities to the developing relationships with her parents and caregivers.

The newborn infant develops a series of signals to help adults become aware of her emotional needs and desires. When a newborn has become overstimulated, he may close his eyes, sneeze, or turn his head away from the stimuli. Newborns calm themselves from stressful events by placing a thumb or fist in their mouths, or by pulling all their limbs into a flexed position. For those infants born early, many of these responses are the same, but there are some differences. For example, infants who are born premature may need many medical interventions to stay alive. During this time they may be less alert and less available for interaction with their parents. In some cases, it may be weeks before parents are able to hold their infant. Because interactions are limited, the infant's responses are more indicative of stress than of pleasure. It may be weeks before both the infant and parents can participate in the reciprocal interactions that form attachment.

Bowlby (1982) defined *attachment* as a warm, continuous relationship with a mother or maternal substitute. Ainsworth (1969), who was influenced by him and his researchers in the early years of her career, has become identified with the concept of the "strange situation," a series of eight types of separation and reunion between the mother and child that evaluate the attachment relationship. These episodes classify individual differences according to five interactive categories.

Temperament has been defined as individual differences in behavioral style (Thomas & Chess, 1977). Emotionality relates to infants' ability to soothe themselves or to be soothed once they are upset or irritable. Activity refers to both the tempo and vigor of the infant's behavior. Sociability refers to the infant's response to caregivers and strangers.

Mastery motivation is a theoretical construct that can be related to both cognitive and social competence in the young child. It is most often measured as the child's persistence in challenging goal-directed tasks. Mastery motivation may be observed through the infant's exploratory behavior. For example, an infant who pushes a toy and activates the musical chime is engaged in a mastery task.

One issue in examining mastery motivation in infants and toddlers with disabilities is that developmental age plays a role in the definition of mastery. For example, a one-year-old child with Down syndrome may explore toys in the same way as a typical six-month-old. Therefore, what may be a mastery task for one child may not be challenging for another. Service providers must combine their skills of observation and knowledge of the developmental level of the child in order to evaluate mastery behavior. Children who have accomplished a mastery task will often smile or sigh in response to successful completion.

Infants who are unable to explore their environment visually or physically will find alternative ways to develop sensorimotor skills that are similar to those of typically developing infants. Caregivers learn to match their interactive style with the unique needs of their infants. With the help of service providers, infants also explore the world through eating and tasting. Good nutrition is essential for optimal growth and development. Learning self-help skills for eating leads a child toward a sense of independence and success.

This chapter examined the first year of life as seen through some key concepts for understanding young children. It provided a lens for understanding individual differences within this period. The complexity of parenting is often increased when a child has a disability. A firm understanding of the parenting process is necessary in order to help with parental concerns during the first year of life.

REFERENCES

Ainsworth, M. D. S. (1969). Object relations, dependency and attachment: A theoretical review of the infant-mother relationship. *Child Development, 40,* 969–1025.

Allen, M. C. (1996). Prematurity. In A. J. Capute & P. J. Accardo (Eds.), *Developmental disabilities in infancy and childhood, Vol. 1: Neurodevelopmental diagnosis and treatment* (2nd ed., pp. 159–173). Baltimore: Paul H. Brookes.

Allen, M. C., & Capute, A. J. (1986). The evolution of primitive reflexes in extremely premature infants. *Pediatric Research, 20,* 1284–1289.

Allen, M. C., Donohue, M. S., & Dusman, A. E. (1993). The limit of viability: Neonatal outcome of infants born at 22 to 25 weeks' gestation. *New England Journal of Medicine, 329,* 1597–1601.

Als, H. (1982). Towards a synactive theory of development: Promise for the assessment of infant individuality. *Infant Mental Health Journal, 3,* 229–243.

Als, H., & Gilkerson, L. (1995). Developmentally supportive care in the neonatal intensive care unit. *Zero to Three, 15(6),* 1–9.

Als, H., Lester, B. M., Tronick, E. Z., & Brazelton, T. B. (1982). Manual for the assessment of preterm infants' behavior (APIB). In H. E. Fitzgerald, B. M. Lester, & M. W. Yogman (Eds.), *Theory and research in behavioral pediatrics,* pp. 35–63. New York: Plenum.

Apgar, V. (1953). A proposal for a new method of evaluation of the newborn infant. *Current Research in Anesthesia and Analgesia, 32,* 260–265.

Batshaw, M. L., & Shapiro, B. K. (1997). Mental retardation. In M. L. Batshaw (Ed.), *Children with disabilities* (4th ed., pp. 335–339). Baltimore: Paul H. Brookes.

Bayley, N. (1993). *The Bayley Scales of Infant Development.* San Antonio, Tex.: Psychological Corporation.

Belsky, J., Garduque, L., & Hrncir, E. (1984). Assessing performance, competence, and executive capacity in infant play: Relations to home environment and security of attachment. *Developmental Psychology, 20,* 406–417.

Belsky, J., Good, M., & Most, R. (1980). Maternal stimulation and infant exploratory competence: Cross-sectional correlational and experimental analyses. *Child Development, 51,* 1163–1178.

Belsky, J., & Most, R. K. (1981). From exploration to play: A cross-sectional study of infant free play behavior. *Developmental Psychology, 17,* 630–639.

Blasco, P. A. (1992). Normal and abnormal motor development. *Pediatric Rounds, 1(2),* 1–6.

———. (1994). Primitive reflexes: Their contribution to the early detection of cerebral palsy. *Clinical Pediatrics, 33,* 388–397.

Blasco, P. M., Bailey, D. B., & Burchinal, M. A. (1993). Dimensions of mastery in same-age and mixed-age integrated classrooms. *Early Childhod Research Quarterly, 8,* 193–206.

Blasco, P. M., Hrncir, E. J., & Blasco, P. A. (1990). The contribution of maternal involvement to mastery performance in infants with cerebral palsy. *Journal of Early Intervention, 14,* 161–174.

Bottos, M. (1986). Clues in neonatal behavior of severely handicapped infants and young children. *Infant Mental Health Journal, 7(4).*

Bowlby, J. (1982). *Attachment.* New York: Basic Books.

Brazelton, T. B. (1992). *Touchpoints: The essential reference.* Reading, Mass.: Addison-Wesley.

Brazelton, T. B., & Cramer, B. G. (1990). *The earliest relationship.* Reading, Mass.: Addison-Wesley.

Brazelton, T. B., & Nugent, J. K., (1995). *Neonatal Behavioral Assessment Scale* (3rd ed.). London: MacKeith Press.

Brownell, C. A. (1990). Peer social skills in toddlers: Competencies and constraints illustrated by same-age and mixed-age interaction. *Child Development, 61,* 838–848.

Bruner, J. S. (1973). Organization of early skilled action. *Child Development, 44,* 1–11.

Buss, A. H., & Plomin, R. (1975). *A temperament theory of personality development.* New York: Wiley.

Capone, G. T. (1996). Human brain development. In A. J. Capute & P. J. Accardo (Eds.), *Developmental disabilities in infancy and childhood* (2nd ed., pp. 25–75). Baltimore: Paul H. Brookes.

Capute, A. J., & Accardo, P. J. (1996). *Developmental disabilities in infancy and childhood.* Baltimore: Paul H. Brookes.

Capute, A. J., Accardo, P. J., & Vining, E. P. G. (1978). *Primitive reflex profile.* Baltimore: Paul H. Brookes.

Capute, A. J., Shapiro, B. K., and Accardo, P. J. (1982). Motor functions: associated primitive reflex profiles. *Developmental Medicine and Child Neurology, 24,* 662–669.

Chen, D. (1996). Parent-infant communication: Early intervention for very young children with visual impairment or hearing loss. *Infants and Young Children, 9,* 1–12.

D'Apolito, K. (1991). What is an organized infant? *Neonatal Network, 10*(1), 97–105.

Dubowitz, L. M. S., Dubowitz, V., & Goldberg, C. (1970). Clinical assessment of gestational age in the newborn infant. *Journal of Pediatrics, 77*(1), 1–10.

Dubowitz, V. (1995). Chaos in the classification of SMA: A possible resolution. *Neuromuscular Disorder, 5*(1), 3–5.

Eliason, L. (1995). The physical management of students with disabilities: Training for school personnel. Masters project. St. Paul, Minn.: University of St. Thomas.

Emde, R. N., Plomin, R., Robinson, J., Corley, R., DeFries, J., Fulker, D. W., Reznick, J. S., Campos, J., Kagan, J., & Zahn-Waxler, C. (1992). Temperament, emotion, and cognition at fourteen months: The MacArthur longitudinal twin study. *Child Development, 63,* 1437–1455.

Fagan, J. F. (1984). The intelligent infant: Theoretical implications. *Intelligence, 8,* 1–9.

Field, T. M., Cohen, D., Garcia, R., & Greenberg, R. (1984). Mother-stranger face discrimination by the newborn. *Infant Behavior and Development, 7,* 19–25.

Forouzan, I., Morgan, M. A., & Batshaw, M. (1997). In M. Batshaw (Ed.), *Children with disabilities* (4th ed., pp. 71–91). Baltimore: Paul H. Brookes.

Frodi, A., Bridges, L., & Grolnick, W. (1985). Correlates of mastery-related behavior: A short-term longitudinal study of infants in their second year. *Child Development, 56,* 1291–1298.

Ganiban, J., Wagner, S., & Cicchetti, D. (1990). Temperament and Down syndrome. In D. Cicchetti & M. Beeghly (Eds.), *Children with Down syndrome* (pp. 63–100). New York: Cambridge University Press.

Greenspan, S., & Thorndike-Greenspan, N. (1985) *First feelings: Milestones in the emotional development of your baby and child.* New York: Penguin.

Haley, S. M., Baryza, M. J., Troy, M., Geckler, C., & Schoenberg, S. (1991). In M. Lister (Ed.), *Contemporary management of motor control problems: Proceedings of the II-STEP Conference* (pp. 237–245). Alexandria, Va.: Foundation for Physical Therapy.

Harris, S. R. (1997). The effectiveness of early intervention for children with cerebral palsy and related motor disabilities. In M. J. Guralnick (Ed.), *The effectiveness of early intervention* (pp. 327–347). Baltimore: Paul H. Brookes.

Harrison, M. J. (1990). A comparison of parental interactions with term and preterm infants. *Research in Nursing and Health, 13,* 173–179.

Harter, S. (1975). Developmental differences in the manifestation of mastery motivation on problem-solving tasks. *Child Development, 46,* 370–378.

Harter, S., & Zigler, E. (1974). The assessment of effectance motivation in normal and retarded children. *Developmental Psychology, 10,* 169–180.

Hauser-Cram, P. (1996). Mastery motivation in toddlers with developmental disabilities. *Child Development, 67,* 236–248.

Heriza, C. B., & Sweeney, J. K. (1994). Pediatric physical therapy: Part 1. Practice scope, scientific basis, and theoretical foundation. *Infants and Young Children, 7,* 20–32.

Horak, F. B. (1991). Assumptions underlying motor control for neurological rehabilitation. In M. J. Lister (Ed.), *Contemporary management of motor control problems* (pp. 11–27). Alexandria, Va.: Foundation for Physical Therapy.

Hrncir, E. J., Speller, G. M., & West, M. (1985). What are we testing? *Developmental Psychology, 21,* 226–232.

Hunt, J. (1965). Intrinsic motivation and its role in psychological development. *Nebraska Symposium on Motivation, 13,* 189–282.

Hupp, S. C., & Abbeduto, L. (1991). Persistence as an indicator of mastery motivation in young children with cognitive delays. *Journal of Early Intervention, 15,* 219–225.

Jennings, K. D., Connors, R. E., Stegman, C. E., Sankaranarayan, P., & Mendelsohn, S. (1985). Mastery motivation in young preschoolers: Effect of a physical handicap and implications for educational programming. *Journal of the Division of Early Childhood, 9,* 162–169.

Jennings, K. D., Harmon, R. J., Morgan, G. A., Gaiter, J. L., & Yarrow, L. J. (1979). Exploratory play as an index of mastery motivation: Relationship to persistence, cognitive functioning, and environmental measures. *Developmental Psychology, 15,* 386–394.

Klaus, M., (1993). Prematurity and serious medical illness in infancy: Implications for development and intervention. In C. J. Zeanah (Ed.), *Handbook of infant mental health* (pp. 105–130). New York: Guilford.

Klaus, M. H., & Kennell, J. H. (1970). Mothers separated from their newborn infants. *Pediatric Clinics of North America, 17,* 1015–1037.

Klaus, M. H., & Kennell, J. H. (1976). *Maternal infant bonding.* St. Louis: Mosby.

Klaus, M. H., & Kennell, J. H. (1982). *Bonding: The beginnings of parent-infant bonding.* St. Louis: Mosby.

Krakow, J. B., & Kopp, C. B. (1982). Sustained attention in young Down syndrome children. *Topics in Early Childhood Special Education, 2*(2), 32–42.

Leach, P. (1987). *Babyhood.* New York: Alfred A. Knopf.

Lester, T. M. (1985). Data analysis and prediction. In T. B. Brazelton (Ed.), *Neonatal Behavioral Assessment Scale,* (2nd ed., pp. 85–91). London: Spartica International.

Levy, J. (1993). *Mother-infant bonding: A scientific fiction.* New Haven, Conn.: Yale University Press.

Lowman, D. K. (1999). Adaptive equipment for feeding. In D. K. Lowman & S. M. Murphy (Eds.), *The educator's guide to feeding children with disabilities* (pp. 141–154). Baltimore: Paul H. Brookes.

MacTurk, R. H., Hunter, F., McCarthy, M., Vietze, P., & McQuiston, S. (1985). Social mastery motivation in Down syndrome and nondelayed infants. *Topics in Early Childhood Special Education, 4,* 93–103.

MacTurk, R. H., McCarthy, M. E., Vietze, P. M., & Yarrow, L. J. (1987). Sequential analysis of mastery behavior in 6- and 12-month-old infants. *Developmental Psychology, 23,* 199–203.

MacTurk, R. H., Vietze, P. M., McCarthy, M. E., McQuiston, S., & Yarrow, L. J. (1985). The organization of exploratory behavior in Down syndrome and non-delayed infants. *Child Development, 56,* 573–581.

Main, M., & Hesse, E. (1990). Parents' unresolved traumatic experiences are related to infant disorganized attachment status: Is frightened and/or frightening parental behavior the linking mechanism? In M. T. Greenberg, D. Cicchetti, & E. M. Cummings (Eds.), *Attachment in the preschool years: Theory, research, and intervention* (pp. 161–182). Chicago: Chicago University Press.

Main, M., & Solomon, J. (1990). Procedures for identifying infants as disorganized/disoriented during the Ainsworth strange situation. In M. T. Greenberg, D. Cicchetti, & E. M. Cummings (Eds.), *Attachment in the preschool years: Theory, research, and intervention* (pp. 121–160). Chicago: Chicago University Press.

Maslin, C. A., Bretherton, I., & Morgan, G. A. (1986, April). *The influence of attachment security and maternal scaffolding on toddler mastery motivation.* Paper presented at the Fifth International Conference on Infant Studies, Los Angeles.

Messer, D. J., McCarthy, M. E., McQuiston, S., MacTurk, R. H., Yarrow, L. J., & Vietze, P. M. (1986). Relation between mastery behavior in infancy and competence in early childhood. *Developmental Psychology, 22,* 336–372.

Murphy, S. M., & Caretto, V. (1999). Anatomy of the oral and respiratory structures made easy. In D. K. Lowman & S. M. Murphy (Eds.), *The educator's guide to feeding children with disabilities* (pp. 35–64). Baltimore: Paul H. Brookes.

Nickel, R. E., & Widerstrom, A. H. (1997). Developmental disorders in infancy. In A. H. Widerstrom, R. A. Mowder, & S. R. Sandall (Eds.), *Infant development and risk* (2nd ed., pp. 89–121). Baltimore: Paul H. Brookes.

Nugent, K. J. (1985). *Using the NBAS with infants and their families.* White Plains, N.Y.: March of Dimes Foundation.

——— (1989). Preventive intervention with infants and families: The NBAS model. *Infant Mental Health Journal, 10*(2), 84–99.

Pascalis, O., de Schonen, S., Morton, J., Deruelle, C., & Fabre-Grenet, M. (1995). Mother's face recognition by neonates: A replication and an extension. *Infant Behavior and Development, 18,* 79–85.

Piaget, J. (1952). *The origins of intelligence in children.* New York: International University Press.

Pianta, R. C., Marvin, R. S., Britner, P. A., & Borowitz, K. C. (1996). Mothers' resolution of their children's diagnosis: Organized patterns of caregiving representations. *Infant Mental Health Journal, 17*(3), 239–256.

Redding, R. E., Morgan, G. A., & Harmon, R. J. (1988). Mastery motivation in infants and toddlers: Is it greatest when tasks are moderately challenging? *Infant Behavior and Development, 11,* 419–430.

Rosenblith, J. F. (1992). *In the beginning: Development from conception to age two* (2nd ed.). Newbury Park, Calif.: Sage.

Sameroff, A. J. (1985). Environmental factors in the early screening of children at risk. In W. K. Frankenburg, R. N. Emde, & J. W. Sullivan (Eds.), *Early identification of children at risk: An international perspective* (pp. 21–44). New York: Plenum Press.

Scalise-Smith, D., & Bailey, D. (1992). Facilitating motor skills. In D. B. Bailey & M. Wolery (Eds.), *Teaching infants and preschoolers with disabilities* (pp. 407–440). New York: Merrill.

Schmidt, R. A. (1991). Motor learning principles for physical therapy. In M. J. Lister (Ed.), *Contemporary management of motor control problems* (pp. 49–63). Alexandria, Va.: Foundation for Physical Therapy.

Schwethelm, B., & Mahoney, G. (1986). Task persistence among organically-impaired mentally retarded children. *American Journal of Mental Deficiency, 90,* 432–439.

Seifer, R., & Vaughn, B. E. (1995). Mastery motivation within a general organizational model of competence. In R. H. MacTurk & G. A. Morgan (Eds.), *Mastery motivation: Origins, conceptualizations, and applications, Vol. 12: Advances in applied developmental psychology* (pp. 95–115). Norwood, N.J.: Ablex Publishing.

Self, P. A., & Horowitz, F. D. (1979). The behavioral assessment of the neonate: An overview. In J. Osofsky (Ed.), *The handbook of infant development* (pp. 127–133). New York: Wiley.

Shore, R. (1997). *Rethinking the brain: New insights into early development.* New York: Families and Work Institute.

Smilansky, S. (1968). *The effects of socio-dramatic play on disadvantaged preschool children.* New York: Wiley.

Stroufe, L. A. (1996). *Emotional development: The organization of emotional life in the early years.* New York: Cambridge University Press.

Tappero, E., & Honeyfield, M. E. (1993). *Physical assessment of the newborn: A comprehensive approach to the art of physical examination.* Petaluma, Calif.: NICU Publications.

Thomas, A., & Chess, S. (1977). *Temperament and development.* New York: Bruner/Mazel.

Wachs, T. D. (1987). Purdue free play mastery motivation manual. Department of Psychological Sciences. West Lafayette, Ind.: Purdue University.

Wachs, T. D. (1987). Specificity of environmental action as manifest in environmental correlates of infant's mastery motivation. *Developmental Psychology, 23,* 782–790.

White, R. W. (1959). Motivation reconsidered: The concept of competence. *Psychological Review, 66,* 297–333.

Wolf, L. S., & Glass, R. P. (1992). *Feeding and swallowing disorders in infancy: Assessment and management.* Tucson, Arizona: Communication Skill Builders.

Worobey, J. and Brazelton, T. B. (1990). Newborn assessment and support for parenting: The neonatal behavioral assessment scale. In E. D. Gibbs, & D. M. Teti (Eds.), *Interdisciplinary assessment of infants, A guide for early intervention professionals* (pp. 33–41). Baltimore: Paul H. Brookes.

Yarrow, L. J., McQuiston, S., MacTurk, R. H., McCarthy, M. E., Klein, R. P., & Vietze, P. M. (1983). Assessment of mastery motivation during the first year of life: Contemporaneous and cross-age relationships. *Developmental Psychology, 19,* 159–171.

Yarrow, L. J., Morgan, G. A., Jennings, K. D., Harmon, R. J., & Gaiter, J. L. (1982). Infants' persistence at tasks: Relationship to cognitive functioning and early experience. *Infant Behavior and Development, 5,* 131–141.

York, J., Rainforth, B., & Giangreco, M. (1990). Transdisciplinary teamwork and integrated therapy: Clarifying the misconceptions. *Pediatric Physical Therapy, 2,* 73–79.

Zirpoli, S. (1997). Issues in early childhood behavior. In T. J. Zirpoli & K. J. Melloy (Eds.), *Behavior management: Applications for teachers and parents* (2nd ed., pp. 383–417). Upper Saddle River, N.J.: Merrill.

CHAPTER FOUR

TODDLERS: THE SECOND AND THIRD YEARS

- To introduce the theoretical approaches to learning in infants and toddlers with and without disabilities
- To understand social development, including social mastery motivation and social competence, and the impact of social development on all developmental domains
- To understand pretend play and its role in development for all toddlers, including children at risk
- To understand prosocial behavior and the expression of feelings during the toddler years
- To understand the impact of language and alternative communication systems for toddlers
- To understand the impact of motor development and new approaches to understanding motor development in toddlers
- To understand the impact of risk status on young children

EXPLORATION THROUGH MENTAL AND PHYSICAL PROCESSES

The second year of life is a time of challenges for the child and challenging behavior for the adults. The busy life of the toddler can readily be observed in all areas of development: the physical, the emotional, language, and cognition. Providing children with the supports they need to grow and learn will promote self-esteem and independence. Cognitive psychologists see thinking and learning as an interactive process between a person and her environments. Over the last three decades, knowledge of child development and, particularly, intellectual development had been greatly influenced by the writings of Piaget (1960).

According to Piaget, from birth to approximately 18 months, children progress through the sensorimotor period. During this period the child is actively engaged in exploring the environment through the sensory modalities of speech and hearing, and touch. Children between the ages of 12 to 18 months often exhibit the following characteristics:

- Engages in trial and error (attempts various methods to gain a response)
- Activates a novel toy after a demonstration
- Understands object permanence (knows when a toy is concealed under a cover)
- Practices placing and removing objects in a container
- Combines actions to complete a task or goal

Children with disabilities also go through the sensorimotor period but may do so at different rates, depending on the disability. For example, data showed that children with Down syndrome progressed through the same stages of sensorimotor development, yet complex competencies were demonstrated at a later age (Dunst, 1990).

Wishart (1995) argued that infants with Down syndrome engage in specific exploration behaviors that are counterproductive to learning. For example, many children with Down syndrome engage in repetitive activities with objects. Currently researchers are exploring the possibility that such repetition may be a step in the process of acquiring knowledge (Lender, Goodman, & Linn, 1998). According to Batshaw and Shapiro (1997), children with severe cognitive impairments do not progress beyond the sensorimotor period.

Children with physical disabilities experience sensorimotor development through the use of technology and with the physical assistance of adults. The application of technology is discussed in detail in Chapter 10. In Vignette 4.1, a child with cerebral palsy communicates his need for help to his mother.

> **VIGNETTE 4.1   JUSTIN AND HIS MOM**
> Justin is an 18-month-old with hemiplegic cerebral palsy. He is play-
> ing with a Fisher-Price garage toy and he needs assistance bringing
> the car up in the elevator and releasing it onto the "down" ramp. His
> mother watches as Justin pushes the car into the elevator. He
> touches the crank and then gazes at his mother to request help.
> Justin's mother asks, "Should we raise the elevator?" and waits for a
> verbal or physical response (often he will raise his eyebrows and
> vocalize "ah" for yes). She then places her hand over Justin's hand to
> try the crank. When the elevator reaches the top floor, the car is
> released down the ramp. Justin laughs as he watches the car speed
> across the floor.

Although Justin's mother gave physical assistance when requested, she did not complete the task for him. This strategy is referred to as partial participation, and is discussed further in Chapter 7. It is important to give Justin the opportunity to succeed at a task involving problem-solving, despite his physical limitations. In the past, parents of children with disabilities were rated by practitioners and researchers as being more directive in their interactions with their children (Jennings, Connors, Stegman, Sankaranarayan, & Mendelsohn, 1985). However, service providers may have inadvertently contributed to this interactive style by requiring parents to set goals and attain them before the next home visit. Recent studies have shown that the parents' behavior may also be reflective of their attempt to adapt the environment so their child may be more successful (Blasco, Hrncir, & Blasco, 1990; Marfo, 1991; Hauser-Cram, 1996). In any event, current trends in services would include supporting parent/caregiver–child interaction by helping parents and caregivers interpret and change their or their child's behavior. As McCollum (in McCollum & Hemmeter, 1997) stated, with this approach the parent becomes an observer, interpreter, and hypothesizer.

Piaget described the period between the ages of two to seven as the preoperational stage, when children gain skills in problem-solving. This is the time when all six layers of the cortex and of the structures that link the two hemispheres of the brain mature (Batshaw & Shapiro, 1997). Children engage in pretend play on an increasingly sophisticated level. They can begin to sort and match objects. For many children, this is a time for language explosion. For children with disabilities and at-risk children, language delay can have serious repercussions in all other areas of development.

A hallmark of Piagetian theory is that the growth of the young child's cognitive skills is gradual and continuous. Each period of development builds on the previous one in a process Piaget called "the growth of mental structures." Finally, Piaget believed that the toddler is engaged in constructing a plan. The concept of "intentionality" gradually emerges as the child selects objects, plays with them, repeats actions on them, and finalizes a plan for interacting with them (Gonzalez-Mena & Widmeyer Eyer, 1993).

THE BEHAVIORAL APPROACH TO LEARNING

A second approach to understanding early conceptual development in toddlers is reflected in the work of Skinner (1953), which formed the basis for the behavioral approach to learning. These scholars believed that behavior was conditioned or learned. Under this approach, the adult manipulates the environment to change the child's behavior. Skinner (1953) believed that overt behaviors are measurable using direct observation. His work formed the foundation for the use of operant conditioning and reinforcement contingencies in working with children with disabilities. Operant conditioning emphasizes the relationship between specific events in the environment and changes in a target behavior (Zirpoli & Melloy, 2001). Antecedent events precede a specific behavior, and consequences are events that occur after the event. For example, when a caregiver brings a spoon of food toward the toddler's mouth, the toddler will open his mouth to receive it. The consequences of opening his mouth are the taste of the food and the response of the caregiver. When a child refuses to accept the food, the antecedent behavior may need to be evaluated and changed. The consequences can be negative for both the child and the caregiver (the child is undernourished, and the caregiver is stressed). Special educators are traditionally taught a behaviorist approach to managing behavior as part of their training program: that is, most behavior is learned and stimulus-specific. Treatment involves teaching specific strategies to chance behavior. This approach may be viewed as narrowly focused when compared with a more developmental or sociocultural theory of learning that commonly provides the foundations for early childhood education.

SOCIAL LEARNING

Recently, scholars have challenged the argument advanced by both behavioral theory and Piagetian theory that children's conceptual development is more dependent on the development of insights or skills that are domain, task, and context specific than on the development of sequential, logical structures (Case, Okamoto et al., 1996). Following Vygotsky's (1962) view that children's thought development is more influenced by external sources and social interaction, some researchers believe that cognitive abilities are dependent on both linguistic and conceptual frameworks that children inherit from their culture and the physical and social principles associated with these frameworks (Case, Okamoto et al. 1996).

The hallmark of Vygotskian theory is that children learn in the "zone of proximal development," which is defined as "a phase of mastery created in the course of social interaction in which the child has partially acquired a skill but can successfully apply it only with the assistance and supervision of an expert partner (Berk & Winsler, 1995, p. 108).

By exploring familiar environments, children engage in problem-solving through the use of their senses. Although they do need some guidance from adults to explore these environments, the caregivers must understand the children's agenda and make decisions aimed at supporting them within the context of learning and appropriate interactional play. As Berk and Winsler (1995) have written, "the social environment is the necessary scaffold, or support system, that allows the child to move forward and continue to build new competencies" (p. 26).

SOCIAL DEVELOPMENT

Social Mastery Motivation

In Chapter 3, we discussed the importance of mastery motivation for infants who are typically developing as well as for infants with disabilities. Mastery motivation continues to be a key developmental framework for understanding the young child. However, as a child enters the second year of life, explorations take on a more social component. During the second year, the infant expands on relationships with others and engages in increasingly sophisticated social behavior. Social mastery motivation is defined as engagement in appropriate social interaction with adults and/or peers by initiation of contact and appropriate response to others (Blasco, 1995a). It is demonstrated by the child's "motivation to generate, maintain, and influence the course of social interaction" (MacTurk, Hunter, McCarthy, Vietze, & McQuiston, 1985, p. 94). According to Boat (1995), social mastery motivation reflects the child's ability to engage in goal-directed social behavior and is nontask specific. Guralnick (1994) pointed out that although the process of developing meaningful and constructive relationships continues throughout the life cycle, the early years are critical if children are to develop the skills that are essential for their daily routines.

Children with disabilities may have difficulty engaging in social interactions as a result of either innate and/or environmental influences (Blasco et al., 1990; Hauser-Cram, 1996). For example, a child with a seizure disorder may have a hard time interacting with his environment due to the high levels of medication necessary to control the seizures (Hauser-Cram, 1996).

Studies have pointed out that as children with disabilities grow into the preschool years, they need more than proximity to other children in order to engage in appropriate social interactions (Odom, McConnell, & McEvoy, 1992). It is imperative that caregivers (both parents and service providers) help scaffold the child's early attempts at social mastery motivation. In two previously published studies, researchers found that caregivers could directly affect on the child's ability to engage in mastery motivation through scaffolding the child's play (see Blasco et al., 1990; Hauser-Cram, 1996).

Social Competence

The roots of peer interaction are now observable as the toddler starts to move from parallel play to complementary and reciprocal play. This behavior occurs sequentially after the toddler has developed the ability to engage in symbolic (pretend) play (Howes, 1988). Complementary play may include give-and-take activities and turn-taking. The child's ability to sustain her own wants and needs in order to share with others begins to increase as the child reaches her second birthday. Although the toddler is now engaging in reciprocal play, that play is typically directed toward one or two children within a group or toward a familiar adult.

Howes (1988) developed a construct for understanding early social competence by describing it as being composed of two independent but related dimensions: social interaction skills and friendship. Social interaction skills include, but are not limited to, the ability to join a play group, play with peers, and demonstrate affective expressions. Friendships are defined as stable, interactive relationships that demonstrate reciprocity and shared positive affect (Howes & Farver, 1987). Table 4.1 demonstrates the sequence of development in terms of social competence with peers.

THE EMERGENCE OF PRETEND PLAY
IN INFANTS AND TODDLERS

Between the second and third year, young children continue to expand their interactional capacities toward others. Piaget (1960) described this period (which for many children starts around 18 months), as the preoperational stage. Characteristics of this stage include increased use of language and increasingly sophisticated pretend play. Toddlers now have the ability to store mental images, and they have increased their memory capacity.

This tendency toward reaching out is precipitated by increasing skills in all developmental domains, particularly in the area of language development. For children with disabilities, an inability to attain or gain communication skills can inhibit all areas of development and the achievement of independence. When an

TABLE 4.1   Constructs Representing Social Competence with Peers

AGE	SOCIAL INTERACTION	FRIENDSHIP FORMATION
13–24 months	Imitative	Beginning friendship
	Complementary and reciprocal play	All social overtures directed to same child
25–36 months	Communication of meaning (cooperative friendships, social pretend play)	Flexibility of friendship (in choice of partner)

Adapted from *Peer Interaction in Young Children* by C. Howes, 1988, Monographs of the Society for Research in Child Development, 53 (1, Ser. No. 217), p. 94; and "Toddler's Emerging Ways of Achieving Social Coordinations with a Peer" by C. O. Eckerman, C. C. Davis, & S. M. Didow, 1989, *Child Development, 60,* 440–453.

infant or toddler has not developed the social skills needed to become engaged in appropriate interactions with others, she is at risk for further developmental delay.

Pretend play develops from the simple manipulation of objects during the first year of life. Vondra and Belsky (1989) found that simple manipulative play declined significantly from 12 to 13 months of age in typically developing children. At the same time, there was a substantial increase in the pretend play of these children. In addition, unfocused play decreased in children from 18 to 24 months, while complex pretend play increased. In contrast, Blasco, Bailey, and Burchinal (1993) found that children with disabilities tended to engage in less sophisticated play at one, two, and three years of age. Thus the inability to engage in increasing levels of pretend play puts children with disabilities at a disadvantage. To complicate the matter further, File (1994) found that teachers in early intervention programs were more likely to support cognitive play than social play in classroom settings.

Play behavior in typical developmental milestones for infants and toddlers was derived by theorists such as Gesell (1925) and Piaget (1960). These milestones provide a basis for understanding typical behavior. For children with disabilities, however, skills may be scattered in terms of developmental level, and it is often difficult to interpret their play. Thus it is important for the team to evaluate and document such children's play behavior through a combination of observations, anecdotal records, and family interviews. In Table 4.2 play behavior is documented by age.

Children with disabilities generally learn to play in the same ways as their typically developing peers but at different rates. However, there is a noticeable dif-

TABLE 4.2 Play Behavior During Infancy and Toddlerhood

AGE	PLAY BEHAVIOR	ACTIVITIES
B–12 months	Sensorimotor/perceptual	mouthing, looking, banging, locating, localizing
12–24 months	Sensorimotor/exploratory	simple manipulation, stacking, imitating simple gestures
24–36 months	Exploration becomes integrated with constructive play and dramatics	simple pretend play, substitutes objects
36–48 months	Familiar fantasy themes	role play, planned play activities
48–60 months	Complex themes	multiple planned sequences, substitutions, simple board games

Adapted from "Play-Based Assessment" by P. M. Blasco & M. LaMontagne, 1996, in L. J. Johnson, M. J. LaMontagne, P. M. Elgas, & A. M. Bauer (Eds.), *Early Childhood Education: Blending Theory, Blending Practice,* Baltimore: Paul H. Brookes.

ference in the ability of children with disabilities to engage in more sophisticated levels of play that involve social roles (Blasco, 1995a). In other to understand the social components of play, service providers should utilize a categorical hierarchy of play behavior. Although developed in 1932, Parten's categories of social play continue to provide the standard for evaluating dimensions of social play. Table 4.3 lists the categories of social play.

Children with disabilities tend to play alone or engage in parallel play (Blasco et al., 1993; Bailey, McWilliam, Ware, & Burchinal, 1992). It is important for caregivers and service providers to realize that children with disabilities may need help in reaching more sophisticated levels of social play.

If a toddler or young child is in a center-based program, service providers should observe that child as well as other children to determine the level of play encouraged in the setting. Child care centers should have toys, materials, and dress-up clothes to encourage social play.

The caregiver can provide the scaffolding needed to help the child engage in social play. For example, if the child offers the adult a cup, the caregiver can pretend to drink from the cup and talk about the contents. "Yum, milk! I love to drink my milk in the morning. Thank you, may I have more milk?" As the child pretends to pour more milk for the caregiver, the caregiver could say, "Timmy [another child] might like to have some milk too. Can you ask Timmy if he would like some milk?"

By observing all children in the setting, the level of play most children engage in can be determined. If children in the setting are not encouraged to move

Discriptive language
- interactions

TABLE 4.3   Parten's Categories of Play

TYPE	BEHAVIOR
Unoccupied	Distracted, looking all around the room.
Solitary	Plays alone and independently with toys. Pursues own interests despite others playing nearby.
Onlooker	Watches the play of others. May talk to other children but makes no attempt to join play.
Parallel	Plays independently but activity is like others' activity. May use same toys as another child but in a different way.
Associative	Plays with other children. May exchange toys and comments, but there is no organization to the play.
Cooperative	Play is organized to make a product or to attain a goal, such as games.

Adapted from "Social Participation among Preschool Children" by M. Parten, 1932, *Journal of Abnormal and Social Psychology, 27,* 243–269.

beyond parallel or solitary play, the early intervention team may want to implement some changes. Vignette 4.2 describes one family's experience with the day care center attended by their son, who was diagnosed with autism.

> **VIGNETTE 4.2   DON'T ASK, DON'T TELL**
>
> Max had been attending a neighborhood child care center. At first, Max's parents were delighted and optimistic about the program, but with time they became increasingly frustrated with his lack of progress. They said that the teachers and children did not interact with Max. When they came to school to pick him up, the teachers would say he had a great day. Eventually, the parents came to realize that a great day occurred when Max did not "disrupt the class." Max's father felt that the teachers were not prepared to work with children with disabilities, so they simply ignored him.

Many service providers have a better opportunity than family members to see a child's progress or lack of progress over time in center-based programs. If the child's needs are not being met, the service provider should encourage the family to make a visit and advocate for a better placement.

Interventions aimed at helping children develop pretend skills and providing means of communication can serve as preventive measures for future failures. For example, young children who cannot express themselves or engage in play with others are less likely to be successful in inclusive environments.

Children acquire the skills to engage in pretend play after they have practiced imitating simple actions that they have observed others performing. For example, a child sees an adult comb his hair. The child picks up the comb and brings it toward his hair. Later, as the child matures and develops pretend skills, he will repeat the action by brushing a doll's hair or by offering to brush Mommy's or Daddy's hair. Vignette 4.3 shows how an 18-month-old with cerebral palsy demonstrated his sophisticated knowledge of pretend play.

VIGETTE 4.3   JASON AND HIS DOLL

Jason was lying on the floor in his favorite play position. He has spastic dyplegia, which affects both his legs and one arm. He uses his right hand to reach for a small doll. He finds a baby bottle and feeds the baby using the bottle. He follows this interaction by feeding himself from the bottle. Jason looks around at his toys and finds a bed for his doll. He puts the doll into bed and places a sponge on top of the doll as a substitute for a blanket. The sponge falls off the doll and Jason looks around and finds a piece of felt cloth to cover the doll. He then pats the baby and says, "Ni-ni."

Jason thus demonstrated that he could use sequence pretend play and substitution, which are appropriate for his age. Yet his degree of cerebral palsy makes it difficult for him to show his abilities on typical measures of development. His strong demonstration of successful pretend play will help others know Jason's capabilities as well as his disabilities.

TABLE 4.4   Intervention Strategies to Promote Symbolic Play

- Observe and then identify experiences that the child enjoys in daily events or activities and use toys to represent these events or activities.
- Respond to the child with pretend actions. For example, when the child lies down on the floor, cover her with a blanket, say "night-night," and sing a lullaby.
- Encourage representation of family members. Use play sets that are culturally sensitive and represent the world the child lives in.
- Substitute one object for another. Use a block for a bed. Use a washcloth or napkin for a blanket.
- Elaborate on the child's pretend play. If he gets into a car, ask, "Where are the keys? Can you turn the motor on? Do we have enough gas?"
- Make use of "breakdowns" by using symbolic solutions to fix things or deal with frustration or anger (e.g., a doctor's kit to make things better).
- Uses cues to prompt an action using a least intrusive to most intrusive strategy. For example, "uh-oh" to "you better turn it around."
- Let the child lead the action and follow her lead.
- Pay attention to the starting and ending of pretend sequences. Let the child decide when and how to end a sequence or begin a new theme.

Adapted from "Creating Connections: Intervention Guidelines for Increasing Interaction with Children with Multisystem Developmental Disorder (MSDD)" by S. Wieder, 1997, *Zero to Three, 17,* 19–29.

Opportunities for pretend play with others help young children develop the prerequisite skills for engaging others. As toddlers gain independence through motor skills (e.g., walking, picking up items, climbing), they become more willing to separate from the caregiver and play near other toddlers. Toddlers engage in parallel play when they play next to other children, using materials and toys that may be similar, but do not interact with one another. In Chapter 5, the various types of play are discussed as part of the exploration of the assessment process. Table 4.4 presents intervention strategies designed to promote symbolic pretend play.

THE EMERGENCE OF PROSOCIAL AND UNDESIRABLE BEHAVIOR

All children learn both positive and undesirable or oppositional behaviors that are a natural part of development. Adults smile and acknowledge the toddler who hugs a sibling or a crying child. Conversely, they frown at or punish the child who bites or hits another child in a play situation. It is important that both positive and oppositional behaviors are acknowledged and that alternative methods for dealing with undesirable behaviors are found and demonstrated.

The Division for Early Childhood's (DEC) position paper on discipline stated that many young children engage in challenging behaviors in the course of early development. In order for all young children to participate in the least restrictive environment with their typically developing peers, the DEC recommends:

- Designing environments and activities to prevent challenging behavior and to help all children develop appropriate behavior
- Utilizing effective behavioral interventions that are positive and addressing the form and function of a young child's challenging behavior
- Adopting curriculum modification and accommodation strategies designed to help young children control their behavior
- Accessing consultation and technical assistance or additional staffing when necessary

It is particularly important for adults to model appropriate behavior toward children and other adults in order to effectively influence children's positive behaviors. All too often, we have seen child care workers speak negatively to groups of two- and three-year-olds or to other adults in front of young children. Children will imitate the behaviors that they observe and that are covertly or overtly reinforced by adults.

Beginning Feelings

Young children's ability to demonstrate sympathetic feelings or caring is an exciting developmental milestone. Radke-Yarrow and Zahn-Waxler (1975) pioneered research in sympathetic behavior. They found that children as young as 14 months would try to do something to alleviate the distress of others. These behaviors might include stopping an activity and observing, patting the person in distress, or bursting into tears. It may be that the demonstration of sympathetic behavior emerges after children have acquired the ability to imitate.

Sympathetic behavior appears to be related not only to the child's developmental level, but also to individual differences among children and the physical and social setting in which young children are placed (Barclay-Murphy, 1992). In a day care setting, where mishaps are common, children will have opportunities to engage in sympathetic behavior. The attitudes and actions of the staff will influence a child's willingness to demonstrate sympathy. Teachers and parents who model and display affection and caring and reinforce affection and caring in young children will more likely make a difference.

Fear is another behavior that takes on new meaning during the toddler years. Although children exhibit fear in infancy by demonstrating stranger anxiety or startling and crying to a loud noise, the cause of fear changes as the child enters the toddler years. At this point the child is more likely to exhibit fears of imaginary creatures or physical harm. Brazelton (1992) observed that even a somewhat familiar person can induce fear in the toddler. For example, a relative visiting from out of state or a newcomer to a day care center may produce a quiet response in the toddler. If that person gets too close or speaks too loudly, the child may burst into uncontrollable tears.

The two-year-old begins the third year in relative peace. His newly acquired language skills have gained him some control over his emotions (Lally, Provence, Szanton, & Weissbourd, 1987). However, at two and two and a half, the child continues to exhibit mood swings that are difficult to trace to specific antecedent events (Brazelton, 1992). He frequently displays aggressive behaviors toward others. The traces of sharing noted as he approaches his second year seem to be gone again. Everything is a definite *"mine"*. The feelings of fearfulness discussed above increase, and night terrors may be noted. Brazelton (1992) described night terrors as out-of-control screaming and thrashing, sometimes accompanied by sweating. The child typically calms down when an adult comes to his rescue and will return to sleep after some cuddling. Night terrors could be reflective of a "bad" or stressful day and may be one way the child works off emotional steam.

The two- to three-year-old is capable of empathic behavior. Her feelings of empathy grow as she observes that others have feelings too. As stated, language helps the child to express her feelings of empathy toward others. In child care settings, children ranging in age from 16 to 33 months will respond to signals of distress 93 percent of the time. However, in order for empathy to exist, the child must have developed a clear sense of self in relationship to others and the cognitive ability to understand that another person is experiencing distress or pain (Barclay-Murphy, 1992; Campos et al., 1983; Howes & Farver, 1987). Lewis (1987) stated that both ecocentric thought (the use of self to infer actions and feelings of others) and decentered thought (the ability to consider that all selves are not like oneself) need to develop before the child is capable of demonstrating and maintaining empathy and sharing.

Other emotions that arise during the two- to three-year age span include guilt, shame, and pride (Lewis, 1992). Similar to empathy, these emotions emerge concurrently with more sophisticated cognitive thought processes and are contingent on socialization practices. As previously mentioned, Lewis described the child's ability to evaluate his own actions, thoughts, and feelings as a prerequisite for demonstrating many of these feelings. In addition, the child must evaluate his performance according to some precondition or standard that is either met or failed.

According to Lewis, shame and hubris (pridefulness) are the result of global self-evaluation, whereas guilt and pride are the result of attribute-specific self-evaluation. With the former, the child decides that she is bad because of the things she does; with the latter, the child decides that she should have said "no" instead of hitting Dashay when she took her car.

Given the complexity of feelings and emotions that the two- to three-year-old is capable of experiencing, the ability to express those feelings in functional ways is of vital importance. The increasing sophistication of language allows the child to express his feelings, but sometimes caregivers must rely on body signals, as when a child withdraws from a group snack after spilling his milk. Observing children and their facial and body responses to situations will help caregivers be more in tune with their emotional responses, particularly if the children are not comfortable vocalizing their feelings.

Modeling empathic behavior is also a way to encourage children to demonstrate some of their own feelings. For example, if a child falls in the block area and cries, a reassuring hug and gentle encouragement from an adult will create a more positive influence than ignoring the child or telling her not to cry. Although this may seem like common sense, in a busy classroom it is only too easy to ignore children's expression of emotions unless they are disruptive to the entire group. Helping children find ways to vent their feelings in a positive way can lead to successful future interactions for both the caregiver and the child.

COMMUNICATION IN TODDLERS

The ability to communicate effectively can be enhanced or defeated during the second year of life. During this time young children learn the power of words and use them to let the adult know what they want and how they may feel (Blasco, 1995b). Communication skills are interrelated with all domains of development: social, cognitive, motor, and adaptive. However, in terms of toddler behavior, communication and the social domain seem to be inseparable. Crais and Roberts (1996) stated, "communication is a social act, the function of which is interaction with another living being" (p. 336). Researchers have found that facilitating communication skills in the early years may prevent or ameliorate future learning problems, including emotional/behavioral issues (Wetherby & Prizant, 1993).

Development of Gestures

Infants and toddlers learn to communicate their needs and desires through preverbal aspects of language, in particular gestures and symbolic play. Infants exhibit behaviors that are labeled "communicative intent" prior to the use of actual verbal communication and words. These gestures are purposeful movements that can communicate meaning to a caregiver (Blake, McConnell, Horton, & Benson, 1992).

Reaching is one of the first gestures to come under the infant's control, at around four months of age. The infant then develops a gesture that pairs movement with reaching. Gradually she develops this gesture into pointing, which serves its purpose for obtaining and showing objects. Pointing at pictures in a book begins at about nine months (Sweeney, 1996). Blake et al. (1992) found that the development of gestures appeared to be an indicator of the later nonreferential as well as referential words that develop about six months later. Gestures are often combined with spoken words to form the first true two-word symbol utterances, which occur before verbal two-word combinations are heard (Kennedy, Sheridan, Radlinski, & Beeghly, 1991).

Language and Speech

When a toddler wants a drink, she may point at the refrigerator and make sounds. If the caregiver asks, "What do you want? Would you like some juice?," the toddler may respond with an approximation of the word *juice.* This dialogue continues until the toddler can say "juice" and then expands the request by saying "more juice" and "more juice, please."

So the toddler has developed the ability to use language as a means of communication. This language is particular to the child. Children who are deaf learn to communicate using sign language. In order to acquire language, children must learn a fairly complex system of rules that govern sounds, grammar, meanings, and uses (Crais & Roberts, 1996).

According to the American Speech-Language-Hearing Association (1993):

> a language disorder is impaired comprehension and/or use of spoken, written and/or other symbol systems. The disorder may involve (1) the form of language (phonology, morphology, syntax), (2) the content of language (semantics), and/or (3) the function of language in communication (pragmatics) in any combination. (p. 40)

The components of the form of language are defined as follows:

- Phonology, the rules for the formation of sounds and sound combinations. Phonemes are sounds that join together to form words. This is demonstrated when the child says, "See."
- Morphology, the rules for the structure of words and the construction of word forms. This is demonstrated when the child says, "Mommy, help."

- Syntax, the rules for combining words to form sentences and for establishing the relationships among the components within a sentence. This is demonstrated when the child says, "Help me."

Semantics refers to the rules for meanings of words and sentences. This is demonstrated when a caregiver pushes a ball toward a toddler who then says, "Ball Go." Pragmatics refers to the rules for combining language components into functional and socially appropriate communication. For infants, pragmatic components of language include eye contact, turn-taking, and verbal interchange. From 12 to 15 months, toddlers begin to use words to state their desires. These words are typically single-word utterances that the child has learned from previous feedback. When the child wants to go outside to play, she may say "go" or "out." From 18 to 24 months, toddlers begin to use word combinations such as "go out." Toddlers approximately 18 months of age know about 50 words and comprehend around 300 words (Crais & Roberts, 1996). In Chapter 5, instruments for evaluating communication skills are listed.

Although there is a lack of research on the timing of intervention for language delays with very young children, approximately one-fourth of young children who are eligible for early intervention services are identified as having a communication disorder (McLean & Cripe, 1997). Children with communication concerns may have specific disabilities that are the primary cause of their disorder. On the other hand, some children exhibit no deficits in other developmental areas.

Hearing Loss

It is particularly important that the early intervention team rule out hearing loss as a source or contributor to language delay. Young children may experience a common childhood infection known as otitis media. Otitis media with effusion may include fluid in the middle ear that can lead to a mild to moderate hearing loss (American Academy of Audiology, 1988; Roberts, Burchinal, Davis, Collier, & Henderson, 1991). During the first year of life, the infant develops skills in localizing, recognizing, discriminating, and categorizing sounds (Peck, 1995). The results of these efforts include increased speech during the second year. We know from recent research on the brain that human communication develops at a rapid rate between birth and 36 months of age.

The importance of early detection and identification of hearing loss cannot be overestimated. One study of 203 young children referred for early intervention services found that 35 percent had some degree of hearing loss (Anderson, 1996). One concern is that children with hearing loss sometimes go unidentified or they are referred instead for communication or behavioral issues. In the United States, the delay between the time a hearing loss is suspected by the parents or service providers and confirmed by a hearing test is usually one year (American Academy of Audiology, 1988).

It is important to remember that communication skills go hand in hand with other areas of development. In planning interventions and activities for the child, the service provider should include activities to enhance all areas of development. Although parents may suspect autism when a child is turning two, most children with autism and other multisensory disorders are diagnosed in the second to third year.

ALTERNATIVE METHODS OF COMMUNICATION

Children who are unable to utilize expressive language skills due to a disability can learn alternative communication methods at an early age. For example, the toddler with Down syndrome who is nonverbal can learn to use sign language to communicate with his family, service providers, and peers. Very young children can also use assistive devices such as push-button communicators and computers for expressive language. These devices are discussed in Chapter 10.

TODDLERS WHO EXPERIENCE DIFFICULTY IN COMMUNICATION AND SOCIAL INTERACTIONS

For children diagnosed with autism or an autism-spectrum disorder, the pretend-play activities that are an integral part of toddler development may appear to be delayed or nonexistent. Lifter, Sulzer-Azaroff, Anderson, and Cowdery (1993) found that young children with autism were more likely to learn and generalize pretend-play activities when they matched their developmental level. Some researchers found that a direct instruction approach using modeling and imitation increased the frequency of and/or duration in which the child will play with objects (Rettig, 1994). Toys that inspire social interaction between the adult and child or between the child and a peer are more likely to lead to increases in social behavior, particularly modeling and imitation (Martin & Brady, 1991). Social toys would include dramatic-play toys, puppets, toy vehicles, and balls. In contrast, isolative toys would include puzzles, pegboards, and stacking toys.

MOVEMENT FOR TODDLERS

Parents will remember the first time their child walked, including the details surrounding the main event. Children who are typically developing begin to walk sometime between 11 and 15 months (*Bayley Scales*, 1993). When parents of a newborn or very young child just diagnosed with a disability discuss expectations for their child, one of the first questions is, "Will he walk?" (Blasco & Johnson, 1996). The ability to become mobile facilitates the child's exploratory skills and leads to independence. The child's ability to produce and control a wide range of movements is related to the child's ability to engage in problem-solving (Wood, 1995). Movement also allows the toddler to experiment with separating from the primary caregiver for brief periods that increase over time.

When a child has a disability that impedes movement, it is crucial to find alternative methods that promote her active exploration of her environment and provide opportunities for independence. The literature on motor development has recently changed its recommended practices for young children with motor delays. In the past, movement ability was said to develop in a predictable sequence that followed a hierarchical model (Scalise-Smith & Bailey, 1992). Motor control was seen as developing in a cephalocaudal direction (head to feet).

However, new theories emerged with the advancement of technology that monitored muscle behavior and the nervous system (VanSant, 1991). Therapists became increasingly aware of the complex interactions between the individual and the environment. This led to decreased emphasis in hands-on manipulation of the child and an increased emphasis on problem-solving to determine the expectations, constraints, and support available for functional movement (Heriza & Sweeney, 1994).

NEW THEORIES ABOUT MOTOR DEVELOPMENT

The contemporary view of motor development focuses on the belief that motor development is determined by multiple factors (Thelen, 1995). A dynamic systems approach to understanding motor development is a process-oriented theory that addresses the development, learning, and control of behavior (Heriza & Sweeney, 1994). At the core of this theory is the view that behavior develops from the dynamic interaction and coordination of many subsystems, including the cognitive, biomechanical, neuromotor, environmental, maturational, and social. Heriza (1991) outlined six basic principles of the dynamic systems theory:

- Multiple systems cooperate to produce useful motor patterns such as walking.
- New forms of movement result when changes in the body occur over time or with a particular task or in a particular environment.
- Movement patterns adapt to the demands of the task and the environment.
- Coordinated movement patterns use less energy as they become preferred movement patterns.
- Children develop comfortable patterns of movement.
- The variables that influence the shift from one form of movement to another change over time.

Intervention using this approach emphasizes the practice of functional tasks within a natural environment. Outcomes are designed to achieve these functional tasks. A child's ability to produce and control a wide range of movements is related to his or her ability to practice problem-solving skills. As a result, motor problem-solving should involve cognitive, perceptual, and motor skills in a variety of functional, environmental situations (Higgins, 1991). Table 4.5 compares traditional versus contemporary theories of motor development, learning, and control.

Another similar approach to motor intervention was described by Horn, Warren, & Jones (1995). Neurobehavioral motor intervention combines behav-

TABLE 4.5   Comparison of Traditional and Contemporary Theories of Motor Development, Learning, and Control

TRADITIONAL	CONTEMPORARY
Central nervous system is hierarchical	Cooperative interaction of subsystems heterarchical (distributed among subsystems)
Movement patterns hard-wired Movement for movement's sake	Movement patterns adaptable to task Movement functionally outcome-directed
Passive motor learning with little emphasis on other systems	Active motor learning with emphasis on other systems and problem-solving

Adapted from "Pediatric Physical Therapy. Part II: Approaches to Movement Dysfunction" by C. B. Heriza & J. K. Sweeney, 1995, *Infants and Young Children*, 7(2), 20–32.

ioral modification with neuromotor intervention strategies. In this approach, service providers identify the movement components missing from the child's repertoire, identify functional skills and activities requiring the ability to use these movements, and then develop intervention strategies that use both behavior and neurodevelopmental programming.

There are many different types of equipment that can help children with motor impairments to function successfully in the environment. Several studies have shown that positioning in adaptive seating devices has improved functional skills such as eating and drinking (Hulme, Shaver, Acher, Mullette, & Eggert, 1987), pulmonary function (Nwaobi & Smith, 1986), and visual tracking and grasping (Hulme, Gallagher, Walsh, Niesen, & Waldron, 1987). Other researchers have found higher test scores for preschoolers with cerebral palsy who were positioned properly (Miedaner & Finuf, 1993).

In addition, the use of inhibitive ankle-foot orthoses (AFOs) for young children with cerebral palsy increased the duration of their standing balance and improved the symmetry of their weight bearing in standing (Harris & Riffle, 1986). Children who use four-wheeled posterior rolling walkers rather than two-wheeled rolling walkers had improved ambulation (Levangie, Chimera, Johnston, Robinson, & Wobeskya, 1989). When children without locomotor abilities were provided with power mobility, they showed increased activity, curiosity, exploratory play, and child-initiated behaviors (Butler, 1986).

SUBSTANCE ABUSE AND ITS LONG-TERM IMPLICATIONS FOR TODDLERS

In 1989, the National Association for Perinatal Addiction Research and Education (NAPARE) published a survey of 36 hospitals nationwide and reported that approximately 11 percent of women who delivered babies tested positive for substance abuse. However, for poor women in inner-city neighborhoods, the levels are even higher. For example, 70–75 percent of the mothers of 200 children followed in an East Baltimore clinical study continued to test positive for substance abuse (personal communication, Dr. Harolyn Belcher, October 15, 1997).

The debate over the impact on long-term development of in utero exposure to substances other than alcohol continues to raise questions about long-term effects. Most studies reporting two- to three-year outcomes of children prenatally exposed to cocaine and other drugs showed little difference in their scores on developmental or behavioral outcome measures compared to children who weren't exposed (Carta et al., 1994; Hurt et al. 1995; Hurt et al., 1996).

The findings of studies on the effect of prenatal exposure to substance abuse on children's play are mixed. In a controlled study, Hurt et al. (1996) found no difference in the play behavior at 18 and 24 months between toddlers exposed to cocaine prenatally and a matched group of unexposed toddlers. Other researchers found that toddlers prenatally exposed to substance abuse showed less age-appropriate play and more irritability during play than controls (Metosky & Vondra, 1995).

A more immediate concern for the infant or toddler is the ongoing environmental effects of living with adults who continue to engage in substance abuse. These families may have fewer resources to deal with the stresses of everyday life. They may not trust service providers who represent a different culture or economic group. For many of these families, the delivery of services must be individually tailored and may not reflect the typical procedures of the agency. These families will need attention to basic needs before they can follow a plan to help their child (Coles, 1995).

Striessguth (1997, p. 11) describes the protective environmental factors that are associated with better outcomes for children exposed to substance abuse:

1. A stable and nurturing home
2. Fewer changes in living arrangements or family membership
3. A home free of domestic violence
4. Recipient of early intervention
5. Diagnosis prior to age six

Substance abuse can also affect the parent-child relationship. When mothers and fathers continue to abuse substances, the consequences for the young child can be devastating. Young children are often the innocent bystanders to family and community violence. The parents may also be affected by mental health issues that go largely untreated. Thus, it is important to consult with members of the team who deal with mental health issues so they can follow up on referrals for mental health care. In Chapter 5, criteria for assessing the effects of violence on young children are discussed in detail.

Service providers need a firm understanding of parent-child relationships in order to help families who need external support and guidance. Positive relationships enable the adult to model, guide, and emotionally support the child (Poulson, 1995), and help the toddler to develop a sense of self that is vitally important in becoming able to persist at difficult tasks (mastery motivation), learn delayed gratification, and develop skills to handle both internal and external frustrations (Poulson, 1995).

MENTAL HEALTH ISSUES

Many service providers working in inner-city environments are increasingly finding that infants and toddlers who qualify for early intervention services due to a language delay also have mental health issues. The service providers often feel unprepared for assisting these children and their families based on their training in either special education or a related field.

One of the best resources for understanding mental health issues in infants and toddlers is the Zero to Three organization, which publishes a newsletter on topics that often deal with mental health (see the references in this book).

Traumatic stress disorder provides an umbrella term for a continuum of symptoms exhibited by children who have experienced a single traumatic event or chronic stress (Wieder, 1994). Children who are experiencing traumatic stress disorder may exhibit aggressive and agitated behavior or socially withdrawn behavior. In Chapter 5, we discuss procedures for evaluating children who may be experiencing the syndrome. It is important to seek qualified help for a diagnosis and to keep ongoing records of the child's daily behavior in all possible settings. The effect on the child's behavior should be understood within the following framework:

- The impact of the trauma
- The child's temperament and personality
- The parent's or guardian's ability to help the child understand and cope with the situation
- The need for protection and safety
- The possibility for working through the experience (Wieder, 1994, p. 19)

MALTREATMENT OF INFANTS
AND TODDLERS WITH DISABILITIES

Child maltreatment is a general term used to describe neglect, physical and sexual abuse, and emotional and psychological abuse by caregivers. Of children who are the victims of physical abuse, one-third are estimated to be less than one year of age. Pianta, Egeland, and Erickson (1989) have suggested that some children under the age of three are the victims of multiple forms of abuse.

Risk factors that are related to child maltreatment include both parental/caregiver and child characteristics and environmental influences. In terms of parental risk factors, the following characteristics have been perceived to be associated with child maltreatment:

- Negative maternal attitude toward the pregnancy
- High levels of perceived social stress
- Social violence modeled within families over generations
- Ongoing substance abuse
- Maternal mental health issues
- Absence of social support and social isolation

Environmental characteristics that may contribute to child maltreatment include low socioeconomic status, homelessness, and unemployment. However, no one should assume that families facing these environmental pressures are likely to abuse their children. Child characteristics, including difficulty in feeding, poor sleeping patterns, and challenging behavior are also consider risk factors. For parents who do not have the resources or support to parent or who are not ready to be parents, the child's characteristics may exacerbate an already volatile situation (Pianta et al., 1989). No one risk factor will lead to child maltreatment. It is the combination of the multiple factors cited above that leads to the problem.

SUMMARY

Increased mobility, a beginning understanding of cause and effect, and initial control over expressive language characterize the second year of life. Emotional and behavioral development is largely influenced by development in three areas (physical, cognitive, and language). The toddler learns that he can control his environment and the sequence of events with an emphatnic "No!" The once placid infant will now squirm and turn during a diaper change or get up and walk away. The toddler spends his time engaging in activities he determines to be important.

This is also a very frustrating time for the child because, although she understands a great deal, she is limited in her ability to communicate and often will revert to screeching or lying on the floor when she cannot effectively express herself. Expressive communication typically occurs through facial expression, pointing or gesturing, and one-word statements such as "more" or "bye-bye."

During the second year of life there is an explosion in language development as well as in the ability to move around freely in many environments. For children with disabilities, the lack of language skills and motoric ability may place them at a disadvantage in learning new skills as well as in engaging in pretend play, which is crucial in helping children to gain the cognitive and social skills that will allow them to be more successful in future relationships.

Children who are at risk and children who have been abused may exhibit the inability to engage in simple play activities. They may need help in utilizing play as a tool for learning. Service providers may find that the parents of at-risk children may not have learned to play as children. In addition, children who have disabilities may experience maltreatment. Many early childhood centers provide opportunities for parents and children to play together.

In this chapter, we discussed the changes that occur in children during the toddler years that equip them with both the cognitive and social skills they need to form relationships with others.

REFERENCES

American Academy of Audiology. (1988). *Audiologic guidelines for the diagnosis and treatment of otitis media in children* (Position Statement).

American Speech-Language-Hearing Association. (1993). Definition of communication disorders and variations. *Asha, 35 (*Suppl. 10), 40–41.

Anderson, G. (1996, April). Hearing loss in children referred to early childhood special education. Paper presented at the American Academy of Audiology, Salt Lake City, Utah.

Bailey, D. B., McWilliam, R. A., Ware, W. B., & Burchinal, M. A. (1993). The social interactions of toddlers and preschoolers in same-age and mixed-age play groups.

Barclay-Murphy, L. (1992). Sympathetic behavior in very young children. *Zero to Three, 12,* 1–5.

Batshaw, M. L., & Shapiro, B. K. (1997). Mental retardation. In M. L. Batshaw (Ed.), *Children with disabilities* (4th ed., pp. 335–359). Baltimore: Paul H. Brookes.

Bayley Scales of Infant Development (BSID II) (1993). San Antonio, TX: Psychological Corporation.

Beckman, P. J., & Lieber, J. (1992). In S. L. Odom, S. R. McConnell, & M. A. McEvoy (Eds.), *Social competence of young children with disabilities* (pp. 65–92). Baltimore: Paul H. Brookes.

Berk, L. E., & Winsler, A. (1995). *Scaffolding children's learning: Vygotsky and early childhood education.* Washington, D.C.: National Association of Education for Young Children.

Blake, J., McConnell, S., Horton, G., & Benson, N. (1992). The gestural repertoire and its evolution over the second year. *Early Development, 24,* 127–136. *Journal of Applied Developmental Psychology, 14,* 261–276.

Blasco, P. A., & Johnson, C. P. (1996). Supports for parents of children with disabilities. In A. J. Capute & P. J. Accardo (Eds.), *Developmental disabilities in infancy and childhood* (2nd ed, pp. 443–464). Baltimore: Paul H. Brookes.

Blasco, P. M. (1995a). *Community-based service models: For children with and without disabilities.* Minneapolis: Minnesota Department of Health.

Blasco, P. M. (1995b). Understanding the emotional and behavioral development of young children: Birth to 3 years. In T. J. Zirpoli (Ed.), *Understanding and affecting the behavior of young children* (pp. 35–59). Englewood Cliffs, N.J.: Merrill.

Blasco, P. M., Bailey, D. B., & Burchinal, M. A. (1993). Dimensions of mastery in same-age and mixed-age integrated classrooms. *Early Childhood Research Quarterly, 8,* 193–206.

Blasco, P. M., Hrncir, E. J., & Blasco, P. (1990). The contributions of maternal involvement to mastery performance of infants with cerebral palsy. *Journal of Early Intervention, 14,* 161–174.

Blasco, P. M., Lynch, E., Trimbach, K., & Scheel, C. (1994). *Community-based service models for young children with disabilities: Final report.* St. Paul: Minnesota Department of Children, Families, and Learning.

Boat, M. (1995). *Defining social mastery motivation in young children with or without disabilities.* Unpublished doctoral dissertation. University of Minnesota.

Brazelton, T. B. (1992). *Touchpoints: The essential reference.* Reading, Mass.: Addison-Wesley.

Butler, C. (1986). Effects of power mobility on self-initiated behaviors of very young children with locomotor disability. *Developmental Medicine and Child Neurology, 28,* 3325–3332.

Campos, J. J., Barrett, K. C., Lamb, M. E., Goldsmith, H. H., & Stenberg, C. (1983). In M. M. Haith & J. J. Campos (Eds.), *Infancy and development psychobiology* (4th ed., pp. 784–857). New York: Wiley.

Carta, J. J., Sideridis, G., Rinkel, P., Guimaraes, S., Greenwood, C., Baggett, K., Peterson, P., Atwater, J., McEvoy, M., & McConnell, S. (1994). Behavioral outcomes of infants and young children prenatally exposed to illicit drugs: Review and analysis of the experimental literature. *Topics in Early Childhood Special Education, 14*(2), 184–216.

Case, R., Okamoto, Y., et al. (1996). Introduction: Reconceptualizing the nature of children's conceptual structures and their development in middle childhood. In R. Case & Y. Okamoto (Eds.), *The role of central conceptual structures in the development of children's thought* (pp. 1–130). Chicago: Monographs of the Society for Research in Child Development.

Cole, P. M., Barrett, K. C., & Zahn-Waxler. (1992). Emotion displays in two-year-olds during mishaps. *Child Development, 63,* 314–324.

Coles, C. D. (1995). Children of parents who abuse drugs and alcohol. In G. H. Smith, C. D. Coles, M. K. Poulson, & C. K. Cole (Eds.), *Children, families, and substance abuse* (pp. 3–23). Baltimore: Paul H. Brookes.

Crais, E. R., & Roberts, J. E. (1996). Assessing communication skills. In M. Mclean, D. B. Bailey, & M. Wolery (Eds.), *Assessing infants and preschoolers with special needs* (2nd ed., pp. 334–397). Englewood Cliffs, N.J.: Merrill.

Dawson, G., & Osterling, J. (1997). Early intervention in autism. In M. J. Guralnick (Ed), *The effectiveness of early intervention* (pp. 307–326). Baltimore: Paul H. Brookes.

Division for Early Childhood. (1998). *Position statement on interventions for challenging behavior.* Denver: Author.

Dunst, C. J. (1990). Sensorimotor development of infants with Down syndrome. In D. Cicchetti & M. Beeghly (Eds.), *Children with Down syndrome: A developmental perspective.* Cambridge: Cambridge University Press.

Eckerman, C. O., Davis, C. C., & Didow, S. M. (1989). Toddlers' emerging ways of achieving social coordination with a peer. *Child Development, 60,* 440–453.

File, N. (1994). Children's play, teacher-child interactions, and teacher beliefs in integrated early childhood programs. *Early Childhood Research Quarterly, 9,* 223–240.

Gesell, A. (1925). *The mental growth of the preschool child: A psychological outline of normal development from birth to the sixth year, including a system of developmental diagnosis.* New York: MacMillan.

Gonzalez-Mena, J., & Widmeyer Eyer, D. (1993). *Infants, toddlers, and caregivers.* (3rd ed.). Mountain View, Calif.: Mayfield.

Greenspan, S. I. (1992). Reconsidering the diagnosis and treatment of very young children with autistic spectrum or pervasive developmental disorder. *Zero to Three, 13,* 1–9.

Guralnick, M. J. (1994). Social competence with peers: Outcome and process in early childhood special education. In P. L. Safford, B. Spodek, & O. N. Saracho (Eds.), *Yearbook in early childhood education: Early childhood special education* (Vol. 5, pp. 45–71). New York: Teachers College Press.

Haas, L., Baird, S. M., McCormick, K., & Reilly, A. (1994). Infant behaviors interpreted by their mothers. *Infant-Toddler Intervention: The Transdisciplinary Journal,* pp. 203–220.

Harris, S. R., & Riffle, K. (1986). Effects of inhibitive ankle-foot orthoses on standing balance in a child with cerebral palsy: A single-subject design. *Physical Therapy, 66,* 663–667.

Hauser-Cram, P. (1996). Mastery motivation in toddlers with developmental disabilities. *Child Development, 67,* 236–248.

Heriza, C. B. (1991). Motor development: Traditional and contempory theories. In M. J. Lister (Ed.), *Contemporary management of motor control problems.* (pp. 99–126). Alexandria, Va.: Foundation for Physical Therapy.

Heriza, C. B., & Sweeney, J. K. (1994). Pediatric physical therapy: Part 1. Practical scope, scientific basis, and theoretical foundation. *Infants and Young Children, 7*(2), 20–32.

Higgins, S. (1991). Motor skill acquisition. In J. M. Rothstein (Ed.), *Movement Science* (pp. 64–180). Alexandria, Va.: American Physical Therapy Association.

Horn, E. M., Warren, S. F., & Jones, H. A. (1995). An experimental analysis of a neurobehavioral intervention. *Developmental Medicine and Child Neurology, 37,* 697–714.

Howes, C. (1987). *Peer interaction of young children.* Monographs of the Society for Research in Child Development, 53 (1, Ser. No. 217).

Howes, C., & Farver, J. (1987). Social pretend play in 2-year olds: Effects of age of partner. *Early Childhood Research Quarterly, 2,* 305–314.

Hulme, J. B., Gallagher, K., Walsh, J., Niesen, S., & Waldron, D. (1987). Behavioral and postural changes observed with use of adaptive seating by clients with multiple handicaps. *Physical Therapy, 67,* 1060–1106.

Hulme, J. B., Shaver, J., Acher, S., Mullette, L., & Eggert, C. (1987). Effects of adaptive seating devices on the eating and drinking of children with multiple handicaps. *The American Journal of Occupational Therapy, 4,* 81–89.

Hurt, H., Brodsky, N. L., Betancourt, L., Braitman, L. E., Belsky, J., & Giannetta, J. (1996). Play behavior in toddlers with in utero cocaine exposure: A prospective, masked, controlled study. *Developmental and Behavioral Pediatrics, 17,* 373–379.

Hurt, H., Brodsky, N. L., Betancourt, L., Braitman, L. E., Malmud, E., & Giannetta, J. (1995). Cocaine-exposed children: Follow-up through 30 months. *Developmental and Behavioral Pediatrics, 16*(1), 29–35.

Jennings, K. D. Connors, R. E., Stegman, C. E., Sankaranarayan, P., & Mendelsohn, S. (1985). Mastery motivation in young preschoolers: Effect of a physical handicap and implications for educational programming. *Journal of the Division of Early Childhood, 9,* 162–169.

Kennedy, M., Sheridan, M., Radlinski, S., & Beeghly, M. (1991). Play-language relationships in young children with developmental delays: Implications for assessment. *Journal of Speech and Hearing Research, 34,* 112–122.

Lally, R., Provence, S., Szanton, E., & Weissbourd, B. (1987). Developmentally appropriate care for children birth to age 3. In S. Bredekamp (Ed.), *Developmentally appropriate practice in early childhood programs serving children from birth through age 8.* Washington, D.C.: NAEYC.

Lender, W. L., Goodman, J. F., & Linn, M. I. (1998). Repetitive activity in the play of children with mental retardation. *Journal of early Intervention, 21*(4), 308–322.

Levangie, P. K., Chimera, M., Johnston, M., Robinson, R., & Wobeskya, L. (1989). The effects of posterior rolling walkers *vs* the standard rolling walker on gait characteristics of children with spastic cerebral palsy. *Physical and Occupational Therapy in Pediatrics, 9,* 1–17.

Lewis, M. (1987). Social development in infancy and early childhood. In J. Osofsky (Ed.), *Handbook of Infant Development* (2nd ed., pp. 419–493). New York: Wiley.

Lewis, M. (1992). Shame, the exposed self. *Zero to three: Bulletin of National Center for Clinical Infant Programs, 12,* 6–10.

Lifter, K., Sulzer-Azaroff, B., Anderson, S. R., Cowdery, G. E. (1993). Teaching play activities to preschool children with disabilities: The importance of developmental considerations. *Journal of Early Intervention, 17*(2), 139–159.

McCollum, J. A. (1991). At the crossroad: Reviewing and rethinking interaction coaching. In K. Marfo (Ed.), *Early intervention in transition: Current perspectives on programs for handicapped children* (pp. 137–176). New York: Praeger.

McCollum, J. A., & Hemmeter, M. L. (1997). Parent-child interaction intervention when children have disabilities. In M. J. Guralnick (Ed.), *The effectiveness of early intervention.* Baltimore: Paul H. Brookes.

McLean, L. K., & Cripe, J. W., (1997). The effectiveness of early intervention for children with communication disorders. In M. J. Guralnick (Ed.), *The effectiveness of early intervention* (pp. 349–428). Baltimore: Paul H. Brookes.

MacTurk, R. H., Hunter, F., McCarthy, M., Vietze, P., & McQuiston, S. (1985). Social mastery motivation in Down Syndrome and nondelayed infants. *Topics in Early Childhood Special Education, 4,* 93–103.

MacTurk, R. H., Vietze, P. M., McCarthy, M. E., McQuiston, S., & Yarrow, L. J. (1985). The organization of exploratory behavior in Down syndrome and non-delayed infants. *Child Development, 56,* 573–581.

Marfo, K. (1991). The maternal directiveness theme in mother-child interaction research: Implications for early intervention. In K. Marfo (Ed.), *Early intervention in transition: Current perspectives on programs for handicapped children* (pp. 177–203). New York: Praeger.

Martin, S., & Brady, M. (1991). Effects of toys on social behavior of preschool children in integrated and nonintegrated groups: Investigation of a setting event. *Journal of Early Intervention, 15,* 153–161.

Metosky, P., & Vondra, J. (1995). Prenatal drug exposure and play and coping in toddlers: A comparison study. *Infant Behavior and Development, 18,* 15–25.

Miedaner, J., & Finuf, L. (1993). Effects of adaptive positioning on psychological test scores for preschool children with cerebral palsy. *Pediatric Physical Therapy, 5,* 177–182.

Nickel, R. E., & Widerstrom, A. H. (1997). Developmental disorders in infancy. In A. H. Widerstrom, B. A. Mowder, & S. R. Sandall (Eds.), *Infant development and risk* (2nd Ed., pp. 89–121). Baltimore: Paul H. Brookes.

Nwaobi, O. M., & Smith, P. D. (1986). Effect of adaptive seating on pulmonary function of children with cerebral palsy. *Developmental Medicine and Child Neurology, 28,* 351–354.

Odom, S. L., McConnell, S. R., & McEvoy, M. A. (1992). *Social competence of young children with disabilities: Issues and strategies for intervention.* Baltimore: Paul H. Brookes.

Peck, J. E. (1995). Development of hearing: Part III. Postnatal development. *Journal of the American Academy of Audiology, 6,* 113–123.

Piaget, J. (1960). *Psychology of intelligence.* Totowa, N.J.: Littlefield, Adams.

Pianta, R., Egeland, B., Erickson, M. F. (1989). The antecedents of maltreatment: Results of the mother-child interaction project. In D. Cicchetti, & V. Carlson (Eds.), *Child maltreatment: Theory and research on the cause and consequences of child abuse and neglect* (pp. 203–253). New York: Cambridge University Press.

Poulson, M. K. (1995). Building resilience in infants and toddlers at risk. In G. H. Smith, C. D. Coles, M. K. Poulson, & C. K. Cole (Eds.) *Children, families, and substance abuse* (pp. 95–119). Baltimore: Paul H. Brookes.

Radke-Yarrow, M., & Zahn-Waxler, C. (1975). *The emergence and functions of prosocial behavior in young children.* Washington, D.C.: National Institute of Health.

Rettig, M. (1994). Play behaviors of young children with autism: Characteristics and interventions. *Focus on Autistic Behavior, 9,* 1–6.

Roberts, J., Burchinal, M., Davis, B., Collier, A., & Henderson, F. (1991). Otitis media in early childhood and later language. *Journal of Speech and Hearing Research, 34,* 1158–1168.

Rosetti, L. (1990). *The Rosetti Infant-Toddler Language Scale.* East Moline, Ill.: LinguiSystems Inc.

Scalise-Smith, D., & Bailey, D. B. (1992). Facilitating motor skills. In D. B. Bailey & M. Wolery (Eds.), *Teaching infants and preschoolers with disabilities* (pp. 407–440). New York: Macmillian.

Skinner, B. F. (1953). *Science and human behavior.* New York: Free Press.

Streissguth, A. (1997). *Fetal alcohol syndrome: A guide for families and communities.* Baltimore: Paul H. Brookes.

Sweeney, C. (1996). *The development of gestures and their relations to communication in infants and toddlers.* Unpublished paper. St. Paul, Minn.: University of St. Thomas.

Thelen, E. (1995). Motor development: a new synthesis. *American Psychologist, 50*(2), 79–95.

VanSant, A. (1991). Motor control, motor learning, and motor development. In P. Montgomery & B. Connolly (Eds)., *Motor control and physical therapy* (pp. 13–27). Hixson, Tenn.: Chattanooga Group, Inc.

Vondra, J., & Belsky, J. (1989). Infant play at one year: characteristics and early antecedents. In J. Lockman & A. Hazen (Eds.). *Action in a social context: Perspectives on early development* (pp. 173–206). New York: Plenum Press.

Vygotsky, L. S. (1962). *Thought and language* (E. Hanfmann & G. Vaker, Trans.). Cambridge: Massachussetts Institute of Technology Press.

Wetherby, A. M., & Prizant, B. M. (1993). Profiling communication and symbolic abilities in young children. *Journal of Childhood Communication Disorders, 15*(1), 23–32.

Wieder, S. (1994). *Diagnostic classification of mental health and developmental disorders of infancy and early childhood. Diagnostic Classification: 0–3.* Arlington, Va.: Zero to Three/National Center for Clinical Infant Programs.

Wishart, J. G. (1995). Cognitive abilities in children with Down syndrome: Developmental instability and motivational deficits. In C. Epstein, T. Hassold, I. T. Lott, L. Nadel, & D. Patterson (Eds.), *Etiology pathogenesis of Down syndrome* (pp. 57–92). New York: Wiley.

Wood, S. (1995). *Dynamic systems theory and motor learning.* Unpublished master's thesis. St. Paul, Minn.: Unversity of St. Thomas.

Zirpoli, T. J. (1995). Introduction: A framework for understanding and affecting the behavior of young children. In T. J. Zirpoli (Ed.), *Understanding and affecting the behavior of young children* (pp. 1–33). Englewood Cliffs, N.J.: Merrill.

Zirpoli, T. J., & Melloy, K. J. (2001). *Behavior management: Applications for teachers* (3rd ed.). Upper Saddle River, N.J.: Merrill.

CHAPTER FIVE

SCREENING AND ASSESSMENT

WITH M. J. LaMONTAGNE

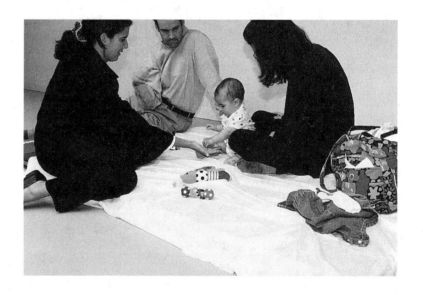

OBJECTIVES

- To understand eligibility requirements for early intervention services and child-find for screening young children

- To understand the theoretical approaches to assessment of young children with disabilities

- To become familiar with issues regarding measurement of young children and their families, including the reliability and validity of assessment instruments

- To understand the utility of alternatives to standardized assessments, including play-based and curriculum-based instruments

- To develop rapport skills in order to discuss assessment results with families in a sensitive and appropriate manner

- To understand the dynamics of caregiver-child interaction and how these relationships influence learning and development

- To understand the approach to assessment with preterm infants

- To become familiar with alternative assessment instruments for specific populations (e.g., children with autism, children exposed to violence)

"Assessment is a generic term that refers to the process of gathering information for the purpose of making a decision"

—McLean, 1996, p. 12.

This definition offers a global interpretation of a very complex task. Assessment is used to make multiple decisions regarding the diagnosis, placement, continuing evaluation, and programmatic strengths and needs of individual young children with disabilities.

Service providers are required by law to document the assessment of children referred for services. The federal government, under the reauthorization of IDEA (Individuals with Disabilities Education Act of 1996, PL 101–476) implemented in July 1998, has enacted Part C legislation, which includes a general definition for eligibility of infants and toddlers. The Part C lead agency in each state is responsible for defining the diagnostic procedures to be used.

The 1997 amendments to IDEA provided that states may include, at their discretion, an "at-risk" infant or toddlers in their definition of "infant or toddler with a disability." This change to the law has led to a reexamination of the eligibility criteria used by states that do not offer funding to children at risk. States that do provide services for infants and toddlers at risk must describe those services in their applications for federal funds. Table 5.1 presents eligibility definitions mandated in Part C.

According to the law, evaluation means documentation, by qualified personnel using appropriate procedures, of the need for services by an infant or toddler

TABLE 5.1   Eligibility under IDEA

(a) As used in this part, infants and toddlers with disabilities means individuals from birth through age 2, who need early intervention services because they—

1) Are experiencing developmental delays, as measured by appropriate diagnostic instruments and procedures in one or more of the following areas:
    (i) Cognitive development
    (ii) Physical development
    (iii) Communication development
    (iv) Social or emotional development
    (v) Adaptive development; or

2) Have a diagnosed physical or mental condition that has a high probability of resulting in developmental delay.

(b) The term may also include, at the State's discretion, children from birth through age 2 who are at risk of having substantial developmental delays if early intervention services are not provided.

The phrase "a diagnosed physical or mental condition that has a high probability of resulting in developmental delay," as used in paragraph (a)(2) of this section, applies to a condition if it typically results in developmental delay. Examples of these conditions include chromosomal abnormalities; genetic or congenital disorders; severe sensory impairments, including hearing and vision; inborn errors of metabolism; disorders reflecting disturbance of the development of the nervous system; congnital infections; disorders secondary to exposure to toxic substances, including fetal alcohol syndrome; and severe attachment disorders.

With respect to paragraph (b) of this section, children who are at risk may be eligible under this part if a State elects to extend services to that population, even though they have not been identified as disabled.

Under this provision, States have the authority to define who would be "at risk of having substantial developmental delays if early intervention services are not provided." In defining the "at risk" population, States may include well-known biological and environmental factors that can be identified and that place infants and toddlers "at risk" for developmental delay. Commonly cited factors include low birth weight, respiratory disress as a newborn, lack of oxygen, brain hemorrhage, infection, nutritional deprivation, and a history of abuse or neglect. It should be noted that "at risk" factors do not predict the presence of a barrier to development, but they may indicate children who are at higher risk of developmental delay than children without these problems.

Early Intervention Program for Infants and Toddlers with Disabilities, 34 C.F.R. § 303.16 (July 1, 1999).

and his family. Moreover, early intervention services must be provided by qualified personnel, including:

- Audiologists
- Family therapists
- Nurses

- Nutritionists
- Occupational therapists
- Orientation and mobility specialists
- Pediatricians and other physicians
- Physical therapists
- Psychologists
- Social Workers
- Special educators
- Speech and language pathologists

Early Intervention Program (1999), § 303.12

This list is not exhaustive. Qualified personnel may also include such personnel as vision specialists, paraprofessionals, and parent-to-parent support personnel.

All commercially available measurement tools recommend qualifications for users in order to maintain the validity and reliability of the instrument. For example, the Bayley Scales of Infant Development (1993) recommend that examiners have formal instruction in administering standardized assessments in a graduate or professional training program. Other tests list qualified personnel by professional field and may include trained educational assistants. This and other instruments must be administered in the native language of the parent. Service providers must use multiple procedures for determining eligibility, including observation. States require observation in the natural environment along with the use of standardized assessments and other procedures. In many states, informed clinical judgment as well as standardized results help determine eligibility.

A full comprehensive assessment is required for the following reasons:

1. To identify and diagnose children for program eligibility according to federal and state guidelines.
2. To plan programs and provide appropriate services as required by the Individualized Family Service Plan.
3. To monitor the child's progress on an ongoing basis. Although used for different purposes, both evaluation and assessment are critical parts of service delivery. Assessment refers to the actual procedures used to develop the Individualized Family Service Plan, including periodic review (McLean, 1996). Part C regulations for the IFSP require the evaluation and assessment of the child along with documentation of family resources, priorities, and concerns.

Part C legislation also mandates that state and local lead agencies actively seek infants and toddlers who may qualify for services. Through this mandate, service providers structure a series of evaluation procedures to provide developmental information to families, health care providers, human services professionals, and education interventionists known as child-find activities.

CHILD-FIND

Child-find is a state-regulated system of locating children who are eligible or may be eligible for early intervention services (McLean, 1996). Children with known disabilities such as cerebral palsy or Down syndrome are typically easier to find because of referrals from medical and other agencies. Children who may have a disability that is not as obvious in infancy and during the toddler years or who are at risk for developmental delay are harder to identify. Providing families with guidelines for typical development often helps caregivers who are unsure if their child has a delay. Many states have created multiple ways for identifying hard-to-find children. A common procedure is to place brochures or ads in settings families are likely to visit (e.g., a doctor's office, school, or mall). Some states use television and radio advertisements to help families who may have questions about their child's development.

SCREENING

Many local early intervention services have a central telephone number that accepts referrals and assigns a service provider to do initial screening. Related to the assessment process, screening is a brief and inexpensive method of identifying children who may need further and more extensive evaluation. Screening usually takes 10 to 20 minutes, and can be done with a formal screening instrument, such as the *Denver II* (formerly the *Denver Developmental Screening*) (Frankenburg et al., 1990), or an informal screening examination completed by the child's physician or another professional.

As a result of federal and state requirements for the identification and evaluation of all children with disabilities, mass screening is offered by many local school systems. These are collaborative community events (including multiple agencies such as Head Start, Early Childhood Special Education, social services, and public health) using advanced advertisements in the local media (newspapers, radio, and television). Many states offer screening for children three years of age and older prior to entering kindergarten. In some states screening is mandatory before the child attends kindergarten. During the screening process, children and their families go from one assessment area to another in order to identify developmental issues, vision problems, and hearing concerns. In addition, some programs include questionnaires or interview formats to elicit family concerns regarding the child's health or developmental status (Wright & Ireton, 1995). Parents play an important role in screening, because they can provide more reliable information about their child's behavioral characteristics than an abbreviated screening instrument (Diamond & Squires, 1993).

Tracking is a part of comprehensive child-find system that provides continuous monitoring of infants and toddlers who are at risk for developing disabilities (Blackman, 1986). An example of this type of service is the premature infant follow-up clinic. Several states have implemented statewide systems. Iowa, for example, has developed a statewide screening and tracking system for infants with biological risk factors. This system represents a cooperative effort by many state agencies, including the University of Iowa and child health specialty clinics. Infants with medical records indicative of neonatal risk factors, including very low birth weight, hypotonia, or seizures, are referred for screening at 4, 9, 18, and 20 months of age. The infants undergo a series of screening and assessment measures, including the *Denver Developmental Screening (DDST) II*, a physical and neurological examination, and an unstructured assessment of psychosocial behaviors and environmental conditions.

THEORETICAL APPROACHES TO ASSESSMENT

The development of assessments for young children is guided by three overlapping theoretical approaches to assessment. The first is the developmental approach. The Gesell Developmental Schedules (Gesell, 1925) established the importance of milestones in the developing child. Over the next two decades Bayley continued to refine this approach and first published the *Bayley Scales of Infant Development* in 1969. This test was renormed in 1992, but continues to be plagued by problems, and though the Bayley Scales continue to be used, no one has ever replicated her work.

The second approach to testing young children is the behavioral approach, which examines the behavioral responses of the child in relation to the environment. The Bayley Scales was one of the developmental scales that examined the child's behavioral repertoire during assessment. Another example of a behavioral assessment is the Brazelton Neonatal Assessment Scale (BNAS) (Brazelton & Nugent, 1995). A primary goal of the BNAS is to demonstrate the newborn's capabilities in terms of the caregiving environment.

The third type of approach to assessment is the ecological approach, which examines the child's abilities and needs in terms of the multiple environments in which the child interacts on a daily basis. The Assessment, Evaluation, and Programming System (AEPS) (Bricker, 1993) is an example of an ecological assessment tool. This approach recognizes the importance of child and family variables that affect development and learning. It also takes into consideration the connection between the child, family, community, and society. By using this approach, the assessment team can probe environmental factors that the family perceives as important (Bricker, 1993).

Standardized assessments generally follow the developmental milestones approach that include specific guidelines for administration, scoring, and interpretation of test results. The instruments are developed using sampling procedures to ensure that all children within a certain age group are represented across race, sex, geographic location, and (in some cases) socioeconomic status. These tests are also called norm-referenced tests because they compare the child's performance to that of a normative group.

Criterion-referenced assessments may also follow a developmental milestone approach, but they measure the child's performance according to a certain level of mastery rather than to a normative group.

Curriculum-based assessment may incorporate all three approaches to assessment. In addition, the assessment is directly linked to a curriculum so that intervention plans can be drawn from the results. The Transdisciplinary Play-Based Assessment (Linder, 1993) is an example of a curriculum-based assessment.

For many service providers working in the field, play has always provided the best window into viewing a child's capacity.

For years, service providers have struggled with federal and state requirements to use standardized assessments with infants and toddlers because these instruments continued to penalize children with disabilities (Blasco, 1989). However, with the passage of Part C, many states have added the requirement of observation-based assessment in the natural environment, and some states do not require standardized assessment at all. However, since many states continue to require a formal assessment procedure, service providers must be familiar with scoring and interpreting these tests.

STANDARDIZED ASSESSMENT

Standardized assessment of young children has been used in this country since the 1930s. The California First Year Mental Scale (Bayley, 1933) was the precursor to the Bayley Scales of Infant Development (BSID) (Bayley, 1993). Standardized measures adhere to required protocols, materials, and procedures for scoring and interpretation (Bailey & Nabors, 1996). As stated, these tests give normative data on children who fall into the age range specified by their developers, who administered the test to a sample population. Such norm-referenced tests can therefore give developmental age scores, developmental quotients, standard scores, and percentile ranks. It is important to realize that some assessments give information on developmental age that is not based on a normative sample. The information in the guidelines or preface to the test should be read carefully to ensure that it is norm-referenced.

Developmental age scores indicate the average age at which 50 percent of the children in the sample population received a particular raw score on the test. A problem with this measurement is that it relies on the raw score and does not differentiate the child's performance on specific items. For example, if one child scored a 2 on three of five items and a 1 on the last two items, and another child scored a 1 on the first two items and a 2 on the last three items, they would have the same score but different needs for learning and skill acquisition. Bailey and Nabors (1996) also pointed out that although a child may exhibit skills typical of an 18-month-old, there is wide variability in the abilities of an 18-month-old, and thus the information is not very helpful in planning intervention.

A developmental quotient (DQ) can be computed by dividing the child's developmental age (DA) by her chronological age (CA), and multiplying by 100. For example, the DQ of an 18 month-old toddler who scores developmentally at 18 months would be as follows:

$$\frac{18 \text{ months (DA)}}{18 \text{ months (CA)}} \times 100 = 100$$

Many physicians use the developmental quotient because it is easy to deliver a small sample of items (Peter A. Blasco, personal communication, March 3, 1996).

Some researchers, however, believe it is problematic because of the disparity between a child's DQ at different ages (Bailey & Nabors, 1996), which, unlike an IQ score, is likely to change as the child grows older. There continues to be a great deal of debate regarding infant assessments that attempt to predict later intelligence. However, infant assessments with items that assess memory, discrimination, or attention correlate highly with intelligence tests given at later ages (Siegel, 1999).

The assessment of infants can be influenced by the temperament of the child and his response to the examiner and to the items. For example, children with difficult temperaments score lower than children with easier temperaments. In addition, infants and toddlers vary greatly in their mood depending on the time of day, their energy level, and their nutritional status. Parents can also influence the child's performance on a standardized assessment. If the parent is overly anxious, the child may sense this and become distraught. It is important for the examiner to establish rapport not only with the child (to overcome any stranger anxiety) but also the parent. Parents may need reassuring from time to time, especially if the child is failing items. In Vignette 5.1, a father expresses his concern about his daughter's performance.

VIGNETTE 5.1   SHE CAN DO BETTER THAN THAT!

Gary and Mary brought 18-month-old Gina in for her assessment after she failed on a preschool screening exam. Gina was born eight weeks prematurely and had developed bronchopulmonary dysplasia while in the Neonatal Intensive Care Unit (NICU). Both parents were anxious about the outcome of this assessment, although they knew they would gain access to services for Gina. Sara, the examiner, pointed out Gina's successes and smiled at both parents to reassure them. After about 10 minutes, Gina was not able to perform many of the items. Her father had played pat-a-cake with her many times, but the examiner could not get her to play the game. Then she tried to get Gina to play peeka-boo. She still was unsuccessful, and it was obvious that this item would not be scored as a pass. Gary was furious, for he had seen Gina play both games many times. He began to move about in his seat restlessly and made several comments about the inadequacy of the test. Gina sensed something was wrong and began to cry. She wouldn't take any interest in the items and wanted to be held. The examiner suggested that Mary give her a hug to help her calm down. Gary said, "No, I'll take her." This action only increased Gina's anxiety. The examiner suggested that they continue the assessment on another day.

Although the situation in Vignette 5.1 does not occur frequently, it is likely that parental anxiety will be heightened during testing. In the above situation, the examiner could have explained beforehand that the assessment required her to continue even after the child began to fail items, or she could have commented that children don't always perform during assessments as they would in a less strange situation. Unfortunately, given the nature of many standardized assessments, families do not participate as equal partners in the assessment process. For example, although a parent report is included on the BSID II, it cannot be used for scoring purposes. It is important for families to have equal status in the assessment process in order to establish a sense of trust (McLean & Crais, 1996). Most curriculum-based and play-based assessments include a parent report as part of the assessment process.

In a perfect world, assessments would occur at the optimal time for both children and parents. But this can be impractical in some situations, especially for the examiner who feels he has an overburdened caseload and does not have time to reschedule assessments. Thus, examiners may be cutting corners to complete an assessment as scheduled, particularly if they are more experienced with assessing older children and do not understand the needs of infants and toddlers.

UNDERSTANDING STATISTICAL PROPERTIES

In order to use all assessment measures correctly, service providers should have a firm background in measurement. Service providers who do not understand procedures are likely to make both administration and scoring errors. In one study, Bailey, Vandiviere, Delinger, and Munn (1987) found that out of 79 teachers, only 11 (14.5 percent) had no scoring errors on the Battelle Developmental Inventory (BDI), a widely used assessment instrument (Newborg, Stock, Wnek, Guidubaldi, & Svinicki, 1984).

There is no replacement for the study of a thorough text on test and measurement. However, at the very least, a few key terms should be reviewed before using assessments in early intervention. Most assessments in early childhood use a standard score for interpreting the overall performance on a test. A standard score provides a mean and standard deviation that is represented on a normal bell-shaped curve that provides a model for the theoretical distribution of scores. Any introductory textbook on statistics will provide an example of the bell curve. With a standardized assessment, most children will score near the mean. A standard deviation provides numeric information on how far a child's score deviates from the mean.

Many states use standard deviations for determining eligibility for special education services. For example, to receive early childhood special education services in Minnesota, a child must receive a score 1.5 standard deviations below the mean on a standardized developmental assessment, or, if the child is younger than 18 months old, a motor score 2.0 standard deviations below the mean.

In addition, the state requires systematic observation in the routine environment and a developmental history and medical history. Percentile ranks are also used to compare a child's score with a population (Bailey & Nabors, 1996). If a child has a percentile score of 70, this would indicate that she scored higher than 69 percent of the normative population.

Reliability and Validity

The developers of a standardized test must supply information regarding its reliability and validity. Reliability refers to the extent to which individual differences are measured consistently. Reliability is the ratio of true variance divided by obtained variance. When the ratio is 1, then reliability is perfect.

There are several types of reliability. Stability, also known as test-retest reliability, examines the relationship of an individual's score on the first administration of the test to her score on the second administration of the same test. A coefficient of stability is reported. For example, for the BSID II, test-retest scores are reported for the mental, motor, and behavior scales as well as for several subscales. The testing was completed on a sample of infants (N = 48) at 12 months of age. The two tests were administered within one to 16 days, with a median retest date of four days. The stability coefficient was .83 for the mental scale and .77 for the motor scale (Bayley, 1993). One concern with test-retest reliability is the influence of practice and memory. Tests scheduled close together give the child opportunities to practice items that were similar.

Another type of reliability examines the internal consistency within the test. Split-half reliability assesses two halves (such as all odd-numbered items and all even-numbered items) by correlating the scores obtained in the comparison of the two halves for each individual. Two statistical procedures for computing internal consistency are the Spearman-Brown and Kuder-Richardson formulas. Interrater (interobserver) reliability examines the relationship between items passed or failed, using percentage of agreement between two independent observers. One problem in using interrater reliability with rating scales is that it does not indicate the discrepancy between two scores. For example, one scorer gave a child a 5 and the other scorer a 1 on the same item. However, when the total was calculated, the observers agreed more than disagreed, so the reliability was high. One solution is to use a statistical procedure called the G-coefficient that also takes into account the variability within the scores between observers.

Validity is the degree to which a test measures what it is supposed to measure. Very few assessments give an indication of their face validity, or their attractiveness to the user. But, as one psychologist pointed out, face validity can make or break an assessment. "I've seen tests where the staff just didn't like the looks of it. They could never give a good explanation for why they didn't like the test, but you can be certain it ended up in a closet collecting dust!"

Content validity measures the intended content area of the test. One question to ask is whether the items on the test correspond to its objectives. All standardized tests include information on their content.

Construct validity measures an intended hypothetical construct. For example, Sell, Figueredo, and Wilcox (1995) completed a confirmatory factor analysis to validate behavioral domains on the Assessment of Preterm Infants' Behavior (APIB). With a sample of 145 infants who required neonatal intensive care, they confirmed six behavioral constructs: overall modulation of behavior, availability for examination, motor competency, sociability, habituation, and reactivity.

Criterion validity relates performance on the test to performance on another criterion. For example, Siegel, Cooper, Fitzhardinger, and Ash (1995) compared a subtest of expressive language items on the Bayley Scales of Infant Development with the Reynell Developmental Language Scales (RDLS-R), using 137 low-birth-weight preterm infants at two years of age. Both tests were scored both with age correction for prematurity and with no correction by using the child's chronological age (corrected scores implies full correction for age). The correlations were .66 for uncorrected comprehension scores and .79 for uncorrected expressive scores. The correlations were .67 for corrected comprehensive scores and .80 for corrected expressive scores.

ALTERNATIVES TO STANDARDIZED ASSESSMENTS

Assessment for early intervention is not a test-based process, primarily; early childhood assessment is a flexible, collaborative decision-making process in which teams of parents and professionals repeatedly revise their collective judgments and reach consensus about the changing developmental, educational, medical, and mental health service needs of young children and their families.

—Bagnato & Neisworth, 1991, p. xi

Recommended practice in both early intervention and early childhood education recognizes the importance of a link between assessment and curriculum in order to ensure program content is meeting the needs of the child and the concerns of the family (Bagnato, Neisworth, & Munson, 1997; Bredekamp & Rosegrant, 1995; Bricker, 1993). No single assessment can make that link. It is the responsibility of the team, including the parents, to make the decisions that affect the child's learning experience. In Chapter 9, we discuss in depth the role of the team in early intervention and the ways in which teams are formed. Over the past decade, teams have found formal assessments to be inappropriate for program planning based on individual needs. As a result, there has been a shift away from the use of formal assessments and toward the use of informal assessments. This has meant increased reliance on criterion-referenced assessments, which focus on mastery of specific skills, rather than making a comparison to a norm sample (Benner, 1992). These types of assessments can be simple checklists that provide a baseline for program planning as well as ongoing evaluation. Although such a checklist can be useful for planning IFSP outcomes, service providers should be cautious about "teaching to the test," since IFSP outcomes should reflect the child's needs as well as the family's priorities.

There are many curriculum-based assessments for infants and toddlers on the market. These tools are designed to link assessment and curriculum. The items on the assessment protocol follow a typical developmental progression. The curriculum activities that correspond to test items teach functional skills related to the identified needs of the individual child. Many of these measures are introduced in Chapter 7. The Carolina Curriculum for Infants and Toddlers with Special Needs (Johnson-Martin, Jens, Attermeier, & Hacker, 1991), for example, provides developmental markers for assessing infants and toddlers across developmental domains. The Carolina Curriculum also provides suggestions for modifying test items for children with motor or sensory impairments. Similarly, the Hawaii Early Learning Profile (HELP) provides developmental assessment for infants and toddlers from birth to three. In addition to curriculum activities, HELP at Home provides activity sheets for parents across the developmental domains (Parks et al., 1992).

The AEPS (Bricker, 1993) was designed as an intervention model that links assessment, intervention, and evaluation processes. According to Bricker (1993):

> Assessment refers to the process of establishing a baseline or entry level measurement of the child's skills and desired family outcomes. The assessment process should produce the necessary information to select appropriate and relevant intervention goals and objectives. Intervention refers to the process of arranging the physical and social environment to produce the desired growth and development specified in the formulated intervention plan for the child and family. Evaluation refers to the process of comparing the child's performance on selected intervention goals and objectives before and after intervention, and comparing the family's progress toward established family outcomes. (p. 12)

Curriculum-based assessment provides the team with an opportunity to plan outcomes for each individual child based on the results of the assessment. Both practitioners and families find this approach to assessment more functional and meaningful in meeting the needs of the child. Because play is such an integral part of the curriculum for very young children, play-based assessment can help to identify the learning needs of children regardless of disability.

PLAY-BASED ASSESSMENT

We suggest that the motivation/competence relationship can be
measured in spontaneous play because in spontaneous play children
are free to show or not show their most sophisticated behaviors.
—Hrncir, Speller, & West, 1985, p. 227

The dynamic nature of infants and toddlers with disabilities has presented many challenges to interventionists charged with the task of assessing their skills, abilities, and behaviors. Young children exhibit characteristics that are often not compatible with standardized assessments (Linder, 1993; McLean, 1996; Peterson, 1988; Fewell, 1983). Infants and toddlers appropriately display anxiety and fear in the presence of strangers who are structuring interactions with them. Unfamiliar settings can create an atmosphere of discomfort for the infant or toddler, resulting in refusal and avoidance behaviors. An assessment environment that is not responsive to the daily routine of a child may impose misjudgments of an infant or toddler who is ready for a nap or a feeding rather than interactions with an adult. In addition, the field of early intervention has become more attentive to infant and toddler characteristics that frame the performance of a skill. The understanding of characteristics such as temperament, states of arousal, motivation, engagement, interactional patterns, and interests has proved to be valuable for designing and implementing individual family service programs. There is also recognition that the interdependence of developmental systems is a major characteristic of infancy that must be addressed if a complete understanding of infant functioning is to be obtained (Teti & Gibbs, 1990).

Acknowledging the limitations of using standardized assessment instruments with infants and toddlers has led to the development of alternative approaches to identifying present levels of functioning in this population. Campbell (1991) concisely articulated the challenge by defining the purpose of assessment as identifying the unique needs of the infant or toddler with disabilities, with the understanding that these needs are constantly changing due to the child's status as an infant or toddler. A particularly effective means of achieving this is through the use of play-based assessment, which has evolved from a transdisciplinary assessment process developed by the United Cerebral Palsy Association (1976) to gather information to use in planning programs for individuals with moderate or severe cerebral palsy.

This transdisciplinary approach transforms the assessment process to a more supportive environment that accesses the competencies and identifies the needs of the infant or toddler with disabilities and her family. In play-based assessment, a single individual interacts with the infant or toddler, while professionals and family members observe the child's performance of skills (Linder, 1993). The observers become active participants as they request the elicitation of specific behaviors during the play session. Play-based assessment is thus a systematic method of viewing a young child's skills and abilities through the medium of play (Blasco & LaMontagne, 1996; Lifter, 1996; Linder, 1993; Woodruff, 1980).

Components of Play-Based Assessment

The five basic components of a play-based assessment (Blasco & LaMontagne, 1996; Linder, 1993; Woodruff, 1980) are described in Table 5.2.

Each of these components contributes to the successful implementation of a play-based assessment. Team membership should reflect the concerns presented by the family during the intake or referral process. A transdisciplinary approach requires that all of the professionals and family members involved assume the various roles in the assessment. If possible, the facilitator should be an individual familiar with the family so that she can gather information from and support the family during the entire procedure. Regardless of the specific format or approach, assessment is stressful for families, and having a familiar facilitator can help to alleviate some of the tension. It is best if the play facilitator is someone who is known to the child and/or who is skilled in working with infants and toddlers in order to be able to follow the child's lead and interests, and be responsive and flexible as the interactions change and as the child's temperament and personality are revealed. In addition, the play facilitator should be comfortable interacting while sitting on the floor or playing at the sand or water table. This person also should be able to provide exaggerated facial responses and to sing or use differing voice tones to engage the child's attention, which are often necessary when interacting with infants and toddlers.

TABLE 5.2 Play-Based Assessment Components

COMPONENTS	ACTIONS
1. Team selection based on child and family characteristics; team members (to include parents if they so choose) define purpose of assessment	Identify and assign roles (e.g., facilitator, play facilitator)
2. Information about priorities, resources, and concerns disseminated to team members; review previous results	Gather information related to child and family background,
3. Selection of appropriate assessment materials	Identify written observation format
	Identify and develop activities to support the child's demonstration of skills
4. Conduct assessment	Structure environment in child- and family-friendly manner
	Review assessment purpose
	Review team member roles
	Play facilitator presents activities to the child and/or allows the child to lead the interactions
	Facilitator supports family members during the assessment and/or gathers additional information from family
	Team members make suggestions for additional activities
	Team members record descriptive information on observation forms and record demonstration of behaviors on developmental checklists
5. Assessment staffing	Include family as team member
	Review past assessment data
	Review information gathered during play-based assessment
	Brainstorm insights and recommendations
	Develop group consensus in relation to IFSP goals and outcomes
	Generate IFSP and/or assessment report

It is important that information about the family and child be disseminated to team members prior to the assessment. This will reduce the length of the assessment and reduce redundancy in gathering data. Such information will also help the team select the appropriate assessment materials. For a play-based assessment to be successful in gathering information needed for program planning, the play facilitator must prepare a series of activities that will allow the infant or toddler to demonstrate his skills and abilities. In many instances, the play facilitator will be able to follow the child's lead, and these preplanned activities may not be needed. However, it is important that activities be available when a team member requests that a specific skill be elicited. For some play-based assessments, team members may want to record demonstration of skills across developmental domains on developmental checklists, with descriptive information logged in available space. For others, observation forms that provide a format for recording running observations of the child throughout the assessment process may be more appropriate.

Conducting the play-based assessment is the most involved component of the process and requires attention to several steps (Blasco & LaMontagne, 1996; Linder, 1993; Woodruff, 1980), as identified in Table 5.3.

TABLE 5.3   The Play-Based Assessment Process

Step 1.   Orient the child and family to the team members and the environment. Let the child hear the voices of the team members so that they will be familiar when heard during the assessment. Introduce the family members to any unknown team member. Allow the family to choose where they would like to sit, and allow the infant or toddler to explore the environment.

Step 2.   Have team members sit around the perimeter of the assessment area so that each has an observational field of the child and play facilitator. Ensure that the environment is child- and family-friendly. Use child-size furniture when appropriate. Have age- and developmentally appropriate toys, including large motor equipment, such as rocking boats, slides, bikes, and push/pull toys. Place a blanket or mat on the floor so that the infant or toddler is comfortable when crawling or lying down.

Step 3.   As the play facilitator engages the child, observers record information on observation forms. Additional information can be gathered from the family as the assessment progresses. When appropriate, observers may request activities and demonstration of specific child skills from the play facilitator. When necessary, observers may talk quietly among themselves but must be careful not to distract the infant or toddler.

Step 4.   If possible, structure the play-based assessment time to include the following interactions: child-family, child-peer, child-sibling, and child-adult. Also include opportunities for the infant or toddler to have a snack or lunch in order to observe self-help/adaptive and feeding skills.

Step 5.   Whenever possible, allow the infant or toddler to dictate the pace, the materials, and the interactions. If the child appears disinterested, ask family members for suggestions for engaging her attention. Use planned activities when requested by team members or when the child is hesitant about initiating an interaction with the play facilitator.

Step 6.   Continue the play-based assessment until: the allotted time is up; the child becomes tired, irritable, or otherwise nonengaged; the observers have acquired all the information of interest; or the family expresses a desire to stop.

It is critical for the family and child to feel comfortable in this assessment environment. As much attention as possible should be paid to creating a relaxed and supportive atmosphere. Refreshments such as coffee or soft drinks often serve to relieve anxiety. Using a room that is bright and cheerful can ease the tension for many families. Reviewing the assessment purpose and reminding participants that this is an opportunity for the child to play and "strut his stuff" takes the emphasis off the concept of right or wrong responses and focuses attention instead on the competencies and abilities of the child. During the assessment, the child should be given the opportunity to interact with peers, siblings, and family members in order to obtain insights into the child's social, communicative, and adaptive skills. Scheduling a short snack not only reenergizes the infant or toddler for further play, but also provides a view of mealtime routines and interactions. Throughout the assessment period, observers should focus on what skills the child performs and how the child demonstrates those skills (i.e., what sustained the child's interest, preference, motivation, learning style, and perseverance). Table 5.4 lists areas that can be observed during the assessment. The play-based assessment should continue until the child, family, or team indicates a need for termination.

After the play-based assessment is completed, the team members meet to discuss and integrate all of the child and family information gathered. Family members are an important part of this reflective process, as they are the professionals' guide to the validity of the results. During this team meeting, past information is reviewed and the data gathered from the play-based assessment are examined. It is at this stage that issues related to teaming become meaningful. All teams go through stages of development: forming, storming, norming, performing, and adjourning (Tuckman & Jensen, 1977). As play-based assessment teams form, they identify their membership and discuss their reason for participating on this team. Next comes the storming phase, where roles and responsibilities are negotiated. During this stage, conflict resolution and mediation strategies are critical as team members struggle to present opposing perspectives. It is important to remember that on most play-based assessment teams, each member has her own view of what is in the best interest of the particular child and family. In order for the team to reach consensus, individuals must negotiate, compromise, and collaborate with each other. The performing stage is characterized by the actions needed to complete the play-based assessment, the staffing, and the development of the IFSP. The goals and outcomes documented on the IFSP are generated at the team meeting and reflect the child and family data derived from the assessment. At the successful completion of these tasks, the team adjourns until the next infant or toddler with disabilities and his family is referred for assessment.

Categories of Play

Because play-based assessment uses play to evoke an infant's or toddler's skills and abilities across developmental domains, team members need an understanding of

TABLE 5.4   Observing an Individual Child

BODY MOVEMENTS AND USE OF BODY
Movements are usually quick or slow

Seems at ease with physical self

Small and large muscle skills and movements
are about equally developed or one area is
more developed than the other area

FACIAL EXPRESSIONS
Uses face to express feelings (e.g., smiles,
frowns, neutral)

Reacts to experiences occurring around
her/him

Shows intense feelings most of the time

Shows neutral or "deadpan" expression most
of the time

SPEECH
Uses tone of voice to express feelings

Raises voice or yells when upset

Uses speech as primary communication
method

Uses alternative communication (e.g.,
gestures, adaptive equipment)

Can imitate songs, chants, verbal expressions

Uses fluent, articulate (easy-to-understand)
speech

EMOTIONAL REACTIONS
Method of exhibiting emotional reactions
(e.g., smiles when happy, cries when angry)

Good balance in controlling feelings

Responds appropriately to adults/to other
children

PLAY ACTIVITIES
Frequent and favorite activities

Play initiation skills, and patterns of play (e.g.,
how play progresses and next event)

Persistence during activities or flits from one
activity to another

Avoidance of certain activities (e.g., sensory
materials like clay or glue)

Evidence of mastery pleasure in completing
an activity

Evidence of frustration with activities

Tempo or pace of play remains even or too
slow or fast. Under what circumstances?

Plays alone. Under what circumstances?

Engages in pretend play (indicate with self
or partner)

Engages in dramatic play (list roles)

Tries new things

Shows curiosity about the environment,
including materials, equipment, and
people

Prefers to play in certain areas (list areas or
indoor *vs.* outdoor)

Special skills in one area (e.g., music, art, etc.)

BASIC NEEDS
Typical response to food

Natural bowel and bladder control

Appropriate sexuality

Seems well rested most of the time

Adapted from *A Guide to Observing and Recording Behavior* by W. Bentzen, 1993, Albany, N.Y.: Delmar.

the categories associated with play. There are several hierarchical models of play behavior; perhaps the most familiar in early childhood is Parten's (1932) categories of social play (see Table 4.3). The first level in this taxonomy is unoccupied behavior. On this level the child shows no sustained attention to any material or person. The second level is solitary play, when a child plays by herself with materials unlike those used by other children in the play area. At the onlooker level, the child observes other children at play and will even converse with them without actually engaging in the play routine. In the fourth stage, parallel play, the child plays next to other children, using materials and toys that may be similar. Associative play occurs when the child exchanges materials with other children, discusses the ongoing actions of the play, and invites others to the play situation, yet remains independent in choice and action. The final stage of Parten's social play is cooperative play. At this level, children are organizing, directing, assigning roles, dividing labor, and working together for some purpose.

Belsky and Most (1981) have identified categories of play activities that focus on how the infant or toddler uses objects. Their first category is mouthing, which is categorized by the haphazard mouthing of objects. Simple manipulation occurs when the infant or toddler intentionally moves or turns objects or materials. In the next stage, functional, the manipulation becomes appropriate to the object or material. When an infant or toddler demonstrates a relational play activity, he brings two unrelated objects together in an action; and when the infant or toddler combines objects or materials in an appropriate fashion, the activity becomes functional-relational. Enactive naming is a behavior that approaches pretend use of objects or materials. For example, a child may bring a telephone receiver or flip-phone up to her shoulder but does not bring it to her ear and say, "Hello." On the next level, the toddler engages in pretend play. Pretend self-play is characterized by behavior directed toward the self, such as picking up a spoon and eating pretend food. Pretend external play is characterized by behavior directed toward another, such as feeding a doll or offering to feed an adult. Substitution happens when the child creatively uses an object or material to give it new meaning. For example, the child may substitute a stick for a baby bottle or a sponge for a blanket.

Next in the hierarchical progression are play behaviors related to sequence. The first, sequence pretend, is displayed when the child links different pretend schemes together, and the second, sequence pretend substitution, occurs when the child makes a substitution in one of the pretense schemes he is linking. An example of sequence pretend is when the child pours pretend milk in a cup and then takes a drink; an example of sequence pretend substitution is when the child places a baby doll in a bed and covers it with a sponge that serves as the blanket. In the final level of play behavior, double transformation, the child uses two substitute materials in a single act. An example is when the child substitutes a stick for a baby doll, places the stick in a bed, covers it with a sponge, and says, "Night-night."

Blasco and LaMontagne (1996) have summarized play behaviors with associated activities and ages to provide an easier framework for using play as the medium for assessment (see Chapter 4). When assessing a young child with a disability through a play-based approach, the play facilitator must have an understanding of what to expect from the child during play interactions and what types of play activities will entice the child into interactions with their environment (e.g., materials, objects, and people). If the play assessment team is observing a 24-month-old infant with suspected developmental delays, then planned activities will include sensorimotor and exploratory activities. In addition, the play facilitator will need to have a few activities that represent more integrated exploration (the next level) in order to challenge the toddler's upward movement to more complex play behaviors. If the assessment is for a 24-month-old infant whose past evaluations indicate a 12-month-old developmental level, then planned activities will focus on sensorimotor/perceptual and/or beginning sensorimotor/exploratory play.

Advantages of Play-Based Assessment

Many of the advantages of play-based assessment are related to the particular characteristics of infants and toddlers. A play-based approach is less intrusive to the child and provides an interactive and engaging format that capitalizes on an infant's or toddler's natural curiosity, exploration, and interests. Play-based assessment has an inherent flexibility and responsiveness that match the child's activity level, temperament, and states of arousal. With this approach, all children, regardless of disability level or age can be assessed. Team members observe the child's interactions and gain insight into his skills and abilities, while family members are available to comment and expand on their child's performance of developmental behaviors. Play-based assessment reduces redundancy, as the play facilitator elicits child behaviors for every team member to observe. Because such assessment focuses on the child's demonstration of abilities, stress is reduced for the child and the family, since there is no right or wrong answer in play. Through observations, team members record the assessment events, and triangulation of data collection is achieved when three or more observers document the same child behavior. This validation of observations strengthens the integrity of the play-based assessment results. The transdisciplinary foundation of play-based assessment brings a richness to the process not found in standardized assessments. The sharing of information before, during, and after the play-based assessment integrates information in an extensive and holistic manner and creates a base of knowledge from which to generate a meaningful and realistic individualized family service program.

Disadvantages of Play-Based Assessment

Although it is an innovative approach to assessing infants and toddlers with disabilities, play-based assessment has certain limitations. As discussed, team-building and consensus can make or break the process. The degree to which individual team members perceive this approach as a valid and reliable method for assessing this population and are committed to the process has a direct impact on the success of the team. The use of specialized jargon that is specific to a discipline can contribute to communication barriers and confusion. Arranging the schedules of various professionals and family members so they can all be in the same place at the same time can be a monumental task. Time commitment is another potential limitation, especially for beginning teams. A play-based assessment can take from one to two hours to complete, depending on the child's age and level of disability, and the presenting concerns of the family. Furthermore, the objectivity of observational data is often questioned, since biased interpretations of play-based assessment events can be recorded as factual. Recognizing the limitations of this observational approach provides early interventionists with a clear view of the potential barriers that may interfere with its successful implementation.

ASSESSING FAMILY ISSUES AND CONCERNS

Sharing Sensitive Information— Saving the Messenger

Most service providers can tell horror stories about their attempts to deliver a diagnosis to parents. In the traditional medical model, the idea was to spill the beans and run out the door. Medical education programs that concentrated on disease but provided little or no training in community resources, human service agencies, or home visiting (Sharp & Lohr, 1994) reinforced this approach. Although medical education is changing with the incorporation of training in community-based and home-visiting programs (Blasco, Kohen, & Shapland, 1999), the push for shorter hospital stays and denial of insurance coverage for certain medical visits make it difficult to practice family-centered care. Families of children with disabilities may find that the first contacts who have time to listen to them are the early intervention team members.

In terms of recommended practice, there is an emphasis on delivering news that is accurate yet respectful of families (Kroth, Olson, & Kroth, 1986). Blasco, O'Leary, Engstrom, Calvin, and Ferski (1996) presented a simple formula for giving news to families—be brief, be gentle, be quiet, and be there. Families often need time to assimilate a child's diagnosis. They may need time to be alone and think things through as a family. However, it is important that service providers be available to answer questions. It is also a good idea to let families know where they can reach you if they have any questions once they return home.

Allowing families to determine their involvement in the assessment process has been advocated as best practice in early intervention (Kjerland & Kovach, 1990; McGonigel, Kaufmann, & Johnson, 1991; McLean & Crais, 1996; Winton & Bailey, 1997). A true family-centered approach to services includes respect for individual decisions. Some families may want to take a very active role in the assessment, while others may be more passive and look to other team members for decision-making. Some families may be less involved in the initial stages and more involved in the implementation and evaluation of services.

It is equally important to realize that family involvement will change over time. Service providers who encounter a family taking a less active role in their early interactions are often surprised when that family wants to be more involved once other resources are in place and needs have been met. Likewise, some families may at times need a break from decision-making or advocacy and rely on professionals to take the lead. If we are to be truly family-guided, then we need to respect family decisions in terms of their involvement. Table 5.5 lists tips for family-guided assessment suggested by the National Center for Clinical Infant Programs.

TABLE 5.5   Tips For Family-Guided Assessment

- Young children should not be separated from their parents during an assessment procedure, if possible. The child may respond to separation by becoming more anxious and cannot give an optimal performance under these conditions.
- Standardized tests should not be the only measurement used with young children. Most standardized tests are designed for children with typical development and will not reflect the abilities and needs of a child with disabilities.
- Other assessment procedures should include parental report and observation of the child and the parent-child relationship.
- Parents should bring an advocate to the child's IFSP meeting. It helps to have the support of a friend or someone who knows the child as well as the parent to offer collaboration and support.
- Parents have a right to disagree, make changes, or ask for clarification in terms of their child's outcomes.

Adapted from S. J. Meisels and E. Fenichel, (Eds.), 1996, *New Visions for the Developmental Assessment of Infants and Young Children*, Arlington, Va.: Zero to Three/National Center for Infant Programs.

Assessing Family Concerns

The IFSP is a document that includes an assessment or inventory of family aspirations for and concerns about their child (Bailey, 1996). Part C of IDEA strengthened the family's role in the assessment process. Families should decide if they think an assessment of their own resources, priorities, and concerns is necessary in order to improve services to the child. Any formal or informal method for gathering information from family members should include the families' own description of these areas. Families will vary in the way they wish to share this information. Some families will prefer checklists or survey options to more informal personal interviews (Bailey & Blasco, 1990).

In order to effectively include family feedback into the process, the service provider should be proficient in both verbal and nonverbal listening skills. Good listening skills include the following:

- Using clarification to restate the content of what a person says in a brief and concise manner
- Using effective questions, both open-ended and closed-ended, as needed
- Reflecting on the feelings expressed by the speaker and demonstrating appropriate empathy and understanding (Winton, 1988; Winton & Bailey, 1993). In addition, nonverbal skills, such as sitting close to the speaker, leaning forward, nodding one's head, and establishing eye contact when appropriate help to keep the conversation going (Winton, 1988; Winton & Bailey, 1993).

In Vignette 5.2, one parent experiences an initial interview with a examiner new to the team. A school psychologist, whose previous work had been with school-age children, the examiner was not used to having parents present during an assessment and was not yet comfortable with this approach.

VIGNETTE 5.2   HE MIGHT AS WELL BE STEVEN

Michael and Ann had brought Shawn, 13 months, in for assessment after a recommendation from the pediatrician, who was concerned that Shawn was showing global developmental delays; he had already ruled out vision or hearing problems. Ann and Michael's first child, Shawn had been born two months prematurely. Both were very anxious about the outcome of the assessment. When the assessment was completed, the examiner said she would score it later and discuss it with them. She asked them to complete an initial interview form for the early intervention program. She said, "Tell me about [she paused to check the name on the folder] Shawn." As she spoke, she continued to write in a folder. Michael and Ann were surprised. They weren't sure what to say. After a brief time, the examiner looked up and said, "What does he like to do, you know . . . play with?" Ann began to talk about his favorite toys, when the telephone rang. The examiner picked up the phone and began talking to someone. She kept looking at her watch and alternatively back at Ann, expecting her to continue. Ann and Michael heard her tell someone that she would be late for the next appointment and to hold the family there until she arrived. The examiner put down the phone and said, "Okay, what are your concerns about Steven?" Both Ann and Michael corrected her at the same time: "His name is Shawn." The examiner offered a brief apology and makes a comment referring to her workload of cases. Ann and Michael took turns talking about the issues raised by the pediatrician and observed by them at home. The examiner seemed to be writing what the parents were reporting, but she was also looking through another file on the desk as if she had misplaced something. When Ann and Michael finished, there was silence as she continued to write in her file. Then she suddenly looked up and said, "Good," and closed the file. She stood up and said, "Someone will be getting back to you soon. It was nice meeting you and Shawn."

In the above vignette, the examiner gave the impression that she was too busy to give her full attention to this family. She was more concerned with completing her paperwork and getting to her next appointment. Although this example paints a dramatic picture that we hope has not occurred in reality, it is intended to underscore the importance of practicing good verbal and nonverbal listening skills with families. It is very easy for overburdened service providers to slip into a pattern of nonlistening when they are in a hurry and overwhelmed. As one psychologist said, "I know all of this sounds like it should come naturally, but it doesn't.

It's just not as easy as it sounds" (Frank Kaufman, School Psychologist, Baltimore City Schools, February 13, 1997).

PARENT-CHILD INTERACTION

Another assessment domain that is included with the birth to three population in particular is parent-child interaction. Many of the well-known measures of this dimension were developed in the late 1970s to mid-1980s, and consisted of either binary checklists or rating scales. The Nursing Child Assessment Feeding Scale (NCAFS) (Barnard, 1978a) examined interaction during feeding, including sensitivity to cues, response to distress and social-emotional and cognitive development, using a binary checklist (yes or no). The Nursing Child Assessment Teaching Scale (NCATS) (Barnard, 1978b) examined these areas when the parent was asked to teach the child. Hauser-Cram (1996) used the NCATS with mothers of toddlers who had developmental disabilities. She found that toddlers whose caregivers gave clear directions and both verbal and nonverbal support and praise while teaching tasks demonstrated more mastery motivation than toddlers whose caregivers did not show these behaviors.

The Parent-Caregiver Involvement Rating Scale (PCIS) (Farran, Kasari, Comfort, & Jay, 1986) examined not only the amount of interaction but also qualitative aspects of the interaction and the appropriateness of the parent/caregiver's behavior along 11 dimensions: physical involvement, verbal involvement, responsiveness of caregiver to child, play interaction, teaching behavior, control activities, directives and demands, relationship among activities, positive statements, negative statements, and goal setting. Professionals trained in the use of the instrument rated these behaviors. In one study, Blasco, Hrncir, and Blasco (1990) used the PCIS with 30 mothers of 18-month-old infants who were diagnosed with cerebral palsy. They found that the mothers scaffolded their children's play behavior by providing appropriate and nonintrusive cues.

In the past, parents (and particularly mothers) of infants and toddlers were consistently rated by researchers to be lacking in their interactions with their children. This research has been challenged by current work that focuses on qualitative aspects of parent-child interaction and evaluation of that interaction when parents/caregivers participate in the evaluation. (see Haas, Baird, McCormick, & Reilly, 1994).

Parent-child interactions may be difficult due to a variety of reasons, including a mismatch in temperaments or the lack of family resources and support. When families are not included as partners in the evaluation process, it is all too common for professionals to make judgments about them that may be inaccurate or misguided. The play-based assessment process allows both professionals and families to observe and evaluate parent-child interaction without the subjectivity of a rating scale or behavioral checklist.

ASSESSMENT WITH SPECIFIC POPULATIONS OF INFANTS AND TODDLERS

Preterm Infants

During the past two decades, medical technology has led to an increase in the number of infants surviving premature birth at earlier and earlier gestational ages. More than 50 percent of infants born prematurely are likely to be referred for early intervention services. For example, Collin et al. (1991) found that 40 to 64 percent of the infants born prematurely qualified for special education. In the past, assessment instruments provided no guidelines for assessing premature infants, because they were developed using a population of full-term infants. When preterm infants are developmentally compared using assessments normed on full-term populations, the results are biased.

Today, several standardized assessments include guidelines for correcting or adjusting age due to premature birth (Bayley II). However, the rationale for these guidelines has not been standardized across instruments. In addition, the length of time to continue age correction has not been clearly defined (Blasco, 1989). There are no state or federal guidelines indicating the best or most accurate procedure. These inconsistencies serve to frustrate families and practitioners as the struggle to provide appropriate services to this population of infants continues.

Allen and Alexander (1990) examined gross motor development in premature infants and believed that full age correction would lead to overdiagnosis of motor delays. Allen (1994) recommended adjusting for prematurity until at least two years of age. In a review of the literature, Blasco (1989) concluded that either full correction or no correction could lead to incorrect diagnosis. He recommended half-correction for the first 6 months of life. After 6 months, partial correction should be made for language skills and visual motor skills. For children with motor delays, full correction should be used after 6 months. However, correction was not necessary after 18–24 months (depending on the degree of prematurity).

Several researchers recommended reporting separate scores for motor development and cognitive/mental development. When these scores are combined into an overall score, motor problems would lower the result (Tvete, 1995). However, many standardized mental assessments for infants are heavily dependent on motor ability. For example, although the Bayley Scales offer a separate motor and mental form, motor skills are used to demonstrate most of the cognitive items on the mental form. Blasco (1989) found that upper dexterity was required to complete 45 percent of the items on the mental form. For infants older than 12 months, several items are scored according to the amount of time needed to complete the task, which would be affected by motor ability.

Infants and Toddlers with Visual Impairments

Infants use their vision to seek out their environment. The newborn's visual system involves the eye, optic nerve, optic radiation, and cerebral cortex. During the first year of life, the focusing power of the cornea and lens becomes very precise and the number of connections between the optic nerves and visual cortex increases significantly. Young children reach levels of 20/20 (adult level) between 3 and 5 years of age (Menacker & Batshaw, 1997).

Most newborns will close their eyes in response to a bright light and will fix their gaze on a person's face when held close to the adult. By two months of age, their ability to focus their attention on a person's face is well developed, and they will follow objects across a vertical and horizontal plane. Between three and six months, infants' unsteady eye movements become smooth.

Infants who have difficulty fixating on an object or who continue to have unsteady eye movements should be referred for further evaluation. In most states, a child must have a medically verified visual impairment that interferes with acquisition of knowledge or interaction with the environment to be eligible for services. A licensed teacher of the visually impaired usually conducts a functional assessment of visual abilities. Children who are legally blind (20/200 or less) will likely have some functional vision. For example, children with less than 20/400 vision may recognize hand movement and light projection (Hoon, 1996).

Infants who display behavioral or physical characteristics that may indicate a visual concern should also be referred for further evaluation. Although these characteristics may be unrelated to the visual impairment, they should serve as a red flag for the early interventionist. Consultation with a vision specialist would be appropriate for any of the following:

- Eyes are crossed or misaligned
- Encrusted lids, red and watery eyes
- Swollen or dropped eyelids
- Frequent styes
- Eyes that move independently of each other

The interventionist should refer the infant for vision evaluation if any of the following behaviors are observed:

- Shows sensitivity to light
- Squints at near and/or distant objects
- Blinks frequently when fixating on an object
- Turns or tilts the head
- Rubs the eyes excessively
- Is unable to locate and pick up small objects that have been dropped
- Stares at light for long periods

Adapted from a checklist used by Intermediate District 287, Minneapolis Public Schools

Infants and toddlers with visual impairments generally receive services from vision experts after initial diagnosis, typically during the first year of life.

Nearsightedness, or *myopia*, occurs when the refractive power of the cornea and lens is too strong, so the individual can see well "near" but has blurred distance vision. Farsightedness, or *hyperopia*, occurs when the refractive power is too weak and the image is focused behind the retina, so near vision is the problem and distance vision is good. *Astigmatism* is the irregularity in the shape of the cornea or lens and not all of the image is sharply focused on the retina (Nickel & Widerstrom, 1997). *Strabismus* is a result of an imbalance of the eye muscles causing one eye or both eyes to turn out. It is often a secondary diagnosis for children with disabilities (Menacker & Batshaw, 1997). *Esotropia* occurs when the eye turns in, and *exotropia* occurs when the eye turns out.

Retinopathy of prematurity (ROP) occurs when there is scarring and detachment of the retina. This condition was a result of too much oxygen being administered to premature newborns. Today, hospitals monitor the use of oxygen closely to avoid ROP (Nickel & Widerstrom, 1997). *Glaucoma* is typically the result of genetic disorder or congenital infection (Menacker & Batshaw, 1997). Fluid builds up in the eye and causes pressure on the retina and damage to the nerve fibers. *Cortical blindness* occurs when there is damage to the visual cortex. This type of blindness is associated with other primary diagnoses such as cerebral palsy (Nickel & Widerstrom, 1997).

Infants and toddlers with visual impairments may be delayed in other areas as well. However, interventions for infants and toddlers have demonstrated a positive impact on increasing developmental skills despite vision impairment.

In order to optimize learning, it is very important that a thorough assessment of visual ability is conducted when the team suspects a problem. Parents and professionals work collaboratively throughout the assessment process to ensure functional outcomes for the young child with visual impairments. Parents will need assistance in learning about the multiple types of evaluations and in interpreting results from ophthalmologists and optometrists (Chen, 1997).

Behavioral Assessment of Infants and Toddlers

Today, more and more children are being referred for services because of behavioral concerns. This trend is not limited to older children. The increase may reflect two societal changes:

1. A better understanding of and more sophisticated instruments to test for behavioral differences
2. An estimated 3.3 million children per year who are exposed to and witness to domestic violence, ranging from verbal abuse to physical assaults with guns (Jaffe, Wolfe, & Wilson, 1990)

Given the age of the child, it is often difficult to tell if the behavior is the sign of a problem or if it is merely a developmental stage. Evaluations for infants and toddlers should include ruling out physical health problems as the cause. As a rule of thumb, there is reason for concern if:

- After four months of age, the infant does not smile or show signs of pleasure when approached or cuddled
- The infant is inconsolable for long periods of time, but this is not related to colic or other physical distress

- After one year of age, the infant does not appear to differentiate between strange and familiar persons
- The infant or toddler has difficulty acquiring typical developmental milestones
- The toddler exhibits self-stimulation behaviors such as hand waving, rocking, or head banging
- The toddler appears sad and shows no appropriate signs of pleasure, fear, anger, or happiness
- The toddler frequently engages in inappropriate behaviors, including hitting or biting, and shows an inability to follow directions or participate in listening activities, even for a brief period (Minnesota Department of Human Services, 1995)

It is important to realize that all infants and toddlers may exhibit the above signs from time to time. It is the frequency and duration of such behavior should be monitored. Another consideration is the environments in which the child spends most of his time. If the child is the victim of or witness to violence or domestic abuse, he may show symptoms of posttraumatic stress syndrome (PTSD) (Scheeringa et al., cited in Gaensbauer, 1996).

For many of the children referred, the concern is that autism or persuasive developmental delay (PDD) may be present. Service providers use a combination of standardized assessments and clinical judgement that follow criteria guidelines outlined by the state in accordance with federal guidelines. In addition, the National Center for Clinical Infant Programs, Zero to Three, has developed a guide for identifying infants and young children who may be presenting mental health concerns (Diagnostic Classification of Mental Health and Developmental Disorders of Infancy and Early Childhood, 1994).

Although children with autism spectrum are often diagnosed by a medical team, following a complete medical and neurological exam, service providers may need to provide functional assessments that facilitate educational placement and individualized programs (Falco, Arick, & Hanzen, 1991). The Autism Screening Instrument for Educational Placement (Krug, Arick, & Almond, 1993) was developed to assist service providers in the identification of children with autism and to develop functional, appropriate learning opportunities. The tool consists of five separate standardized subtests: The Autism Behavior Checklist, The Sample of Vocal Behavior, Interaction Assessment, Educational Assessment, and Prognosis of Learning Rate. These subtests were developed for children between the ages of three months to 49 months (Krug, Arick, & Almond, 1993). The authors provide information on the standardization process for each subtest in the manual. The Child Behavior Checklist & Profile (Auchenbach, 1992) is a three-point rating scale that examines 99 behaviors that can be identified as problematic in two- to three-year-olds. Normed on a sample of 368 typically developing children, this checklist has been used both as a tool to help qualify a child for services and as part of the ongoing evaluation. As with any behavioral assessment, it is important to involve all members of the team, including mental health professionals who are trained to clinically recognize emotional disturbance, when using the checklist. In addition, a checklist adds one source of information, and information gathered from a variety of sources should supplement the findings obtained from any one instrument (Wittmer, Doll, & Strain, 1996). Finally, many behavioral checklists were developed and standardized on children from white, middle-class backgrounds. Some of the items are not appropriate in terms of cultural differences or diversity (e.g., sexual orientation).

Children Exposed to Violence

Infants and young children with disabilities are often the target of physical violence (Zirpoli, 1997). They may also be in homes where poverty and crime impair the abilities of their caregivers. Infants and toddlers who are exposed to or experience personal violence may experience long-term psychological distress (Zeanah & Scheeringa, 1996). Service providers of young children are increasingly baffled by the number of children who are being removed from one child care center to another and referred for special education services due to their aggression or out-of-control behavior as toddlers. One service provider claimed she had a child who was moved from three child care centers in six months because the staff couldn't handle her.

Recent awareness of the influence of domestic violence on young children has led to a new approach to evaluation and subsequent treatment of aggressive, disruptive behavior in infants and toddlers. According to Zeanah and Scheeringa (1996), it is important to assess the antecedent events (both in a child care setting and at home) that preceded the aggressive behavior. For children who have a history of chronic domestic violence, the diagnosis of posttraumatic stress disorder (PTSD) should be considered. Although it takes a qualified team member to make this diagnosis, all members of the team can help in identifying this disorder by the observation and recording of consistent behavioral concerns.

Young children who are affected by traumatic stress disorder may show a numbing of responsiveness. They may lose recently acquired skills, especially in areas such as expressive language and toileting. Children may also show signs of avoidance of adults who remind them of an abuser. They may exhibit increased irritability and temper tantrums that were not observed prior to the experience. Since many children at this age exhibit temper tantrums now and then, it is important that service providers not make assumptions based solely on their observations. Many families experience temporary difficulties, and young children may show signs of distress at such times. Service providers can offer support and assistance to families. Sometimes just listening and acknowledging the difficulties of family life in our society may serve the purpose. However, if there are persistent, ongoing family issues that are unresolved, and if the child exhibits persistently difficult behavior or seems chronically depressed, a complete evaluation of the child and the family situation by qualified professionals should be pursued.

According to Zeanah (1994), the following issues should be addressed in the evaluation of young children who have experienced traumatic events:

1. Ensure that the child is currently living in a safe and stable environment. If the child is not removed from the traumatic situation, intervention and treatment will be more difficult.
2. Consider the developmental skills of the child prior to and after the traumatic event. Knowledge of the child's previous developmental level will help the team understand her perceptions of the event.
3. Review the quality of the pretrauma caregiving environment and the impact of the event on the environment.
4. Examine the nature of the event. Was it acute or chronic in terms of ongoing events? For example, if a caregiver is the victim of ongoing domestic abuse, the situation would be considered chronic.
5. Find out the child's proximity to the event, particularly if a caregiver was involved. An example is a child's presence during a police raid for illicit drugs.
6. Construct a picture of the child's symptoms that appeared after the event.
7. Utilize the strengths and protective factors, especially in terms of relationships, that may help a child deal with a traumatic experience. For example, a grandmother may provide nurturing support.

It is also important to explore how the caregiver responds to violent events (Lewis, 1996). He may think the child is too young to remember what happened. According to Osofsky, Wewers, Hann, and Fick (cited in Lewis, 1996), another concern is the level of intensity of the violence experienced by the child. The child could be either a victim (e.g., sexually abused) or a witness to a violent scene (e.g., gunfire and a corpse in the street).

Finally, a multisystems approach is critical in working with children exposed to violence (Groves, 1996). Because crisis intervention is often necessary, police, the courts, the local crisis nursery, and temporary foster placement may be involved to handle the immediate needs of the situation. Service providers may find themselves working with a whole new team in trying to continue to provide support and services.

SUMMARY

This chapter addressed issues of the screening and assessment of infants and toddlers and their families. Service providers are required by law to document the assessment of children referred for services. The federal government, under the reauthorization of IDEA, enacted Part C legislation, which included a general definition for eligibility of infants and toddlers. Part C regulations also require the evaluation and assessment of the child, along with documentation of family resources, priorities, and concerns, in developing the individualized family service plan.

Child-find is a state-regulated system of locating children who are eligible for or may be eligible for early intervention services (McLean, 1996). Many local early intervention services have a central telephone number that accepts referrals and assigns a service provider to do the initial screening, which is a brief and inexpensive method of identifying children who may need further and more extensive evaluation.

The development of tests for young children is guided by three overlapping theoretical approaches to assessment. The first is the developmental milestones approach, generally followed by standardized tests, which include specific guidelines for administration, scoring, and interpretation of the results. Another approach is the behavioral approach, which assesses the behavioral responses of the child in relation to the environment. The third type of approach to assessment is the ecological approach, which examines the child's abilities and needs in terms of the multiple environments in which the child interacts on a daily basis.

Acknowledging the limitations of using standardized assessment instruments with infants and toddlers has led to the development of alternative means of identifying levels of functioning in this population. In play-based assessment, a single individual interacts with the infant or toddler, while professionals and family members observe the child's performance of skills (Linder, 1993). Such an approach is less intrusive to the child and provides an interactive and engaging format that capitalizes on an infant's or toddler's natural curiosity, exploration, and interests. Play-based assessment also has an inherent flexibility and responsiveness that match the child's activity level, temperament, and states of arousal. The degree to which individual team members perceive this approach as a valid and reliable method for assessing this population, and their commitment to the process, have a direct impact on the success of the play-based assessment team.

Another assessment process that is used with the birth-to-three population in particular is parent-child interaction. In the past, parents (and particularly mothers) of infants and toddlers were consistently rated by researchers to be lacking in their interactions with their children. This research has been challenged by current work that focuses on qualitative aspects of parent-child interaction and parent evaluation of these interactions.

For some, parent-child interactions may be difficult due to a variety of reasons, including a mismatch between their temperaments and lack of family resources and support. When families are not included as partners in the evaluation process, it is all too common for professionals to make judgments about families that may be inaccurate or misguided.

Other assessment procedures relate to special populations of children. Infants who are born preterm may have both medical and later developmental complications that should be addressed through early intervention. Similarly, children with challenging behavior and those children exposed to violence are presenting one of the growing categories of children at risk. Strategies for both prevention and intervention should be addressed from a mental health framework, as outlined in this chapter.

Assessment in early intervention is used for the purposes of eligibility, ongoing evaluation, and annual evaluation. As stated by Bagnato et al., 1997, "most conventional, norm-referenced, standardized materials developed through psychometric procedures do not meet standards for acceptable assessment in early intervention" (p. 3). Many service providers and families rely on curriculum-based and other informal means (e.g., play, parent report) as ways to assess young children. The use of curriculum-based assessments is important for establishing a link between the assessment and intervention. Bagnato and his colleagues provide an excellent guide to identification of assessments that provide this link for children birth to three (see Bagnato et al., 1997).

REFERENCES

Allen, M. C. (1994). Neurodevelopmental follow-up of the preterm infant. *Pediatric Rounds, 3,* 1–4.

Allen, M. C., & Alexander, G. R. (1990). Gross motor milestones in preterm infants: Correction for degree of prematurity. *Journal of Pediatrics, 116,* 955–999.

Auchenbach, T. M. (1992). *Manual for the Child Behavior Checklist/2–3 age and 1992 profile.* Burlington: University of Vermont.

Bagnato, S. J., & Neisworth, J. T. (1991). *Assessment for early intervention: Best practices for professionals.* New York: Guilford Press.

Bagnato, S. J., Neisworth, J. T., & Munson, S. M. (1993). Sensible strategies for assessment in early intervention. In D. M. Bryant & M. A. Graham (Eds.), *Implementing early intervention: From research to effective practice.* New York: Guilford Press.

Bagnato, S. J., Neisworth, J. T, & Munson, S. M. (1997). *LINKing assessment and early intervention: An authentic curriculum-based approach.* Baltimore: Paul H. Brookes.

Bailey, D. B. (1996). Assessing family resources, priorities, and concerns. In M. McLean, D. B. Bailey, & M. Wolery (Eds.), *Assessing infants and toddlers with special needs* (2nd ed., pp. 203–233). Englewood Cliffs, N.J.: Merrill/Prentice Hall.

Bailey, D. B., & Blasco, P. M. (1990). Parents' perspectives on a written survey of family needs. *Journal of Early Intervention, 14,* 196–203.

Bailey, D. B., & Nabors, L. A. (1996). Tests and development. In M. McLean, D. B. Bailey, & M. Wolery (Eds.), *Assessing infants and preschoolers with special needs* (2nd ed., pp. 23–45). Englewood Cliffs, N.J.: Merrill/Prentice Hall.

Bailey, D. B., Vandiviere, P., Delinger, J., & Munn, D. (1987). The Battelle Developmental Inventory: Teacher perceptions and implementation data. *Journal of Psychoeducational Assessment, 3,* 217–226.

Baird, S. M., Peterson, J., & Reilly, A. (1995). Patterns of specific infant behavior interpretation. *Infant-Toddler Intervention: The Transdisciplinary Journal, 5*(3), pp. 255–276.

Barnard, K. E. (1978a). *Nursing child assessment feeding scale.* Seattle: University of Washington.

Barnard, K. E. (1978b). *Nursing child assessment teaching scale.* Seattle: University of Washington.

Barrera, M. E., Rosenbaum, P. L., & Cunningham, C. E. (1987). Corrected and uncorrected Bayley scores: Longitudinal developmental patterns in low and high birth weight infants. *Infant and Behavior Development, 10,* 337–346.

Bayley, N. (1933). *The California first-year mental scale.* Berkeley: University of California Press.

Bayley, N. (1969). *Bayley Scales of Infant Development.* New York: Psychological Corporation.

Bayley, N. (1993). *Bayley Scales of Infant Development—II.* San Antonio, TX: Psychological Corporation.

Belsky, J., & Most, R. K. (1981). From exploration to play: A cross-sectional study of infant free-play behavior. *Developmental Psychology, 17,* 630–639.

Benner, S. M. (1992). *Assessing children with special needs: An ecological perspective.* New York: Longman.

Bernbaum, J. C., & Hoffman-Williamson, M. (1991). *Primary care of the preterm infant.* St. Louis: Mosby.

Blackman, J. A. (1986). *Warning signals: Basic criteria for tracking at-risk infants and young children.* Washington, D.C.: Zero to Three: National Center for Clinical Infant Programs.

Blasco, P. A. (1989). Preterm birth: To correct or not to correct. *Development Medicine and Child Neurology, 21,* 174–177.

Blasco, P. A., Kohen, H., & Shapland, C. (1999). Parents as teachers: Design and establishment of a training programme for paediatric residents. *Medical Education, 33,* 695–701.

Blasco, P. M. (1989). *Comparison of the Bayley Scales and a measure of mastery in infants with cerebral palsy.* Poster presented at the conference of the American Academy for Cerebral Palsy and Developmental Medicine, San Francisco.

Blasco, P. M., Hrncir, E. J., & Blasco, P. A. (1990). The contribution of maternal involvement to mastery motivation performance in infants with cerebral palsy. *Journal of Early Intervention, 14,* 161–174.

Blasco, P. M., & LaMontagne, M. J. (1996, September). *Play-based assessment.* Paper presented at the conference of the American Academy for Cerebral Palsy and Developmental Medicine, Minneapolis.

Blasco, P. M., O'Leary, J., Engstrom, B., Calvin, S., & Ferski, G. (1996, December). *Postconference workshop on prenatal diagnosis.* Presented at the Conference of the International Division for Early Childhood, Phoenix.

Brazelton, T. B., & Nugent, J. K. (1995). *Neonatal behavioral assessment scale* (3rd. ed.). London: MacKeith Press.

Bredekamp, S., & Rosegrant, T. (Eds.). (1995). *Reaching potentials: Transforming early childhood curriculum and assessment.* Washington, D.C.: National Association for the Education of Young Children.

Bricker, D. (1993). *AEPS: Measurement for birth to three years.* Baltimore: Paul H. Brookes.

Campbell, P. H. (1991). Evaluation and assessment in early intervention for infants and toddlers. *Journal of Early Intervention, 15*(1), 36–45.

Chen, D. (1997). What can baby see? Vision tests and interventions for infants with multiple disabilities [videotape and viewers' guide]. New York: AFB Press.

Collin, M. F., Halsey, C. L., & Anderson, C. L. (1991). Emerging developmental sequelae in the "normal" extremely low birth weight infant. *Pediatrics, 88,* 115–119.

Cripes, J., & Bricker, D. (1992). *AEPS: Curriculum for birth to three years.* Baltimore: Paul H. Brookes.

Diagnostic Classification of Mental Health and Developmental Disorders of Infancy and Early Childhood. (1999). Arlington, Va.: Zero to Three/National Center for Clinical Infant Programs.

Diamond, K. E., & Squires, J. (1993). The role of parental report in the screening and assessment of young children. *Journal of Early Intervention, 17,* 107–115.

Early Intervention Program for Infants and Toddlers with Disabilities, 34 C.F.R. 303 (1999, July 1).

Falco, R., Arick, J., & Hanzen, J. (1991). *Quality education services training: Project QUEST.* Portland, Ore.: Portland State University.

Farran, D., Kasari, C., Comfort, M., & Jay, S. (1986). *Parent/Caregiver Involvement Scale.* Nashville, Tenn.: Vanderbilt University.

Fewell, R. (1983). Assessing handicapped infants. In S. Garwood & R. Fewell (Eds.), *Educating handicapped infants.* Rockville, Md.: Aspen.

Frankenburg, W. K., Dodds, J., Archer, P., Bresnick, B., Marshka, P., Edelman, N., & Shapiro, H. (1990). *Denver II.* Denver: Denver Developmental Materials.

Furuno, S., O'Reilly, K., Hosaka, C. M., Inatsuka, T. T., Zeisloft-Falbey, B., & Allman, T. (1994). *Revised HELP checklist: Birth to three years.* Palo Alto, Calif.: Vort.

Gaensbauer, T. (1996). Developmental and therapeutic aspects of treating infants and toddlers who have witnessed violence. *Zero to Three, 16,* 15–20.

Gesell, A. (1925). *The mental growth of the preschool child: A psychological outline of normal development from birth to the sixth year, including a system of developmental diagnosis.* New York: MacMillan.

Groves, B. M. (1996). Children without refuge: Young witnesses to domestic violence. *Zero to Three, 16*, 29–34.

Haas, L., Baird, S. M., McCormick, K., & Reilly, A. (1994). Infant behaviors interpreted by their mothers. *Infant-Toddler Intervention: The Transdisciplinary Journal*, 203–220.

Hauser-Cram, P. (1996). Mastery motivation in toddlers with developmental disabilities. *Child Development, 67*, 236–248.

Hoon, A. H. (1996). Visual impairments in children. In A. J. Capute & P. J. Accardo (Eds.), *Developmental disabilities in infancy and childhood* (2nd ed., pp. 461–478). Baltimore: Paul H. Brookes.

Hrncir, E. J., Speller, G. M, & West, M. (1985). What are we testing? *Developmental Psychology, 21*, 226–232.

Jaffe, P. G., Wolfe, D. A., & Wilson, S. K. (1990). *Children of battered women*. Newbury Park, Calif.: Sage.

Johnson-Martin, N., Jens, K., Attermeier, S., & Hacker, B. (1991). *The Carolina curriculum for infants and toddlers with special needs* (2nd ed.). Baltimore: Paul H. Brookes.

Kjerland, L., & Kovach, J. (1990). Family-staff collaboration for tailored infant assessment. In E. Gibbs & D. Teti (Eds.), *Interdisciplinary assessment of infants: A guide for early intervention professionals* (pp. 287–298). Baltimore: Paul H. Brookes.

Kroth, R. L., Olson, J., & Kroth, J. (1986). Delivering sensitive information, or please don't kill the messenger. *Counseling and Human Development, 18*, 1–11.

Krug, D. A., Arick, J. R., Almond, P. J. (1993). *ASIEP—2: Autism screening instrument for educational planning* (2nd ed.). Austin, Tex.: Pro-ed.

Lewis, M. L. (1996). Trauma reverberates: Psychosocial evaluation of the caregiving environment of young children exposed to violence and traumatic loss. *Zero to Three, 16*, 21–28.

Lifter, K. (1996). Assessing play skills. In M. McLean, D. B. Bailey, & M. Wolery (Eds.), *Assessing infants and preschoolers with special needs* (2nd ed., pp. 435–461). Englewood Cliffs, N.J.: Merrill.

Linder, T. (1993). *Transdisciplinary play-based assessment: A functional approach to working with young children* (2nd ed.). Baltimore: Paul H. Brookes.

McGonigel, M. J., Kaufmann, R., & Johnson, B. (1991). *Guidelines and recommended practices for the individualized family service plan* (2nd ed.). Bethesda: Association for the Care of Children's Health.

McLean, M. (1996). Assessment and its importance in early intervention/early childhood special education. In M. McLean, D. B. Bailey, & M. Wolery (Eds), *Assessing infants and preschoolers with special needs* (2nd ed., pp. 1–22). Englewood Cliffs, N. J.: Merrill.

McLean, M., & Crais, E. R. (1996). Procedural considerations in assessing infants and preschoolers with disabilities. In M. McLean, D. B. Bailey, & M. Wolery (Eds.), *Assessing infants and preschoolers with special needs* (pp. 46–68). Englewood Cliffs, N.J.: Prentice-Hall.

Meisels, S. J., & Fenichel, E. (Eds.) (1996). *New visions for the developmental assessment of infants and young children*. Arlington, Va.: Zero to Three/National Center for Clinical Infant Programs.

Meisels, S. J., & Provence, S. (Eds.). (1996). Screening and assessment: Guidelines for identifying young disabled and developmentally vulnerable children and their families [Special issue]. *Zero to Three*.

Menacker, S. J., & Batshaw, M. L. (1997). Vision: Our window to the world. In M. L. Batshaw (Ed.), *Children with disabilities* (4th ed., pp. 211–239). Baltimore: Paul H. Brookes.

Minnesota Department of Human Services. *Children and youth at risk of emotional disturbance* (1995). St. Paul, Minn.: Mental Health Division.

Newborg, J., Stock, J. R., Wnek, L., Guidubaldi, J., & Svinicki, J. (1988). *The Battelle Developmental Inventory (BDI)*. Dallas, Tex.: DLM Teaching Resources.

Nickel, R. E., & Widerstrom, A. H. (1997). Developmental disorders in infancy. In A. H. Widerstrom, B. A. Mowder, & S. R. Sandall (Eds.), *Infant development and risk* (2nd ed.). Baltimore: Paul H. Brookes.

Parks, S., et al. (1992). *Help at home: Activity sheets for parents*. Palo Alto, Calif.: Vort.

Parten, M. (1932). Social participation among preschool children. *Journal of Abnormal and Social Psychology, 27,* 243–269.

Peterson, N. (1988). *Early intervention for handicapped and at-risk children.* Denver: Love.

Reynell, J. (1985). Reynell Developmental Language Scales. Los Angeles, Calif.: Webster Psychological Services.

Scheeringa, M., Zeanah, C. H., Drell, M., & Larrieu, J. (1995). Two approaches to the diagnosis of post-traumatic stress disorder in infancy and early childhood. *Journal of the American Academy of Child and Adolescent Psychiatry, 34,* 191–200.

Sell, E. J., Figueredo, A. J., & Wilcox, T. G. (1995). Assessment of preterm infants' behavior (APIB): Confirmatory factor analysis of behavioral constructs. *Infant Behavior and Development, 18,* 447–457.

Sharp, M. C., & Lohr, J. A. (1994). The nature of teaching hospitals. In S. L. Hostler (Ed.), *Family-centered care: An approach to implementation* (pp. 72–88). Charlottesville: Children Rehabilitation Center, University of Virginia.

Siegel, D. J. (1999). *The developing mind: Toward a Neurobiology of interpersonal experience.* New York: Guilford Press.

Siegel, L. S., Cooper, D.C., Fitzhardinger, P. M., Ash, A. J. (1995). The use of the mental developmental index of the Bayley Scale to diagnose language delay in 2-year-old high-risk infants. *Infant Behavior and Development, 18,* 483–486.

Teti, D. M., & Gibbs, E. D. (1990). Infant assessment: Historical antecedents and contemporary issues. In E. D. Gibbs & D. M. Teti (Eds.), *Interdisciplinary assessment of infants: A guide for early intervention professionals* (pp. 3–13). Baltimore: Paul H. Brookes.

Tuckman, B. W., & Jensen, M. A. C. (1977). Stages of small group development revisited. *Group and Organization Studies, 2,* 419–427.

Tvete, J. M. (1995). *When and how long to adjust for prematurity? Assessment of premature infants for early childhood special education.* Unpublished manuscript. St. Paul, Minn.: University of St. Thomas.

United Cerebral Palsy Association. (1976). *Staff development handbook: A resource for the transdisciplinary process.* New York: Author.

Winton, P. J. (1988). The family-focused interview. A mechanism for collaborative goal-setting with families. *Journal of the Division for Early Childhood, 12,* 195–207.

Winton, P. J., & Bailey, D. B. (1993). Communicating with families: Examining practices and facilitating change. In J. Paul & R. J. Simeonsson (Eds.), *Children with special needs: Family, culture, and society* (pp. 210–230). Baltimore: Paul H. Brooks.

Winton, P. J., & Bailey, D. B. (1997, February). Family-centered care: The revolution continues. *Exceptional Parent,* 16–20.

Wittmer, D., Doll, B., & Strain, P. (1996). Social and emotional development in early childhood: The identification of competence and disabilities. *Journal of Early Intervention, 20,* 299–318.

Woodruff, G. (1980, June). Transdisciplinary approach for preschool children and parents. *Exceptional Parent,* 13–16.

Wright, A., & Ireton, H. (1995). Child development days: A new approach to screening for early intervention. *Journal of Early Intervention, 19,* 253–263.

Zeanah, C. H. (1994). The assessment and treatment of infants and toddlers exposed to violence. In J. D. Osofsky & E. Fenichel, (Eds.). *Caring for infants and toddlers in violent environments: Hurt, healing, and hope.* Arlington, Va.: Zero to Three: National Center for Clinical Infant Programs.

Zeanah, C. H., & Scheeringa, M. (1996). Evaluation of posttraumatic symptomatology in infants and young children exposed to violence. *Zero to Three, 16,* 9–14.

Zirpoli, S. (1997). Issues in early childhood behavior. In T. J. Zirpoli & K. J. Melloy (Eds.), *Behavior management: Applications for teachers and parents* (2nd ed., pp. 383–417). Upper Saddle River, N.J.: Merrill.

CHAPTER SIX

NATURAL ENVIRONMENTS FOR INFANTS AND TODDLERS AND PREPARING FOR TRANSITIONS

- To understand the importance of service provision in a variety of natural environments for infants and toddlers

- To present a framework for a family-centered approach within these environments (e.g., home, center-based, community-based)

- To consider the interventionist's role in home visiting, especially with regard to ethical and cultural issues in working with families

- To apply knowledge of the use of outdoor space for all children to promote growth and learning

- To apply knowledge of the transition process from early intervention services to school-aged services, and to understand its effect on the child, family, and service providers

This chapter was written, in tandem with a graduate seminar, with Betsy May, Dolly Lastine, Debra Bomberg, Katherine Eldevik, and Stacy Rovick. The chapter contains more vignettes than the other chapters do, and these vignettes reflect the experiences of these service providers as they worked in early intervention.

Today, more than ever, service providers are working with infants, toddlers, and their families in many different environments. Historically, services for infants and toddlers were primarily provided in the family's home. Most often service providers worked with the mother or father (or both parents) and child for a set period of time every week. This model of service provision falls short in our present society, where 60 percent of all women with children under the age of six are in the workforce (Children's Defense Fund, 1999).

Given the increase in the number of households with both parents working, early intervention services are often provided outside the home in center-based programs such as child care or family home care settings. In addition, the increase of children identified as "at risk" (National Center on Child Abuse and Neglect, 1988) may require visits in other settings, including foster homes and shelters. One service provider reported that a family came to her office because they were living in their car. The purpose of this chapter is to discuss the many environments currently utilized by service providers in the field of early intervention. *Parent* will be used to refer to the primary caregiver, who may or may not be a biological parent. In addition, the impact of transition from early intervention services to school-aged services will be discussed.

In Chapter 1, we looked at the addition of the "natural environments" clause in Part C of the Individual with Disabilities Education Act (IDEA). That is, to the maximum extent appropriate, early intervention services must be provided in natural environments, including the home and community settings in which children without disabilities participate. This law expands systems of support for infants and toddlers and their families in natural environments. Research studies suggest that toddlers with disabilities who are served in inclusive settings do as well as those who are served in segregated settings (Bruder, 1998). Challenges in meeting the requirement of the law include finding quality child care settings and designing a statewide system of training for child care staff. Bruder (1998) also pointed out that time constraints, staff turnover, children with diverse needs, and a lack of fiscal resources in some states may affect the transition from segregated settings to inclusive settings. Chapter 9 discusses the importance of training service providers in collaboration skills as states move toward the use of natural environments.

SERVICES PROVIDED IN THE HOME SETTING

> *Home visiting programs function within a context shaped*
> *by both their underlying theory and their organization.*
> —Powell, 1993, p. 24

McWilliam and Bailey (1993) defined three philosophical tenets that are characteristic of home-based family-centered services: (1) recognizing differences among families; (2) using a family systems approach; and (3) respecting the family's priorities. Today, the very definition of the word *family* implies diversity. A family can range from a single parent and a child to extended multigenerational caregivers who are raising a child. Recognizing the diversity of family units is necessary for professionals working in the home environment (Lynch & Hanson, 1998). As discussed in Chapter 1, just as family function is related to individual uniqueness, there is no single way to raise a child. Values, roles, and priorities differ in each family. Strategies for service provision should meet the family's particular styles of functioning within the child's natural environments.

From a family systems approach, the interventionist must believe that every family has strengths. These strengths may not be easy to recognize from one's own perspective. The family's values may differ radically from the mainstream concepts of a strong family unit, and it may be easier to focus only on the family's needs and deficits. Their strengths may also be overshadowed by unemployment, lack of resources, lack of educational opportunities, or other societal factors. In a world of increasing cultural diversity, service providers should examine their own beliefs and values and how they might be inadvertently projecting them onto families.

When visiting in the home, autonomy of the family should also be respected. According to federal law, families have the right to determine their priorities and needs to the extent that they are willing and able. It is up to the service provider to help the family explore options, to advocate for the family, to mediate, and to consult with other professionals. The family should be able to decide what is important not only for their child but also for the whole family system. Some families may be ready and eager to accept services and make changes, while others may need more time to ponder options. Still others may not want services at all or may discontinue services for a variety of reasons. The service provider, therefore, must tailor the services to meet the family's concerns and resources (Kjerland & Corrigan Eide, 1990). Vignette 6.1 demonstrates a situation that requires flexibility on the part of the service provider.

VIGNETTE 6.1   IS ANYBODY HOME?

In my first home visit with an isolated rural family, I had been told that this family rarely left the home. They had four preschoolers whom a doctor had thought were nonverbal. So, although I had spoken with the mother very briefly on the phone to set up the visit, I was still surprised when she just opened the door a crack and didn't make eye contact with me as we spoke. I saw three little faces peering at me through an upstairs screen as I approached the house. There was complete silence as I stood vainly attempting to establish some kind of rapport with the mother. She didn't invite me in and when I asked if I could meet the children, she hesitated and said, "They're kind of shy. We've only had their grandparents come to our house before; Virgil [the father] goes to the store when we need something." I arranged to come back the next week and said I hoped I could meet the children. I left a list of a few activities for her do with the children as well as some toys that they could borrow until the next visit.

Although those first visits were extremely short, they were very intense for both the mother and myself because of the family's extreme social isolation. Over the course of the next several months, I was able to get the children to come into the same room with me and to very tentatively explore the toys. By the year's end, I had built a trusting relationship with the family. The two eldest preschoolers were happily enrolled in a preschool and their mother had started volunteering in their classroom.

In Vignette 6.1, the service provider was able to make a breakthrough with the family over an extended period of time. This type of experience may not be valued by an administrator who wants the child assessed and then enrolled in a center-based program for a variety of reasons. Service providers are often left to use their own initiative in handling a difficult situation. It is a good idea to get feedback from team members and to know the policies of the agency in which you are employed before making a decision.

Goals of Family-Centered, Home-Based Programs

In recent years the frequency of the question "Who is the client?" has reflected the shift from a child focus to a family focus and from an individual focus to a family systems focus (Wasik, Bryant, & Lyons, 1990; Roberts, Akers, & Behl, 1996; Roberts, Behl, Akers, & 1996). The purpose of family support is to enhance the ability of families to work toward their own goals and deal effectively with their own concerns. Advocates of self-determination believe that persons with disabilities and their family members should strive to attain the goals of independence and self-efficacy despite societal setbacks (Mike Ward, personal communication, October 2, 1999).

Because complex interactions exist among members of a family, a change in any family member will affect other relationships within the family (Blasco, 1995).

A family-centered focus means that the client may change as different needs emerge among family members. Programs centered on the broader base of parent, family, and environmental factors that directly or indirectly influence outcomes for the child are more likely to experience success. In Table 6.1, home visiting from a family's point of view was captured by staff at Project Dakota.

In a comprehensive review of the experimental literature on the effectiveness of various types of home visiting programs, Olds and Kitzman (1993) concluded that clarifying the purpose and goals of a particular program was an important requisite for successful outcomes. This sense of mission is exemplified by the broadening focus of existing programs.

Likewise, as Bronfenbrenner (1979) indicated, a shift toward looking at the family in the context of the larger web of extended family, neighborhood, and community is necessary. Because changes in the larger system may also affect the family, awareness of the full extent of the family's involvement and dependence upon the larger community is crucial. An effective program will enable families to recognize their strengths, to make decisions that benefit their family unit, and to provide an optimal environment for their children. Many interventionists find themselves wearing more than one hat, including that of the advocate who helps the family deal with the day-to-day stress received from a variety of sources.

Role of the Interventionist in the Home Environment

When PL 99-457 was passed in 1986, it held strong implications for interventionists already serving families in their homes. Service providers reexamined their

TABLE 6.1   A Family's View of a Good Home Visit

- Be clear about agenda and roles.
- Give choices in scheduling that are convenient and flexible.
- Provide a record of the visit using writing, pictures, or toys.
- Give ideas for activities, then help parents brainstorm.
- Be flexible with the family's daily schedule: pitch in, change agenda, and reschedule.
- Don't use jargon, and let the family know it's okay to ask questions.
- Use modeling and reminding; don't overload with information.
- Explain what you are doing and why.
- Include others, e.g., siblings, grandparents, etc., in activities and conversations.
- Explain paperwork and point out progress/changes that are made.
- Be sensitive to the family's need for someone to take over.
- Be courteous; call if you are going to be late, absent, etc.
- Respect the family's values; don't judge.
- Be prepared; don't waste the family's time and energy.
- Be honest with the family.

Adapted by permission from Project Dakota Outreach, Training and Consultation Services, Eagan, Minn.

traditional roles and the way in which they implemented services to promote mutual respect and a partnership with families. Dunst, Trivette, and Deal (1988) were clearly ahead of their time when they defined the multiple roles of service providers described in Table 6.2.

Establishing Rapport with Families.   Opening lines of communication with parents and families is a necessary first step toward fulfillment of these roles. Building a trusting relationship with a family means showing mutual respect and a willingness to share ideas, feelings, and information. A way to begin this process is to drop one's preconceived ideas about the family and to begin with an optimistic focus. As Turnbull and Turnbull (1988) noted, "being open to new views allows one to expand their repertoire of skills and creativity." (p. 4)

Well-meaning colleagues may wish to advise us on what to expect from a family, but such comments only serve to ignite negative feelings. Instead, emphasizing the family's strengths rather than weaknesses can focus attention where it can best benefit both the family and the interventionist.

> **VIGNETTE 6.2   JOHN**
>
> John was a three-year-old boy in my early childhood special needs classroom who had physical and visual impairments. As I read his school records, I discovered that John had been a normally developing, healthy child until his young mother with limited resources had attempted to smother him. I felt enormous revulsion at this act. I knew that I was obligated to make home visits, but it was very difficult for me. I had to leave my own values on the doorstep and try to see John's mother as a person who desperately needed support.

TABLE 6.2   Primary Helping Roles

ROLE	CHARACTERISTICS
Empathetic listener	Listens active and reflectively
Teacher/therapist	Instructs and intervenes
Consultant	Offers information and opinions in response to family requests
Resource person	Provides information about support resources and services
Enabler	Helps family acquire competencies they need to mobilize resources to meet their needs
Mobilizer	Mobilizes resources and support services
Mediator	Acts as an intermediary between family and others
Advocate	Provides knowledge and skills for proactive advocacy

Adapted from *Enabling and Empowering Families: Principles and Guidelines for Practice* by C. J. Dunst, C. Trivette, & A. Deal, 1988, Cambridge, Mass.: Brookline Books, pp. 91–94.

A person who is hurting, either physically or emotionally, needs care and support. When working with families, it may be very obvious that the parent is the one most acutely in need of care, as Vignette 6.2 demonstrates. Relying on other team members and/or other agencies in the mental health field is important for home visitors. An interventionist must be responsive to the immediate needs of a family member. At the same time, it is important to provide an appropriate learning opportunity for the child. As Ramey and Ramey (1993) stated, "limiting the focus in home visiting programs to supporting the family first, without special efforts to target the child's early development as well, may be self defeating." (p. 133)

Gathering Information.   Because the interventionist's role is dependent upon the input of the families, establishing expectations early in the relationship is paramount. This can be accomplished by an informal, preliminary discussion or through a formal checklist or assessment (Winton, 1988). Whatever method is used, the crucial ingredient is that the expectations should be two-way: what the interventionist can expect of the family and what the family can expect of the interventionist. Families should have an opportunity to select the method of sharing information (Bailey & Blasco, 1990). Some families prefer written surveys, whereas others prefer informal interviews.

Some interventionists like to use an open-ended questionnaire that can be filled in as each item is discussed and that includes very general categories. A benefit of this approach is that it not only serves as a vehicle for opening communication with the family, but it also will be a written communication that the parent can discuss with family members who may not be present for the home visit. For those families who have never had a service provider work in their home, the use of an open-ended interview can help to establish trust and ease the uncertainty about having an unfamiliar person visit. In Vignette 6.3, one parent recollects the first home visit she received.

VIGNETTE 6.3   COMPANY COMING

I spent hours cleaning my house before the home teacher came. I didn't know if she'd stay in the living room or want to see Nathan's room. I made coffee and cookies, but she said she'd just eaten. She said she'd come for an hour, but by the time she finished with all the paperwork it was closer to two hours, and I'd forgotten half of what she said. Nathan was fussy and ready for his nap, and my three-year-old had just interrupted us for the umpteenth time. I wasn't sure that home visits were going to be such a good idea.

For this mother, it was obvious that the interventionist had her own agenda and was not sensitive to the family's priorities. Winton (1988) suggested that service providers can reduce parental anxiety by reconfirming the allotted time for the visit before arriving. This interventionist could have asked the mother if she should continue or if she should reschedule the visit for another time.

Practical Aspects and Scheduling

Flexibility is a key factor in providing services to families on a least intrusive schedule for visits (Wasik, Bryant, & Lyons, 1990). The timing of the interventionist's visit needs to reflect the child's own schedule as well as the schedule of the family. If the child has a difficult time with feeding, the most efficient time for a visit would be during the child's naturally occurring feeding schedule. Modeling the activity for the parent and responding with feedback are more beneficial when the child is actually hungry. However, a home visit may hinder communication and optimal collaboration with the parent if, for example, it's scheduled during the parent's scheduled recreation activity, or when the parent is preparing dinner in the late afternoon. Finding the best time is not always easy and may necessitate compromise on the part of the service provider and the family. Service providers should yield to family preference when possible. Many early intervention programs allow for flexible working hours so that service providers can meet family timelines.

Another aspect to consider is the family's working schedule during the day. Families that work may prefer evening visits or, conversely, may be too exhausted for an interventionist to come to their home after they have been working all day. Creative scheduling may include a home visit in the morning, before the parent goes to work, or a visit in the child's child care setting with the parent present during his or her lunch hour or in the evening. Vignette 6.4 describes an evening visit to one family's home.

> **VIGNETTE 6.4   NIGHT VISITS**
> Jean was a single mother of four children ages two to seven. She was planning to return to work and was worried about having to forgo home visits for her two-year-old son, Ronald, who had developmental delays and nonorganic failure to thrive diagnosed at 15 months. Jean, a recovered addict who had been separated from her children for extended periods of time, found the visits not only beneficial for her son but organizing for herself as well. We discussed how visits may be hard after a long day for the children and herself. We chose shorter visits every other week with a phone call in between to discuss Ronald's child care and developmental concerns.

The frequency and length of home visits must reflect the needs of the child and family. It may be necessary to come once a week or bimonthly to exchange ideas and find out what is working with the child. In planning the visit, the interventionist must consider the family's circumstances, the energy level of the child, the focus of the parent, and unforeseen events that may happen in the home. In one situation, the parent spent the entire visit setting limits for her two-and-a-half-year-old. The one-hour visit was too stressful for him and his mother. The interventionist shortened her visit to a half hour, and the toddler was much less oppositional.

Table 6.3 offers several tips to keep in mind when visiting a family in their home. Compiled from several sources, they are based on the practical skills that service providers have found useful over the years.

Clearly, it is essential to try to follow the recommendations given in Table 6.3 when working with families. However, the interventionist will need to have Plan B ready in case Plan A does not work. The schedule may not go as planned due to a crisis in the home, an illness with a child, the parent's focus on another issue, or an activity that isn't working with the child. Therefore, flexibility is crucial when considering the child's schedule, the family's schedule, and the professional schedule of the interventionist.

Materials

Many homes contain an amazing array of possible teaching tools for infants and toddlers, yet many interventionists continue to rely on store-bought educational toys. In doing so they may inadvertently give the parents the message that in order to help their child, they must spend a lot of money and buy a wide variety of toys. On the other hand, when an interventionist brings in a homemade rattle, or, better yet, shows the parent how to make one, she is modeling resourcefulness. Sim-

---

TABLE 6.3   Suggestions for Home Visitors

- Greet each family member or day care provider as well as other children.
- Confirm the allotted time and discuss the plan for the visit.
- Begin and end the home visit on time.
- Prepare an activity for the siblings or include siblings and other children in day care in the activity.
- Take time to acknowledge pets, favorite toys, or household items.
- Confirm information with the parent about recent or upcoming medical or other appointments.
- Share developmental information and review developmental progress.
- Evaluate suggested activities.
- Discuss and model activities.
- Encourage parents to show how they ordinarily interact or play with their child.
- Listen to parents' concerns and offer support.
- Share problem-solving strategies.
- Share a sense of humor.
- Locate community resources.
- Schedule and discuss the next visit.
- Remain calm and focused despite distractions.
- Be flexible if the activity is not working with the child.

Adapted from "The Art of Home Visiting," by G. Calvello, 1990, in F,. Otto (Ed.), *Parents and Visually Impaired Infants*, Louisville, Ky.: American Printing House for the Blind; "Learning Together: A Parent Guide to Socially Based Routines for Visually Impaired Infants" by D. Chen, C. T. Friedman, and G. Cavello, 1990, in F. Otto (Ed.), *Parents and Visually Impaired Infants*; and *Adapting Early Childhood Curricula for Children in Inclusive Settings* by R. E. Cook, A. Tessier, & M. D. Klein, 2000, Englewood Cliffs, N.J.: Merrill/Prentice-Hall.

ple items found at home can be turned into valuable teaching tools. If one of the parents' goals for the toddler is that he learn to match objects, the interventionist and parents might consider functional objects around the house that could be used for this purpose (socks, shoes, etc.).

When items commonly found in the home are used in teaching, they can be easily incorporated in the family's routine and can make learning a natural occurrence. By suggesting that the child sort laundry, find matching socks, or place all the boxes of macaroni and cheese on the same shelf, parents are enriching the experiences for their children as well as providing a sense of self-determination. In addition, toddlers who are frustrated or tired often delight in an activity that they can do together with a parent. The activity helps them refocus their energy into a productive task.

Family Routines

Calvello (1990) emphasized the importance for the interventionist to spend time and observe the child during naturally occurring routines in the home environment. Such observations offer an insight into the family's life and routines and allow the interventionist to provide services within that framework. When working collaboratively with the parent during routines that are not taken out of context, a natural opportunity for learning will occur. Likewise, if the parent provides the child with learning experiences during everyday routines (e.g., meals, play, bath, bedtime), the activities will have more meaning to the child (Bricker, Pretti-Frontczak, & McComas, 1998; Chen, Friedman, & Calvello, 1990).

Siblings

Siblings or playmates in the child's child care are invaluable teachers. They are able to engage in repetitive games with the child to encourage social interaction in a natural setting. The interventionist should, with the parents, plan activities to occupy the siblings or playmates, or, more important, to design strategies to include the other children in the visit. Vignette 6.5 describes how one service provider accomplished this goal.

> **VIGNETTE 6.5   GO PLAY**
> Katie is a one-year-old with a severe visual impairment, who attends a family day care setting. Jane (the child care provider) expressed concern about the amount of time she spent with Katie alone and felt guilty about telling her two-year-old daughter, Kara, to go play while she worked with Katie. The interventionist had brought toys and materials to facilitate Katie's development, and Jane wanted to spend time working with Katie doing the activities. The interventionist explained how Kara would be a wonderful role model and playmate for Katie and could help in developing Katie's play skills. The interventionist developed play strategies with Jane to include her daughter and other children in playing with Katie.

Meyer and Vadasy (1994) reported that when siblings are involved in their brother's or sister's intervention, the entire family benefits. With planning from the interventionist and parent, the sibling can assume an active role in the child's intervention at home. The interventionist needs to view the family as a system and understand that all family members are influenced by events affecting one member of the family (Wasik, Bryant, & Lyons, 1990).

Environmental Intrusions

Many home visits follow a smooth schedule, as described in the previous examples. However, the service provider needs to be prepared for challenging intrusions and then must either adapt to the changes or develop strategies with which to handle them. These intrusions can take innumerable forms, ranging in seriousness from a blaring television set to an act of violence during a home visit. Vignette 6.6 portrays a crisis in one home.

> **VIGNETTE 6.6   TELL ME WHAT'S REALLY IMPORTANT!**
> A referral from the public health nurse was received to assess the developmental skills of Erik. After numerous tries to contact the parent to schedule a convenient time to visit, his mother finally agreed to a date scheduled in the later part of an afternoon. Upon arriving at their home, Erik's mother, Jody, was busy feeding her eight-week-old daughter. Erik was asleep on the sofa because he had been up all night after choking on a piece of candy. The phone rang and it was the phone company informing Jody of their intent to disconnect her phone. Jody told the phone company that her check was in the mail and begged them not to disconnect the phone. After her phone call, Jody stated that she was moving to another apartment soon. We set up a time the following week to see Erik and Jody. The day before we were scheduled to come, we tried to call Jody. Her phone had been disconnected.
>
> Eventually the assessment team did contact Jody through the mail and set up another date to come and see Erik. After completing the assessment and sharing the results, Jody decided that she did not want any services for Erik and she would take care of his needs.

Although Jody and Erik would benefit from services, it was difficult for this mother to reach out for help. She was preoccupied with providing the most basic needs for her family. Perhaps when her living situation is more stable, she will see the importance of getting services for Erik. At this point, does the service provider have other options for the family? Possibly the public health nurse could continue to contact or visit the family to establish rapport and trust to encourage some form of communication regarding Jody and Erik's situation. The assessment team could try to reassess Erik in six months and offer services again.

Often situations cannot be changed and instead need to be adapted for a successful home visit. Some intrusions are a necessary part of the child's daily routine.

Consider Vignette 6.7, which illustrates medically related intrusions for one child and her family.

VIGNETTE 6.7 OLIVIA

Olivia is a three-year-old with a significant birth history: born premature at 24 weeks. She spent six months in NICU and three additional months in the infant critical care unit before discharge. Medically she has been followed for bronchopulmonary dysplasia, tracheostomy with ventilator assistance, and retinopathy of prematurity. Olivia was weaned from mechanical ventilation at two and a half years. Just recently, at age three, she had successful surgery for decannulation and now has a stable airway.

Olivia has had many environmental intrusions. Each day, she requires nebulizing treatments every four hours for respiratory difficulties (at times, they can be every two hours), feedings through a gastrostomy tube, and medication. Home visits are scheduled when Olivia is most rested and does not need medical therapy or medication. Her mother, Cheryl, is also affected by intrusions, which may include the home health nurse's own agenda and phone calls from the pediatrician or pulmonologist, from the home health care agency to reschedule or inform Cheryl of changes in nursing staff, and from friends who call during Olivia's therapy to chat or make plans.

Developmentally, Olivia is ready to interact and play with other children. However, her pediatrician has recommended that she not participate in a play group or preschool program for at least one year due to the possibility of a respiratory infection. Cheryl feels that the medical demands and the threat for illness with a medically at-risk child have led to a very isolating experience for Olivia and her family. Olivia's parents are pursuing play groups with other medically at-risk children whose parents understand what precautions are needed to allow the children to play together.

Although Olivia's environmental intrusions are very necessary, Cheryl has coordinated Olivia's schedule so that Olivia has opportunities to explore and learn in her environment with minimal interruptions. Therapists, nurses, doctors, and friends have been asked not to call during Olivia's home visits with the interventionist. Communication, collaboration, and flexibility are key factors in working around the many environmental intrusions on families in order to facilitate successful home visits (Wasik, Bryant, & Lyons, 1990).

Advocacy

Families can become their child's best advocate. With advocacy skills, families are better able to help their child obtain appropriate resources and intervention services (Turnbull & Turnbull, 1990). In Vignette 6.7, Cheryl shared how she coordinated and communicated with all professionals involved in Olivia's medical and educational needs. When asked how she advocates for Olivia, Cheryl chuckled and said, "I'm a bully." Seriously, Cheryl and her husband, Steve, continue to ask questions of doctors, nurses, therapists, and other parents. They research information to help them be more knowledgeable in making informed decisions about Olivia's medical and educational needs.

Many families feel intimidated and may not be comfortable communicating to professionals their particular issues regarding intervention or medical services. It may be helpful for the family to compile a running list of questions or concerns and then share it at an appropriate time (for example, during a home visit, at an IFSP meeting, or in the doctor's office). Families need to be encouraged to ask questions, request additional information, and positively assert their needs as a family (Armenta, 1993).

Networking

Families can be a valuable resource to other families. Networking may help them to identify with other families whose child has a similar disability, offer or gain support, create additional resources, establish a friendship, lessen the sense of isolation, and provide opportunities to learn from each other (Armenta, 1993). Informal or formal networking may occur through the interventionist, the pediatrician, and local or national organizations.

However, families with few supports often have difficulty negotiating the system independently. The process of getting the appropriate social services is very time-consuming and bureaucratic. Likewise, the process of finding child care, transportation, housing, and a job can be very complicated. Some parents may question why they should even attempt to become more self-sufficient when struggling with so many demands and expectations. In Vignette 6.8, a parent loses her job and gives up hope.

> **VIGNETTE 6.8   NO HOPE LEFT**
> Mary had lost her job due to her inability to transport herself to her job site. The loss of her job meant she had to apply for housing assistance and food stamps. It also meant the loss of a child care subsidy, which had paid for the majority of the child care for Jason, who is autistic. With no car, no child care, and mounting worries about providing shelter and sustenance for her family, she contemplated whether or not to try to find a job. The stress of this situation caused increased frustration for Jason. Because she had lost her child care, she was taking him along to apply for assistance and jobs. Jason was unable to sit and wait with her. He would scream and cry and try to run from the room. Mary often had to leave the office before completing the application.

This is an all-too-familiar story in the lives of many families. If Mary had access to reliable transportation, she might have been able to prevent her situation from deteriorating. What is particularly frustrating is that Mary's son was not getting his needs met. How can the early interventionist help parents function more autonomously? Providing opportunities and encouraging parents to network with others are essential in promoting independence. Doss and Hatcher (1996) discussed the importance of being involved in parent organizations. They found that these organizations helped parents learn the latest philosophies guiding services and supports for their children. Many parents find that making a connection with others who have similar experiences is empowering as well as validating in that they are able to hear the success stories.

ETHICAL ISSUES IN HOME VISITING

Home visiting gives the early interventionist another opportunity to enhance the quality of life for a child. Working outside the professional domain of classroom or clinic presents many situations in which a skilled home visitor must be able to operate independently. By allowing professionals into their home, families are giving up a considerable amount of privacy and may view home visits as invasive. The situation places them in a vulnerable position that may require a significant amount of adjustment. Some parents may feel inadequate about providing a home for their child or be worried that the professional will discover some negative information about the family, such as drug abuse or domestic violence. Building a strong, trusting relationship with the family can help the home visitor provide appropriate services. Critical in this process is establishing the boundaries that are necessary for home visiting to take place (Powell, 1993).

Most professional organizations provide a set of ethical guidelines that members are encouraged to follow. The American Psychiatric Association (APA) and the National Association of Social Workers (NASW) are examples of helping professions that have adopted a set of standards to be applied when situations of an ethical nature arise in servicing clients. These standards outline appropriate conduct and rules for the delivery of services. The Council for Exceptional Children (CEC) has developed a Code of Ethics, and requires compliance by all members. Early interventionists should follow these guidelines when serving children and their families. Compliance will help professionals provide support for the actions they may take in serving clients.

Table 6.4 is drawn from a number of sources in order to provide a comprehensive view of the major ethical issues for home visitors. Reamer (1982) developed guidelines more specific to situations that may involve conflict or require a judgment call. These guidelines were further elaborated on by Wasik, Bryant, and Lyons (1990) for home visitors. Additional guidelines were added to address other current issues in home visiting, such as the client's legal rights and your rights as a professional.

It is important to follow and understand safety procedures established by the service organization. In many states, early intervention agencies have worked closely with police and others to ensure the safety of home visitors. Some of the

TABLE 6.4   Ethical Issues in Home Visiting

- Rules against basic harms to necessary preconditions (e.g., life, health, food, safety) take precedence over rules against lying or revealing confidential information. In other words, a professional may lie about the whereabouts of a mother and child to an abusing spouse who may be threatening him or her.
- An individual's right to basic well-being takes precedence over another individual's right to freedom. If a parent is engaged in self-destructive behavior, they may do so without interference from the professional unless someone else's well-being is at stake.
- An informed individual's rights to choose an unsafe action takes precedence over his or her own right to basic well-being. A home visitor may provide resources, information, and even transportation to a mental health agency for a parent with a mental illness, but the parent has the right to refuse assistance. The visitor should enlist other family members and mental health professionals in determining a solution.
- The obligation to obey laws, rules, and regulations that the home visitor has voluntarily consented to takes precedence over one's right to engage in actions that conflict with these laws, rules, and regulations. Thus, home visitors must abide by the rules and regulations stipulated by their agency.
- An individual's right to well-being may take precedence over laws, rules, regulations of the agency in a case of conflict. It may be an agency rule to wait for police before taking a family to a shelter. However, if the family is in immediate danger, the home visitor may need to take faster action.
- The obligation to prevent basic harms such as starvation, and promote public education, assistance, and adequate housing overrides the right to keep one's property. Home visitors often face the dilemma of using their own resources to assist the families they are working with. They try to find a balance between providing resources and disempowering families.
- Home visitors must demonstrate cultural sensitivity and adaptation of visiting goals to diverse family ecologies.

Adapted from *Ethical Dilemmas in Social Service* by F. G. Reamer, 1982, New York: Columbia University Press, pp. 72–79; *Home Visiting: Procedures for Helping Families* by B. H. Wasik, D. M. Bryant, & C. M. Lyons, 1990, Newbury Park, Calif.: Sage, pp. 203–206; "Home Visiting Programs and the Health and Development of Young Children" by C. T. Ramey & S. L. Ramey, 1993, in R. E. Behrman (Ed.), *The Future of Children: Home Visiting,* Los Altos, Calif.: Center for the Future of Children, David and Lucille Packard Foundation, p. 134.

strategies used by programs include the use of cellular phones for all home visitors, required reporting of arrival and departure times at the agency, teaming up for visits in questionable neighborhoods, using reliable, safe transportation, and leaving valuables in the trunk or at the agency.

Data Privacy

Another important issue in serving families with special needs is how information is used and shared among those involved in delivering services. Special care must be taken to uphold client confidentiality and respect their privacy. Medical information, environmental considerations, personal history, and families' goals and issues must be considered confidential and only shared with permission by parents. It is important that the information shared is pertinent to the professional who is receiving it. However, there are times when confidentiality guidelines should be bypassed (Corey, Corey, & Callanan, 1993). If the professional is concerned for the safety of an individual, confidentiality may be overlooked. For example, professionals are mandated by law to report suspected cases of abuse or neglect of a child.

Child Abuse and Neglect

Maltreatment of children is one of the most complex issues faced by professionals working with families. Children with disabilities are at an increased risk of abuse because of the stress that exceptionality may create in families (T. J. Zirpoli, 1986, 1995). Other risk factors include the child's temperament; maternal and paternal variables such as age, socioeconomic status, race, marital status, and education level; social isolation; and environmental stressors (Willis, Holden & Rosenberg, 1992). Home visiting is a valuable tool in prevention of child abuse. Research supports the positive impact early intervention can have in the home (Olds, Henderson, Chamberlain, & Tatelbaum, 1986). Visitors should be knowledgeable about the indicators of abuse and the correct procedures in reporting cases to child welfare and law enforcement. Information for each state should be available from the respective state department of human services.

Cultural Diversity and Sensitivity

Effective communication is the basis for working across cultures. A home interventionist will convey many messages, not only through words but also with body language, gestures, eye contact, and facial expressions. Researchers have outlined strategies to enhance communication with families from diverse cultures, as summarized in Table 6.5.

TABLE 6.5   Cross-Cultural Effectiveness

- Acknowledging one's own cultural heritage and its impact on your work.
- Investigating the cultural norms and traditions of specific groups through literature and a community inventory.
- Recognizing differences in communication styles within various cultures.
- Recognizing nonverbal communication styles.
- Showing respect and openness toward other cultures.
- Being willing to tolerate ambiguity.
- Approaching others with a desire to learn.

Adapted from *Developing Cross-Cultural Competence: A Guide from Working with Young Children and Their Families* by E. W. Lynch & M. J. Hanson, 1998, Baltimore: Paul H. Brookes; and *Strategies for Working with Culturally Diverse Communities and Clients* by E. Randall-David, 1989, Washington, D.C.: Association for the Care of Children's Health.

Even if communication is optimized, differences in basic beliefs may need to be addressed. For example, one of the main assumptions of early intervention programs is that change is not only possible but also valued (Hanson, 1992). Thus, families from diverse cultures immediately come up against mainstream values about change and action. In some cultures, changes may be viewed as undesirable or unnecessary. Families may prefer to take a "wait and see" approach. An early interventionist who moves ahead with inquiries and assumes that the family will actively participate may find that those good intentions are not in accordance with the family's dynamics and beliefs, thus alienating the family from the start.

Table 6.6 illustrates how beliefs that are an everyday part of the mainstream Anglo-American psyche may be extremely different from those of other cultural groups.

The values listed in Table 6.6 are such an integral part of a person's being that daily actions and interactions are unconsciously guided by them. When working with families from cultures dissimilar to our own, it is prudent to pause and question these assumptions. For example, if the interventionist is from the mainstream culture, it might seem natural to assume that informal attire is appropriate for home visits because, more than likely, one may end up on the floor working with a child. Yet some cultural groups might take this as a sign of disrespect, because for them more formal attire is appropriate when entering another person's home.

VIGNETTE 6.9   THE LEE FAMILY
Louise knocked politely on the door of the Lee family's apartment. Upon entering, she introduced herself to the family, and shook hands

TABLE 6.6   Contrasting Beliefs, Values, and Practices

DIVERSE CULTURAL VALUES	ANGLO-AMERICAN VALUES
Fate	Personal control over environment
Tradition	Change
Human interaction dominates	Time dominates
Hierarchy/rank/status	Human equality
Group welfare	Individualism/privacy
Birthright inheritance	Self-help
Cooperation	Competition
Past orientation	Future orientation
"Being" orientation	Action/goal/work orientation
Formality	Informality
Indirectness/ritual/"face"	Directness/openness/honesty
Idealism/theory	Practicality/efficiency
Spiritualism/detachment	Materialism

Adapted from "Cross-Cultural Counseling: A Guide for Nutrition and Health Counselors" United States Department of Agriculture & United States Department of Health and Human Services, 1986, Washington, D.C.: Author, p. 3.

with Mr. Lee, Mrs. Lee, and Mr. Lee's father. She was offered both food and drink; but declined, saying she had eaten just before coming. She felt slightly uneasy with this new family, and because the Lees seemed so reserved and quiet, Louise tried to fill in the uncomfortable pauses with animated questions and talk. Louise's queries were politely answered, but she felt she was somehow not connecting with the family.

How would you prepare yourself?

If Louise had attempted to understand and respect the family's cultural background, she probably would have been more successful in her first visit. But she inadvertently offended the family numerous times in her ignorance of their cultural customs, which dictate that shoes be taken off at the door, that women typically do not shake hands with men or anyone significantly older than themselves, that food or a beverage is always graciously accepted, and that laughter, informality, and personal questions are inappropriate when initially meeting someone (Chan, 1998).

On the other hand, just because a family has roots in another culture or is of a different race, this doesn't necessarily mean that they adhere to the customs and values typical of that culture. Several generations of a family might live in a mainstream culture without ever acculturating to it, while other, recently immigrated families may immediately embrace the new ways and values even though they may not speak the language.

Wayman, Lynch, and Hanson (1991) developed a comprehensive set of guidelines that address in detail the family's structure, childrearing practices, language and communication systems, and attitudes and that can be extremely helpful in determining the concerns, priorities, and resources of a family (see Table 6.7). These guidelines can serve to ease the process toward understanding a family's perspective.

TABLE 6.7   General Guidelines for Cultural Sensitivity in Home Visiting

- Don't overgeneralize about members of any specific cultural group.
- Realize that cultural differences as well as similarities are common.
- Find out about the culture and the family's degree of acculturation before you make your first contact.
- Use resources written by members of the culture.
- Be respectful of the family's belongings and ask where they would like you to sit, work with the child, etc.
- Be especially sensitive to social structure and hierarchy.
- Accept food or drink graciously, even if only a token amount.
- Be aware that the family's childrearing practices may be directly at odds with mainstream norms.
- Use reflective listening often to check if you are hearing what the family intended to communicate, as language differences may impair communication.

Adapted from "Home-Based Early Childhood Services: Cultural Sensitivity in a Family Systems Approach" by K. Wayman, E. Lynch, & M. Hanson, 1991, *Topics in Early Childhood Special Education, 10,* 65–66.

SERVICES IN OTHER SETTINGS

Infants and toddlers expend much of their energy adjusting to the behavioral styles of their primary caregivers (Blasco, 1995). Research shows that both the infant and the adult are active partners who affect each other's behavior over time (Sameroff & Fiese, 1990). For the infant or toddler with disabilities, this interactive dance often becomes difficult and frustrating for both partners. Given the increase in out-of-home care, infants and toddlers with disabilities must learn to interpret and respond to a variety of behavioral characteristics of those who care for them in many different settings (Belsky, 1988). Therefore, it is important to understand and evaluate the quality of attachment and the care that young children receive outside the home.

Bowlby (1982), and Ainsworth (in Ainsworth, Blehar, Waters, & Wall, 1978) were pioneers in developing attachment theory and highlighting its importance in the field of child development. Their efforts have resulted in attention to attachment issues in caregiving situations outside the home. Belsky (1988) looked at the amount of time infants spent in child care and its impact on infant-parent attachment. Using the "strange situation" method developed by Ainsworth, he found that infants who were in nonparental care for more than 20 hours per week showed higher rates of insecure attachment behaviors when reunited with parents.

Further studies indicate the importance of secure parental attachment for success in child-caregiver relationships (Barnas & Cummings, 1994; Howes & Hamilton, 1992). "When children are distressed, attachment figures can serve as an effective source of security, and in routine play they may facilitate functioning by serving as a secure base for infants' explorations" (Barnas & Cummings, p. 141).

From a practical standpoint there are three critical factors in determining whether a child care situation is going to be a positive social and emotional experience for a child: (1) daily transitions of departing and reuniting, (2) the quality of the child's emotional experiences in the course of the day, and (3) the quality of the parent's relationship with the caregiver (Lieberman, 1993, p. 203).

All these are important regardless of the setting—in-home care, center care, or family home care. Family home care is defined as care provided for a child by someone other than the parent in the other adult's home. It is a form of care for infants and toddlers highly used in the United States. Until recently, it also was the least supported and regulated type of care for children. Typically, family day care is a mixed-age setting with one caregiver responsible for the well-being of all children in her care. States have implemented licensing guidelines for family day care operations that help to ensure safe environments for children, but these guidelines are inconsistent (Adams, 1995). There are many family day care settings that are operating without frequent inspections. Parents may choose those settings due to their low cost or proximity to work (Bryant & Graham, 1993).

Although developmentally appropriate practices are paramount for family day care, the environment differs from the atmosphere of a center. "Toys and equipment are available for children, but children's interactions, rather than explicit planning and involvement of the provider, form the core of the day's activities" (Jones & Meisels, 1987, p. 2). Family day care providers should be trained and experienced in child development and should have the opportunity to build skills and network with other providers on a continuous basis. Providers need to have firm guidelines and limits, which parents should follow in regard to hours of service, sickness policies, and payment.

Among the barriers to quality child care that social policy needs to address are training and qualification standards of providers, networking and support systems for providers, and financial assistance for parents and providers (NAEYC, 1999). Another area for growth would be increasing training and support for family day care.

Staff Qualifications

In an ideal world, infants, toddlers, and their families could find child care staffed by individuals who are highly skilled and knowledgeable about typical and atypical development and family structure. Currently, there is much interest in developing a career ladder in early childhood education that extends from technical colleges providing child care certificates to institutions of higher education preparing students on the baccalaureate, master, and doctoral levels. The National Association for the Education of Young Children (NAEYC) and the Division for Early Childhood (DEC) have developed specific guidelines and recommended practices for teachers working with young children. These guidelines offer specific recommendations regarding the following core content: child development and learning, curriculum, family and community partnerships, assessment and evaluation, practical and field experiences, and diversity (Bredekamp, 1995; Odom & McLean, 1993). Field experiences to demonstrate competency include but are not limited to child care environments, including center-based and home-based education. Working professionals receive continuing education through local and state sponsored in-services and training efforts. One way that professionals can keep current in their field is through affiliation with organizations such as the NAEYC and DEC. Both of these provide service providers with current knowledge of the best practice and networking opportunities.

The American Speech and Hearing Association (ASHA), the American Occupational Therapy Association (AOTA), the Physical Therapy Association, and the American Medical Association (AMA) have all developed guidelines for their disciplines regarding practice with families and young children.

Staff-to-child ratios are a critical factor in the quality of care. The NAEYC recommendations for classes of typical developing children are 1:3 for infants, 1:6 for toddlers (24–36 months), and 1:8 for 3-year-olds (Bredekamp, 1993). DEC recommendations suggest that ratios provide the highest quality care possible to meet the safety, health, and educational goals of the specific group of children (Odom & McLean, 1993). Group size may vary depending on the needs of children and individual state guidelines. However, a small-group approach for toddlers has been shown to foster independent choice-making, self-worth, and conflict resolution (Elgas & Barber Peltier, 1998). The small-group format used in many programs today is modeled on the Reggio Emilia approach to learning. The philosophical basis for this approach was mentioned in Chapter 1. Important components of this approach include self-determination, relationship-based learning, and emergent curriculum (Rinaldi, 1993).

Appropriate Materials and Curriculum

The use of materials and curriculum for child care centers is discussed in Chapter 7. However, it is important to consider curriculum within the context of the environment. As previously mentioned, developmentally appropriate practice (DAP) (Bredekamp & Copple, 1998) provides guidelines to meet children's individual developmental needs. DAP is implemented through planned curriculum and design of the environment. "Infants and toddlers learn by experiencing the environment through their senses by physically moving around and through social interaction" (Bredekamp, 1993, p. 5). DAP recommendations include encouragement of cognitive learning and healthy social emotional development, in part by service providers and parents providing appropriate play experiences in a safe, nurturing environment.

Children with disabilities may require more structure and guidance in their play from the caregiver. Fox, Hanline, Vail, and Galant (1994) pointed out that early intervention programs focus on the remediation of skills and the prevention of future developmental problems. These programs tend to emphasize developing individualized goals for children and designing learning activities to achieve those goals. Incorporating recommended practices with DAP is appropriate for children with disabilities. "This best practice is echoed in the Early Childhood Special Education (ECSE) literature in that teaching through routines and in natural contexts is promoted as a functional approach that will yield generalized responding. A developmentally appropriate curriculum provides ample opportunity for child-directed play with objects and peers, during which specific skills can be targeted for young children with special needs" (Fox et al., 1994, p. 244).

Designing Environments for Child Care

The overall environment of a child care center can set the stage for optimal growth and learning by young children. McEvoy, Fox, and Rosenberg (1991) pointed out that there are two important considerations in designing the environment: in addition to establishing a social environment, the physical layout of the center needs to be considered very carefully to include all children. In the past, child care centers have had to take what they could get in terms of physical space. Although centers must meet certain legal requirements for their buildings and grounds, many struggled to meet the bare minimum. Because of the need for quality child care, there has been a vast improvement in the design of child care centers.

According to Bailey and Wolery (1992, p. 200), a responsive environment should incorporate the following teaching strategies:

- Provide opportunities for children to use appropriate materials for problem-solving and mastery;
- Provide opportunities for children to understand and respond to verbal and nonverbal signals from other children as well as adults;
- Encourage autonomy through appropriate adaptive equipment, assistive technology, and child-size furniture.

Child care centers should provide children with separate active and quiet spaces. Quiet activities such as storytelling or "reading" (looking at a book) should be located near other quiet activities. The block area should be in a distant part of the room, perhaps near the dress-up area to encourage symbolic play within these two sections (S. B. Zirpoli, 1995). With very young children, it is important to consider how each area will be utilized so that appropriate behavior occurs. For example, hanging a mobile or placing bright color pictures on the ceiling in the diaper-changing area can create opportunities for conversation and avoid the battles that may arise during a change. The aisle in the room should be wide enough for a wheelchair but not so wide that it creates a runway for toddlers. It is a good idea to define spaces using tables, shelving, or furniture. Different areas and materials can be identified with picture and name labels. A good physical layout of a center for toddlers is illustrated in Figure 6.1.

Adaptive equipment allows a child with a physical disability to participate in typical center routines. For example, a corner chair or a floor seat can be used to position a toddler during group time. Wedges and prone standers can be useful when the child is looking at books or participating in table activities. The team should spend time making sure the equipment is used properly and not for an overextended period. To use the previous example, young children may have difficulty staying in a straight-leg position during group time. Children should be monitored for head, back and trunk stability when sitting in a group (Nwaobi & Smith, 1986). Lofts and platforms are very popular in child care centers today, yet one must consider the difficulty that children with disabilities encounter in negotiating such spaces. A good rule is to plan ahead with the team (including parents, of course) to make the optimal use of the space for all children.

Outdoor Environments

The opportunity for play in a safe outdoor environment is very important for all children. Rivkin (1995) noted the lack of available, appropriate space for young children in many center-based programs.

Most centers begin by taking stock of what is available and deciding what are the priorities in meeting children's needs. Outdoor play should provide lots of opportunity for children to engage in large muscle activities, and also serve to increase their exploratory behavior by using interesting materials and equipment.

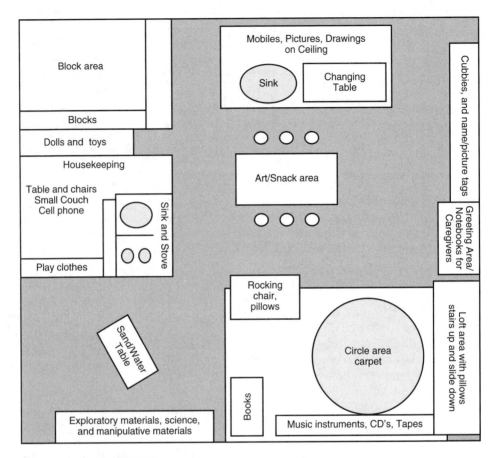

FIGURE 6.1   Toddler Room

Source: From "Designing Environments for Optimal Behavior" by Susan B. Zirpoli, 1995, in T. J. Zirpoli (Ed.), *Understanding and Affecting the Behavior of Young Children*, Englewood Cliffs, N.J.: Merrill, pp. 122–150.

Such equipment should be of appropriate size for toddlers and should include adaptive devices for children with physical disabilities. Tricycles and pull wagons can be modified to hold adaptive seating. It is important to consider access to a play area for children with disabilities. For example, Levangie, Brouwer, McKeen, Parker, and Shelby (1989) found that posterior rolling walkers helped children with motor impairments to walk with close to a normal gait. Young children are encouraged to use their walkers to negotiate hallways and playgrounds. Because many centers do not have a stable walkway leading to the play area, the team needs to problem-solve a way to get the child to these areas as independently as possible.

Another consideration for making the most of outdoor play is the role of staff, including assistants, all of whom must stay actively involved with the children. Outdoor time is not a "break time" for adults. S. B. Zirpoli (1995) offered suggestions to manage behavior on the playground:

- Separate play areas for younger and older preschoolers. (In some states, this is now required by law.) Toddlers need especially close supervision and should play on equipment designed for them.
- Allow for adequate monitoring and supervision. For example, an extra adult should be available to take children indoors when necessary for toileting or other needs.
- Make sure there is adequate equipment to go around. Otherwise, limiting the number of children on the playground may eliminate waiting for a turn on the swing or slide.
- Teach children how to use the playground equipment. For example, showing children the correct way to walk around swings and other hazards will decrease injuries and conflicts. (p. 133)

TRANSITIONS IN NATURAL ENVIRONMENTS

Transitions within early childhood environments are used to move children to and from various locations (Dee-Tourdot, 1995). Researchers have found that preschool-age children spend as much as 20 to 30 percent of time in center-based programs moving from one activity to another (Sainato, Strain, Lefebvre, & Rapp, 1987). Too many transitions within a classroom may be frustrating for very young children. When activities are structured and planned appropriately, they can provide opportunities for very young children to learn and develop self-management skills (Dee-Tourdot, 1995). Elements that promote smooth transitions include: an organized and easily accessed environment, staff planning and preparation, and routine timing and procedure (Larson, Henthorne, & Plum, 1994). For example, toddlers can get their blankets from cubbies in preparation for napping if the cubbies are at their height level.

When not planned, transitions can increase disruptive behavior and decrease the effective use of instructional time (Carta et al., 1992). "Down" time occurs when children are waiting or nonengaged in appropriate activities. Vignette 6.10 shows how this behavior, coupled with ambiguous instructions, creates a chaotic atmosphere.

> **VIGNETTE 6.10   CHANGES AND STAGES**
> Martha's class of older toddlers was required to stand in line by the sink to wash hands after outdoor play. The children had difficulty maintaining the line and staying within their own space. The transition was trying for both the children and staff. Martha's solution was to have another staff member help the children wash hands in small groups of two or three while the others were seated for a short singing activity. The stress was greatly reduced by this change in the routine.

Much of the research on transitions within the classroom focused on decreasing "down" time and increasing independence. Strategies to improve transitions within the classroom include organization of the environment to enhance learning and specific instructional strategies (Sainato & Lyon, 1989).

As an example, S. B. Zirpoli (1995) listed physical elements of a center-based program that can facilitate organization and structure including the following:

- Separating active and quiet activity spaces
- Providing obvious boundaries of all play spaces, using furniture and/or space dividers
- Labeling activity areas with word labels and picture symbols
- Limiting the number of children per activity area (e.g., through use of chairs, tickets, activity necklaces, carpet squares, and pictures noting how many children are allowed in the area)
- Using child-size furniture and bathroom fixtures to promote independence.

In Vignette 6.11, one child humorously illustrates his knowledge of a two-person area.

VIGNETTE 6.11   TWO-PERSON AREA
Joey has a great understanding of how many children are allowed to play in each area of the classroom. Recently, Joey went on a class field trip to the History Center. At the center, he saw an exhibit involving a large model cow. All of the children were crowding in awe around the cow. Joey reminded everyone that it was "a two-person cow!"

Classroom Schedule

A critical component for a smooth transition is an effective and predictable schedule (Dee-Tourdot, 1995). The daily schedule includes the times of various activities and events throughout the day. It is helpful to include information on where events will be held and which staff members will be responsible for different activities (Sainato, 1990). Daily schedules can promote learning across content areas (e.g., language, preacademics, gross motor) by sequencing high- and low-activity periods, grouping by skill components, and building reliance on established routines (Ostrosky, Skellenger, Odom, McConnell, & Peterson, 1994).

Defining the responsibilities of staff in relation to the schedule will help to eliminate confusion. The "zone" procedure assigns staff to specific areas within the classroom, while the children are free to move around the room. In the "man-to-man" procedure, children must wait until everyone has completed an activity before moving on to another area. The zone method was more effective in decreasing the time children spent in transitions and increasing their level of engagement in planned activities (Zirpoli, 1995).

When developing strategies for classroom transitions, the team must consider what is developmentally appropriate for the child. Linking transition plans with the child's individual education program (IEP) or individual family service plan (IFSP) is an effective way to build successful transitions within the classroom.

HELPING FAMILIES WITH CHILD CARE

Most centers follow state guidelines in meeting standards for child care. However, parents sometimes feel forced to choose between quality child care and less expensive or more convenient services. It is often difficult for service providers who are working with children as consultants to see them placed in a questionable setting. Several options exist in these situations. You may want to offer suggestions or share strategies and curriculum ideas with the child care center. If this does not help, you may want to visit the center with the parents and indicate areas that need improvement. There are several tools available to assess quality in child care programs and environments for infants and toddlers. The Family Day Care Rating Scale (Harms & Clifford, 1989), The Infant/Toddler Environment Rating Scale (Harms, Cryer, & Clifford 1990), and *Barriers and Supports to Early Childhood Inclusion* (Wesley & Buysse, 1994a) are three such instruments that assess environments by looking at all domains of child development, interactions with parents, and general structure of routines. These tools are applicable to inclusive settings and match current guidelines on quality care.

TRANSITION FROM PROGRAM TO PROGRAM

In most states, when children turn three years of age, they are often "moved" from early intervention services to early childhood special education. The difference in approach to services between the two forms may reflect more than a change from the IFSP to the IEP. For one thing, families no longer have access to a service coordinator. As mandated by federal law, the early intervention program staff will help them with the transition to a preschool program. This can be a joyous but also stressful time for families and their young children. It is also sometimes difficult for service providers who have to let go of a child and family after three years of building a relationship.

A successful transition is a primary goal for service providers working with young children and their families. PL 99-457, Part H (1986), placed a spotlight on the transition process for young children. When the Individuals with Disabilities Education Act (IDEA), Part C, was passed in 1991 and reauthorized in 1997, states were required to define how they will assure a smooth transition for the family when applying for federal funds for early intervention programs.

To secure a smooth transition, the law states that an Individual Education Plan (IEP) must be developed and implemented by the child's third birthday. In states that have adopted the IFSP (Individualized Family Service Plan) through age five, such as Oregon, the new program uses the IFSP unless an annual review is due. A description of the family's role in the transition process must be included in the documentation. At least 90 days before the child's third birthday, a meeting between the sending and receiving personnel and the family must occur (Rosenkoetter, Hains, & Fowler, 1994). The trend in early childhood services is to collaborate within the community and become family-centered. Furthermore, state and local agencies need to service families and their children in natural and least intrusive environments (Rosenkoetter et al., 1994).

Transition is a time of change that can lead to growth and at the same time add stress in families' lives. Planning successful transitions leads to positive experiences (Odom & McLean, 1993). Rosenkoetter and colleagues suggested several key ideas for bridging the transition process, including (1) ensuring program continuity by using developmentally appropriate curriculum for all age levels in all settings; (2) maintaining ongoing communication and cooperation between staff at both programs; and (3) helping children and families prepare for the transition (Rosenkoetter et al., 1994).

Parents have legal rights to be involved in the decisions made regarding the IFSP and ensuring that adequate steps are made in the transition process. Information should be given to the parents about future placements, educational options, and training. Families have many concerns regarding transitions. Table 6.8 lists some of these concerns.

In addition, families need to evaluate philosophies and practices in the new program that may be different from those in the previous program. For example, moving from a teacher who may work as a member of a transdisciplinary team to a single contact person who represents the other members of the team involves a change in philosophies. A trusting relationship with a particular service coordinator/provider may have evolved, and in a transition, the family is forced to form a new relationship. To open the lines of communication, the child, the parents, and the new teacher may choose to hold informal meetings, thus giving everyone the opportunity to share information and visit the future environment (Rosenkoetter et al., 1994).

TABLE 6.8   Families' Concerns Regarding Transitions

- Changes in service delivery, including focus, types, and coordination of services
- Differences in service personnel
- Eligibility for services
- Labeling
- Social acceptance
- Transportation issues
- No or fewer home visits
- Schedule/routine changes
- Change from family-centered to child-centered environment

Adapted from *Bridging Early Services for Children with Special Needs and Their Families: A Practical Guide for Transition Planning* by E. S. Rosenkoetter, H. A. Hains, and A. S. Fowler, 1994, Baltimore: Paul H. Brookes.

The degree to which families are involved in the decision-making process during the transition may differ from family to family and from situation to situation. Some families may choose to advocate strongly for their child, while other parents may prefer to take a backseat in the process. In any case, educators need to be sensitive to the families' preferences and concerns by providing them with information and support during the transition (Rosenkoetter et al., 1994). Families can also provide valuable information about their child and should be considered an equal member of the transition team (Odom & McLean, 1993). Summers (cited in Rosenkoetter et al., 1994) stated that "professionals need to remember, however, that families may not always be *ready* to hear, understand, or accept some information, but it should be available for later use." (p. 88)

Through collaborative efforts, agencies should establish a timeline to ensure that policies and procedures have been followed. By providing a continuum of services for children and families, duplication can be avoided. A plan should define fiscal responsibilities, guidelines, and constraints of each agency. This plan should include both formative and summative evaluation (Rosenkoetter et al., 1994).

Transition means change, which is a part of life. To provide positive experiences with change, professionals need to be sensitive to strategies that families and children can use to cope with the transitions. Children need to be prepared for environments that are structured differently and to be taught functional skills that can be integrated into the new setting (Odom & McLean, 1993). For families, leaving the child at child care, joining a new play group, and meeting new friends are all steps that promote successful transitions in the future.

Rosenkoetter and colleagues (1994) have suggested strategies, presented in Table 6.9, to help prepare children and families for transitions.

Transitioning from program to program can be a challenge. However, with collaboration on the part of administrators, teachers, and the sending and receiving programs, it can be done with success. Interagency planning is necessary to develop working agreements between agencies, form the transition team, and allocate a timeline to accomplish transition tasks. In addition, team responsibilities must be assigned and carried out. Intraagency planning is necessary to designate the responsibilities of the service coordinators/providers and to allow adequate time to plan a successful transition (Odom & McLean, 1993).

It is important to evaluate the transition process from the family's perspective. Were support services coordinated throughout the process? Families can be extremely helpful in identifying what worked and what needs to be improved for future transitions. Formal and informal means of collecting information from families regarding the transition process have been used. Questionnaires and observations are a few tools used in developing the evaluation plan. The evaluation team may consist of families, staff members, and agency representatives. Eliminating any biases while forming and implementing the evaluation plan will lead to an accurate outcome. Communicating the evaluation findings to the appropriate persons in various programs is vital to implementing change for future transitions (Rosenkoetter et al., 1994).

TABLE 6.9   Preparing Children for Transition from Program to Program

- Help the child anticipate the situation by talking about the new program, providing concrete experiences, and providing opportunities for the child to ask questions and express emotions.
- Read picture books about children undergoing changes in their environment that may be stressful.
- Volunteer to visit the new program with the parent or, if preferred by the parent, alone.
- Review changes in routines and schedules and the impact on all family members.
- If possible, videotape a new situation for viewing by the child. For example, videotape group time if the child hasn't sat in a group before, and let them watch the videotape as often as they like.
- Discuss separation from parents and other caregivers who may have been involved with the child.
- Facilitate social skills so the child is comfortable with social initiations and interactions with peers.
- Target new skills that can be learned in natural situations and easily transferable to a new environment (e.g., carrying a backpack to the library).
- Practice familiar skills in multiple settings.
- Assist the family with the preparation of the child's paperwork and portfolio.

Adapted from *Bridging Early Services for Children with Special Needs: A Practical Guide for Transition Planning* by S. E. Rosenkoetter, A. H. Hains, and S. A. Fowler, 1994, Baltimore: Paul H. Brookes, pp. 129–146.

SUMMARY

This chapter highlighted the many environments in which infants and toddlers grow and develop. Traditionally, children under three received services in the home. The teacher or other staff member worked with the parent in developing goals and objectives for the child. Today, the involvement of all family members in every stage of early intervention from planning to implementation reflects recommended practice. Families can be as involved as they want to be. However, there is an emphasis on helping them achieve independent problem-solving skills and a sense of self-determination.

Service providers working with families in the home must be trained in helping skills, including the ability to access resources, provide empathic listening, and act as a mediator and advocate for the family. Service providers should be flexible and willing to adjust schedules to fit the family's concerns. Another area of concern is environmental intrusions that interfere with the provision of regular services. These intrusions can range from minor ones, such as the use of loud entertainment devices during home visits, to life-threatening ones, such as domestic abuse. A successful home visitor uses communication strategies, collaboration skills, and flexibility in dealing with environmental intrusions. The home visitor should be aware of each agency's policy on ethical dilemmas and act quickly if a family or family member is viewed as being in danger. It is important to be respectful of cultural differences when visiting in a family's home and to respect and protect the integrity of the family. Ethical decisions during home visiting may become a necessity, and service providers should be aware of state reporting procedures regarding child abuse and neglect.

An increasing number of infants and toddlers are receiving care outside of the home. Given this increase, infants and toddlers must learn to interpret and respond to a variety of behavioral characteristics of those who care for them in many different settings (Belsky, 1988). This effort may be compounded when the infants and toddlers have disabilities.

Service providers may assist families in locating quality early childhood centers in their communities. Both the NAEYC and the DEC offer guidelines on best practices in early childhood intervention. Parents should be aware of regulations regarding staffing and staff qualifications. There may be occasions when a family chooses a child care setting that is not the best environment for the child but may be convenient to the family's home or work. In such situations, the service provider offers consultation or technical assistance. If the environment continues to be a poor match for the child's needs, the service provider may want to document his or her concerns and share them with the family.

The structure of the environment and the daily schedule are important considerations in observing and evaluating center-based programs. In addition, young children may have difficulty when there are no established routines or no clear method for handling transitions to and from activities or other environments, such as outdoor play. Several suggestions were given for helping young children make smooth transitions within early intervention or preschool programs.

Another type of transition to consider for young children is the movement from birth-to-three services to preschool services when the child turns three. This transition can present new challenges to the family and to the service providers. It is helpful when service providers inventory the future setting to assess the necessary skills the child will need. It is also a good idea to have the receiving service provider (usually a teacher) visit in the home or the child care center.

Often the process is further complicated because the agency currently working with the child may be different from the receiving agency. For example, the public health nurse may have been the primary service provider and now the child will receive services through the school system. Agencies must coordinate their efforts to help the child and the family move through the stages of transition as smoothly as possible. Finally, all stakeholders, including the family, should engage in the evaluation of the process to ensure satisfaction and implement any changes necessary for future transitions.

It is important to remember that both families and service providers may need time to say good-bye. Many families will have worked with a primary caregiver and/or service provider for three years. Families may have feelings of anger and frustration at having to develop new relationships. They may need time to build a sense of trust with the new agency and its representatives. Service providers can help families accept the changes and move on to the new program. Service providers who have not recognized their own need to say good-bye may inadvertently undermine the transition by making it more difficult for the new staff to step in. By keeping the concerns of the child and family as the primary focus of transitions, service providers can balance their loss with the family's gains.

REFERENCES

Adams, G. (1995). *How Safe? The status of state efforts to protect children in child care.* (ERIC Document Reproduction Service No. ED 406059).

Ainsworth, M. D. S., Blehar, M., Waters, E., & Wall, E. (1978). *Patterns of attachment: A psychological study of the strange situation.* Hillsdale, N.J.: Erlbaum.

Armenta, F. (1993). The family. In *First steps: A handbook for teaching young children who are visually impaired* (pp. 35–56). Los Angeles: Blind Children's Center.

Bailey, D. B., & Blasco, P. M. (1990). Parent's perspectives on a written survey of family needs. *Journal of Early Intervention, 14,* 196–203.

Bailey, D. B., & Wolery, M. (1992). *Teaching infants and preschoolers with disabilities* (2nd ed.). New York: Macmillan.

Barnas, M. V., & Cummings, E. M. (1994). Caregiver and toddlers' attachment-related behavior towards caregivers in day care. *Infant Behavior and Development 17,* 141–147.

Belsky, J. (1988). Infant day care and socioemotional development: The United States. *Journal of Child Psychology and Psychiatry, 29,* 397–406.

Blasco, P. M. (1995). Understanding the emotional and behavioral development of young children: Birth to three years. In T. J. Zirpoli (Ed). *Understanding and affecting the behavior of young children* (pp. 34–59). Englewood Cliffs, N.J.: Merrill.

Bowlby, J. (1982). *Attachment and loss.* New York: Basic Books.

Bredekamp, S. (1993). *Developmentally appropriate practice in early childhood programs serving children from birth through age 8.* Washington, D.C.: National Association for the Education of Young Children.

Bredekamp, S., (1995). What do early childhood professionals need to know and be able to do? *Young Children, 50*(2), 67–69.

Bredekamp, S., & Copple, C. (1998). Developmentally appropriate practice in early childhood programs (rev. ed.). Washington, D.C.: National Association for the Education of Young Children.

Bricker, D., Pretti-Frontczak, K., & McComas, N. (1998). *An activity-based approach to early intervention* (2nd ed.). Baltimore: Paul H. Brookes.

Bronfenbrenner, U. (1979). *The ecology of human development: Experiments by nature and design.* Cambridge: Harvard University Press.

Bruder, M. B. (1998). A collaborative model to increase the capacity of child care providers to include young children with disabilities. *Journal of Early Intervention, 21,* 177–186.

Bruder, M. B., & Staff, I. (1998). A comparison of the effects of type of classroom and service characteristics on toddlers with disabilities. *Topics in Early Childhood Special Education, 18*(1), 26–37.

Bryant, D. M., and Graham, M. A. (1993) *Implementing early intervention.* New York: Guilford Press.

Calvello, G. (1990). The art of home visiting. In F. Otto (Ed.), *Parents and visually impaired infants* (10 pp.). Louisville, Ky.: American Printing House for the Blind.

Carta, J., Elliot, M., Orth-Lopes, L., Scherer, H., Schwartz, I., & Atwater, J. (1992). *Skills for learning independence in diverse environments: Project SLIDE.* Lawrence, Kans.: The University of Kansas Juniper Gardens Children's Project.

Chan, S. (1998). Families with Asian roots. In E. W. Lynch and M. J. Hanson (Eds.), *Developing cross-cultural competence: A guide for working with young children and their families* (pp. 251–344). Baltimore: Paul H. Brookes.

Chen, D., Friedman, C. T., & Calvello, G. (1990). Learning together: A parent guide to socially based routines for visually impaired infants. In F. Otto (Ed.), *Parents and visually impaired infants* (29 pp.). Louisville, Ky.: American Printing House for the Blind.

Children's Defense Fund. (1999). *The state of America's children yearbook.* Washington, D.C.: Author.

Cook, R. E., Tessier, A., & Klein, M. D. (2000). *Adapting early childhood curricula for children in inclusive settings* (5th ed.). Englewood Cliffs, N.J.: Merrill.

Corey, G., Corey, M. S., & Callanan, P. (1993). *Issues and ethics in the helping professions* (4th ed.). Pacific Grove, Calif.: Brooks/Cole.

CEC standard for professional practice in special education (1994). Reston, Va.: Council for Exceptional Children.

Dee-Tourdot, D. S. (1995). *Classroom transition strategies in early childhood.* Unpublished master's thesis. St Paul, Minn.: University of St. Thomas.

Doss, B., & Hatcher, B. (1996). Self-determination as a family affair: Parents' perspectives on self-determination. In D. J. Sands & M. L. Wehmeyer (Eds.), *Self-determination across the lifespan* (pp. 51–63). Baltimore: Paul H. Brookes.

Dunst, C. J., Trivette, C., & Deal, A. (1988). *Enabling and empowering families: Principles and guidelines for practice.* Cambridge, Mass.: Brookline Books.

Elgas, P. M., & Barber Peltier, M. B. (1998). Jimmy's journey: Building a sense of community and self-worth through small group work. *Young Children, 53*(2), 17–21.

Fox, L., Hanline, M. F., Vail, C. O., & Galant, K. R. (1994). Developmentally appropriate practice: Applications for young children with disabilities. *Journal of Early Intervention, 18*(3), 243–257.

Fraiberg, S. H. (1959). *The magic years.* New York: Charles Scribner's Sons.

Greenman, J. (1988). *Caring spaces, learning places: Children's environments that work.* Redmond, Wash.: Exchange Press.

Hanson, M. J. (1992). Ethnic, cultural, and language diversity in intervention settings. In E. W. Lynch & M. J. Hanson (Eds.), *Developing cross-cultural competence: A guide for working with young children and their families.* Baltimore: Paul H. Brookes.

Harms, T., & Clifford, R. M. (1989). *The Family Day Care Rating Scale (FDCRS).* New York: Teachers College Press.

Harms, T., Cryer, D., & Clifford, R. M. (1990). *Infant/Toddler Environment Rating Scale (ITERS).* New York: Teachers College Press.

Howes, C., & Hamilton, C. E. (1992). Children's relationships with caregivers: Mother and child care teachers. *Child Development, 63,* 859–866.

Jones, S. N., & Meisels, S. J. (1987). Training family day care providers to work with special needs children. *Topics in Early Childhood Special Education 7*(1), 1–11.

Kjerland, L., & Corrigan Eide, K. (1990). *Project Dakota: Early intervention tailor-made.* Eagan, Minn.: Project Dakota Outreach.

Larson, N., Henthorne, M., & Plum, B. (1994). *Transition magician: Strategies for guiding young children in early childhood programs.* St. Paul, Minn.: Redleaf Press.

Levangie, P. K., Brouwer, J., McKeen, S. H., Parker, K. L., & Shelby, K. A. (1989). The effects of the standing rolling walker and two posterior rolling walkers on gait variables of normal children. *Physical and Occupational Therapy in Pediatrics, 9,* 1–17.

Lieberman, A. F. (1993). *The emotional life of the toddler.* New York: Free Press.

Lynch, E. W., & Hanson, M. J. (1998). *Developing cross-cultural competence: A guide from working with young children and their families.* Baltimore: Paul H. Brookes.

McEvoy, M. A., Fox, J. J., & Rosenberg, M. S. (1991). Organizing preschool environments: Suggestions for enhancing the development/learning of preschool children with handicaps. *Topics in Early Childhood Education, 11*(2), 18–28.

McWilliam, P. J. & Bailey, D. B. (1993). *Working together with children and families.* Baltimore: Paul H. Brookes.

Meyer, D. J., & Vadasy, P. F. (1994) *Sibshops: Workshops for siblings of children with special needs.* Baltimore: Paul H. Brookes.

National Association for the Education of Young Children (NAEYC). (1999). *Developing and implementing effective public policies to promote early childhood and school-age care program accreditation* [On-line]. Available: www.naeyc.org/accreditation/position/htm

National Center on Child Abuse and Neglect (1988). *Study of national incidence and prevalence of child abuse and neglect: 1988.* Washington, D.C.: U.S. Department of Health and Human Services.

Nwaobi, O. M., & Smith, P. D. (1986). Effect of adaptive seating on pulmonary function of children with cerebral palsy. *Developmental Medicine and Child Neurology, 28,* 351–354.

Odom, L. S., & McLean E. M. (1993). DEC recommended practices: Indicators of quality in programs for infants and young children with special needs and their families (pp. 96–103). Reston, Virg.: Division for Early Childhood of the Council for Exceptional Children.

Olds, D., & Kitzman, H. (1993). Review of research on home visiting for pregnant women and parents of young children. In R. E. Behrman (Ed.), *The future of children: Home visiting* (pp. 53–94). Los Altos, Calif.: Center for the Future of Children, David and Lucille Packard Foundation.

Olds, D. L., Henderson, C. R., Chamberlin, R., & Tatelbaum, R. (1986). Preventing child abuse and neglect: A randomized trial of nurse home visitation, *Pediatrics, 78,* 65–78.

Ostrosky, M., Skellenger, A. C., Odom, S. L., McConnell, S. R., & Peterson, C. (1994). Teachers' schedules and actual time spent in activities in preschool special education classes. *Journal of Early Intervention, 18*(1), 25–33.

Powell, D. R. (1993). Inside home visiting programs. In R. E. Behrman (Ed.), *The future of children, 3* (3) (pp. 23–38). Los Altos, Calif.: Center for the Future of Children, David and Lucille Packard Foundation.

Ramey, C. T., & Ramey, S. L. (1993). Home visiting program and the health and development of young children. In R. E. Behrman (Ed.), *The future of children: Home visiting* (pp. 127–139). Los Altos, Calif.: Center for the Future of Children, David and Lucille Packard Foundation.

Randall-David, E. (1989). *Strategies for working with culturally diverse communities and clients.* Washington, D.C.: Association for the Care of Children's Health.

Reamer, F. G. (1982). *Ethical dilemmas in social service.* New York: Columbia University Press.

Rinaldi, C. (1993). The emergent curriculum and social constructivism. In C. Edwards, L. Gandini, & G. Forman (Eds.), *The hundred languages of children* (pp. 101–111). Greenwich, Conn.: Ablex.

Rivkin, M. S. (1995). *The great outdoors: Restoring children's right to play outside.* Washington, D.C.: National Association for the Education of Young Children.

Roberts, R. N., Akers, A. L., & Behl, D. D. (1996). Family-level service coordination within home visiting programs. *Topics in Early Childhood Special Education, 16*(3), 279–301.

Roberts, R. N., Behl, D. D., & Akers, A. L. (1996). Community-level service integration within home visiting programs. *Topics in Early Childhood Special Education, 16*(3), 302–321.

Roberts, R. N., and Wasik, B. H. (1990). Home visiting programs for families with children birth to three: Results of a national survey. *Journal of Early Intervention, 14*(3), 274–284.

Rosenkoetter, E. S., Hains, H. A., Fowler, A. S. (1994). *Bridging early services for children with special needs and their families. A practical guide for transition planning.* Baltimore: Paul H. Brookes.

Sainato, D. M. (1990). Classroom transitions: Organizing environments to promote independent performance in preschool children with disabilities. *Education and Treatment of Children, 13,* 288–297.

Sainato, D. M., & Lyon, S. R. (1989). Promoting successful mainstreaming transitions for handicapped preschool children. *Journal of Early Intervention, 13,* 304–314.

Sainato, D. M., Strain, P. S., Lefebvre, D., & Rapp, N. (1987). Facilitating transition times with handicapped preschool children: A comparison between peer mediated and antecedent prompt procedures. *Journal of Applied Behavior Analysis, 20,* 285–292.

Sameroff, A. J., & Fiese, B. H. (1990). Transactional regulation and early intervention. In S. J. Meisels & J. P. Shonkoff (Eds.), *Handbook of early childhood intervention* (pp. 119–149). Cambridge: Cambridge University Press.

Turnbull, A. P., & Turnbull, H. R. (1988) Toward great expectations for vocational opportunities: Family-professional partnerships. *Mental Retardation, 26*(6), 337–342.

Turnbull, A. P., & Turnbull, H. R. (1990). *Families, professionals, and exceptionality: A special partnership* (2nd ed.). Columbus, Ohio: Merrill.

Wasik, B. H., Bryant, D. M., & Lyons, C. M. (1990). *Home visiting: Procedures for helping families.* Newbury Park, Calif.: Sage.

Wayman, K., Lynch, E., & Hanson, M. (1991). Home-based early childhood services: Cultural sensitivity in a family systems approach. *Topics in Early Childhood Special Education, 10,* 65–66.

Wesley, P., Buysse, V. (1994a). *Barriers and supports to early childhood inclusion.* Chapel Hill, N.C.: Frank Porter Graham Child Development Center.

Wesley, P., & Buysse, V. (1994b). *Self-assessment for child care professionals.* Chapel Hill, N.C.: Frank Porter Graham Child Development Center.

Willis, D. J., Holden, E. W., & Rosenberg, M. (1992). *Prevention of child maltreatment, Developmental and ecological perspectives.* New York: Wiley.

Winton, P. J. (1988). The family-focused interview: An assessment measure and goal-setting mechanism (pp. 185–205). In D. B. Bailey & R. J. Simeonsson (Eds.), *Family assessment in early intervention.* Columbus, Ohio: Merrill.

Zirpoli, S. B. (1995). Designing environments for optimal behavior. In T. J. Zirpoli (Ed.), *Understanding and affecting the behavior of young children* (pp. 122–151). Englewood Cliffs, N.J.: Merrill.

Zirpoli, T. J. (1986). Child abuse and children with handicaps. *Remedial and Special Education, 7*(2), 39–48.

Zirpoli, T. J. (1995). *Understanding and affecting the behavior of young children.* Englewood Cliffs, N.J.: Merrill.

CHAPTER SEVEN

CURRICULUM AND TEACHING STRATEGIES IN EARLY INTERVENTION

OBJECTIVES

- To apply knowledge of curriculum-recommended practices from both the Division for Early Childhood (DEC) and National Association for the Education of Young Children (NAEYC)
- To understand emergent curriculum and its implication for children with disabilities
- To understand individually appropriate skills and activities across ages for children with disabilities
- To understand the role of parents in designing and implementing curriculum objectives
- To be knowledgeable about the most current curriculum guides for infants and toddlers
- To understand the importance of skill acquisition, fluency, generalization, and maintenance
- To understand the use of milieu teaching strategies as well as prompting and modeling techniques to increase skill acquisition
- To understand the implementation of IFSP outcomes through functional curricula across settings (e.g., home, child care)
- To maintain ethical standards for instruction as specified by the Council for Exceptional Children (CEC) and the National Association for the Education of Young Children (NAEYC)

The behavior of children cannot be fragmented into isolated segments since play, exploration, and a variety of other activities continuously flow from one another.
—Hughes, 1991, p. 46

One of the most important aspects of service provision is supplying young children and their families with appropriate, functional activities that promote optimal growth and development for each child. It is important that service providers and families work together to identify outcomes that have meaning and relevance within the child's real-life environment of home and community (Cook, Tessier, & Klein, 2000; Kaiser, Hester, Harris-Solomon, & Keitiz, 1994). Young children are active learners and benefit from activities that promote multiple learning opportunities across developmental domains.

The statements above reflect the thrust of the theoretical beliefs as well as the policy that guide the development of curriculum in early intervention (Spodek & Brown, 1993). In order to meet the need of coordinated services for young children with disabilities and their families, professional organizations developed and refined standards for practice in early intervention (McLean & Odom, 1993; Odom, McLean, Johnson, & LaMontagne, 1995). The Division for Early Childhood (DEC) of the Council for Exceptional Children (CEC) offered recommended practices for curriculum and intervention (McLean and Odom, 1993) that include the following:

ECE Practice

- Support and encouragement of family values and participation
- Responsiveness to infants'/childrens' interests, preferences, motivation, interactional styles, developmental status, learning histories, cultural variables, and level of participation
- Ability to integrate information and strategies from different disciplines
- Provision of structured learning activities in all relevant environments
- Ability to select a balance between child- and adult-initiated/directed activities
- Ability to integrate skills from various domains within routine activities in the classroom
- Ability to design a plan for the acquisition (initial learning, fluency, proficiency), maintenance (retention), and generalization (application, utilization across settings) of important outcomes or goals

As stated in Chapter 6, given the number of families with both parents (over 60 percent) in the workforce (Children's Defense Fund, 1999), and the emphasis on inclusion practice for children in child care settings, it is important to consider curriculum designed for all young children in these settings. The National Association for the Education of Young Children (NAEYC) has established guidelines for curricula that promote recommended practice for all young children, including the following:

- Address a broad range of content that is relevant, engaging, and meaningful to children.
- Respect and support individual, cultural, and linguistic diversity.
- Support and encourage positive relationships with children's families.
- Provide conceptual frameworks for children so that their mental constructions based on prior knowledge and experience become more complex over time.
- Focus on a particular topic or content while allowing for integration across traditional subject-matter divisions by planning around themes and/or learning experiences that provide opportunities for rich conceptual development.
- Provide for development across domains—physical, emotional, social, cognitive, and psychological—through an integrated approach.
- Strengthen children's sense of competence and enjoyment of learning by providing experiences for them to succeed from their point of view.
- Enable teachers to adapt to individual children or groups. (Bredekamp & Rosegrant, 1995, p. 16)

EMERGENT CURRICULUM

Curriculum that develops when exploring what is "socially and culturally relevant, engaging, and important to a young child is referred to as emergent curriculum" (Gestwicki, 1999). In the field of early education, this type of curriculum is considered recommended practice. Ideas for curriculum emerge from interactions within a particular environment, by a particular group of children and adults. Although children's interests are followed, the values and concerns of all those involved (including staff and parents) help to form the classroom culture (Cassidy & Lancaster, 1993). Thus a service provider or parent may follow up on a child's ideas by introducing new materials to sustain his or her interest and engagement.

Infants and toddlers with disabilities may require more flexibility and adaptability on the part of service providers when using curricula (Wolery, Werts, & Holcombe, 1994). Ongoing opportunities for young children to learn and practice skills should be available at intervals throughout the day during naturally occurring routines (Bricker, Patti-Frontczak, & McComas, 1998). Outcomes should be incorporated into all daily activities, as specified by the family (Cook et al., 2000).

ENVIRONMENTAL CONSIDERATIONS

In Chapter 6, we discussed the impact of the environment on young children's learning. For infants and toddlers, this environment is typically the home, a child care center, or a family day care arrangement. Providing services in natural environments that are effective, efficient, and nonintrusive follows the original intent of normalization (Bailey & McWilliam, 1990). The normalization principle promotes services that build on naturally occurring routines and events in the child's life. All routines have a beginning (preparation stage), middle (participation stage), and end (termination stage) (Stremel, Matthews, Wilson, & Holston, 1992). Functional, developmentally appropriate activities can be naturally grouped into each stage. In Vignette 7.1, an interactive game between a father and his eight-month-old son demonstrates all three stages.

VIGNETTE 7.1   PEEK-A-BOO

Tony was born 10 weeks premature after a difficult labor. By three months of age, his parents knew that something was not right. Tony was very stiff and hard to hold. He was diagnosed with cerebral palsy after a visit to the local pediatrician and a follow-up visit to a developmental clinic. Tony and his parents began to receive services from an early intervention program in the home. As part of the IFSP, Susan (the occupational therapist), and the family wanted to try simple interaction games. Gary, the dad, liked to play peek-a-boo with Tony because when he smiled his entire face lit up. Today, Gary was in a hurry to get to work, but as he approached Tony, who was still lying in his crib, he looked down and smiled. Tony focused on his father's face in anticipation of interaction. Gary slowly brought his tie up to cover his eyes and said, "Peek-a-boo!" Tony instantly smiled and shrieked, ready to enter the game. He batted at the tie each time Gary brought it to his face. When the game was over, his father said gently, "All done. Daddy has to go to work. Bye-bye, big boy."

In this vignette, the simple interaction between Tony and Gary had a stage-setting time, a play time, and an ending. Although the activity was brief, it occurred in a natural setting when both Tony and Gary would be highly interested in a successful interaction. Service providers can help families realize that activities and learning experiences do not have to be regimented for most young children. Learning should be fun and conducted at a time that is convenient and natural for the family.

Today there are many commercial curriculum guides that promote functional and individually appropriate activities for young children from birth to three (Johnson-Martin, Jens, Attermeier, & Hacker, 1991; Linder, 1993; Bricker, 1993). These curricula provide excellent assistance with designing intervention strategies, but, as with other products, the user must be aware of individual differences and responses. Curriculum guides are most useful when the users can adapt the activities to reflect the individual preferences of the child and family. As Sandall (1993) stated, "Curricular sequences help interventionists to organize and plan intervention, but rigid adherence to particular sequences may be counter-productive" (p. 137).

Table 7.1 summarizes the various curricula available today.

When purchasing a curriculum, it is important to consider the long-term benefits of using the materials with children and families. Curriculum books are increasingly expensive and many require that assessment tools and videos be purchased as a package. Table 7.2 provides a guide for deciding which curriculum best fits your program and team needs.

Whether services are provided in the home or in a center-based program, planning for effective, efficient learning opportunities is important. Several steps should be taken before implementing an intervention program. The team should:

- Determine the child's present level of performance
- Identify the child's strengths, interests, and concerns
- Identify family priorities and concerns
- Inventory the child's routines and daily schedule
- Identify multiple learning opportunities throughout the day and across settings
- Identify teaching strategies and materials, making sound decisions regarding curriculum implementation
- Identify team members who can help with implementation
- Implement the intervention and monitor its effectiveness with the team

Adapted from Bailey & Wolery, 1992; Bricker, Pretti-Frontczak, & McComas, 1998.

The IFSP provides a framework for developing lesson plans based on the above components. The team, including the family, should gather ideas for activities based on the outcomes identified in the IFSP. Vignette 7.2 sets the stage for the lesson plan, which is presented in Box 7.1.

TABLE 7.1   Curriculum Guide for Early Services

TITLE	AUTHOR	DATE	PUBLISHER	AGES	PARENTS AS PARTNER	DOMAINS	STRATEGIES	ASSESS LOG
AEPS Curriculum for Birth to Three Years	Cripe, Sluntz, & Bricker	1993	Paul H. Brookes	birth–3	yes	all domains	yes	yes; separate book; also progress charts
Active Learning for Infants, Ones, Twos, and Threes	Cryer, Harms, & Bourland	1987	Addison-Wesley	birth–3	yes	communication, physical/creative	yes	no
Carolina Curriculum for Infants and Toddlers with Special Needs	Johnson-Martin, Jens, Attermier, & Hacker	1991	Paul H. Brookes	birth–3	yes	all domains	yes	yes; separate protocol; also progress charts
Creative Play Activities*	Morris & Schulz	1989	Human Kinetics Books	birth–8	yes	senses, movement, outdoor play	yes	no
Help at Home	Parks et al.	1991	Vort	birth–3	yes	all domains	yes	yes
Instructional Activities for Children at Risk	Dolimar, Boser, and Holm	1994	DLM	2–6	no	all domains	yes	no
Teaching Young Children Using Themes	Kostelnik et. al.	1991	Goodyear Books	2–6	no	themes: social science, numbers, language	no	no
Transdisciplinary Play-Based Intervention	Linder	1993	Paul H. Brookes	birth–5	yes	all domains, including mastery motivation	yes	yes; separate assessment book

*For children with disabilities

TABLE 7.2   Choosing a Curriculum

QUESTION	YES	NO
Is the curriculum developmentally and age appropriate?	____	____
What strategies for modeling does the curriculum use?	____	____
Can the curriculum be used with various group sizes?	____	____
Can the curriculum be implemented by parents/caregivers?	____	____
Is the curriculum culturally sensitive to all families?	____	____
Are assessment procedures included?	____	____
Does the curriculum include supportive, instructive materials such as a videotape or CD-ROM?	____	____
Are strategies that promote generalization and maintenance of skills included?	____	____
Is the cost of the curriculum reasonable?	____	____

Adapted from "Social Skills Curriculum Analysis" by J. Carter and G. Sugai, 1989, *Teaching Exceptional Children, 22*(1), 36–39.

VIGNETTE 7.2   JOHN AND MOMMA

John is a 13-month-old with Klippel-Feil syndrome. He has congenital fusion of the first through fourth cervical vertebrae. This results in very limited range of motion of his neck. Associated conditions include a soft cleft palate and maldevelopment of the inner ear. Thus John was also diagnosed with a severe sensorineural hearing loss and now has a body-mounted hearing aid. John's use of the body aid is inconsistent due to his activity as an infant. He is starting to pull to a stand and uses his hands to manipulate toys. He uses pointing, head nodding, and natural gestures to get his needs met. He has learned a few signs, including "Mom," "Dad," and "bird" (the family pet).

The service provider and John's family planned some activities that could easily be implemented at home, in a child care center, or in the community. Since both parents work full-time, the service provider gave them a copy of the plan so the family day care provider could also try it.

The lesson plan was designed to enhance both infant and family participation. The service provider used visual and auditory cueing as well as a natural game between participants. The activity is easy to implement across environments and results in a pleasurable interaction for both the mother and the child. In addition, the materials used are generally found in the home and are not costly or difficult to obtain. Service providers should always consider both cost and familiarity of use when choosing materials for young children and families.

BOX 7.1

LESSON PLAN FOR JOHN AND HIS FAMILY

Outcome: To help John notice and turn to auditory, visual, and tactile events.

Name of activity: Where is Momma?

Purpose of the activity: To improve the child's orientation to auditory, visual, and tactile stimuli in order to comprehend and develop verbal language and/or sign language.

Materials: rattles, drum, music box, squeeze toys

Procedures:
1. Position the child on the floor on his tummy (prone) or back (supine), sitting or in an infant seat.
2. Mother presents a noisemaking object (i.e., bell, rattle, squeeze toy, drum) close to child and within visual range (approximately three feet).
3. Mother holds the object up to her face and encourages the child to make eye contact through use of vocal cues: "Where's Momma?"
4. After the child makes eye contact, verbally praise the child, nod head, and then touch the child's hands or feet.
5. Allow the child to touch the object and demonstrate to the child how to make the object produce a sound.
6. Incorporate a song to the tune of "Thumbkin," using different voice intonations and pitch to encourage play.
   Where is Momma?
   Where is Momma?
   Here I am.
   Here I am.
   Shake the rattle for me.
   Shake the rattle for me.
   Give it to John.

Variations:
1. The caregiver approaches the child from behind or to the side and calls his name. A noisemaking toy can be used as an additional auditory stimulus.
2. The caregiver moves into the child's line of sight while saying, "Where's Momma?"

For children with severe to profound hearing loss, use a vibrating tactile cue, for example, knocking on the wall, stamping your foot on each step while calling his name and using sign language.

Contributed by Diane Dee-Tourdot, Minneapolis, Minn.: Minneapolis Public Schools, Birth-to-three team.

Other considerations for selecting materials include the following:

- Do they focus on functional behaviors and skills that the child needs to be successful in multiple environments (home, community, center-based program)?
- Are they multipurpose and adaptable? Do they elicit a range of developmentally appropriate responses?
- Do they promote social interaction with either a caregiver or other children?
- Do they promote the efficient learning of important outcomes?
- Are they culturally sensitive and relevant to the individual child?

(Adapted from Bailey & McWilliam, 1990; Rettig, Kallam, & McCarthy-Salm, 1993)

All intervention strategies should result in skill acquisition, fluency, maintenance, and generalization. Skill acquisition refers to the learning of new skills. Fluency refers to a smooth demonstration of the new skill at each observation (Bailey & Wolery, 1992). Once the child has learned the skill, he or she needs to show that the skill can be used in other situations with other people. Maintenance refers to the degree of change in behavior over time following skill acquisition (Zirpoli & Melloy, 1996). Generalization refers to the degree of change in behavior that transfers to other settings, situations, and materials. Maintenance and generalization may not occur spontaneously and must be included in the design of an instructional strategy. The service provider can provide natural opportunities for generalizing in other settings and to other persons or materials.

TEACHING STRATEGIES TO ENHANCE CURRICULUM DEVELOPMENT

In order to establish generalization and maintenance, teaching strategies have been developed to prompt and reinforce the behavior of young children. According to Wolery, Werts, and Holcombe (1994), "although a balance should be maintained between the child- and teacher-initiated activities, the value of teacher-guided learning is especially important for young children with disabilities." (p. 7) This statement seems applicable to all service providers working with young children with disabilities and their families. For many children with disabilities, strategies that include behavioral dimensions such as intermittent reinforcement, variable stimuli, and trials to increase skill acquisition may be necessary. Service providers can provide a scaffold to help the child maximize his or her potential across developmental domains. As discussed in Chapter 4, Vygotsky (1962) advocated the "zone of proximal development" as the window in which the child can learn and continue to grow. If we encourage the child to perform at a level too far above or too far below his or her ability, we miss this window of learning opportunity. *Insight / connection*

Direct Instruction Versus Naturalistic Teaching Approaches

The direct instruction method tends to be adult-directed and offers little room for flexibility in terms of instructional objectives. However, many of the more recent activity-based interventions combine strategies from direct instruction with strategies for early childhood (Bricker et al., 1992). These strategies include various prompting systems and other methods for eliciting appropriate responses. It is important when choosing strategies to apply the most naturalistic approach with young children. Naturalistic teaching approaches occur in the natural environment, can be child- or adult-initiated, and use natural consequences (Kaiser, Ostrosky, & Alpert, 1993).

System of Least Prompts

The system of least prompts is a response-prompting procedure that is effective in teaching a variety of skills linked together through a series of events (Wolery, Ault, & Doyle, 1992). This technique consists of a target stimulus, a prompt hierarchy of least-to-most assistance, an opportunity to respond independently at each level of the hierarchy, and an opportunity for positive reinforcement (Wolery et al., 1992).

An example of the least prompt system is described in Vignette 7.3.

VIGNETTE 7.3   HOLD YOUR HEAD UP

During a home visit, Mary, the occupational therapist, worked with Vicki, the mother, to help Kenisha hold her head up when lying on her tummy (prone). Mary would place a bright red toy apple in front of Kenisha. Then she gently shook the apple so it would make a soft chime. Kenisha showed signs of alertness but did not pick up her head. Mary shook the apple again while Vicki said, "Kenisha, look at my apple." When Kenisha still did not move, Mary waited 10 seconds and then placed her hands gently on Kenisha's shoulders, repeating, "Kenisha, look at my apple." She waited another 10 seconds for a response, then she gently applied pressure to Kenisha's shoulders and guided her head up. Once Kenisha had lifted her head, Mary placed one hand on her bottom to help maintain stability in the head-up position.

This strategy can be used with a task analysis so that an outcome objective can be broken down into a series of simple steps. The number of steps and the difficulty of each step are individually tailored to the needs of the child. In Vignette 7.3, Mary used a system of prompts, starting with a simple auditory cue (the least prompt), then adding a verbal cue, and finally providing physical assistance, to achieve the objective. During this task, the least intrusive prompt was used first. In other prompt systems, the most intrusive prompt may be used first and then faded over time. Finally, the task was a natural, pleasurable activity for Kenisha and her mother.

Simultaneous Prompting

Another natural teaching strategy that can fit into a natural sequence of events is simultaneous prompting (MacFarlane, Smith, Schuster, & Stevens, 1993), in which the service provider presents a prompt simultaneously with the target stimulus. The child is given an opportunity to respond and a correct response is reinforced. At other times, the service provider presents the target stimulus without the prompt to examine the child's response.

Violation of Expectancy

Another strategy that has been used successfully with young children is called violation of expectancy. The service provider may do something incorrectly or out of order for a routine (Bailey & Wolery, 1992), such as helping a toddler to put on a coat by holding the coat upside down. The adult might say, "Is this where your coat goes?" Toddlers will recognize the game and happily join in the fun. This is an excellent way to teach self-help skills. You can easily continue the game by asking, "Where do you put your [hat, gloves, etc.]?"

For this strategy to work, the child needs a solid cognitive understanding of the task. It will not work with a child who does not have the cognitive capability to understand change in routines and should not be used with children who are easily upset by a change in routine. For example, a child with autism may become confused and upset rather than participate in a learning opportunity.

Graduated Guidance

This strategy is more intrusive than some of the other strategies discussed above. However, graduated guidance has been used to teach children with autism to follow a photo schedule and remain on task for longer periods of time (MacDuff, Kasntz, & McClannahan, 1993). This procedure may require much assistance in the beginning. The amount of help is determined by observing the child's response (Noonan & McCormick, 1993). An infant with low muscle tone or poor muscle strength may need help holding a rattle. The service provider might bring the rattle into view and wait to see if the infant will reach for it. If the infant is unable to reach for the toy, the service provider may then use a physical prompt by placing her hand under the infant's elbow to move the hand forward. If the infant is unable to grasp the rattle, she may help the infant hold it by closing her hand over the infant's hand. As the infant becomes stronger, the amount of assistance is decreased.

MILIEU TECHNIQUES

Milieu teaching is a naturalistic approach that encompasses three types of teaching strategies: incidental teaching, mand (task or request)-model, and time delay. Intervention includes teaching opportunities that are infused into typical conversations that follow the child's interest (Warren, 1992). Milieu strategies have been used to teach parents methods of instruction for their infants and toddlers with language delays (Alpert & Kaiser, 1992; Kaiser, Hemmeter, Ostrosky, Alpert, & Hancock, 1995; Simser, 1993) and with children who have disabilities (Warren, Yoder, Gazdag, Kim, & Jones, 1993). Service providers trained in using environmental strategies with milieu teaching that incorporate augmentative communication systems have observed increases in total communication and the use of targets in three preschool-age children (Kaiser, Ostrosky, & Alpert, 1993). Although some parent training programs have been successful, it is important to include family-guided decision-making when designing any intervention program, and especially when developing strategies for use in daily routines (Stremel et al., 1992).

Milieu strategies that have been used to increase social interactions among infants and toddlers with disabilities include those designed to:

- use duplicate toys to encourage parallel play and modeling (imitation)
- use "social" toys (dolls, blocks, bells)
- use words to describe children's play
- use a peer model to demonstrate a play or interaction skill
- facilitate helping relationships among children

    Adapted from Wittmer & Peterson, 1992.

Incidental Teaching

Hart and Risley (1975) originally described incidental teaching as the mutual interaction between an adult and a child that arises naturally within the context of a situation and/or setting. The interaction is child-initiated with the adult responding to the child's interest and cues.

Mand-Model

In this strategy the adult initiates a mand (task or request) related to something of interest to the child. The strategy builds on the child's focus of attention to guide the interaction. For example, a toddler is playing with a red truck by pushing it around a play town set up on the floor. The caregiver approaches and observes the child as she imitates a motor sound. The child looks up and continues to make motor noises. The caregiver smiles and says, "Oh, I see you are playing with something." The child responds by saying, "Car." The caregiver says, "That's right, car," and then expands the conversation: "You have a red car, I have a blue car. Where shall we go today?" If the child does not respond to the initial request, the teacher models the appropriate response. This strategy differs slightly from incidental teaching because the adult does not wait for the child to initiate the interaction (Noonan & McCormick, 1993).

Time Delay

This strategy can be used to increase the amount of time between the introduction of the stimulus and a cue. A cue is a type of prompt that gives a specific command. For example, a parent may say to his toddler, "Eat your food, please." He then waits five seconds before guiding the child's hand to pick up the food. For a child with a severe physical disability, a task analysis can be used to guide him through the steps necessary to bring food to his mouth (see Table 7.3).

When implementing a plan, the team needs to decide the amount of time between each step, and a method for handling correct and incorrect responses. By increasing the amount of time before the prompt is introduced, the service provider can gradually reduce the level of assistance (Bailey & Wolery, 1992; Snell,

TABLE 7.3 Task Analysis for a Toddler with Motor Difficulties

James will bring food to his mouth.

1. Give a verbal cue: *James, pick up the banana.*
2. Physically assist James as he picks up the food.
3. Give a verbal cue: *James, eat your food.*
4. Physically guide James's hand with the food to his mouth.
5. Give a verbal cue: *James, eat your food.*
6. Physically guide James's hand with the food to open his lips.
7. Give a verbal cue: *James, chew your food.*

1987). With infants and toddlers, verbal praise that specifies the correct response is a natural reinforcer. For example, the service provider or parent might say, "Good for you! You put the top on the box." If the child does not perform a step within a predetermined period of time, the adult provides assistance, either verbal, physical, or both, and then continues with the next step.

Naturalistic Time Delay.   Time delay can be used to increase the amount of time between a natural prompt and a teaching prompt (Bailey & Wolery, 1992). For example, a toddler wants more milk and bangs her cup against the table. Her mother says, "Do you want more milk? Say, 'More.'" At the next occasion the child bangs her cup on the table, and the mother waits five seconds before introducing the prompt, "Say 'More.'" She continues to increase the time by five seconds until the toddler says, "More" by herself to the request "Do you want more milk?"

Whatever strategy is used, the team should plan for inappropriate responses. Although reinforcement is a powerful tool for teaching new behaviors, very young children do not have the ability to understand the meaning of withholding of reinforcement for inappropriate behavior. Service providers and parents may instead redirect the child from an inappropriate behavior. For example, a toddler who hits another toddler at the snack table may need to be reminded, "No, hitting, hitting hurts," and then be redirected toward a more constructive activity with a statement such as "Let's pour more milk for Amber."

2, Redirect vs Distract ?,

PROMPTING STRATEGIES TO INCREASE PLAY BEHAVIOR

Strategies that can be used to increase play behavior include pointing to a toy, placing a toy in front of the child and removing other materials, offering the toy, and restructuring the toy's configuration (e.g., if the toy is upside down, turning it right side up). If the child does not respond actively, the adult can model a use for the toy, then ask the child to do it, or activate a toy partially and then let the child complete the task (this is called partial participation) (Lifter, 1993).

ACTIVITY-BASED INTERVENTION

Activity-based intervention is a curriculum approach that was adapted from the instruction of children with severe disabilities (Bruder, 1997). Bricker, Pretti-Frontczak, and McComas (1998) designed activity-based strategies that (1) promote active involvement of the learner; (2) facilitate learning through routines and natural opportunities; and (3) enhance learning through meaningful and functional activities. In addition, activity-based intervention utilizes a behavioral approach by defining antecedents and consequences of behavior and collecting data on a weekly, quarterly, and annual basis.

FAMILY-CENTERED CURRICULUM

Bailey (1997) described an adult-centered view of curriculum content. He suggested that curriculum activities are based on what the adult does or what the environment provides. Alternatively, a child-centered view focuses on what the child perceives or experiences. Bruder (1997) emphasized the importance of the family role in curriculum. A family-centered curriculum would include what the child and family members perceive or experience.

PARENTS AS PARTNERS

Most curricula designed for early intervention are child-centered. The tasks and outcomes designed in these curricula are focused on increasing the child's skills across developmental domains. However, if parents and other caregivers are to be included as partners in early intervention, then curricula should include the family as part of the intervention plan.

A part of curricula unique to early intervention are materials that include parent-child interaction. Since Bell's (1968) seminal paper on parent-infant reciprocity, both researchers and practitioners have recognized the importance of the partnership between the parent and the child during interaction. There needs to be a match between parental intent and the child's response or vice versa for a successful interaction (Sameroff & Fiese, 1990). The transactional model of development described the parent and child as active participants who continue to affect one another's behaviors and renegotiate the partnership (Sameroff & Chandler, 1975; Sameroff & Fiese, 1990).

Early research on parent-child interactions and on children with disabilities often described parents as ineffective partners who could not "read" their child's behaviors and interactive style. However, more recent studies have shown that many parents are able to match their interactive behavior to the needs of their child despite the disability (Baird, Haas, McCormick, Carruth, & Turner, 1992; Blasco, Hrncir, & Blasco, 1990; Hauser-Cram, 1996). The assessment of parent-child interaction was discussed in Chapter 5.

In reviewing the extensive literature on parent-child interaction, it is evident that parents' education and socioeconomic status (SES) are related to levels of appropriate developmental play for children at risk, including children who were born premature and had low birthweight (Bailey, 1997; Fewell, Casal, Glick, Wheeden, & Spiker, 1996). The impact of prenatal (e.g., substance abuse, smoking) and postnatal risk factors (attachment issues) were discussed in Chapters 2, 3, and 4 respectively.

Families will vary in how they use both formal and informal resources and in how they define their concerns to other members of the intervention team. In addition, cultural differences may dictate interactive behavior that may not be viewed as appropriate by members of the mainstream culture.

Thus targeting family members for intervention remains controversial in the early intervention field. As members of the team, should parents determine to what extent they want to be involved directly in intervention? This question is asked as teams are struggling to meet both child and family outcomes. An additional concern is that some team members do not receive training in parent-child interaction and attachment theory. Thus it is important to seek the help of qualified personnel who have had training in both adult learning theory and family-child interaction.

Despite the controversy, service providers working with families cannot ignore a mismatch in parent-child interactive styles. Baird and colleagues (1992) used videotaping to help parents to examine their own interactive style and to identify those behaviors they would like to change and those behaviors of their child that are causing concerns. This strategy gives the interventionist the opportunity to provide recommendations without giving unsolicited advice about the partnership.

There is very little research on the impact of parent-child interaction on curricula. However, several commercial products are available that are geared toward helping parents work with their babies. These include the Partners for Learning (Sparling & Lewis, 1984); Help at Home (Parks et al., 1998); and Best Beginning (Hussey-Gardner, 1999). Both of these curriculum guides offer suggestions and guidelines for understanding the infant's behavior.

CURRICULUM INVENTORY

Even when you have found a curriculum that seems tried and true, it is important to evaluate it periodically to see what the child and family have gained from the experience. Some good questions to think about include:

- What are the features or sensory modalities of the materials that interest and sustain the attention of this child?
- What are the features or sensory modalities that do not attract or sustain the attention of this child?
- Are you currently using verbal or physical prompts to support appropriate problem-solving and engagement in activities? Should you fade support or add support in some areas?
- What level of mastery motivation is exhibited by the child? Does the child persist at problem-solving tasks, give up easily, or become frustrated when he cannot complete a task?
- Does the child exhibit "mastery pleasure" when a task is completed?
- Does the child ask for help (either verbal or physical) when appropriate?
- Does the family find the materials and tasks to be meaningful and appropriate?
- Do the materials and strategies reflect culturally responsive and developmentally appropriate content?

The information needed for a curriculum inventory can be gathered through multiple methods of observation. Examples of informal observation methods include the use of photographs, video, tape recordings, and anecdotal records. In Chapter 5, the various methods of using observations as assessment tools were discussed. These methods include checklists, rating scales, observation narratives (including anecdotal records), informal and formal assessment tools, and samples of children's work (portfolio).

In addition, many curriculum guides have assessment packets that include daily and long-term evaluation of skill acquisition. It is equally important to develop a generalization and maintenance plan. No skill is truly learned unless the child can generalize to other settings, behaviors, and persons. The following strategies promote generalization and maintenance of new behaviors:

- Provide learning opportunities within settings where the behavior is likely to occur and across multiple settings; avoid artificial and isolated teaching of skills.
- Implement learning opportunities among all caregivers who have regular contact with the child.
- Use natural stimuli that occur in the child's natural environment.
- Reinforce generalization and maintenance by telling the child when you notice generalization has occurred. For example, say, "That's right, you use the cup to drink."

All curricula and materials should be evaluated by the team on a continuing basis. This can be done by using formative evaluation, that is, data collected on a daily basis regarding progress of the individual child using a specific curriculum. Service providers should also collect summative evaluation information. This information looks at the overall effectiveness of the curriculum with groups of children. Both forms of evaluation will help the team make informed decisions regarding curriculum.

In providing services, professionals should be careful to offer only those services for which they are trained (Wasik, Bryant, & Lyons, 1990). This ethical standard also applies to implementing curricula. This is not to say that service providers should not engage in role release but that they should be well trained before implementing an activity.

When working in the home, such situations are inevitable, and professionals must be prepared for them (Wasik et al., 1990). Each service provider must be familiar with state and federal regulations regarding children's welfare. It is also helpful to meet with team members trained in crisis intervention. Every team should have a social worker and/or psychologist available for consultation. The impact of ethical issues and standards for ethical conduct were discussed in Chapter 6. It is important to apply these same standards to curricula and materials.

Service providers need to be aware of cultural differences and adapt curricula and materials accordingly. There are several resources available that address cultural diversity in curriculum. One important resource is CLAS (Cultural and Linguistically Appropriate Services, Early Childhood Research Institute, Office of Special Education Programs). This federally funded project provides descriptions and reviews of current early childhood materials and the potential usefulness of these materials with culturally and linguistically diverse children and families. Information is easily accessed through the Web site at *http://www.uius.edu/clas.* Some suggested questions for service providers include:

- How closely does the community you serve resemble those for whom the material was developed?
- Is the material based on assumptions, beliefs, or values that are agreeable to most members of the community you serve?
- Are the family or child roles described in the material consistent with those found in the community you serve?
- If the material is presented in a language other than English, does the language style and dialect match that of the community to be served?

Questions for family members include the following:

- How closely does your family or child resemble those for whom the material was developed?
- If you see many differences, how important are these differences to you?
- Does the material contain assumptions, beliefs, or values that are similar to those of your family?
- Does the language style and dialect match what your family uses?
- Does the material describe provider, family, or child roles that are similar to those in your family?
- Do you have the time, skills, and resources to use this material?

From CLAS (Culturally & Linguistically Appropriate Services) Web site.

TABLE 7.4   Culturally Sensitive Services

1. Reflect on your own cultural heritage and how it influences your life and work.
2. Build on your awareness of other cultures through literature, the media, community events.
3. Meet community leaders of various cultural groups and seek out friends from diverse cultural backgrounds.
4. Conduct a community inventory of the institutions (e.g., churches, food stores, clinics) that are utilized by families from culturally diverse backgrounds.
5. Learn to understand the communicative style of various cultures but don't overgeneralize.
6. Listen to families and respect their choices.
7. Help others see cultural differences as strengths, not weaknesses.
8. Ask questions when you are unsure or unclear. Families will forgive you for not knowing everything.
9. Seek out interpreters with a good understanding of early childhood development.
10. Learn to interpret both verbal and non-verbal communication.

Information from *Developing Cross-Cultural Competence: A Guide for Working with Young Children and Their Families,* 2nd ed., by E. W. Lynch and M. J. Hanson, 1998, Baltimore: Paul H. Brookes; and *Strategies for Working with Culturally Diverse Communities and Clients,* by E. Randall-David, 1992, Bethesda: The Association for the Care of Children's Health.

Table 7.4 provides cultural-sensitivity suggestions for service providers. These strategies help one to become comfortable with his or her own cultural identity.

Although most curricula designed today advocate culturally sensitive material and activities, it is still possible to find materials that are insensitive to different cultural groups or family definitions. This is particularly true when choosing computer software for very young children. Most software is developed for traditional Caucasian, middle-class families, and these programs can inadvertently be insensitive to cultural differences. For example, service providers in one Midwestern town were unable, due to a schoolwide policy, to use software they purchased to teach language skills because there were no culturally diverse role models in the program. It is a good idea to preview materials before using them with families.

SUMMARY

This chapter examined current practices in developing curricula for service providers working with young children and their families. In order to make an impact on a child's individual learning styles, curricula must be flexible, functional, and adaptable. Organizations that support the education of young children, including NAEYC and DEC, offer guidelines on curricula. Whether new to the field or practicing for several years, service providers need to be aware of recommended practices and keep current with changing curricula trends. As pointed out by Cook, Tessier, & Klein (2000), early intervention and early childhood special education are evolving fields. Each decade brings new challenges and new ideas for curriculum development.

Today, many commercial curriculum guides promote functional and individually appropriate activities for young children from birth to age three. It is important to be flexible and adapt materials and activities to individual needs. Service providers should involve family members in planning and implementing services as stipulated by federal law. The IFSP is a document that is family-driven. There should be a match between IFSP-identified outcomes and the choice of curriculum materials.

Service providers should continue to reflect on their own teaching strategies to see if they are meeting the needs of each child and family. Intervention strategies should be recorded through one or several methods of observation. Record keeping and reevaluation are important for meeting the changing needs of children and their families.

Service providers should be mindful of ethical standards within their affiliated organizations, as well as state and federal guidelines. They should also attend to cultural differences when choosing activities and materials. Planning ahead with the family will help avoid potentially embarrassing sessions in which activities and materials are deemed culturally offensive by a family. Using activities and materials that are culturally sensitive and individually appropriate provides current recommended practices in the field today.

REFERENCES

Alpert, C., & Kaiser, A. (1992). Training parents as milieu language teachers. *Journal of Early Intervention, 16,* 31–52.

Bailey, D. B. (1997). Curriculum alternatives for infants and preschoolers. In M. J. Guralnick (Ed.),. *The effectiveness of early intervention* (pp. 227–247). Baltimore: Paul H. Brookes.

Bailey, D. B., & McWilliam, R. A. (1990). Normalizing early intervention. *Topics in Early Childhood Special Education, 10,* 33–47.

Bailey, D. B., McWilliam, R. A., Ware, W. B., & Burchinal, M. A. (1993). The social interactions of toddlers and preschoolers in same-age and mixed-age play groups. *Journal of Applied Developmental Psychology, 14,* 261–276.

Bailey, D. B., & Wolery, M. (1992*). Teaching infants and preschoolers with disabilities* (2nd ed.). Columbus, Ohio: Merrill.

Baird, S. M., Haas, L., McCormick, K., Carruth, C., & Turner, K. D. (1992). Approaching an objective system for observation and measurement: Infant-parent social interaction code. *Topics in Early Childhood Special Education, 12,* 544–571.

Bell, R. Q. (1968). A reinterpretation of the direction of effects in studies of socialization. *Psychological Review, 75,* 1171–1190.

Berk, L. E., & Winsler, A. (1995). *Scaffolding children's learning: Vygotsky and early childhood education*. Washington, D.C.: National Association for the Education of Young Children.

Blasco, P. M., Bailey, D. B., & Burchinal, M. A. (1993). Dimensions of mastery in same-age and mixed-age integrated classrooms. *Early Childhood Research Quarterly, 8,* 193–206.

Blasco, P. M., Hrncir, E., & Blasco, P. B. (1990). The contribution of maternal involvement to mastery performance in infants with cerebral palsy. *Journal of Early Intervention, 14,* 161–174.

Bredekamp, S. (1993). The relationship between early childhood education and early childhood special education: Healthy marriage or family feud? *Topics in Early Childhood Special Education, 13,* 258–273.

Bredekamp, S., & Rosegrant, T. (Eds.). (1995). *Reaching potentials: Transforming early childhood curriculum and assessment* (Vol. 2). Washington, D.C.: National Association for the Education of Young Children.

Bricker, D. (1993). *Assessment, evaluation, and programming system for infants and young children* (Vol. 1). *AEPS measurement for birth to three.* Baltimore: Paul H. Brookes.

Bricker, D., Pretti-Frontczak, K., & McComas, N. (1998). *An activity-based approach to early intervention* (2nd ed.). Baltimore: Paul H. Brookes.

Bruder, M. B. (1997). Curriculum for children with disabilities. In M. Guralnick (Ed.), *The effectiveness of early intervention* (pp. 523–548). Baltimore: Paul H. Brookes.

Cassidy, D., & Lancaster, C. (1993, September). The grassroots curriculum: A dialogue between children and teachers. *Young Children, 48*(5), 47–51.

Children's Defense Fund. (1999). *The state of America's children yearbook.* Washington, D.C.: Author.

Cook, R. E., Tessier, A., & Klein, M. D. (2000). *Adapting early childhood curricula for children in inclusive settings* (5th ed). Englewood Cliffs, N.J.: Merrill.

Cripe, J., Slentz, K., & Bricker, D. (1993). *Assessment, evaluation, and planning system for infants and children: Curriculum for birth to three years.* Baltimore: Paul H. Brookes.

Dolinar, K., Boser, C., & Holm, E. (1994). *Learning through play: Curriculum and activities for the inclusive classroom.* Albany: Delmar.

Doyle, P., Gast, D., Wolery, M., Ault, M., & Farmer, J. (1990). Use of constant time delay in small group instruction: A study of observational and incidental learning. *Journal of Special Education, 23,* 369–385.

Fewell, R. R., Casal, S. G., Glick, M. P., Wheeden, C. A., & Spiker, D. (1996). Maternal education and maternal responsiveness as predictors of play competence in low birth weight, premature infants: A preliminary report. *Developmental and Behavioral Pediatrics, 17,* 100–104.

Fox, L., & Hanline, M. (1993). A preliminary evaluation of learning within developmentally appropriate early childhood settings. *Topics in Early Childhood Special Education, 13,* 308–327.

Gestwicki, C. (1999). *Developmentally appropriate practice: Curriculum and development in Early Education* (2nd ed.). Albany, N.Y.: Delmar.

Hanson, M. J., & Lynch, E. W. (1989). *Early intervention: Implementing child and family services for infants and toddlers who are at-risk or disabled.* Austin, Tex.: Pro-ed.

Hart, B., & Risley, T. (1975). Incidental teaching language in the pre-school. *Journal of Applied Behavior Analysis, 8,* 411–420.

Hauser-Cram, P. (1996). Mastery motivation in toddlers with developmental disabilities. *Child Development, 67,* 236–248.

Hughes, F. P. (1991). *Children, play, and development.* Boston: Allyn & Bacon.

Hussey-Gardner, B. (1999). *Best beginning: Helping parents make a difference through individualized anticipatory guidance (Birth to three).* Palo Alto, Calif.: Vort.

Johnson-Martin, N., Jens, K., Attermeier, S., & Hacker, B. (1991). *The Carolina curriculum for infants and toddlers with special needs* (2nd ed.). Baltimore: Paul H. Brookes.

Kaiser, A. P., Hemmeter, M. L., Ostrosky, M. M., Alpert, C. L., & Hancock, T. B. (1995). The effects of group training and individual feedback on parent use of milieu teaching. *Journal of Childhood Communication Disorders, 16,* 39–48.

Kaiser, A., Hester, P., Harris-Solomon, A., & Keitiz, A. (June, 1994). *Enhanced milieu teaching: An analysis of applications by interventionists and classroom teachers.* Paper presented at the 118th Annual Meeting of the American Association on Mental Retardation, Boston, Mass.

Kaiser, A. P., Ostrosky, M. M., & Alpert, C. L. (1993). Training teachers to use environmental arrangement and milieu teaching with nonvocal preschool children. *Journal of the Association for Persons with Severe Handicaps, 18*(3), 188–199.

Lifter, K., Sulzer-Azaroff, B., Anderson, S., & Cowdery, G. (1993). Teaching play activities to preschool children with disabilities: The importance of developmental considerations. *Journal of Early Intervention, 2,* 139–159.

Linder, T. (1993). *Transdisciplinary play-based intervention: Guidelines for developing a meaningful curriculum for young children.* Baltimore: Paul H. Brookes.

Lynch, E. W., & Hanson, M. J. (1998). *Developing cross-cultural competence: A guide for working with young children and their families* (2nd ed.). Baltimore: Paul H. Brookes.

MacDuff, G., Kasntz, P., & McClannahan, L. (1993). Teaching children with autism to use photographic activity schedules: Maintenance and generalization of complex response chains. *Journal of Applied Behavior Analysis, 26* (1), 89–97.

MacFarlane-Smith, J., Schuster, J., & Stevens, K. (1993). Using simultaneous prompting to teach expressive object identification to preschoolers with developmental delays. *Journal of Early Intervention, 17,* 50–60.

McCollum, J. A., & Stayton, V. D. (1985). Infant/parent interaction: Studies and intervention guidelines based on the SIAI model. *Journal of the Division of Early Childhood, 9,* 125–135.

McLean, M. E, & Odom, S. L. (1993). Practices for young children with and without disabilities: A comparison of DEC and NAEYC identified practices. *Topics in Early Childhood Special Education, 13*(3), 274–292.

Noonan, M. J., & McCormick, L. (1993). *Early intervention in natural environments: Methods and procedures.* Belmont, Calif.: Brooks/Cole.

Odom, S. L., McLean, M. E., Johnson, L. J., & LaMontagne, M. J. (1995). Recommended practices in early childhood special education: Validation and current use. *Journal of Early Intervention, 19*(1), 1–17.

Parks, S., Furuno, S., O'Reilly, K., Hosaka, C., Inatsuka, T., & Zeisloft-Talby, B. (1998). *Hawaii early learning profile at home.* Palo Alto, Calif.: Vort.

Rettig, M., Kallam, M., McCarthy-Salm, K. (1993). The effect of social and isolate toys on social interactions of preschool-aged children. *Education and Training in Mental Retardation, 28,* 258–256.

Sameroff, A. J., & Chandler, M. J. (1975). Reproductive risk and the continuum of caretaking casualty. In F. D. Horowitz, M. Hetherington, S. Scarr-Salapatek, & G. Siegel (Eds.), *Review of child development literature* (pp. 187–244). Chicago: University of Chicago Press.

Sameroff, A. J., & Fiese, B. H. (1990). Transactional regulation and early intervention. In S. J. Meisels & J. P. Shonkoff (Eds.), *Handbook of early childhood intervention* (pp. 119–149). Cambridge: Cambridge University Press.

Sandall, S. (1993). Curricula for early intervention. In W. Brown, S. K. Thurman, & L. F. Pearl (Eds.), *Family-centered early intervention with infants and toddlers: Innovative cross-disciplinary approaches* (pp. 129–151). Baltimore: Paul H. Brookes.

Simser, J. (1993). Auditory-verbal intervention: Infants and toddlers. *Volta-Review, 95*(3), 217–229.

Snell, M. E. (1987). *Systematic instruction of persons with handicaps.* Columbus, Ohio: Merrill.

Sparling, J., & Lewis, I. (1984). *Partners for learning.* Lewisville, N.C.: Kaplan Press.

Spodek, B., & Brown, P. C. (1993). Curriculum alternatives in early childhood education. A historical perspective. In B. Spodek (Ed.), *Curriculum alternatives in early childhood education: A historical perspective* (pp. 91–104). New York: Macmillan.

Stremel, K., Matthews, P., Wilson, R., Holston, J. (December, 1992). *Facilitating infant/toddler skills in family-child routines.* Paper presented at the Division for Early Childhood Conference, Washington, DC.

Vygotsky, L. S. (1962). *Thought and language* (E. Hanfmann & G. Vaker, Trans.) Cambridge: Massachusetts Institute of Technology Press.

Warren, S. F. (1992). Facilitating basic vocabulary acquisition with milieu teaching procedures. *Journal of Early Intervention, 16*(3), 235–251.

Warren, S. F., Yoder, P. J., Gazdag, G. E., Kim, K., & Jones, H. A. (1993). Facilitating prelinguistic communication skills in young children with developmental delay. *Journal of Speech and Hearing Research, 36,* 83–97.

Wasik, B. H., Bryant, D. M., & Lyons, C. M. (1990). *Home visiting: Procedures for helping families.* Newbury Park, Calif.: Sage.

Wittmer, D., & Peterson, S. (1992). Social development and integration: Facilitating the prosocial development of typical and exceptional infants and toddlers in group settings. *Zero to Three, 12,* 14–20.

Wolery, M., Ault, M. J., & Doyle, P. M. (1992). *Teaching students with moderate to severe disabilities: Use of response prompting strategies.* White Plains, N.Y.: Longman.

Wolery, M., Werts, M., & Holcombe, A. (1994). Current practices with young children who have disabilities: Placement, assessment, and instructional issues. *Focus on Exceptional Children, 26*(6), 1–12.

Zirpoli, T. J., & Melloy, K. J. (2001). *Behavior management: Applications for teachers* (3rd ed.). Upper Saddle River, N.J.: Merrill.

CHAPTER EIGHT

MEDICAL CONSIDERATIONS

PETER A. BLASCO, M.D.

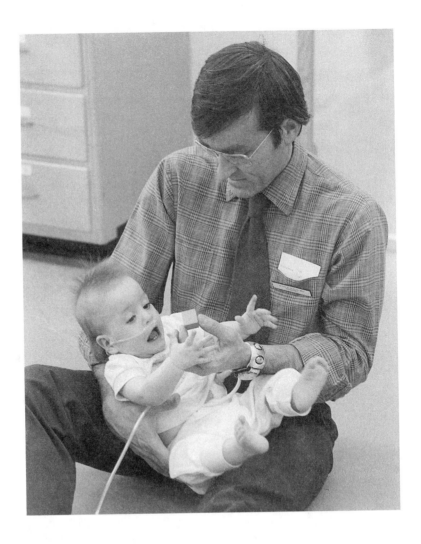

OBJECTIVES

- To recognize the different patterns of growth deficiency and their implications
- To review the spectrum of neurodevelopmental disabilities
- To review in depth the problem of cerebral palsy as a prototype for neurodevelopmental disability in general
- To understand the diagnostic approach to the enormous number of causes of disabilities
- To identify and define specific conditions unique to high-risk infants
- To understand aspects of medical assistive technology
- To review emergency first aid interventions relevant to children with disabilities
- To review important infectious disease considerations
- To go over some issues related to professional communication, including do not resuscitate (DNR) orders

Personnel working in early childhood programs are often faced with children and family issues that are distinctly different from those that primary school teachers are accustomed to with their special education students. The latter group traditionally comes to the attention of educational professionals because of learning and/or behavior problems. These older children with high-prevalence but low-severity disorders tend to have a minimum of medical needs. Diagnostically many of these children have the milder developmental disabilities (e.g., learning disabilities and attention deficit hyperactivity disorder [ADHD]), acquired emotional and behavioral problems, and to a lesser extent chronic medical conditions that by school age are almost always stable. Service providers working with the birth-to-three range, however, see a very different population of children.

Children who are identified early (i.e., during infancy) as being in need of intervention are likely to have neurodevelopmental problems that are more severe and more pervasive than those found in children who present later. In thinking about the medical issues that confront early intervention personnel, the contrast between low-prevalence/high-severity disorders and high-prevalence/low-severity disorders is an important consideration. The infant group often involves children with rare or uncommon conditions that tend to be both complex and severe in their manifestations. Hence, symptoms and signs appear and tend to be identified early. Medical complications and neurodevelopmental problems are prominent features and may even be life-threatening. They are often extremely difficult to manage. Minor acute illnesses, such as a simple upper respiratory infection (a routine "cold"), may severely affect the child's ability to perform or greatly disrupt otherwise stable health functions, such as breathing. Feeding problems and nutritional deficits may be primary factors that are most difficult to treat. These medical issues add an additional level of challenge for the early intervention team and may, indeed, be quite intimidating and anxiety-provoking. In addition, families of such children are typically facing a diagnosis for the first time and have had no prior experience with or even awareness of early intervention services.

The main intent of this chapter is to address the many medical considerations as they pertain to the natural environments of infants and toddlers (e.g., the home, child care center, and community) and to provide some structure for thinking about complex medical problems. A second goal is to provide information about and approaches to accessing and utilizing resources in the medical community that will enhance the relationship between service provider and health care professional and thereby improve everyone's ability to work with children who have various low-prevalence/high-severity disorders, and with their families. All of the case illustrations are real, although some are blended histories. The names of the children and families have all been changed to ensure confidentiality.

GROWTH AND DEVELOPMENT

When thinking about child development in the broadest terms, one usually begins under the encompassing umbrella of "growth and development":

1. Physical growth is precisely measured using standard parameters: height, weight, and head circumference. Occasionally additional measures are of significance, such as the ratio between the upper and lower body segments and skin-fold thickness. The conformation of the body is also examined, and abnormalities are described in terms of dysmorphic features (dysmorphisms).
2. Behavioral development is measured in terms of Gesell's traditional four streams: language, problem-solving, motor, and psychosocial (or affective) sequences of neurobehavioral maturation (Knobloch & Pasamanick, 1974).

The separation of physical growth and development from behavioral growth and development and the further splitting of behavior into four streams, or areas, are representative of the "medical model." This conceptual approach is applied widely in the medical neurodevelopmental world. It provides a very useful construct for logically approaching the child who is brought to the physician because he is viewed as being different in some way (delayed, small, unusual looking, etc.).

Measurement

In general, physical growth milestones are predictable, although they must be viewed within the context of each child's specific genetic and ethnic background. It is essential to plot the child's growth on gender and age-appropriate charts. Fetal weight gain is greatest during the third trimester. There is a continuation of this rapid growth during the first few months of life, after which growth decelerates. Whereas birth weight doubles by four to five months, height does not double until between three and four years of age (Hamill et al., 1979). Head growth during the first five or six months is due to continued neuronal cell division and is remarkably rapid. Later, increasing head size is due to neuronal cell growth and support tissue proliferation, and the rate of head growth decelerates.

Large and small head size are both relative red flags for developmental problems. Microcephaly, or small head size, is associated with an increased incidence of mental retardation, but there is no straightforward relationship between small head size and depressed intelligence. As a reflection of normal variation, microcephaly is not associated with structural pathology of the nervous system or with low intelligence. Furthermore, microcephaly can be seen with above average cognitive capability. Microcephaly associated with genetic or acquired disorders reflects cerebral pathology and almost always carries cognitive implications. Macrocephaly, or large head size, may be due to hydrocephalus, which has an increased incidence of cognitive deficits, especially learning disabilities. Macrocephaly without hydrocephalus, far from being a predictor of advanced intelligence, is also associated with a higher prevalence of cognitive deficits. It may be due to metabolic and/or anatomic abnormalities. About 50 percent of the time, macrocephaly is familial, in which case the implications are benign in terms of intellect. When evaluating infants with isolated macrocephaly, the finding of a large head size in one or both parents is reassuring.

Body size follows the same logic. While the majority of individuals with below or above average size are otherwise normal, there is an increased prevalence of developmental disabilities in these two subpopulations. Many genetic syndromes are associated with short stature; large stature syndromes are less common. Again, in evaluating deviation from the norm in a specific child, family characteristics must be taken into consideration. Knowing the size of the biological parents is useful in determining whether a given child's size is appropriate for his or her familial growth pattern.

VIGNETTE 8.1 DARLENE

Darlene is a 14-month-old who was born at 31 weeks of gestation and weighed 1.29 kilograms (kg). She spent nine weeks in the neonatal intensive care unit. Her course in the unit was relatively benign, but she did experience an intraventricular hemorrhage (IVH). She was identified as motor delayed by nine months of age and was referred for early intervention services at 10 months. At 13 months, a diagnosis of spastic diplegic cerebral palsy was made. At this time, her height is 71.5 centimeters (cm), her weight is 8.7 kg, and her head circumference is 46.5 cm. Her mother is worried because Darlene is small and tends to be a picky eater.

Is this child described in Vignette 8.1 growing adequately? The answer can only be determined by graphing the measured growth parameters (Figures 8.1A and 8.1B). Obviously all preterm babies will be small relative to full-gestation birth heights and weights. Growth parameters at birth are plotted for gestational age on special growth charts developed for premature infants, and, indeed, Darlene's birth weight of 1.29 kg was perfectly appropriate for her gestational age of 31 weeks (not shown). As the child ages, by convention the full number of months preterm is subtracted from the child's chronologic age for the purpose of plotting on the standard growth chart. Because Darlene was born nine weeks early (almost exactly two months), her height and weight are plotted at 12 months rather than 14 months to correct for her degree of prematurity. Plotting these points reveals that she is in the 10th to 25th percentile for both height and weight. This indicates that her height and weight are within the normal range and are relatively proportionate. She is a little below average in terms of size for a 12-month-old, and if her mother is comparing Darlene to 14-month-olds, then it is easy to see why she might perceive her daughter as too small (Figure 8.1B). To help with the assessment of body proportion, weight is plotted against height. On that chart, Darlene ranks at the proper level, in the 50th percentile.

Darlene's head looks a little bit large clinically, and its circumference plots at the 75th percentile. This indicates some body disproportion. Does this child have hydrocephalus? Because she has a motor disability, we know that she sustained a brain injury. We also know that she had an IVH, so hydrocephalus is a real concern. Could it be contributing to her disability or limiting her response to therapy?

The answer is that we don't know from the information given. However, many preterm babies tend to have heads that are relatively large compared to their bodies, without having genuine obstructive hydrocephalus. Most infants who experience an intracranial hemorrhage do not go on to develop hydrocephalus. Nonetheless, an IVH can lead to obstructive hydrocephalus. The two most important additional pieces of information that should be already available are prior head circumference measurements, to document how the head has grown over time, and clinical symptoms. If the *rate* of head growth is increasing, then progressive hydrocephalus is a serious possibility and must be tested for. A neurodiagnostic study of the cranium itself would need to be done to see whether the ventricular fluid spaces are enlarged, which would indicate hydrocephalus. This would most easily be done through a head ultrasound study. A cranial computerized tomogram (head CT) or magnetic resonance imaging (MRI) scan would provide a much more sophisticated and more detailed picture of the brain than the head ultrasound, but would not help answer the question much more accurately. Darlene's ultrasound study was normal, arguing against progressive hydrocephalus.

Failure to Thrive (FTT)

The term *failure to thrive* (FTT) is often applied generically and rather loosely to any situation in which a child is not growing adequately. Precise definitions of failure to thrive have varied in the medical literature. Currently, most growth experts use the term to refer only to those of individuals who are underweight for their height. Older literature tended to use FTT more broadly to encompass individuals who demonstrated generalized growth deficits and behavioral abnormalities.

Regardless of which definition one prefers, the diagnosis of failure to thrive is, once again, absolutely dependent upon accurately measured growth parameters plotted on appropriate growth charts. It is worth noting that growth failure tends to fall into several patterns, the recognition of which can help differentiate the most likely underlying cause of the growth retardation.

VIGNETTE 8.2   TOMMY

Tommy is a 24-month-old who is developmentally delayed, somewhat slow and lethargic in his general demeanor, and small. He was born at full term and was of average size at birth. His current height is 79 cm (less than 5th percentile), and his weight is 11.1 kg (10th percentile) (Figure 8.2A). His head circumference is 48.5 cm (25th percentile) (Figure 8.2B). By inspection of the growth curves alone, one would anticipate that this boy is perhaps a bit on the chubby side. In other words, he is short but appears far from malnourished. Inspection of the weight-for-height chart confirms that he is indeed above average, plotting just over the 50th percentile (Figure 8.2B).

In the scenario described in Vignette 8.2, organic etiologies are high on the list of the causes of Tommy's condition, the most likely being endocrine abnormalities or disturbances of skeletal growth that are causing retardation in linear growth but have no effect on appetite or weight gain. It turns out Tommy had acquired thyroid deficiency. This was easily diagnosed by a blood test, and, when he was treated with thyroid hormone, his linear growth returned to a normal rate. His state of alertness and developmental profile also improved, although he was left with some mild permanent cognitive deficits.

Another growth pattern seen in the broad category of failure to thrive includes children who are small for both height and weight. If their head circumferences are normal and their development is appropriate, these tend to be simply normal, small children. This pattern usually has a familial basis and is sometimes referred to as constitutional or familial short stature. On the other hand, if the head circumference is below the 5th percentile and/or the child is developmentally delayed, this pattern represents a subgroup that will often fall into the category of a syndrome diagnosis, especially if some dysmorphic features are also present.

VIGNETTE 8.3   PETER

Peter is a 12-month-old who is small and developmentally delayed. He was born at 38 weeks of gestation (considered full term). Recently, he has been placed in foster care with his aunt, having been abandoned by his biological mother. At the time of placement his height was 75 cm (25th percentile) and his weight was 7.8 kg (below the 5th percentile) (Figure 8.3A). His head circumference was 47 cm (50th percentile) (Figure 8.3B). His weight-for-height measurement is well below the 5th percentile.

A

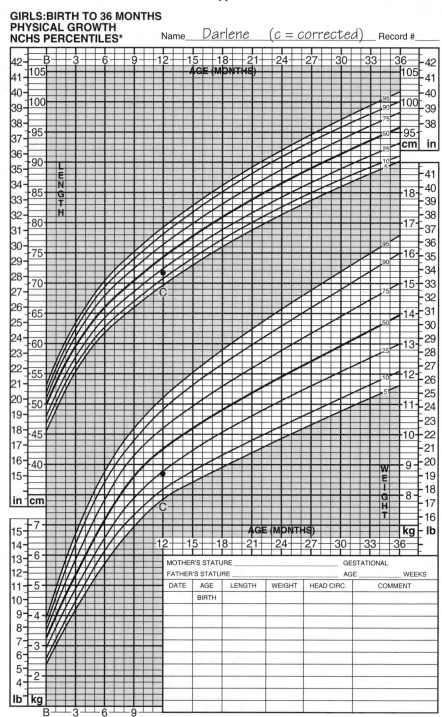

FIGURE 8.1 Case 1: Darlene. Standard infant girl growth chart plotted at Darlene's corrected age (12 months). **A,** Height = 71.5 cm, weight = 8.7 kg. **B,** Head circumference = 46.5 cm, height = 71.5 cm, weight = 8.7 kg.

B

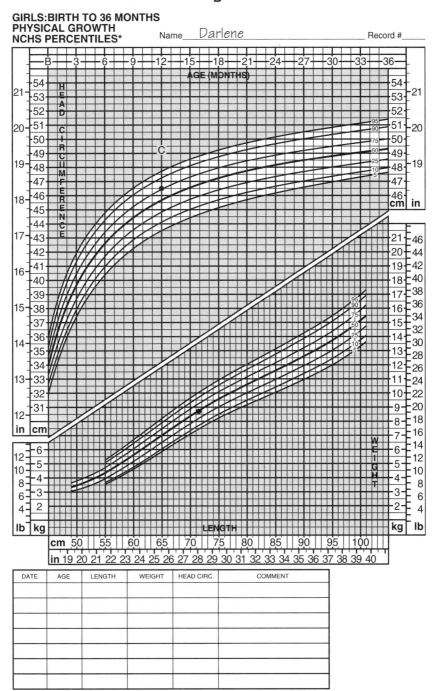

GIRLS:BIRTH TO 36 MONTHS
PHYSICAL GROWTH
NCHS PERCENTILES*

Name Darlene   Record #

DATE	AGE	LENGTH	WEIGHT	HEAD CIRC.	COMMENT

Source: From "Physical Growth: National Center for Health Statistics Percentiles" by P. V. V. Hamill, T. A. Drizd, C. L. Johnson, R. B. Reed, A. F. Roche, and W. M. Moore, 1979, *American Journal of Clinical Nutrition, 32,* 607–629. Data from the Fels Longitudinal Study, Wright State University School of Medicine, Yellow Springs, Ohio. Copyright 1982 Ross Products Division, Abbott Laboratories. Adapted by permission.

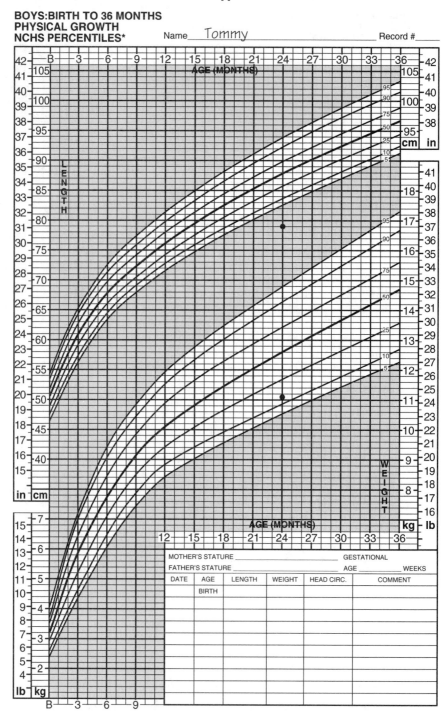

A

BOYS:BIRTH TO 36 MONTHS
PHYSICAL GROWTH
NCHS PERCENTILES*

Name___Tommy_____ Record #_____

FIGURE 8.2   Case 2: Tommy. Standard infant boy growth chart plotted at
Tommy's chronologic age (24 months). **A,** Height = 79 cm, weight = 11.1 kg. **B,**
Head circumference = 48.5 cm, height = 79 cm, weight = 11.1 kg.

B

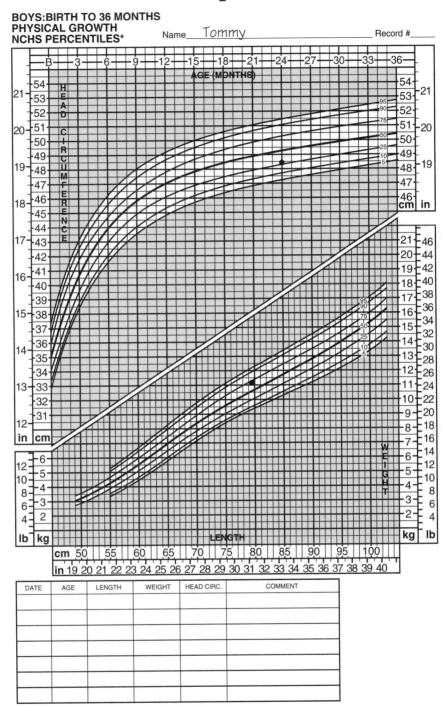

BOYS:BIRTH TO 36 MONTHS
PHYSICAL GROWTH
NCHS PERCENTILES*

Name _Tommy_____ Record #_____

DATE	AGE	LENGTH	WEIGHT	HEAD CIRC.	COMMENT

Source: From "Physical Growth: National Center for Health Statistics Percentiles" by P. V. V. Hamill, T. A. Drizd, C. L. Johnson, R. B. Reed, A. F. Roche, and W. M. Moore, 1979, *American Journal of Clinical Nutrition, 32,* 607–629. Data from the Fels Longitudinal Study, Wright State University School of Medicine, Yellow Springs, Ohio. Copyright 1982 Ross Products Division, Abbott Laboratories. Adapted by permission.

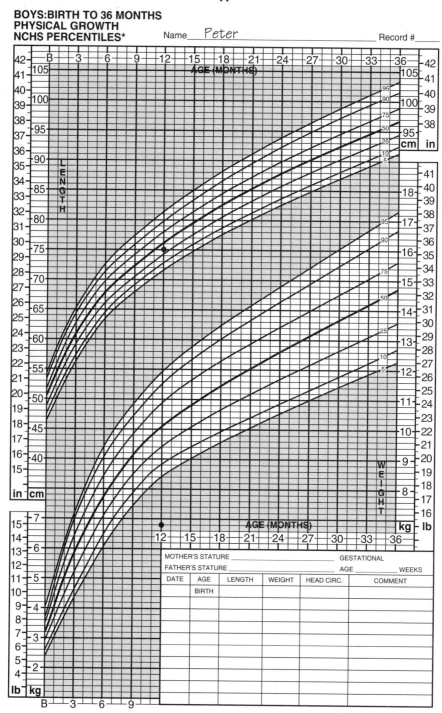

FIGURE 8.3   Case 3: Peter. Standard infant boy growth chart plotted at Peter's chronologic age (12 months). **A,** Height = 75 cm, weight = 7.8 kg. **B,** Head circumference = 47 cm, height = 75 cm, weight = 7.8 kg.

B

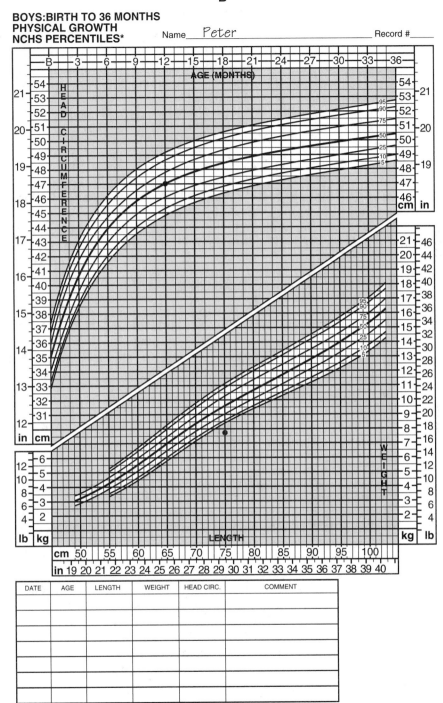

BOYS:BIRTH TO 36 MONTHS
PHYSICAL GROWTH
NCHS PERCENTILES*

Name Peter   Record #_____

DATE	AGE	LENGTH	WEIGHT	HEAD CIRC.	COMMENT

Source: From "Physical Growth: National Center for Health Statistics Percentiles" by P. V. V. Hamill, T. A. Drizd, C. L. Johnson, R. B. Reed, A. F. Roche, and W. M. Moore, 1979, *American Journal of Clinical Nutrition, 32,* 607–629. Data from the Fels Longitudinal Study, Wright State University School of Medicine, Yellow Springs, Ohio. Copyright 1982 Ross Products Division, Abbott Laboratories. Adapted by permission.

In the situation presented in Vignette 8.3, simple inspection of the height and weight graphs (Figures 8.3A and 8.3B) would lead one to expect to see a thin infant, which was indeed true clinically. If we also performed some measure of body fat, for example, by using the skin-fold thickness test, it would have been below normal as well. In this case we are dealing with genuine malnutrition. Malnutrition results from one of three processes: (1) inadequate intake of calories and nutrients, (2) excessive loss of calories and nutrients (such as occurs with diarrhea), or (3) excessive or ineffective utilization of absorbed nutrients (such as results from chronic lung disease, congenital heart disease, and other medical conditions). In this situation, Peter was simply not being fed adequately in the home. Most cases of failure to thrive are caused by inadequate intake due to parent-child feeding difficulties that are not organic in nature, which is the source of the often-used term *nonorganic failure to thrive* (NOFTT). Peter rapidly and dramatically gained weight when his home environment was altered and he was fed an appropriate diet by his foster family. NOFTT is a troubling and complex disorder with many difficult, long-term social and behavioral subissues. For a thorough review of the subject, see Stevenson (1992).

The last group is composed of those children who are close to or below the lower limit for height, usually below the margin for weight, and far below the 5th percentile for head circumference. The lack of head growth, out of proportion to body growth, is usually a reflection of substantial brain damage, and these children typically have severe associated neurodevelopmental deficits that are permanent. The brain dysfunction may be the result of a malformation of the nervous system or an acquired injury to the developing nervous system. There may also be a superimposed component of undernutrition related to oral motor dysfunction and resultant difficulty with feeding and swallowing.

VIGNETTE 8.4   EDDIE

Eddie is a 15-month-old born at full term with Down syndrome and congenital heart disease, which is believed to be relatively mild. However, he is a slow feeder and has been gaining weight slowly. His height is 69 cm and his weight is 7.4 kg, both under the 5th percentile on the growth curves (Figure 8.4A).

Do the data presented in Vignette 8.4 suggested that Eddie is undernourished? This boy's height and weight are both well below the 5th percentile, which is not in itself too surprising, given that we know he has a genetic syndrome. Could his heart condition be causing additional growth deficiency? Determining whether or to what degree he is undernourished requires looking at the appropriateness of his weight for his particular height. Inspecting the weight-for-height curve reveals that he is, in fact, doing reasonably well and is proportionate (Figure 8.4B). This should be apparent from visual inspection as well. Will feeding him more help his growth? On the contrary, Eddie is adequately nourished, and increasing his calorie intake may lead to greater weight gain but is unlikely to increase his linear growth, which is deficient as a consequence of his genetic constitution, not as a consequence of malnutrition and/or heart disease.

Could there be other factors at play? If one has the advantage of following Eddie's growth over time, a consistent pattern of slow but steady, proportionate length and weight increments would most likely be seen. Children with Down syndrome do, however, have a high rate of thyroid deficiency, something the astute pediatrician would be routinely screening for with blood tests done at regular intervals. As an added assist, a number of syndrome-specific growth charts have been developed to allow comparisons against more appropriate norms (for example, for Down syndrome, see Cronk et al., 1988; for Prader-Willi syndrome, see Butler & Meaney, 1991). When plotted on such a chart, Eddie's height and weight are roughly in the 10th percentile, which is within the average range (Figure 8.5).

In summary, the approach to determining adequacy of growth is straightforward and depends on accurate measurement of growth parameters for height, weight, and head circumference, followed by careful plotting on the appropriate growth curves. The weight-for-height curve is exceedingly valuable in helping to determine adequacy of nutrition. For the child who is failing to grow at an appropriate rate in any (or all) parameters, the pattern of deficiency and the presence of additional factors (developmental deficits, dysmorphisms, etc.) help direct the clinician toward an etiologic explanation for the growth problem.

DEVELOPMENTAL DIAGNOSIS

VIGNETTE 8.5   DANIEL

Daniel is a 13-month-old referred for developmental delay, mainly because he is not sitting independently. His mother had been worried about him since he was about four to five months old because "he just didn't seem right." The family doctor believed Daniel would "grow out of" his delays. He was a first child.

On examination the child is quite hypotonic (floppy). Developmentally he is close to sitting while propped and has a gross motor level of four to five months. His fine motor, problem-solving, and language levels are all in the same range, indicating severe delays in motor and cognitive domains. Additionally, he has a number of subtle dysmorphic facial features and some unusual palmar increases noted on physical examination.

Based on the history of slow developmental progress, this seemed most likely to be a case of static encephalopathy. A salient feature was that Daniel's mother had experienced approximately 15 spontaneous abortions. During the etiologic workup, the child's chromosome analysis showed a translocation of genetic material between two chromosomes. His mother's chromosomes revealed a "balanced" translocation of the same genetic material, permitting her to be normal but making all of her ova either nonviable or characterized by a severe abnormality. The translocation coupled with Daniel's clinical features did not conform to a known syndrome.

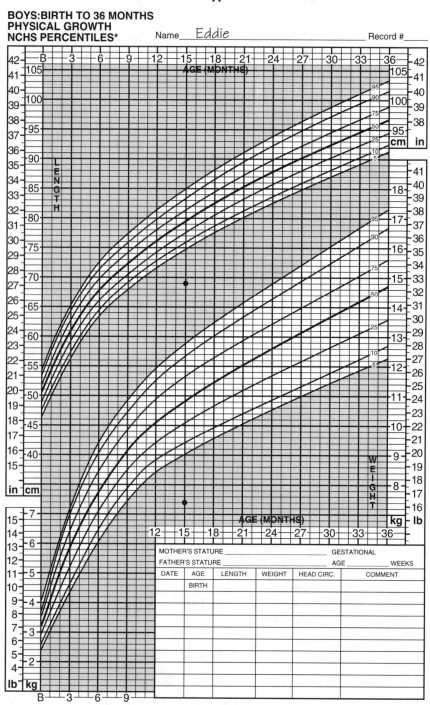

FIGURE 8.4 Case 4: Eddie. Standard infant boy growth chart plotted at Eddie's chronologic age (15 months). **A,** Height = 69 cm, weight = 7.4 kg. **B,** Height = 69 cm, weight = 7.4 kg.

226

B

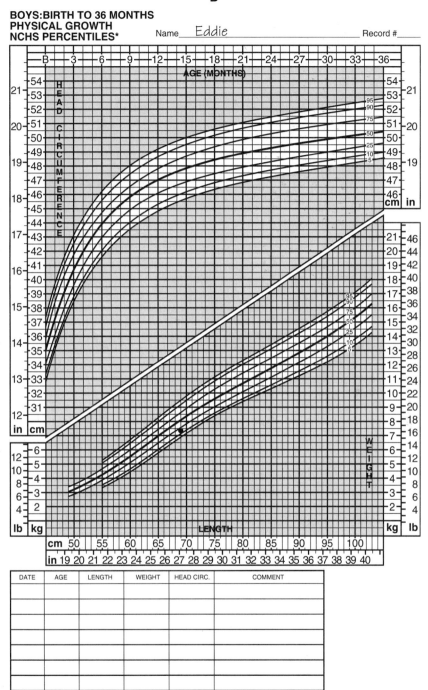

BOYS:BIRTH TO 36 MONTHS
PHYSICAL GROWTH
NCHS PERCENTILES*   Name _Eddie_ _____ Record #____

DATE	AGE	LENGTH	WEIGHT	HEAD CIRC.	COMMENT

Source: From "Physical Growth: National Center for Health Statistics Percentiles" by P. V. V. Hamill, T. A. Drizd, C. L. Johnson, R. B. Reed, A. F. Roche, and W. M. Moore, 1979, *American Journal of Clinical Nutrition, 32,* 607–629. Data from the Fels Longitudinal Study, Wright State University School of Medicine, Yellow Springs, Ohio. Copyright 1982 Ross Products Division, Abbott Laboratories. Adapted by permission.

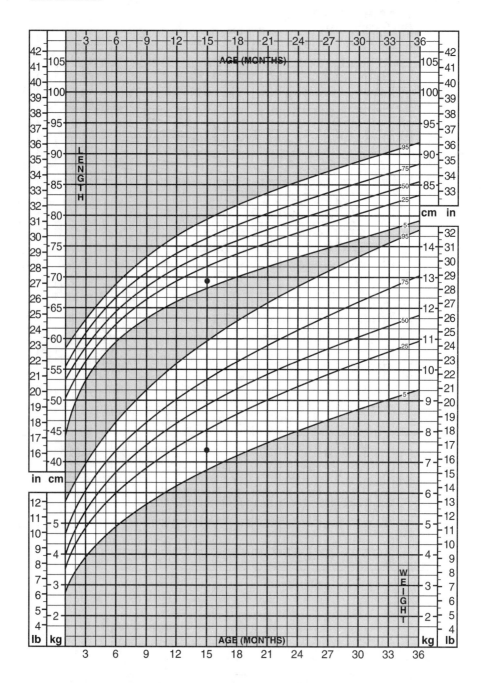

FIGURE 8.5   Case 4: Eddie. Eddie's weight (7.4 kg) and height (69 cm) plotted on a Down syndrome growth chart for boys.

Source: From "Growth Charts for Children with Down Syndrome: 1 Month to 18 Years of Age" by C. Cronk et al., 1988, *Pediatrics, 81*, 102–110. Reprinted by permission.

Developmental disabilities include a spectrum of disorders whose underlying substrate is the presence of chronic and nonprogressive neurological impairment at a cerebral level, clinically known as a static encephalopathy as illustrated in Vignette 8.5 (Capute & Palmer, 1980). Such cerebral dysfunction can exist on the basis of a central nervous system (CNS) that has not developed properly right from the start, referred to as a central nervous system anomaly, or, alternatively, can be the consequence of an injury to a developing nervous system that, up to the point of the insult, was normal. The neurodevelopmental disabilities are presented in Table 8.1. Cerebral palsy refers to *significant* motor dysfunction due to a nonprogressive cerebral insult. The definition indicates nothing about intellectual function. Mental retardation refers to significantly below average general intellectual ability, likewise due to cerebral dysfunction.

Communication disorders span a spectrum of primary language disorders that may be congenital or acquired. Among the congenital communication disorders, which are usually very subtle in their early symptoms, the severe end of the spectrum is autism. The acquired disorders are commonly referred to as aphasias and are rarely subtle in their onset. In the past the low-severity spectrum of dysfunction was known as minimal brain dysfunction or minimal cerebral dysfunction and now is more specifically referred to as learning disability (LD) and/or attention hyperactivity deficit disorder syndromes. Blindness and deafness are self-explanatory. For most of these conditions, an essential criterion for the diagnosis is the fact that the nervous system lesion is static, that is to say, not progressive in nature.

Hence, as a broad group these conditions are referred to as the static encephalopathies. In violation of this general principle, however, we do tend to use the terms *blindness* and *deafness* regardless of whether the underlying process is static or, as it is in a minority of cases, progressive in nature. However, progressive cognitive

TABLE 8.1   Developmental Disabilities

Cerebral palsy

Mental retardation

Communication disorders

Autism

Aphasia

Learning disabilities/ADHD

Blindness

Deafness

Chronic childhood neurological disorders (which may *masquerade as* developmental disabilities) (e.g., seizures, degenerative CNS disease, myopathies)

deficit and progressive motor deficit should never be referred to as mental retardation or cerebral palsy. (Progressive mental deterioration is termed *dementia*.) Many slowly progressive neurological conditions are notorious for masquerading as static encephalopathies, but the implications are vastly different for progressive (also known as degenerative) disorders. The neurodevelopmental clinician must always be alert to the possibility of mistaking a progressive disorder for a static one and must be certain to reaffirm that the condition is not one of deterioration over time. Seizure disorders are very common among individuals with developmental disabilities, but by convention seizures are not classified among the developmental disabilities. Seizures do not *of necessity* affect development. They also have a wide variety of causes, some static and some progressive.

Prevalences of the neurodevelopmental disabilities vary (Table 8.2). The LD/ADD/ADHD complex is most common, found in 5–7 percent of all school-aged children. Mental retardation, by statistical definition, must occur in a little over 2.5 percent of the population, and empirically it is present in roughly 3 percent of individuals. There is considerable debate (especially in the education profession) about this number, which may be as low as 1 percent. In any case, the distribution is greatly skewed toward the mild end of the spectrum. What the lay public commonly thinks of in terms of mental retardation is not the mildly impaired individual but rather the 10–15 percent of the retarded population that falls in the moderate, severe, and profound range.

Diagnostic Levels

An area of confusion for nonmedical professionals and the lay public often centers around the issue of diagnosis. It is important to keep in mind that diagnosis occurs on two separate conceptual planes. Problem diagnosis, the first level of developmental diagnosis, relates to the problem at hand. Cerebral palsy, for example, is a disorder of movement and posture; in other words, it is a motor function problem.

The second level of diagnosis relates to etiology; or is the cause of the neurologic dysfunction. An extraordinary number of conditions—basically anything that can affect the brain or brain development—can cause any type of developmental disability (Table 8.3).

TABLE 8.2   Prevalence of Developmental Disabilities

DISABILITY	PERCENT
Learning disabilities/ADD syndromes	5–7
Mental retardation	3
Cerebral palsy	.2–.5
Deafness	.1
Blindness	.05
Autism	.04

TABLE 8.3   Causes of Developmental Disabilities

CONGENITAL	ACQUIRED
■ Genetic (e.g., Down syndrome, neurocutaneous syndromes, dyslexia)	■ Perinatal (e.g., hypoxic-ischemic insult, prematurity)
■ Infectious (e.g., TORCHS)	■ Head trauma
■ Toxic/metabolic (e.g., maternal PKU, maternal iodine deficiency, fetal alcohol syndrome)	■ Spinal cord injury
■ Other (e.g., unexplained CNS malformations)	■ Infectious (e.g., encephalitis, or secondary effect on CNS, as with sepsis and shock or pneumonia and hypoxia)
	■ Toxic/Metabolic (e.g., inborn errors of metabolism; hypothyroidism; lead poisoning)
	■ Neoplastic
	■ Other diseases (e.g., vascular accidents [strokes], nutritional deficiency, collagen vascular disease)

The causes of any given developmental disability (for example, cerebral palsy) are innumerable, and any given insult (for example, meningitis) can in general result in almost any developmental disability. A broad classification of cause categories, with a few more common specific examples, is presented here. Etiologic investigation in these conditions can be extremely difficult and not infrequently unrewarding. The medical workup for etiology relies heavily on the history and the physical and neurological examinations. Finding a cause cannot depend on completing an all-inclusive laboratory investigation for every child. There are too many possibilities to rule out every one with a test. The approach is, rather, to rely on clues that point toward a specific etiology.

Age

How early can one make a specific developmental diagnosis? The neurodevelopmental disabilities are not recognized and diagnosed as early as we would all like. Cerebral palsy is diagnosed at a mean age of 12 months. Disorders that are heralded by communicative dysfunction are referred for evaluation and diagnosed considerably later—closer to two and a half years for mental retardation and even later for learning disabilities and autism (Table 8.4).

These data come from a community with a long and strong history of exceptional developmental teaching in the local medical schools and pediatrics residencies. Hence, the pediatricians in the area are probably more attuned to neurodevelopmental problems than most. The numbers may be worse in other communities. The most flagrant example of delay in developmental diagnosis is

TABLE 8.4   Mean Age of Presentation (Referral) of Developmental Disabilities

DISABILITY	AGE
Cerebral palsy	12 months
Mental retardation	27 months
Communication disorder	32 months
Attention deficit disorder	7 years
Learning disability	9½ years

From "Age of Presentation of Developmental Disabilities" by T. H. M. Lock, B. T. K. Shapite, A. Ross, and A. J. Capute, 1986, *Journal of Developmental and Behavioral Pediatrics, 7*, 340. Adapted by permission.

deafness. Most deafness is inherited and therefore congenital. However, the mean age of diagnosis of congenital deafness ranges from 20 to 27 months and has not changed for four decades (deSchweinitz, Miller, & Miller, 1959; Robinson, Willits, & Benson, 1965; Shah, Chandler, & Doll, 1978; Coplan, 1987; Drews, Yeargin-Allsopp, Murphy, & Decoufle, 1994).

Cerebral Palsy

From an academic and conceptual standpoint, cerebral palsy (CP) represents the prototypical developmental disability, because it encompasses the entire spectrum of cerebral dysfunction. For that reason it is singled out for a more detailed review as an illustration of the nature of this entire class of disorders. As noted previously, the diagnosis of CP refers to a group of motor dysfunctions arising from a nonprogressive cerebral insult. The motor disability is subclassified based on pattern of involvement diplegia, hemiplegia, and certain qualitative neurological features, spasticity and ataxia (cf. Baird & Gordon, 1983; Batshaw, 1997). The majority of children with CP have additional problems, referred to as associated deficits (Table 8.5).

The hallmarks of the primary motor dysfunction are abnormalities of muscle tone, imbalance of various muscle groups, and aberrant movement patterns. These abnormalities generate forces on developing muscles and bones that were never meant to be, and as a result frequently produce deformities of the soft tissues (muscles and tendons), the bones themselves, and the joints. These alterations produce mechanical disadvantages that further interfere with functional ability and in addition can result in substantial pain, not to mention cosmetic deformity. More than half of the children with CP have cognitive dysfunction (mental retardation and learning disabilities). Oral-motor involvement can lead to a broad spectrum of serious impairments: poor speech intelligibility due to articulation problems, feeding difficulty leading to nutritional deficits, and swallowing dysfunction with drooling and/or aspiration. Blindness, deafness, and seizures will be much more common in children with CP than in the general population. Both

TABLE 8.5   Cerebral Palsy: Associated Disorders

Orthopedic deformities
- Muscle/tendon contracture
- Bone deformity/malalignment
- Joint dislocation and degeneration
- Scoliosis
- Osteoporosis and fracture

Cognitive deficits
- Mental retardation
- Learning disability

Oral-motor performance impairments
- Speech dysfunction
- Feeding and swallowing problems
- Drooling
- Malnutrition

Special sensory losses
- Hearing impairment
- Visual impairment

Seizures

Peripheral sensory impairment

Behavioral/emotional problems
- Organic
- Acquired

innate behavioral disorders (i.e., ADHD) and acquired behavioral/emotional disturbances are also more prevalent.

Evaluation of the child with CP, of necessity, must be quite comprehensive and, to be efficient, ought to be highly interdisciplinary. Just as communication among the professionals involved is critical, so is communication with the family, particularly at the time of initial diagnosis. Counseling parents at this sensitive time is a difficult process and a learned skill (Klein, 1993; Krahn, Hallum, & Kime, 1993). A family-centered approach to care should ideally be the governing principle for all interactions (Brewer, McPherson, Magrab, & Hutchins, 1989; Blasco & Johnson, 1996).

Treatments covering the primary disorder and the multitude of associated problems in some children may be very extensive and exceedingly complex. Treatment approaches for the motor disorder alone can be classified into five types of intervention (Table 8.6).

Counseling refers to providing information to the parents, as well as to the involved child and siblings. Written materials can be a tremendous adjunct to this process (see Kraft, 1985), but one needs to be discerning in their selection (Blasco, Baumgartner, & Mathes, 1983). The hands-on therapies include occupational,

TABLE 8.6   Interventions for Children with Cerebral Palsy

Counseling

Hands-on Therapy
- Physical Therapy
- Occupational Therapy
- Speech Therapy
- Recreational Therapy

Equipment
- Braces
- Adaptive Devices
- Electronics

Drugs

Surgery

---

physical, and speech therapy. Often short-changed on the list are the recreational therapists and their close counterparts, adaptive physical education professionals. Recreational activities can have the advantage of providing treatment while building self-esteem; for example, sitting astride a horse is beneficial for stretching one's adductor and hamstring muscles, but it also represents a powerful mastery experience for a young child.

An extensive—in truth, bewildering—array of equipment is available to help the disabled child function better. These can be grouped into braces and splints, whose purpose is to provide mechanical stability and prevent deformity; adaptive equipment, such as wheelchairs, seating systems, potty and bath chairs, etc.; and electronic devices, from the simplest mercury switch for activating a toy to the most sophisticated computerized augmentative communication systems (see Chapter 10). Medications have a role in the treatment of muscular hypertonus and movement disorders. Although there are a huge number to choose from, they are often rather unpredictable in terms of effects and side effects. Different drops are administered by different routes to achieve the best effect: orally (most drugs; see Pranzatelli, 1996), into the muscle itself (botulinum toxin; see Koman, Mooney, & Smith, 1996), or even into the spinal canal (intrathecal baclofen; see Albright, Cerri, & Singletary, 1991). Surgical interventions encompass an extensive array of orthopedic operations (Bleck, 1987) and a smaller group of neurosurgical procedures, with the most currently popular being dorsal rhizotomy (Peacock, Arens, & Berman, 1987). The surgical goals are always first and foremost to facilitate function and prevent deformity. Once a deformity has already developed, surgical outcomes are destined to achieve less and expectations are more limited: to correct deformity (as much as possible), to relieve discomfort, and to enhance care. Cosmesis is occasionally a consideration but is never primary.

Individuals unfamiliar with developmental disabilities, both lay and professional, often mistakenly assume that treatments are undertaken in a hierarchical fashion. In other words, one begins with talk therapy and progresses to physical therapy, occupational therapy, and so on. If those are unsuccessful, one moves on to braces and other equipment. The next intervention would be drugs, and one would look to surgery only as a last resort. Of course, this is not at all the case. The key to management of the child with any type of physical disability is applying the right treatment at the right time. When, for example, surgery is indicated to promote a function, then it is time to intervene surgically, regardless of what treatment has or has not preceded it. In many instances, surgery can be viewed as a necessary precursor to intensive hands-on therapy. The clinical experience and expertise of the interdisciplinary habilitation team are critical to arriving at these timely judgments.

MEDICAL DIAGNOSIS

The causes of developmental disabilities are numerous and include basically anything that can do injury to the brain, the eyes, or the ears. Table 8.3 outlined the broad spectrum of potential causes and offered a few examples. As noted, the search for the cause (etiology) of a particular developmental problem must be somehow narrowed for the process to be an efficient exercise. The diagnostic approach is outlined in Table 8.7. Such a list is, of necessity, incomplete, presenting only some of the more common tests.

TABLE 8.7   Medical Approach to Etiological Diagnosis Developmental Disabilities

CLINICAL ASSESSMENT	LABORATORY DIAGNOSTIC STUDIES	
■ History	*Blood tests*	*X-ray/imaging studies*
■ Physical examination	■ CBC, diff, plt, smear	■ Hips
■ Neurodevelopmental examination	■ SMAC	■ Skull
■ Consults	■ LFTs	■ Spine
■ Other	■ Amino Acids	■ Long bones
	■ Lead/FEP	■ Bone age
	■ Chromosomes	■ CT scan
	■ Thyroid and other endocrine tests	■ MRI
	■ CK, other muscle enzymes	
	■ Antibody titers, TORCH, HIV	*Other neurodiagnostic studies*
	■ Drug levels	■ EEG
		■ EMG
	Urine tests	■ NCV
	■ Urinalysis	■ SSEP
	■ Amino acids (also mother)	■ BAER
	■ Metabolic screen	■ VEP
	■ Organic acids	■ PET scan
	■ Culture (esp. virus)	

A fundamental truth of etiologic investigation in the developmental disabilities is that one does not always arrive at an answer. For cerebral palsy, for example, this occurs about 20 percent of the time—a disconcerting circumstance for clinicians and a frustrating one for parents. Another general truth is that the greater the severity of disability, the more likely one is to find an etiology. Thus, most of the time mild mental retardation goes unexplained (and is often referred to as "idiopathic"), whereas severe and profound degrees of retardation will almost always have some identifiable organic pathology.

Another key point for parents is that arriving at an etiology very often does not mean that one can do anything about the condition. Nonetheless, just knowing the cause provides some degree of satisfaction and perhaps relief. There may also be important genetic and prognostic implications that come with a specific etiologic diagnosis.

VIGNETTE 8.6   MICHAEL

Michael is an 18-month-old referred to a child neurologist by his pediatrician because of a four-month history of gradually increasing irritability and a two-week history of repeated bouts of vomiting. The child is extremely irritable at times without obvious reason, and has otherwise been listless with no interest in food and little interest in play. He frequently holds or hits his head. Among other things, the examination shows a head circumference that is barely at the 5th percentile in a child who is in the 50th percentile for height and the 25th percentile for weight. The head shape is elongated in the anterior-posterior dimension.

Neurodiagnostic tests measure some aspect of neuroanatomic structure or neurophysiologic function. Neuroimaging studies are those that provide a neuroanatomic picture. The simplest such example would be a skull X ray, which gives a picture not of the brain directly but of the box enclosing it. This provides indirect information about the contents by indicating whether the skull is for example too big or too small (although you could get similar information by simply inspecting and measuring the head circumference). Skull X rays can also help explain neurological symptoms (e.g., irritability, vomiting, or a misshapen skull). In Vignette 8.6, skull X rays showed stenosis (premature closure) of the child's skull bones along the sagittal suture line, known as craniosynostosis. Because this event limits growth directed laterally, the skull is elongated in the anterior-posterior direction (known as scaphocephaly or dolichocephaly). Despite the growth that does take place, there is still encroachment on the rapidly growing brain with resulting symptoms of increased intracranial pressure, which could have caused Michael's irritability and vomiting, and probably made his head ache. The treatment for this condition is fairly urgent surgical splitting of the involved sutures.

The head ultrasound (HUS) test can provide a very crude picture of brain anatomy by bouncing sound waves off different surfaces, such as the fluid-filled ventricles and the skull. Because the HUS requires a "window" through the bony skull, its greatest utility is in neonates and infants who still have open fontanels. The ultrasound machine is portable and can be brought to the patient, a great advantage when one is dealing with small, fragile, premature infants. The HUS could not be done with Michael because his fontanels were closed. Indeed, it would not have been very useful anyway, because in his case the skull bones themselves were of primary interest. Pictures of brain anatomy are best supplied by magnetic resonance imaging and computed tomography scans. Computed cranial tomography (CT scan) of the head would have shown the same thing as the skull X rays as well as some of the compression effects going on in the brain. The CT scan involves a large series of X rays that are computer analyzed and reconstructed to give a three-dimensional picture of the brain and skull. It provides much more information than does a simple skull X ray but also involves a much greater exposure to radiation. MRI scanning takes advantage of the ability of an extremely high-powered magnet to alter the orientation of tissue water molecules. When the magnet's electronic field is changed, the molecules change orientation in space and then flip back, releasing energy in the process. This energy can be captured and converted to create a picture. The anatomic detail of the brain shown by an MRI is superior to that of a CT (in most respects), and it has the added advantage of no radiation exposure. While both are capable of producing very refined pictures of brain (and other organ) anatomy, they do not tell us everything. The great disadvantage of both the MRI and the CT is that the patient needs to hold perfectly still for about 15 minutes, which means that young children must be well sedated.

The electroencephalogram (EEG) measures electrical activity generated by brain neurons at multiple points along the scalp. It provides very little information about structure and is a fairly crude test of neurophysiologic function. Its greatest utility is in determining the presence and subtype of seizure disorders, but even here it has limitations (Lewis & Freeman, 1977). Variations on the EEG are used to gather information on visual pathway integrity (VER, or visual evoked response) and on auditory function (AEP, auditory evoked potential, and BAER, brainstem audiometric evoked response). Cortical evoked potentials, both visual and auditory, have fairly limited utility in young children. Brain stem audiometry is particularly helpful in screening for or documenting hearing levels in subjects with limited or no ability to cooperate with earphone or behavioral testing.

Other neurodiagnostic tests provide increasingly sophisticated information about brain metabolism and blood flow (NMR spectroscopy, nuclear magnetic resonance, and PET, positron emission tomography scanning, respectively,) but are not widely available and are never first-line investigative tools.

The electromyogram (EMG) and nerve conduction velocity (NCV) studies specifically define the electrophysiology of muscles and peripheral nerves. Innumerable blood and urine tests for normal and abnormal chemical constituents can provide clues in the diagnosis of metabolic disorders, infectious exposures, and genetic makeup. These tests are too numerous to review here and are only undertaken when a specific, small category of diagnoses or a single diagnosis is being sought.

SPECIFIC MEDICAL CONSIDERATIONS

High-Risk Infants

The baby born prematurely is at extremely high risk to experience complications while in the neonatal intensive care unit (NICU) and to acquire a broad spectrum of clinical problems. These complications will at times be fatal, and among survivors long-term, sometimes lifelong, problems can result. The chronic disorders associated with preterm birth fall into four domains: medical problems, growth deficits, neurodevelopmental disabilities, and emotional/behavioral issues.

The service provider who has reviewed a discharge summary from the NICU may be confronted by a cryptic "alphabet soup" of diagnoses (IVH, BPD, ROP, CP, NEC, etc.). Organizing one's thoughts about these problems and understanding a little about their nature can greatly assist the provider in terms of realistic program planning, hands-on activities for the child, and coordination of services for the family.

Medical Problems

Neonates who are sick can develop chronic conditions involving any organ system, but most typically it is the lungs. In the immature lung, respiratory insufficiency results from inadequate surfactant coating the surface of the pulmonary alveoli (where respiratory gas exchange between the inspired air and the circulating blood takes place). This acute condition is known as the respiratory distress syndrome (RDS), aptly describing the clinical appearance of these very sick babies. Without surfactant, the alveoli tend to collapse and cannot easily snap back open during inspiration. As a result, the neonate must work extremely hard to breathe and even with great effort may still inadequately oxygenate her blood, causing a bluish color to the skin and lips (cyanosis). Surfactant replacement treatment has become widely available in recent years and greatly ameliorates the situation. Nonetheless, most of these infants need to be treated with oxygen, and some need to be mechanically ventilated. Under conditions of high inspired oxygen concentration, high ventilation pressures, and prolonged need for ventilator assistance, damage accumulates in the lung tissue, resulting in bronchopulmonary dysplasia (BPD), the chronic lung disease of infancy. Although an occasional child will succumb early to RDS or later to BPD, or at any time to other conditions, especially infection, the ultimate outlook is quite good. Home cardiac and respiratory monitoring and home oxygen use will be necessary for many months in some children. The illness itself and to some extent these additional devices restrict activities, limit stamina, and interfere with growth, especially weight gain. Children with BPD are more likely to become ill, even critically ill, with what would otherwise be a mild respiratory infection in the healthy infant.

Even those infants who leave the hospital without pulmonary sequelae are at increased risk for acute respiratory illness, especially during the first winter at home. They are more likely to wheeze with an upper respiratory infection, more likely to experience a moderate-to-severe respiratory syncytial virus infection, and more likely to come down with pneumonia. As many as 45 percent of infants with birthweight less than 1,500 grams who required mechanical ventilation in the neonatal period will be rehospitalized in the first year. Family members, physicians, and service providers should be vigilant about early signs and symptoms of respiratory illness. Because of the inevitable greater exposure to infectious agents, there is good reason to think twice about center-based early intervention programming, especially for infants with known BPD. Everyone around the infant should be counseled about passive smoke exposure, be diligent about hand washing, and try to decrease the infant's exposure to adults and children during the cold/influenza season.

An acute gastrointestinal problem commonly encountered in the preterm baby is necrotizing enterocolitis (NEC). Providing nutrition to the sick preterm infant is an enormous clinical challenge. One of the pitfalls associated with introducing feeding is the development of NEC, which is linked to a large number of factors centered around exposing the immature gut to food. In severe cases, NEC results in death of portions of the bowel. This requires surgical excision of the necrotic tissue and aggressive treatment of the accompanying massive infection. If enough small intestine is involved, the baby may survive with little or no ability to absorb nutrients. Such a child could be dependent on complicated tube feedings given by slow drip and/or intravenous feeding for years, potentially indefinitely. Chronic heart disease, liver problems, bone or joint damage, and palatal and dental problems are also among the problems that can plague the high-risk neonate.

Many premature infants, especially those with very low birthweight (VLBW), defined as less than 1,500 grams, develop moderate to severe anemia. In the first six to eight weeks of life, this usually represents anemia of prematurity, a poorly understood delay in bone marrow responsiveness. The hematocrit may drop to very low levels, but most infants tolerate anemia well. Others may present with symptoms of poor feeding, poor weight gain, or apnea, and require blood transfusions. After two months of age, the infant may become iron deficient, further worsening anemia.

Umbilical and inguinal hernias are common in premature infants. Rarely will an umbilical hernia require surgical correction. Inguinal hernias, on the other hand, pose a significant risk of incarceration. Once recognized, timely referral for surgical repair is important due to this risk.

Growth Deficits

Most infants will have demonstrated adequate weight gain as a condition for discharge from the neonatal unit. Some preterm infants, however, remain too small. They grow poorly, for reasons that are not well understood. It is not unusual for the infant with extremely low birthweight (ELBW), defined as less than 1000 grams, to gain weight and length at a pace below the 5th percentile and to parallel that curve through the first 18 to 24 months of life. This may be a "normal" pattern of growth for some premature infants, who, due to illness and/or relatively poor nutrition at a critical period of life, have lost some growth potential. As long as the infant's growth rate and caloric intake are appropriate, no additional therapy or investigation is necessary.

Occasionally, premature infants will demonstrate a growth curve that begins to drop across percentiles or falls further below the 5th percentile. Poor weight gain may result from the infant's inability to keep up with increased caloric requirements due to ongoing respiratory problems, thermal instability, malabsorption secondary to necrotizing enterocolitis, or feeding difficulty consequent to neurodevelopmental deficits. Often the failure to thrive is complicated by problems that are behavioral in nature and need to be addressed with a consistent behavior management program (Singer et al., 1996).

Premature infants, especially VLBW and ELBW infants, have nutritional needs beyond those of the full-term infant. The premature infant should receive a daily multivitamin supplement until he is consuming at least 28 to 32 ounces of formula each day. The infant also requires iron supplementation. Some neonatal nutritionists recommend continuing the premature infant on a special premature infant formula, with its increased mineral, vitamin, and protein content, at least until the infant is approximately 40 weeks postconception.

Breast-feeding is strongly encouraged for the premature infant. Many of these infants will leave the hospital fully breast-fed. Some, however, will be making the transition from bottle to breast, while a few will remain dependent on some formula supplementation for several weeks or months. The breast-fed premature infant requires both multivitamin and iron supplementation, and the breast-feeding mother may require additional support and encouragement during this period. Service providers can be extremely helpful in this regard, even by simply promoting the benefits of breast-feeding and acknowledging the priority of a "good meal" (be it at the breast, bottle, or table) in an intervention session. Mothers receive valuable assistance from lactation support groups, lactation consultants, and other mothers of premature babies.

Neurodevelopmental Disabilities

The brain of the premature baby is extremely fragile and is routinely exposed to hypoxic stresses, rapid metabolic events, and wide swings in intracranial blood pressures that would virtually never be experienced in the uterus. What is perhaps most remarkable about high-risk preterm infants is that any of them survive neurologically intact. Major neurodevelopmental deficits (CP, mental retardation, blindness, deafness) occur in roughly 20–25 percent of surviving ELBW infants. Minor dysfunctions (learning disability, ADHD, lesser vision and hearing problems) probably occur in close to 50 percent, leaving the remainder, approximately 25 percent, apparently entirely normal and presumably having suffered no ill effects from their preterm birth (Allen, 1994; Halsey, Collin, and Anderson, 1996).

The prototypical neurodevelopmental deficit in the preterm infant is cerebral palsy. Sorting out what may be minor deficits or insignificant motor delays from CP in the first 12–18 months can be clinically difficult, and early intervention may be desirable before a firm diagnosis can be established. Mental retardation as a consequence of perinatal cerebral insult almost always occurs in concert with CP. It is quite uncommon to see significant cognitive impairment without equal or greater motor impairment unless there is some other explanation (e.g., a syndrome). In the mid-1950s, there was an epidemic of blindness in this country related to the use of high concentrations of life-saving oxygen in premature infants with RDS. The blindness was due to damage to the developing retina, then called RLF (retrolental fibroplasia). Oxygen toxicity is one of a number of factors that can contribute to this condition, which we now term ROP (retinopathy of prematurity). ROP still occurs, but with much less frequency, and generally only in the smallest and sickest premies. Since the link to oxygen was discovered back in the 1950s, blood oxygen levels have been monitored with great attention in order to keep them down to safe levels.

All premature infants who weighed less than 1,500 grams at birth (or any baby receiving oxygen therapy in the newborn period) should have an ophthalmologic examination for ROP at five to seven weeks of age and at least once again, due to the unpredictable course of ROP. In addition, premature infants are at increased risk, independent of the history of retinopathy, for strabismus and myopia. Careful evaluation of the eyes and the infant's vision is a part of routine well-child care, and service providers need to document their observations on how the infant uses his eyes in the intervention/play setting.

Published studies estimate a 1–5 percent incidence of hearing loss in preterm infants, especially in association with specific risk factors—birth weight less than 1,500 grams, intracranial hemorrhage, persistent fetal circulation (PFC), also called persistent pulmonary hypertension, or PPH exposure to ototoxic drugs, and meningitis. Many newborn units routinely screen infants falling into these risk categories. All preterm infants should have an audiologic screening evaluation prior to discharge. An abnormal screen may indicate an immature central nervous system or may be secondary to transient and reversible conductive deficits. Repeat evaluation is often necessary. As with vision, attention to and documentation of auditory performance by early intervention providers are most helpful.

Emotional/Behavioral Issues

Almost all parents will attest that the birth of one's child is a special, emotionally charged event. Surrounding this impression has risen a large and at times contentious literature related to these process of attachment, also known as "bonding" (Chess & Thomas, 1982; Lamb, 1982; Minde, 1986). The process is enormously disrupted by the birth of a sick and/or premature infant. High-risk infants have more developmental and behavioral problems as children, and the contribution of disrupted bonding to long-term behavioral/emotional disturbances is unknown. Anecdotally many parents seem strongly attached to their sick babies despite prolonged separations, and as these babies grow they seem equally attached to their parents (Chang et al., 1982). But for some more vulnerable parents, especially the younger, poorer, and less socially supported, interventions to foster attachment may have an extremely important effect on the attachment process (Anisfeld & Lipper, 1983)

Technology Assistance

Any apparatus that augments or replaces a bodily function is considered medical assistive technology. Many are internal (e.g., a shunt for hydrocephalus or a pacemaker). This section will address only the more common external devices, the vast majority of which are related to breathing or feeding functions.

Intravenous Lines.   Fluids, nutrients, or medications that must be delivered by direct infusion require an intravenous (IV) access route. IV catheters may be placed peripherally, whereby the tip of the catheter is in an extremity, or centrally, in which case the catheter is actually in the heart or in a major vein directly adjacent to it. Infection involving intravenous lines, especially central lines, is a major hazard. Therefore meticulous care is required to avoid contamination. These lines should be manipulated only by those specifically trained to do so.

Suctioning.   Children with severe oral motor dysfunction will have difficulty handling their own secretions. In this instance, feeding may be fraught with difficulty and may even be hazardous. Suctioning secretions from the mouth is intended to clear the airway and make breathing easier. Suctioning can be accomplished in easily accessible portions of the mouth and nose using the standard rubber bulb syringe. Deep suctioning to reach secretions that are in the back part of the mouth (the pharynx) requires a longer and relatively firm but not stiff tube and an electrically driven suction machine. Deep suctioning will almost always cause the patient to gag and can do damage to the throat if the tube is too stiff and is handled too vigorously. Suctioning is done as often as necessary, which may vary tremendously from child to child and will always increase when a child has an upper respiratory illness.

Tube Feeding.   For children who are unable to maintain adequate nutrition by oral feeding, the use of feeding tubes becomes a necessity. Tubes that are passed into the stomach through the nose (nasogastric) or mouth (orogastric) are generally employed for relatively short durations of time. These types of tubes are common in neonatal intensive care units, where the infant is expected to eventually acquire the ability to suck and swallow and sustain herself by the oral route. Gastrostomy tubes, on the other hand, should be considered in situations where longer-term oral feeding inadequacy is anticipated. The tube itself goes directly through the abdominal wall and through the stomach wall, where it is secured by means of a small, soft balloon. Feeding is accomplished directly into the stomach, bypassing the mouth and esophagus entirely. The gastrostomy tube (g-tube) itself is cumbersome; it gets in the way of prone activities, and it is at risk to be accidentally pulled out. After a relatively short period of time (usually 6–12 weeks), it can almost always be replaced with a gastrostomy button device that acts as a sealable port into which a feeding tube can be intermittently passed and then withdrawn. Button devices avoid the problems with positioning and prone activities. Often, children have gastrostomies performed in combination with a gastric fundoplication. This is a procedure designed to inhibit the reflux of stomach contents up the esophagus, with resultant vomiting and sometimes aspiration. Gastroesophageal reflux (GER) is particularly common in children with more severe neurodevelopmental problems. Care and management of the g-tube or button is influenced by whether the child has also had a fundoplication. A superb gastrostomy care manual for parents and other caretakers has been developed by clinicians at the University of Virginia (Paarlberg, Atkinson, Bella, & Kocher, 1991).

Monitors. Monitoring devices are used to continuously measure breathing or heart rate performance in children who are prone to have respiratory or cardiac events that may be life-threatening. Monitors generally rely on sensitivity to the respiratory rate, the pulse rate, or a measure of blood oxygen content (oximetry) through a sensor located on the skin, usually the earlobe or the fingertip. These devices are often mechanically troublesome because the wires and body attachments involved can easily become detached and may produce frequent false alarms. They are used almost exclusively during sleep and, therefore, should not interfere with active intervention programming.

Oxygen. Many children with chronic respiratory failure require supplemental oxygen in order to maintain an oxygen saturation in their blood at a level adequate for growth and well-being. Room air contains 21 percent oxygen; additional oxygen may be administered by a nasal cannula (a tube with short prongs inserted into the nostrils), face mask, oxygen tent or hood, or an artificial airway, such as a tracheostomy. A child requiring oxygen can go to school or to a therapy program with an oxygen source and delivery system.

There is a common misconception that oxygen is explosive. Oxygen itself is not combustible, but it is essential to support the combustion of other materials. Hence, a higher concentration of oxygen will make any fire burn *faster* (and therefore hotter), but oxygen itself does not explode in the presence of a flame.

Ventilators. Mechanical ventilation becomes necessary when, for any reason, the thoracic cage is unable to move air adequately into and out of the lungs, or when the lung tissue itself is diseased to such a point that oxygen and carbon dioxide cannot be effectively exchanged. An example of the latter would be the respiratory distress syndrome outlined previously. An example of the former situation would a high spinal cord injury paralyzing the respiratory muscles of the rib cage and/or diaphragm. For almost all purposes, mechanical ventilation involves delivering positive pressure through the airway, although negative pressure can be used (and was extremely important back in the days of the "iron lung" respirator for polio). Air can be pumped through the natural airway (via a mask), or, in a more invasive fashion, it can be delivered directly into the trachea via a tube inserted through the mouth, the nose, or a tracheostomy opening created surgically.

The tracheostomy incision is made in the cartilage of the trachea just below the larynx ("Adam's apple"). A tracheostomy is by far the most likely artificial ventilation system that a teacher would need to learn to deal with in the classroom. The tube is secured with adhesive or foam-padded strings around the neck. This open airway is then attached to a small mask, a ventilator machine, or a continuous pressure device with tubing that provides humidified air alone or mixed with extra oxygen. The tracheostomy permits access for suctioning secretions or removing of other obstructions, accomplished easily by disconnecting the ventilator tubing from the tracheostomy tube.

A blocked tracheostomy tube must be replaced or unobstructed immediately. A dislodged tube must be correctly repositioned immediately. This is especially true for children with narrowed tracheas who are at extra risk for a catastrophe because they have less (or no) natural airway passage to fall back on if the tube is blocked or dislodged. Children with tracheostomies should be closely observed and electronically monitored when human surveillance is limited (i.e., when sleeping). It is helpful for classroom personnel to be aware of the specifics of the child's airway in order to know the degree of response urgency needed.

The ventilator itself contains an alarm system that sounds under conditions of low or high pressure. The most common reason for a low-pressure alarm is accidental disconnection of the tracheostomy tube from the ventilator tubing. A high-pressure alarm most commonly sounds because something is obstructing the flow of gas into the child. The cause may be external to the child (e.g., kinked or obstructed tubing), or it may be within the child (e.g., mucus plugging the tracheostomy tube). Mucus plug formation is usually prevented by humidifying the gas mixture that passes through the tubing. If there is a mucus plug, it requires removal by suctioning. Ventilators typically are powered via standard wall socket electricity; they also have their own built-in power source (a battery) for emergency and temporary-use situations. The alarm system also will go off when there are electrical problems, when the battery is low, and so on.

Developmental complications of long-term mechanical ventilation include language deficits and behavior and feeding problems. A number of studies have pointed to deficits in language production, syntax, and articulation related to the presence of a tracheostomy during the period of early language development (Simon, Fowler, & Handler, 1983; Singer, et al., 1989). A speech-language pathologist should provide alternative methods of communication that are developmentally appropriate for the child. These include sign language and the use of medical or nonmedical technology assistance, such as a speaking tracheostomy valve or an augmentative communication system (e.g., picture board, language board, or computer).

Ventilator-dependent children may have behavior problems. The absence of audible speech leads to frustration in attempts at communication and may result in aggressive or acting-out behavior. Noncompliance and attention-getting behaviors (such as intentionally disconnecting the ventilator hose from the tracheostomy tube) can appear as well. All these issues should be managed in a formal way with an emphasis on consistency of approach in the school, home, and any other environments where they occur.

EMERGENCIES AND FIRST AID

Fifth-grade teacher: "Kevin, how do you define 'first aid'?"
Kevin: "First aid is what you can do for yourself before the doctor gets a hold of you."

This section of the chapter will provide a quick overview of how to react to certain situations that are *more likely* to arise among children with neurodevelopmental disabilities. Teachers in any classroom setting need to be prepared to respond to any and all pediatric/childhood emergency situations. For a concise, wonderfully illustrated resource, see the *Baby and Child Emergency First Aid Handbook* (Einzig, 1992).

All personnel working with medically fragile children should be trained in the performance of cardiopulmonary resuscitation (CPR). In fact, it is highly desirable for *all* day care, preschool, and early childhood professionals to be trained and to maintain proficiency in CPR. Respiratory arrest almost always precedes cardiac arrest in children. This fact cannot be stressed enough, because the ease and likelihood of successful resuscitation and the outlook following successful resuscitation are all tremendously more optimistic with children than with adults. Proper technique for mouth-to-mouth and bag-and-mask resuscitation is an essential skill for early interventionists and caretakers. With a little practice, the techniques become quite easy and unforgettable (like riding a bicycle).

Infant or young child CPR should be initiated as soon as someone becomes aware that a child is not breathing. As with all emergencies, the single most important factor is keeping one's equanimity when panic is the usual immediate reaction. The "ABC" (*airway,* rescue *breathing,* cardiac chest *compression*) basics and the need to call for help should be heeded, and will become automatic with regular recertification. For further details, the reader is encouraged to review guidelines for the performance of CPR (see American Heart Association, 1980, or other resources) and to become officially certified in the technique.

Allergic Reactions/Latex Allergy

Allergic reactions to medications and environmental allergens are common in children and are generally minor. Rashes, areas of swelling, flushing, sneezing, and running eyes and noses are the most common symptoms and are uncomfortable but never life-threatening.

More serious reactions include vomiting, wheezing, respiratory distress, and even cardiovascular shock. While these are exceedingly rare, they can be life-threatening. All caretakers and intervention personnel need to be aware that certain subgroups of special needs children, most notably those with spina bifida, are at very high risk to have serious allergic reactions to an extremely common substance—rubber (Cotter et al., 1996; Landwehr & Boguniewicz, 1996). This is the problem of latex allergy. Children with spina bifida are exposed repeatedly to latex-containing hospital supplies (catheters, rubber gloves, etc.) in an invasive manner. Many become sensitized, and once sensitized they can experience a life-threatening response to what would seem a trivial exposure (i.e., a toy balloon). The problem is so widespread and so serious that medical personnel treat all children with spina bifida under the assumption that they are latex allergic. School personnel should do the same. Table 8.8 provides an incomplete list of the innumerable common objects that contain latex.

As with children known to have anaphylactic reactions to insect stings (venom allergy), children known to have severe reactions to latex should carry an epinephrine administration device (Epi-Pen) for immediate injection. Caregivers and intervention personnel should be trained in its use. The records and health-information forms of such children should be conspicuously labeled. Also note that a recent report emphasizes that there is strong cross-reactivity between latex allergen and avocado proteins (Ahlroth et al., 1995).

Choking

Infants have frequent minor bouts of choking and gagging, usually on food. Children with neuromotor abnormalities are more likely to experience choking episodes, and

TABLE 8.8   Latex*-Containing Objects

MEDICAL SUPPLIES	CLASSROOM AND PLAYGROUND ITEMS
Adhesives	Art supplies: paints, glues
Bandages and dressings	Balloons
Catheters	Clothing: appliqués, elastic
Crutch tips and pads	Diapers, nipples, and pacifiers
Diapers, nipples, pacifiers	Dishwashing gloves
Elastic wraps and cuffs	Erasers
Enemas	Inner tubes
Gloves	Newspaper, coupons
Reflex hammers	Numerous toys (e.g., car wheels)
Syringe stoppers	Playground surfaces (shredded tires)
Tubing	Pool gear (e.g., goggles, thongs)
	Shoe soles
	Sports equipment (e.g., balls, handle grips)
	Stretch toys

NB: *Cross-reaction with banana, kiwi, and avocado can occur.

The Spina Bifida Association updates an exhaustive list of latex-containing and latex-free materials on a yearly basis. For a copy write to:

SBAA, Suite 250
4590 MacArthur Blvd. NW
Washington, DC 20007

some will be less able to spontaneously clear the obstruction on their own. If a significant choking episode appears to be under way, the key things to remember are:

1. Do not be too aggressive if the child can still cough, breathe, or cry.
2. Get help (call 911).
3. Avoid reaching in for the obstructing object.
4. Initiate CPR beathing, if necessary, *after* the airway has been cleared (cf. Einzig, 1992).

Fractures

Children who do not bear weight on their bones (e.g., the nonambulatory child with cerebral palsy or myelodysplasia), who are malnourished, or who have metabolic bone disorders (e.g., osteogenesis imperfecta) are at risk to break bones under circumstances that would usually be considered mildly traumatic or nontraumatic. These breaks can be relatively silent—accompanied by relatively mild discomfort and only minor swelling and/or a barely perceptible deformity. Additionally, a child may not be able to clearly express degree of pain or its localization.

School personnel need to be aware of children under their care who have had recurrent fractures or who are osteoporotic (have weakened, poorly calcified bone structure) and, therefore, are at risk for fracture. Basic splinting and immobilization techniques are useful to know and employ when a probable or definite fracture is recognized. Immobilization with a splint will greatly decrease pain and also limit additional tissue damage, bleeding, and swelling.

Drug Effects and Overdose/Poisoning

Every medication produces both beneficial and undesirable effects. Drug effects refer to the desirable, hoped-for benefits that prompted initiation of the medication. The measure of how well any given medication is accomplishing this is the objective (at least as much as possible) change in the target symptom, such as a decrease in muscle tone or increase in hand coordination from being placed on diazepam (Valium), or a decrease in seizure frequency from an anticonvulsant. Documentation of effects by nurses (who check, e.g., blood pressure), therapists (who check, e.g., tone and positioning, articulation), teacher (who checks, e.g., seizures, tone, positioning, attention span, etc.), parents, and other caregivers, and timely communication of these data are critical if the physician is to make a well-informed decision about changes in drug dosage.

The side effects of drugs are those signs and symptoms that are not the intended reason for using the medication and are usually (although not always) undesirable. Most side effects are predictable or at least can be somewhat anticipated; some will be unexpected. Their presence and severity (once again, well documented) must be balanced against the benefits of the medication in determining which way to go with dosing.

Some parents and many nonmedical professionals like to use the *PDR* (*Physicians' Desk Reference*) to help them understand a medication, anticipate its undesirable effects, and get a feel for its safety; however, a word of caution is in order. For the nonphysician, nonnurse, or nonpharmacist, a very limited amount of information about drug usage and drug effects is accessible in the *PDR*. On the other hand, an enormous amount of side effect information is presented without discrimination. Basically, every drug can produce multiple damaging effects on every organ system, a very large number of which are potentially life-threatening. The same litany of deathly consequences is more or less repeated for every drug in the compendium. This aspect of the information is virtually useless. What is of importance in decision-making is the discrimination of which side effects are most likely to occur, how persistent or transient they typically are when they appear, and how much of a problem they might cause the particular patient. Additionally, one needs to know how frequently the truly serious, life-threatening side effects are known to occur.

Children with cognitive deficits may be more likely to ingest medication or other harmful substances as a result of pica (the tendency to mouth and eat nonfood objects). More commonly, the child who is taking medication (e.g., anticonvulsant drugs for seizures) may gradually become toxic due to rising blood levels of the drug, even without any change in the dose. This phenomenon can occur due to changes in drug metabolism resulting from drug interference (from another medication), an unrecognized *brand* change, or a minor illness. A dose change (intentional or accidental) is also distinctly possible. The only indication of drug toxicity may be behavioral change in the classroom, once again pointing out the importance of knowing a child's baseline and making note of observed changes therefrom.

Head Injury

Head trauma in special needs children should be managed as it would be for any other child. Minor injuries can be treated with cold compresses, pressure for bleeding, cleaning, and covering for abrasions. More severe injuries that require possible suturing or have associated neurological symptoms will require medical attention.

Seizures

A seizure is the clinical manifestation of paroxysmal electrical activity in the brain. Seizures may be extremely subtle, as with *petit mal* epilepsy (characterized by very brief staring and/or perhaps a few rapid blinks), or frighteningly explosive, as with *grand mal* epilepsy (typified by falling to the ground, rigidity and violent shaking, stridorous breathing, and/or cyanosis).

Children with neurodevelopmental disorders are at much higher risk than the general population to experience an isolated seizure or to have epilepsy (repeated seizures). The two key factors in the classroom are observation and basic first aid. Observation is important in order to report the duration, frequency, and exact clinical features of a seizure or seizures as accurately as possible. First aid is important to protect the child from doing further harm to himself as a result of striking the head or limbs or biting the tongue. The old recommendation to put a stick, spoon, billfold, or heaven-knows-what in the mouth so the child does not swallow his tongue is incorrect. Loosening clothing, removing eyeglasses, keeping the child (especially the head and extremities) out of harm's way, and positioning the child on his side are the basic measures to be followed. Many children who experience "hard" seizures for more than two or three minutes will turn blue, but as this occurs the seizure tends to lessen and their breathing will improve. When the seizure finally ceases, they usually resume normal breathing, often with a deep sigh or two. If good breathing and improved skin color do not return, then the CPR sequence (ABC, with special attention to A) should be initiated.

For children with a known seizure disorder, having reliable knowledge of the usual type and frequency of seizures is essential if the teacher is to be able to respond appropriately to a spell that is out of the ordinary. As a rule, any first seizure requires urgent medical attention. In a child with known seizures, a spell that lasts five minutes or more generally deserves medical evaluation. This guideline may be too short for some individuals known to typically have slightly longer seizures. On the other hand, even four minutes may be troubling in a child whose usual pattern is much briefer. This also reemphasizes the importance of observational data on seizures in a child with epilepsy that differ in their manifestations or frequency from that child's usual pattern, which may be a warning that something new or different is going awry (e.g., with a shunt, a metabolic condition, or an anticonvulsant drug). These observations warrant diligent reporting and are extremely useful to the physician treating the child.

AIDS

The human immunodeficiency virus (HIV) is almost always acquired by infants and toddlers from their HIV-infected mother at the time of birth. Recent medical advances in drug therapy for HIV have substantially reduced the chance of transmission from mother to infant. At the time of this writing, if the mother is placed on a special regimen of zidovudine medication and if other general precautions are observed, the risk of transmission from mother to newborn is as low as 5 to 10 percent (American Academy of Pediatrics [AAP] Committee on Pediatric AIDS, 1997).

HIV multiplies in certain cells of the immune system, eventually depleting them and rendering the child almost defenseless against numerous infections, some of which can transform other cells into cancers. Once the child begins to acquire infections, the problem is referred to as the acquired immunodeficiency syndrome (AIDS). Although the various infections can be suppressed or successfully treated with appropriate medications for years, ultimately infection and/or cancer are fatal for the great majority of people with AIDS.

Needless to say, the presence of an HIV-infected child in school and day care settings can be the cause of extreme anxiety for parents, children, health care providers, and educators. HIV is not transmitted through casual contact (sharing toys, food, and eating utensils; hugging; kissing; etc.) nor by contact in the environment with urine, stool, saliva, or vomitus. Under extremely rare circumstances, direct contact of HIV-infected blood with broken skin can produce infection. Because of this possibility, preschoolers and developmentally disabled children who might bite are viewed as a theoretical transmission hazard. Actual transmission of HIV through biting in a day care setting has never been reported. There is one reported "possible" (unconfirmed) case of a sibling being infected at home from the bite of an infected toddler (Shirley & Ross, 1989).

Communities should emphasize their own state and national guidelines in designing school placement policies for HIV-infected children (Table 8.9).

State agencies (e.g., the Virginia Department of Health, 1995a, 1995b), the American Academy of Pediatrics (AAP Task Force on Pediatric AIDS, 1992), and others (Crocker & Cohen, 1990; Santelli, Birn, & Linde, 1992) have prepared guidelines in regard to developmental services and school and day care attendance for children with HIV infection and AIDS. Policies work best in the context of a comprehensive program incorporating AIDS education and care (Santelli et al, 1992).

TABLE 8.9   National Guidelines Regarding School Placement for Human Immunodeficiency Virus (HIV)-Infected Children*

1. In general, infected school-age children should be allowed to attend school in an unrestricted setting. The benefits of school attendance outweigh the remote possibility of transmission occurring in school.
2. Some children, such as preschoolers and children with neurologic impairments, with open skin lesions, or with behavior problems such as biting, may need a more restricted setting.
3. In determining an individual educational placement, a team approach should be employed using representatives of health and education departments as well as family members.
4. Staff knowledge about a child's HIV status should be based on a "need to know." The child's and family's right to privacy should be respected.
5. Universal hygiene precautions should be adopted by schools.
6. Mandatory or universal screening is not warranted.
7. Education about HIV/AIDS should be encouraged for parents, students, and educational staff.

*Based on recommendations of the American Academy of Pediatrics and the Centers for Disease Control.

From "School Placement for HIV-Infected Children: The Baltimore Experience" by J. H. S. Santelli, A. E. Birn, and J. Linde, 1992, *Pediatrics, 89,* 843–848. Adapted by permission.

Hepatitis

Hepatitis (inflammation of the liver) can result from a number of causes. As a primary disease, it is most commonly caused by one of several viruses, which are designated by letters (A, B, C, etc.); less commonly, another infection or a toxic agent can be involved. It can be an associated problem of other infections (e.g., infectious mononucleosis). It can be a toxic side effect of therapeutic drugs (e.g., anticonvulsants) or a direct effect of environmental toxins or drug overdoses (e.g., acetaminophen, iron). In the years before the deinstitutional movement began, infectious hepatitis was rampant in institutions for the mentally retarded. Hepatitis A virus is highly communicable by the fecal-oral route. The other hepatitis viruses are more difficult to transmit and usually require blood (via transfusions or contaminated needles) or other intimate exchange. Hepatitis can easily be transmitted from an infected mother to her newborn at birth.

In the early intervention setting, the infant or toddler who has active hepatitis could transmit the infection to staff and to other children as well as to family members. There are two key considerations to understanding the risks and the precautions. First, most people who acquire viral hepatitis resolve the infection and become immune to it. They carry hepatitis *antibody* in their blood indicating a past infection, and they *cannot* transmit the disease. (In fact, they no longer have the disease.) Individuals who are still infected (and therefore potentially infectious) carry hepatitis *antigen* in their blood. The first order of business is to learn whether the child is a "carrier," that is to say, positive for the antigen. The second issue is to learn which viral type is involved. Hepatitis B is not generally transmitted by casual contact, but hepatitis A can be.

COMMUNICATION AMONG PROFESSIONALS

Doctors and the IFSP

Part C of the Individuals with Disabilities Education Act (see Chapter 1) deals with financial incentives offered to states to develop their own comprehensive services for infants and toddlers who are disabled. The services are to be family-centered and truly coordinated among agencies. The IFSP (individualized family service plan) required by Part C reflects a broad and comprehensive human services approach to structuring an efficient array of supports, taking into account all aspects of family life and dynamics. The American Academy of Pediatrics has strongly encouraged pediatricians to participate in the IFSP process (AAP, Committee on Children with Disabilities, 1992).

Pediatricians, however, have often felt left out by the language employed in federal legislation that limits medical services to diagnosis and evaluation only. The Committee on Children with Disabilities has promoted a much broader role for pediatricians, which includes program planning and monitoring, medical supervision, and other aspects of management as well (Purvis, 1991).

Regardless of these language deficiencies at the policy level, at the local level individual school personnel have urged increased pediatrician input into the process. Children who come to light in the under-three age range are likely to have considerable medical needs, as noted. In addition to major medical and neurodevelopmental problems (seizures, technology dependency, etc.), a proportion of them have infectious or related etiologies (e.g., congenital infections, AIDS) that can be highly anxiety-provoking for early interventionists, caretakers, and parents of other children in the same program, as noted in many of the above vignettes.

A cooperative relationship between team members is fundamental to achieving the goal of coordinated family-centered care. Developmental pediatricians and general pediatricians with a special interest in chronic conditions should be key collaborators in the care for young children. The goal is to see that the best supports are made available to the parents of children with any chronic illness or disability. The "medical home" philosophy has dominated new directives adopted by the American Academy of Pediatrics (AAP, Task Force on the Definition of the Medical Home, 1992) and federal funding policies. It implies the essential importance of quality community services in order to achieve successful family-centered care. While medical center–based interdisciplinary clinics will still be needed for comprehensive evaluations, academic pediatricians must better address the need for continuing education programs for community professionals that are up-to-date, comprehensive, and practical.

DNR Orders

If a child has an untoward event that results in the cessation or compromise of respiratory or cardiac function, the immediate response by professional, paraprofessional, and lay observers should be to resuscitate (see the section on CPR above). Do not resuscitate (DNR) orders represent specific instructions, written by a licensed physician, either to not initiate or to limit the extent of resuscitation efforts. There are many children who have DNR orders in place while receiving care in the hospital or at home. Some of these individuals will be in center-based school programs.

Obviously the decision to establish a DNR order must be a carefully considered exercise involving the child (to the extent she is capable), the parents, the attending physician, and other relevant members of the family and the health care team. DNR orders are legally binding! A clear delineation of actions that should or should not be carried out needs to be communicated verbally and in writing to all relevant parties. The health care team doctors, nurses, emergency medical technicians, and so on are clearly implicated. It is less clear how directly these wishes and orders apply to school personnel. Many school administrators have simply declared it to be "school policy" that DNR orders cannot be carried out in school settings, which is probably more a reflection of avoiding the issue than of thoughtfully considering the ethical implications. In the author's discussions with teachers, nurses, and therapists about the topic, it seems that the uneasiness expressed about DNR orders comes down to three issues:

1. The acute psychological distress occasioned by "not doing something"
2. The fear that a simple and easily remediable event could be missed (e.g., choking on thick saliva)
3. The effect on other children in the vicinity

The first issue is one that everyone has to deal with—parent, doctor, teacher, and others. It has a lot to do with understanding death as a natural and necessary end point and with being able to acknowledge that when the time has come, it is permissible to allow death to happen. This viewpoint runs strongly counter to most people's instincts. Thus, the determination *not* to intervene must be a premeditated conclusion arrived at in each individual case. When the decision to limit intervention has been carefully thought out in advance, carrying it out in a palliative, supportive manner is much easier than trying to make such a decision in a crisis mode or intervening in a way or to a degree that one senses is wrong.

The second issue can be broken down into two parts: following explicit orders and being reasonable. A sample set of DNR orders, taken from a current hospital chart, is presented in Table 8.10. These orders are simply and clearly stated and are unequivocal. They are a model for the type of clarity desired. In this particular instance, they allow for examining the patient and "doing something" in the case of a remediable situation. In a different case, where, for example, assisted ventilation were *not* endorsed, it would still be *reasonable* for a classroom aide (or whoever) to check the mouth for an obstruction or to suction the airway of a child who has suddenly and unexpectedly stopped breathing, even if not specified in the orders. (It is hard to imagine suctioning being explicitly prohibited in a child with or at risk for respiratory compromise.) On the other hand, for a teacher, an emergency medical technician, or a physician to initiate and persist with mouth-to-mouth resuscitation and cardiac chest compressions in the face of written DNR orders prohibiting these measures amounts to unreasonable (and disrespectful) behavior.

TABLE 8.10   Sample DNR Orders

The following advanced directive is to be honored per the wishes of the parents (or legal guardians) of _____ (name of patient). In the event of cardiorespiratory dysfunction or arrest:

1. *Support* with assisted ventilation.
2. *Support* with parenteral medications for control of blood pressure or arrhythmias.
3. Do *not* administer intracardiac drugs.
4. Do *not* initiate chest compressions.
5. Do *not* administer electroshock cardioversion.

The final issue is an important one that takes into account the well-being of other children and demands careful consideration. The key to all three issues is advance planning and a willingness to collaborate on a plan that will fairly serve all parties the involved child, parents, school staff, other children, and bystanders. For the benefit of the latter two groups, some effort at comforting and segregating (not hiding) the "patient"; maintaining a calm, controlled, and professional atmosphere; and rendering some type of appropriate explanation all need to be accomplished.

Case managers are central to this entire process, and the county medical examiner needs to be notified *in advance* that a death may occur in the community, be it at home, in school, or in another setting. Otherwise, unnecessary police and/or medical examiner investigations may be imposed on an already difficult situation.

In summary, early interventionists are very likely to encounter children with substantial medical needs, even medical fragility, in their case loads. Early childhood service providers need general medical background information and need support from the medical community with regard to specific issues about each child they are working with. The intent of this chapter has been to provide some of that background and to offer some insights on when and how to effect collaboration and communication among medical and educational professionals.

REFERENCES

Ahlroth, M., Alerius, H., Turjanmaa, K., Makinen-Kiljunen, S., Reunala, T., & Palusno, T. (1995). Cross-reacting allergens in natural rubber latex and avocado. *Journal of Allergy and Clinical Immunology, 96,* 167–173.

Albright, A. L., Cerri, A., & Singletary, J. (1991). Intrathecal baclofen for spasticity in cerebral palsy. *Journal of the American Medical Association, 265,* 1418–1422.

Allen, M. C. (1994). Neurodevelopmental follow-up of the preterm infant. *Pediatric Rounds, 3*(1), 1–4.

Allen, M. C., & Alexander, G. R. (1990). Gross motor milestones in preterm infants: Correction for degree of prematurity. *Journal of Pediatrics, 116,* 955–959.

American Academy of Pediatrics Committee on Children with Disabilities (1992). Pediatricians' role in the development and implementation of an individual education plan (IEP) and/or an individual family service plan (IFSP). *Pediatrics 89,* 340–342.

American Academy of Pediatrics Task Force on Definition of the Medical Home (1992). The medical home. *Pediatrics, 90,* 774.

American Academy of Pediatrics Task Force on Pediatric AIDS (1988). Pediatric guidelines for infection control of human immunodeficiency virus (acquired immunodeficiency virus) in hospitals, medical offices, schools, and other settings. *Pediatrics, 82,* 801–807.

American Academy of Pediatrics Task Force on Pediatric AIDS (1992). Guidelines for human immunodeficiency virus (HIV)-infected children and their foster families (1992). *Pediatrics, 89,* 681–683.

American Academy of Pediatrics Committee on Pediatric AIDS (1997). Evaluation and medical treatment of the HIV-exposed infant. *Pediatrics, 99,* 909–917.

American Heart Association (1980). *Cardiopulmonary resuscitation: CPR.* (2nd ed.) Tulsa: CPR Publishers.

Anisfeld, E., & Lipper, E. (1983). Early contact, social support, and mother-infant bonding. *Pediatrics, 72,* 79–83.

Austin, K. D., & Hall, J. G. (1992). Nontraditional inheritance. *Pediatric Clinics of North America, 39,* 335–348.

Baird, H. W., & Gordon, E. C. (1983). *Neurological evaluation of infants and children* (Clinics in Developmental Medicine No. 84/85). Philadelphia: J. B. Lippincott.

Batshaw, M. L. (1997). *Children with disabilities* (4th ed.). Baltimore: Paul H. Brookes.

Blasco, P. A. (1989). Preterm birth: To correct or not to correct. *Developmental Medicine and Child Neurology, 31,* 816–821.

Blasco, P. A. (1992). Normal and abnormal motor development. *Pediatric Rounds, 1*(2), 1–6.

Blasco, P. A., Baumgartner, M. C., & Mathes, B. C. (1983). Literature for parents of children with cerebral palsy. *Developmental Medicine and Child Neurology, 25,* 642–647.

Blasco, P. A., & Johnson, C. P. (1996). Supports for parents of children with disabilities. In A. J. Capute & P. J. Accardo (Eds.), *Developmental disabilities in infancy and childhood,* 2nd ed. (pp. 443–472) Baltimore: Paul H. Brookes.

Blasco, P. M., Blasco, P. A., & Zirpoli, T. J. (1994). Prenatal diagnosis: Current procedures and implications for early interventionists working with families. *Infants and Young Children, 7,* 33–42.

Bleck, E. E. (1987). *Orthopedic management in cerebral palsy* (Clinics in Developmental Medicine No. 99/100). Philadelphia: J. B. Lippincott.

Blizzard, R. M. (1993). Genetics and growth: New understanding. *Pediatric Rounds, 2*(2), 1–4.

Brewer, E. J., McPherson, M., Magrab, P. R., & Hutchins, V. L. (1989). Family-centered, community-based, coordinator care for children with special health care needs. *Pediatrics, 83,* 1055–1061.

Butler, M. G., & Meaney, F. J. (1991). Standards for selected anthropometric measurements in Prader-Willi syndrome. *Pediatrics, 88,* 853–860.

Capute, A. J., & Accardo, P. J. (1996) *Developmental disabilities in infancy and childhood* (Vols. I & II, 2nd ed.). Baltimore: Paul H. Brookes.

Capute, A. J., & Palmer, F. P. (1980). A pediatric overview of the spectrum of developmental disabilities. *Journal of Developmental and Behavioral Pediatrics, 1,* 66–69.

Capute, A. J., Shapiro, B. K., Palmer, F. P., Ross, A., & Wachtel, R. C. (1985). Normal gross motor development: The influence of race, sex, and socio-economic status. *Developmental Medicine and Child Neurology, 27,* 635–643.

Chang, P. N., Thompson, T. R., & Fisch, R. O. (1982). Factors affecting attachment between infants and mothers separated at birth. *Journal of Developmental and Behavioral Pediatrics, 3,* 96–98

Chess, S., & Thomas, A. (1982). Infant bonding: Mystique and reality. *American Journal of Orthopsychiatry, 52,* 213–222.

Coplan, J. (1987). Deafness: Ever heard of it? Delayed recognition of permanent hearing loss. *Pediatrics, 79,* 206–213.

Cotter, C. M., Burbach, C., Boyer, M., Engelhardt, M., Smith, M., & Hubka, K. (1996). Latex allergy and the student with spina bifida. *Journal of School Nursing, 12,* 14–18.

Crocker, A. C., & Cohen, H. J. (1990). *Guidelines on developmental services for children and adults with HIV infection.* Silver Spring, Md.: AAUAP for Persons with Developmental Disabilities.

Cronk, C., Crocker, A. C., Pueschel, S. M., Shea, A. M., Zackai, E., Pickens, G., & Reed, R. B. (1988). Growth charts for children with Down syndrome: 1 month to 18 years of age. *Pediatrics, 81,* 102–110.

deSchweinitz, L., Miller, C. A., & Miller, J. B. (1959). Delays in the diagnosis of deafness among preschool children. *Pediatrics, 24,* 462–468.

Drews, C. D., Yeargin-Allsopp, M., Murphy, C. C., & Decoufle, P. (1994). Hearing impairment among 10-year-old children: Metropolitan Atlanta, 1985 through 1987. *American Journal of Public Health, 84,* 1164–1166.

Einzig, M. J. (1992). *Baby and child emergency first aid handbook.* New York: Meadowbrook.

Erhardt, R. P. (1994). *Developmental hand dysfunction: Theory, assessment, treatment* (2nd ed.). San Antonio: Therapy Skill Builders.

Halsey, C. L., Collin, M. F., & Anderson, C. L. (1996). Extremely low-birth-weight children and their peers: A comparison of school-age outcomes. *Archives of Pediatrics and Adolescent Medicine, 150,* 790–794.

Hamill, P. V. V., Drizd, T. A., Johnson, C. L., Reed, R. B., Roche, A. F., & Moore, W. M. (1979). Physical growth: National Center for Health Statistics percentiles. *American Journal of Clinical Nutrition, 32,* 607–629.

Jackson, J. F., North, E. R., III, & Thomas, J. G. (1976). Clinical diagnosis of Down's syndrome. *Clinical Genetics, 9,* 483–487.

Jones, K. L. (1996). *Smith's recognizable patterns of human malformation* (5th ed.). Philadelphia: W. B. Saunders.

Kaminer, R. K., & Jedrysek, E. (1983). Age of walking and mental retardation. *American Journal of Public Health, 73,* 1094–1096.

Klein, S. D. (Ed.) (1977). National resources for specific disabilities and conditions. *Exceptional Parent* (Annual Resource Guide), *27,* 9–39.

Klein, S. D. (1993). The challenge of communicating with parents. *Journal of Developmental and Behavioral Pediatrics, 14,* 184–191.

Knobloch, H., & Pasamanick, B. (1974). *Gesell and Amatruda's develpomental diagnosis* (3rd ed.). Hagerstown, Md.: Harper and Row, pp. 3–15.

Koman, L. A., Mooney, J. F., & Smith, B. P. (1996). Neuromuscular blockade in the management of cerebral palsy. *Journal of Child Neurology, 11* (Suppl.1), S23–S28.

Kraft, M. (1985). *A child's guide to cerebral palsy.* Charlottesville: University of Virginia, Kluge Children's Rehabilitation Center.

Krahn, G. L., Hallum, A., & Kime, C. (1993). Are there good ways to give "bad news"? *Pediatrics, 91,* 578–582.

Lamb, M. E. (1982). Early contact and maternal-infant bonding: One decade later. *Pediatrics, 70,* 763–768.

Landwehr, L. P., & Boguniewicz, M. (1996). Current perspectives on latex allergy. *Journal of Pediatrics, 128,* 305–312.

Lewis, D. V., & Freeman, J. M. (1977). The electroencephalogram in pediatric practice: Its use and abuse. *Pediatrics, 60,* 324–330.

Lipkin, P. H. (1996), Epidemiology of the developmental disabilities. In A. J. Capute & P. J. Accardo (Eds.), *Developmental disabilities in infancy and childhood* (Vol. I, 2nd ed.) (pp. 137–156). Baltimore: Paul H. Brookes.

Liptak, G. S., Keller, B. B., Feldman, A. W., & Chamberlin, R. W. (1983). Enhancing infant development and parent-practitioner interaction with the Brazelton Neonatal Assessment Scale, *Pediatrics, 72,* 71–78.

Lock, T. M., Shapiro, B. K., Ross, A., & Capute, A. J. (1986). Age of presentation of developmental disabilities. *Journal of Developmental and Behavioral Pediatrics, 7,* 340–345.

Minde, K., (1986). Bonding and attachment: Its relevance for the present day clinician. *Developmental Medicine and Child Neurology, 28,* 803–813.

Myers, B. J. (1982). Early intervention using Brazelton training with middle-class mothers and fathers of newborns. *Child Development, 53,* 462–471.

Nolan, C. (1987). *Under the eye of the clock.* New York: St. Martin's.

Paarlberg, J., Atkinson, W., Bella, D., & Kocher, A. (1991). *Guide to gastrostomy tubes and their care: A parent instruction manual.* Charlottesville: University of Virginia, Kluge Children's Rehabilitation Center.

Peacock, W. J., Arens, L. J., & Berman, B. (1987). Cerebral palsy spasticity: Selective posterior rhizotomy. *Pediatric Neuroscience, 13,* 61–66.

Peckham, C., & Gibb, D. (1995). Mother-to-child transmission of the human immunodeficiency virus. *New England Journal of Medicine, 333,* 289–302.

Physicians' desk reference (51st ed.). (1997). Montvale, N.J.: Medical Economics Data Production.

Pranzatelli, M. R. (1996). Oral pharmacotherapy for the movement disorders of cerebral palsy. *Journal of Child Neurology, 11* (Suppl. 1), S13–S22.

Purvis, P. (1991). The public laws for education of the disabled: The pediatrician's role. *Journal of Developmental and Behavioral Pediatrics, 12,* 327–339.

Remington, J. S., & Klein, J. O. (Eds.). (1995). *Infectious diseases of the fetus and newborn* (4th ed.). Philadelphia: W. B. Saunders.

Robinson, C. G., Willits, R. E. & Benson, K. I. G. (1965). Delayed diagnosis of congenital hearing loss in preschool children. *Public Health Reports, 80,* 790–796.

Santelli, J. S., Birn, A.-E., & Linde, J. (1992). School placement for HIV-infected children: The Baltimore experience. *Pediatrics, 89,* 843–848.

Shah, C. P., Chandler, D., & Doll, R. (1978). Delay in referral of children with impaired hearing. *Volta Review, 80,* 206–215.

Shirley, L. R., & Ross, S. A. (1989). Risk of transmission of human immunodeficiency virus by bite of infected toddler. *Journal of Pediatrics, 114,* 425–427.

Simon, B. M., Fowler, S. M., & Handler, S. D. (1983). Communication development in young children with long-term tracheostomies: Preliminary report. *International Journal of Pediatric Otolaryngology, 6,* 37–50.

Singer, L. T., Davillier, M., Preuss, L., Szekely, L., Hawkins, S., Yamashita, T., & Baley J., et al. (1996). Feeding interactions in infants with very low birth weight and bronchopulmonary dysplasia. *Journal of Developmental and Behavioral Pediatrics, 17,* 69–76.

Singer, L. T., Kercsmar, C., Legris, G., Orlowski, J. P., Hill, B. P., & Doershurk, C. (1989). Developmental sequelae of long-term infant tracheostomy. *Developmental Medicine and Child Neurology, 31,* 224–230.

Stevenson, R. D. (1992). Failure to thrive. In D. E. Greydanus & M. L. Wolraich (Eds.), *Behavioral pediatrics* (pp. 298–313). New York: Springer-Verlag.

Virginia Department of Health (1995a). *Recommendations for day care center attendance.* Richmond: Author.

Virginia Department of Health. (1995b). *Recommendations for school attendance.* Richmond: Author.

Widmayer, S. M., & Field, T. M. (1981). Effects of Brazelton demonstrations for mother on the development of preterm infants. *Pediatrics, 67,* 711–714.

CHAPTER NINE

MODELS OF COLLABORATION FOR EARLY INTERVENTION

Laying the Groundwork

VIRGINIA BUYSSE

PATRICIA W. WESLEY

- To describe the expanding roles of early intervention professionals in the context of a changing field
- To apply the concept of quality to early intervention practice as a foundation for identifying consumers and evaluating the effectiveness of services
- To understand the similarities and distinctions among various models of collaboration, including technical assistance, consultation, teaming, training, and supervision and mentorship
- To develop strategies for evaluating the effectiveness of existing collaborative approaches and envisioning new methods for working together in the future.

> *Most of us operate in a small central area of the role which we can call a "zone of comfort." Within this zone of comfort we feel quite safe because we are very sure of our ground and it is a low-risk area. Once we step outside this comfort zone the ground is considerably less firm underfoot. These swampy areas are at the boundary of our expertise, professional knowledge, authority and confidence.*
>
> —Dimock, 1993, p. 45

The field of early intervention has changed and continues to change rapidly. As described in previous chapters, parents and professionals have witnessed the adoption of a family-centered orientation, the unification of early education and early intervention, and the move to serve young children with disabilities in inclusive and natural environments. In addition, a corresponding paradigm shift has occurred in the way early intervention services are designed and delivered from a stimulation or remediation model to one that promotes competence and supports full inclusion and participation in the community through multiagency collaboration. These and other innovations have created new professional roles for early interventionists and redefined the ways in which parents and professionals work together (Buysse & Wesley, 1993).

This paradigm shift has also resulted in a move from direct services to indirect services. Kontos and File (1993) pointed out that "when children with disabilities are placed in integrated community programs, even for part of a day, early interventionists are no longer the only educators working with the children, and, in many instances, the responsibilities of the early interventionist evolve from those of direct service to those of indirect service to the children." (p. 176)

Indirect services are primarily adult-oriented and consist of consultation and collaboration, rather than direct instruction, which focuses on the child. The shift from direct to indirect services requires that early interventionists learn new roles and extend the boundaries of their professional comfort by expanding their partnerships to include not only family members but child care providers, therapists, health care professionals, administrators, social workers, and others with whom children and families interact in a variety of community settings.

The purpose of this chapter is to familiarize the reader with state-of-the-art models of collaboration for early intervention. The specific professional roles and models that have been identified to enhance collaborative work relationships emanate from the fields of business, organizational development, international politics, education, community mental health, and psychology. These include technical assistance, consultation, teaming, training, and supervision and mentorship. Our intent in this chapter is to lay the groundwork to equip early interventionists with the skills to work effectively with parents and adults who serve children and families. In addition to a theoretical framework, each of the collaborative models presented in this chapter contains practical suggestions, as well as a discussion of the process and tools needed to build relationships, communicate effectively, identify and respond to technical assistance needs, and plan strategically for the future. We begin by discussing the concept of quality as it relates to consumers of early education and intervention, and then distinguish among various models of collaboration that promote quality services for young children and families. We conclude with a framework that can be used to integrate and evaluate these approaches.

APPLYING THE CONCEPT OF QUALITY TO EARLY INTERVENTION PRACTICE: WHO ARE THE CONSUMERS?

Sometimes it is difficult to remember that collaboration is a means to an end, not an end in itself. We seek better methods of working together for one basic reason: to improve the quality of our services for young children and families. The focus on improving quality among the human service professions can be viewed as part of a growing quality movement across many institutions throughout the world today. Quality is a term that is, at the same time, both easy to understand and difficult to define. What do we mean by quality services, and what are some benchmarks for measuring it?

Total Quality Management (TQM), which originated in business and manufacturing, offers one approach for understanding ideas related to quality. The ideas inherent in TQM were introduced by Demming, Juran, and others in the 1930s and 1940s, but were not widely accepted in the United States until recently (Sallis, 1993). TQM is a philosophy and a methodology for managing institutional change with the goal of improving quality (Sallis, 1993). The main idea behind the concept is quite simple: quality is a function of customer satisfaction. To assess whether our customers are satisfied, we must first determine who the customer is and then decide what the product is. As mentioned earlier, the consumers of early intervention are young children and their families, as well as a growing number of professionals and assistants from a variety of settings: homes, child care centers, preschool classrooms, family child care homes, hospitals, and clinics. The product is more difficult to define. Drawing a distinction between human services and other types of products, Sallis (1993) noted that human services are both intangible and relationship-based, making quality an even more challenging notion to define and measure.

One concept from TQM that has implications for improving the quality of early education and intervention services is the assessment of the organizational structure of early education and intervention programs. Programs that rely too heavily on top-down, hierarchical management structures may find it difficult to involve families in decision-making, to create leadership roles for families, or to promote interdisciplinary collaboration through teamwork, which is an essential element of TQM. Developing leadership potential to create a vision and communicate this vision effectively to others is another TQM concept that could be applied in our work with families and other professionals. Creating effective team leaders, supervisors, and program administrators through leadership training and other methods represents an important step in developing high-quality programs and services. Finally, we must embrace teamwork at every level as a building block for improving quality and implementing strategic planning to address current and future needs of young children and families.

In programs that serve young children and their families, the concept of quality must be applied broadly across all aspects of planning, delivering, and evaluating services. National professional organizations have described recommended practices and guidelines to help practitioners and families define and apply notions of quality across each of these areas. As part of the process of improving quality, professionals face particular challenges in developing ways to involve family members and create leadership roles for them. Most professionals now recognize the value of family involvement, but have found it difficult to find ways to encourage broad-based parental participation on boards and planning teams and to promote family decision-making at every level. Another important challenge in making quality improvements lies in developing an awareness of the influence of cultural diversity on collaborative processes. Many programs serving young children and families were influenced by a cultural perspective that is different from that of the clients they serve (Nugent, 1994). Viewing the early childhood fields from different cultural perspectives challenges professional assumptions about child development, raises questions about the appropriateness of program goals and practices, and reveals the rich diversity of child-rearing patterns and beliefs among various ethnic and cultural groups. Although there is general consensus that programs serving young children and their families should be community-based, family-centered, and culturally sensitive, most programs continue to struggle to achieve a balance.

TECHNICAL ASSISTANCE

As community child care and early intervention organizations redefine their mission, target population, and methods of service delivery, it is easy to recognize a need for support and guidance. Technical assistance (TA) can provide helpful tools to programs experiencing these kinds of changes as they reexamine the way they relate to each other and the rest of the community.

Although definitions of TA vary, a common feature is the transfer of "information, methods, tools, and support" (Sullivan, 1991, p. 290) or "specialized knowledge, skills, information, and technologies" (Richman & Clifford, 1980, p. 13) from one system to another that perceives a need for change. Although the terms *in-service training* and *consultation* are often equated with TA, Trohanis

(1982) pointed out that "TA involves the provision of quality content and/or process expertise via a responsive, continuous, and external system to assist clients and their organization to change or improve for the better." (p. 120) Based on this definition, consultation and training are but two strategies that may be employed in a carefully designed sequence of activities to promote systems change. Technical assistance offers a system of strategies that can be used to effect changes that require more intensive and extensive assistance than can be provided through materials, training, or consultation alone (Loucks-Horsley & Mundry, 1991).

As early interventionists expand their collegial networks to include persons who traditionally have been outside the special education field, they can be valuable resources to programs undergoing some of the systems changes described in this chapter. In Vignette 9.1, Julie encounters someone eager to take advantage of her expertise.

VIGNETTE 9.1   BRIGHT BEGINNINGS AND FUTURE NEEDS

Julie is an early interventionist who has been visiting 15-month-old Jorge at Bright Beginnings child care for nearly six weeks, ever since she went with Jorge and his mother to visit the program prior to enrollment. Jorge has cerebral palsy, and his new teacher, Ann, was especially glad to have Julie in the classroom on Tuesday and Thursday mornings. Ann had many questions about how best to adapt routines and activities for Jorge, and about his health and physical condition. But Ann also had questions about toddlers in general, since this was the first year the center had opened a toddler class. Julie made a few suggestions for making more toys and materials accessible to the children by rearranging some low shelves in the room. On a recent visit, Ann told Julie about the center's toddler waiting list. Ann was on a staff committee at the center to look into expanding in the spring—perhaps adding another toddler class and an infant class. She knew Julie also saw an infant in a family child care home in the neighboring county, and she wondered about what other types of programs were available for infants and toddlers, including those with special needs. What did Julie think were the challenges and benefits of serving younger children? What steps could they take to make sure a new class would be appropriate for children with special needs? Ann also had lots of questions about training resources and opportunities for herself and the other staff at the center. She wondered if Julie could do a workshop about child development in the near future for the whole center. She also wanted to learn more about how to work with parents of very young children.

We can imagine how overwhelmed Julie may have felt after this visit. She was comfortable answering the questions Ann had about Jorge, and she was glad to offer suggestions about room arrangement. She wasn't prepared, however, to provide consultation about program expansion or to take on training the whole staff. Julie knew that she would have to draw from a range of resources to be able to help Ann, and that there were some services Ann needed that she could not personally provide. What Julie and Ann both needed was the support of multiple TA services focusing on early childhood issues. In the absence of a formal system of resources and support, Julie would do the best she could to find such assistance for Ann. She could refer Ann and the expansion committee to a child care program in the neighboring county that had expanded its infant-toddler program the previous year. She could loan them a videotape series about child development from her office, and mention their need for a workshop to the nurse who provides training as a part of the public health department's well child clinic. She could also refer Ann to a staff person at the local child care resource and referral agency who was aware of what types of licensed and registered child care centers and family child care homes were operating across their local tricounty area. Finally, Julie and some of her colleagues at the office had just been talking about the challenges of collaborating with parents to meet the needs of their young children. Perhaps they would all benefit from sitting down with someone like Ann and sharing ideas.

Strategies like the ones described above illustrate how flexible TA must be to respond to the diverse needs that arise in early intervention and child care today. Technical assistance providers must draw from a range of options to be effective in a variety of contexts. Some states have responded to the needs of practitioners like Julie and Ann and to the corresponding needs of families by creating statewide systems of TA to support early childhood programs. In other states, regional teams provide support to local communities. In many instances, however, early interventionists find themselves in a position much like Julie's, where their role evolves to include providing TA in specific situations. It is useful to be aware of resources in the community that can help. For example, perhaps a local university sponsors a TA project or offers in-service training on a particular topic, or a mental health agency or child care resource and referral agency may offer a lending library of training materials and other resources. Ways to locate resources include talking with professional colleagues in the community, attending regional and state conferences, and conducting a search on the Internet.

Whether the focus of TA is on facilitating change at the state, regional, community, program, classroom, or individual child or family level, the process involves common goals based on what we know about how change occurs. In the following sections, we will see how these broad goals might apply to Julie and Ann's situation, and we will examine the roles and process of technical assistance.

Goals

Technical assistance providers first must understand and help the people with whom they are working to understand the barriers and facilitators of change in specific situations (Peck, Furman, & Helmstetter, 1993). For example, when programs like Ann's begin to serve children with disabilities, it is necessary to examine program policies, personnel preparation practices, and the adequacy of resources such as special education consultation to determine what obstacles and supports exist for the innovation. Similarly, although the attitudes of the staff at the child care program may be supportive of early childhood inclusion, there may be families of children with and without disabilities who are not comfortable with the idea. Only when these critical issues are examined can change be implemented in an effective way.

Second, TA builds support and commitment for innovation by encouraging the broad participation of all stakeholders in planning, and by creating opportunities for them to listen to and understand the unique perspective that each brings to the process. At Bright Beginnings, a staff committee has been formed to talk about expanding the center to serve more infants and toddlers in the community. If Julie agrees to provide TA during this process, one of her roles might be to help the committee identify who else might have a stake in the center's expansion and to bring them to the table. For example, there may be parents or other early intervention professionals whose experiences and interests would be valuable contributions to the committee's work.

Third, TA provides expertise to help clients develop their vision of what changes are needed and to translate that vision into a written plan of action. In other words, it enhances both content and process. Ann and the committee at Bright Beginnings have a broad vision of serving younger children, including those with special needs. Julie can help link them to the resources they need to fine-tune their vision and long-range plan. Such resources might represent a variety of content areas: child care rules and regulations regarding infant/toddler classrooms, service coordination for young children with special needs, the critical components of quality inclusive infant/toddler care, and building strong relationships with families. Technical assistance could also help the committee identify and implement a step-by-step planning process.

Fourth, TA utilizes and promotes multiple services and methods of working with others that help the client implement the plan of action: consulting on site, coordinating or delivering training and staff development, providing print and audiovisual materials or other self-instructional resources, <u>linking people to others with similar interests and needs</u>, and offering short-term advice and information. The methods and services selected are determined by the unique needs and characteristics of the clients, and will change over time depending on what outcomes are desired (Trohanis, 1986). For example, some services are intended to transmit information. Others, such as consultation, are better suited to assisting in problem-solving or in the development of products and procedures. Inservice training and print and audiovisual materials are used to develop new knowledge and skills. Lasting change stems from variety in TA alternatives and a flexibility that allows the TA and client system to adapt to one another (McLaughlin, 1991). Ann has asked Julie for a combination of services, including information and training. If we imagine TA continuing through the opening of the new classes, we can see how providing on-site consultation and pairing

Ann with other infant/toddler teachers for continued professional development would also be relevant.

A final goal of TA is to build the capacity of the client to evaluate and sustain changes and to identify and solve problems in the future. This is accomplished by engaging the client from the beginning in activities that promote the transfer of responsibility from the external assistance provider to the client staff (Loucks-Horsley & Mundry, 1991). The TA provider encourages the client to compare outcomes with the action plan throughout the TA process. When major systems changes such as the implementation of family-centered practices or early childhood inclusion are involved, TA can support clients as they establish or modify policies, identify funding, design continuing staff development and orientation, or participate in other activities that support the institutionalization of the change. Ongoing support and follow-up are also provided once the initial changes have been implemented.

Let's imagine Julie one year later. She has continued to work with Bright Beginnings as they enroll the infants and toddlers for the new classes, including two of the new children on her early intervention caseload. She has also discovered that Ann is not the only child care provider she is visiting who needs assistance. Because no formal TA system is available in Julie's community, she and the speech and language, physical therapy, and occupational therapy specialists at her agency, along with a consultant from the local child care resource and referral agency, have agreed to work as an informal TA team. Since they are present in the programs on a regular basis to provide services and consultation related to children with special needs, they are in a good position to field a variety of requests related to program-level changes from both center- and home-based child care providers. Their continued presence and support have enhanced the effectiveness of major changes, such as expansion of classes and smaller changes like those related to room arrangement or staff development. Julie realizes that she and her colleagues on the early intervention team enhance their own knowledge and skills when they collaborate with early childhood professionals. Table 9.1 outlines the goals of technical assistance.

TABLE 9.1 Goals of TA

- To help clients clarify their vision of what changes are needed and begin to understand the barriers to and facilitators of change
- To build support for change by encouraging broad participation of community stakeholders in planning
- To help clients translate their vision of what changes are needed into an action plan
- To provide multiple services to support the implementation of the action plan
- To build the capacity of clients to evaluate and sustain the changes

Roles

The above examples clearly illustrate the diverse roles of TA. Crandall (cited in Loucks-Horsley & Mundry, 1991) described a TA provider as a person who must have specialized skills to play various roles and be able to play them in a variety of contexts. A person providing TA may function as an assessor of needs and resources, facilitator, broker or linker, teacher or trainer, helper or coach, capacity-builder, information specialist, regulator or monitor, relationship-builder, morale-booster, communicator or translator, diagnostician, planner, visionary, coordinator, problem-solver, expert, and evaluator (Dimock, 1981; Trohanis, 1986; Loucks-Horsley & Mundry, 1991; Kanter, Stein, & Jick, 1992; Buckley & Mank, 1994). Care should be taken in choosing the appropriate role or combination of roles, depending on the specific needs of the client and the TA relationship. For example, although the client may request assistance from the TA system to evaluate a program or service system, it would not be appropriate for the TA provider to suggest such a role in the early stages of getting to know the client and establishing trust. It is also helpful to consider how directive or nondirective a role may be; the roles of expert or regulator may be less collaborative than those of capacity-builder, linker, or coach. Table 9.2 gives an example of TA roles.

Process

The TA process is not unlike any consultation or strategic planning process in which lasting changes depend on collaboration and ongoing support. Several

TABLE 9.2 TA Roles

Needs assessor: identifies discrepancy between current and desired practice

Capacity builder: encourages clients to identify problems and resources for solving them

Facilitator: assists clients to collaborate and solve problems

Broker: links clients with resources and coordinates the assistance they need

Trainer: teaches new knowledge and skills

Information specialist: gathers and organizes new information and makes it accessible to clients

Helper: delivers services that support the client in making changes

Relationship builder: helps clients build trust and identify effective roles in working together

Morale booster: helps clients feel confident and recognize positive aspects of change

process models have been described in the literature and can be used to deliver in-depth, long-term or short-term TA (Havelock, 1973; Trohanis, 1982; Loucks-Horsley & Mundry, 1991; Kanter et al., 1992). Typically, the following steps are included: (1) establish first contact and build trust with stakeholders; (2) assess attitudes and needs related to change; (3) develop a written plan specifying methods and timelines for change; (4) deliver TA to support implementation of the plan and solve problems along the way; (5) evaluate the outcomes; and (6) consider a plan for ongoing support. These steps may overlap. For example, the TA provider and clients may assess attitudes throughout the process; clients may go back and modify the action plan after implementation has begun; and problem-solving often occurs as soon as Step 2. The trusting relationship that begins at the beginning of the TA process becomes the foundation for subsequent steps toward change and is as important in contributing to effective outcomes as the intrapersonal competencies and personal qualities of the TA provider.

Challenges and Opportunities

Given the complexity of the early intervention and early childhood systems today, it is critical that TA providers recognize the developmental nature of collaboration. Early interventionists who provide community TA in addition to direct services to children and families are challenged to find the time to facilitate a planning process like the one described above. Participants themselves at first may want "quick fixes" and may need help in seeing the benefits of learning strategies for working together to solve their own problems. These skills, however, are of increasing value in the early intervention community as multiple agencies and programs work together to implement early childhood inclusion and improve services for all children and families.

Another challenge of providing TA is the need for participants to develop understanding and respect for each others' diverse perspectives. By utilizing training and awareness activities that build upon the experiences of participants and stimulate discussions about value judgments, TA providers can promote such understanding and identify sources of resistance to change. Personal qualities such as the ability to "speak the language" of the TA participants are also important ingredients for success.

CONSULTATION

The term *consultant* is used so frequently today that there is some danger that people will embrace the title without fully comprehending implications for theory and practice (Hansen, Himes, & Meier, 1990). This is complicated by the fact that consultation is an emerging body of knowledge, and unfortunately, theory and research have not kept pace with practice. Consultation is broadly defined as an indirect service delivery model in which consultant (e.g., physical therapist, speech-language pathologist, early interventionist) and a consultee (e.g., parent, general early childhood educator, child care provider) work together to address a common goal (Brown, Pryzwansky, & Schulte, 1998; Coleman, Buysse, Scalise-Smith, & Schulte, 1991; Buysse, Schulte, Pierce, & Terry, 1994; Wesley, 1994).

According to Hansen et al. (1990), three aspects of this definition distinguish consultation from other types of helping relationships. First, consultation involves any activity in which an expert provides assistance to someone who lacks expertise in a particular area; however, the nature of this interaction differs from the way in which knowledge is transferred through other methods such as supervision, teaching, or counseling. Second, consultation is defined in terms of process. While the process may vary depending on the particular model of consultation that is employed, the stages of consultation generally involve building rapport and establishing a relationship with a consultee; identifying the nature of the problem or defining a common goal; and identifying, implementing, and evaluating strategies to address these needs. Figure 9.1 describes each stage in the consultation process in more detail. Finally, unlike other forms of collaboration, consultation is defined by its triadic nature. The consultant and consultee work together to address a mutually identified goal that benefits the client (e.g., infant with special needs and his or her family).

Various approaches to consultation exist in the consultation literature (Bergan & Kratochwill, 1990; Caplan, 1970). Table 9.3 displays four models of consultation that vary primarily in the expected roles of the consultant and consultee at various stages in the consultation process.

Two other consultation models are worth noting. The *organizational consultation* addresses complex problems and potential solutions from a systems perspective (Conyne & O'Neil, 1992). Any organization, such as an early intervention or child care program, consists of interrelated and interactive components. An organizational consultant might focus on problems within a single component of the program, such as staffing patterns and caseloads, supervision and service delivery, or on the system as a whole. The *process model* of consultation places less emphasis on content knowledge and more emphasis on facilitating problem-solving or serving as a catalyst for change. Thus, the process consultant frequently functions as a coach, encouraging consultees to draw upon their own knowledge, skills, and areas of expertise.

Wesley (1994) described yet another model of consultation that was developed and tested specifically for early intervention to enhance the quality of child care programming. This approach involved a collaborative relationship between trained professionals (e.g., those with a master's degree in early childhood education or early childhood special education) and child care teachers who lack experience or training in serving young children with disabilities. During a series of visits over a four- to six-month time span, the consultant collects data on the concerns, needs, and resources of the staff and provides hands-on assistance as needed. Key components of the model include:

- Providing effective strategies for meeting the needs of children with disabilities in inclusive settings;

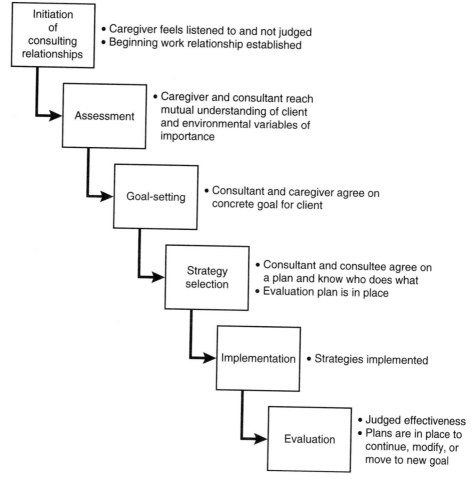

FIGURE 9.1   Stages of Consultation

Source: From *Information from Psychological Consultation: Introduction to Theory and Practice,* 3rd ed., by D. Brown, W. B. Pryzwansky, and A. C. Schulte, 1998, Boston: Allyn & Bacon.

- Completing a joint assessment using the Infant/Toddler Environment Rating Scale (Harms, Cryer, & Clifford, 1997);
- Identifying specific consultation goals and empowering goal-related activities;
- Evaluating both the changes made and the consultation process itself.

The on-site model offers multiple resources to support collaborative consultation. These include providing print and audiovisual materials, helping to arrange visits to exemplary inclusive programs, and working with child care staff to make improvements in the physical and social environment (Wesley, 1994).

TABLE 9.3 Models of Consultation

	COLLABORATION	MENTAL HEALTH	MEDICAL	EXPERT/ BEHAVIORAL
Consultant goal	Work with consultee to identify problem, plan and carry out recommendations	Increase consultee's ability to deal with similar problem in future	Identify problem and develop recommendations for consultee to carry out	Plan and carry out recommendations for problem identified by consultee
Problem identification	Both consultee and consultant identify problem	Consultant helps consultee identify problem by clarifying his/her perceptions of it	Consultant identifies problem	Consultant identifies problem
Intervention recommendations	Consultee and consultant suggest intervention recommendations	Consultee plans intervention with consultant acting as facilitator	Consultant offers recommendations for consultee to implement	Consultant plans intervention which he/she will implement
Implementation of recommendations	Consultee and consultant may each implement some recommendations	Consultee implements recommendations he/she developed	Consultee implements recommendations developed by consultant	Consultant implements his/her recommendations
Nature and extent of follow-up	Consultee and consultant engage in continuous follow-up to modify intervention if necessary	Further consultation may be initiated at request of consultee	Consultant may offer further advice to consultee	None

Reprinted with permission from "Models of Consultation: Preferences of Educational Professionals at Five Stages of Service" by N. L. Babcock and W. B. Pryzwansky, 1983, *Journal of School Psychology, 21,* 359–366.

Because these approaches vary on a number of dimensions (e.g., theoretical underpinnings, goals, intervention strategies), Gallesich (1985) proposed a framework for unifying these dimensions by developing three broad categories to encompass all consultation models. In the *scientific-technological* model, the consultant's goal is to address knowledge deficits of the consultee through training and knowledge dissemination (e.g., a care provider is taught clean intermittent catheterization techniques); whereas the *human development* model emphasizes the consultee's needs for human growth and professional development (e.g., a care provider and a consultant work together to create a professional development plan), and the *social-political* model is concerned with facilitating change within the consultee's organization or work orientation (e.g., a consultant introduces a team-building model to all early intervention personnel). To further elucidate the similarities among various consultation models, Gallesich (1982, 1985) identified characteristics that are common to most consultation practice:

- Consultants have expertise or content knowledge that the consultee lacks;
- Consultants focus primarily on the consultee's work-related problems or goals;
- Consultants work directly with consultees, and only indirectly with clients;
- Consultants are frequently external to the consultee's organization;
- Consultation typically involves collaboration between peers whose areas of responsibility and expertise differ;
- Consultation is governed by philosophies, ideologies, or values;
- Consultation involves a set of processes by which consultation goals can be accomplished; and
- Consultees are free to accept or reject the advice offered by consultants and have primary responsibility for implementing the consultant's suggestions.

File and Kontos (1992) suggested that there is "no one right model of consultation." (p. 226.) However, a number of studies have shown that service providers and other professionals have a preference for a collaborative approach to consultation, one that involves direct help-giving in the form of offering specific strategies to parents and care providers, as well as facilitation of the consultation process (Buysse et al., 1994; Babcock & Pryzwansky, 1983; Schulte, Osborne, & Kauffman, 1993; West, 1985). This means that effective consultation should stress content (e.g., knowledge of infant development, recommended practices regarding assessment and selection of curriculum materials) as well as process (e.g., relationship building, conflict resolution, facilitative communication).

Service providers who function as consultants to parents and other professionals wear a number of different hats, depending on the particular consulting roles that they assume. It is important to note that these roles are apt to change throughout the consultation process. What are the various roles that consultants play and how do they select the appropriate role for each stage of consultation? Figure 9.2 presents some options for selecting a consulting role. These roles are constructed along two axes. The X axis presents a continuum of roles designed to help the consultee grow professionally. The Y axis displays roles designed to help the consultee obtain positive results for the client. To illustrate, if the goal of consultation is to provide more opportunities for a toddler with delays to interact successfully with her environment, the consultant may choose to model strategies for arranging the environment or demonstrate methods for adapting toys. On the other hand, if the consultant's goal is to increase the caregiver's capacity to perform these functions independently, the consultant may elect to serve as a facilitator or a coach.

Vignette 9.2 presents a typical scenario for consultants in early intervention. In this vignette, the consultant must consider the human and professional needs

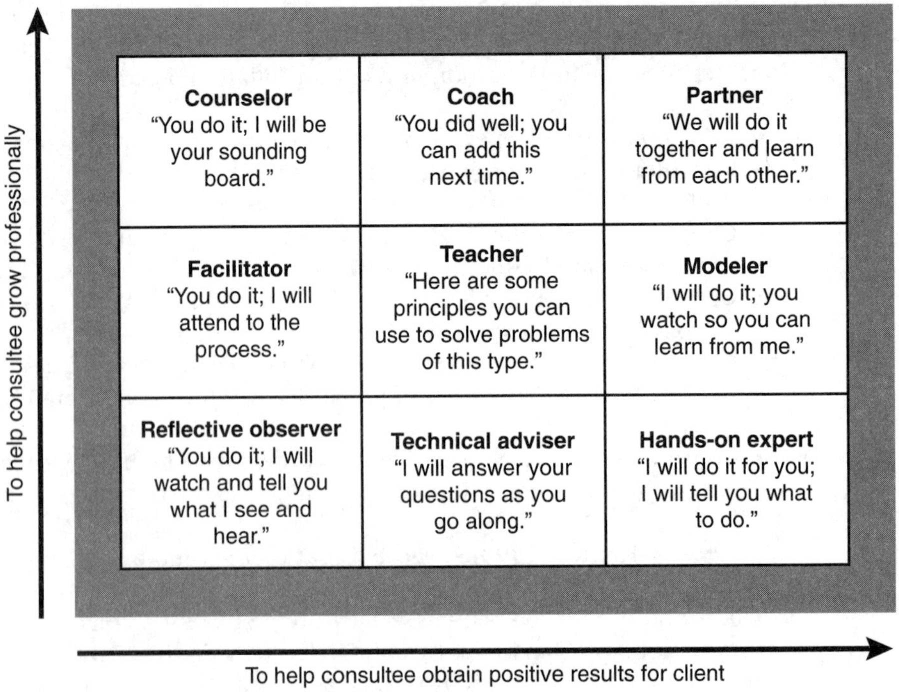

FIGURE 9.2   Consulting Role Grid

Source: From "Choosing a Consulting Role" by D. P. Champion, D. H. Kiel, and J. A. McLendon, March 1990, *Training and Development Journal*, 66–69. Copyright March 1990, Training & Development, American Society for Training & Development. Reprinted with permission. All rights reserved.

of the teacher as well as appropriate and effective intervention strategies to address the social-emotional goals for the child.

VIGETTE 9.2   ORLANDO

Marianna watched in horror as one of her two-year-old charges, Orlando, reached out and pulled the hair of another toddler, who was playing with blocks. "Get out of his hair," Marianna demanded. Orlando did not acknowledge his teacher's reprimand, nor did he appear to notice the loud protests of his most recent victim. Marianna walked quickly across the classroom and pulled Orlando away from the other child. "Don't pull hair," she repeated firmly. But Orlando only squirmed out of her arms and retreated to the other side of the classroom, where he joined a group of toddlers on the climbing structure.

Later, as she watched how effortlessly a parent volunteer organized snacktime and led a story-time activity, Marianna confided in an early intervention consultant who had been observing Orlando's behavior in the classroom. Why, she wondered, did Orlando respond so well to other adults? The consultant listened sympathetically. She had been working with Marianna to help her deal more appropriately with Orlando's challenging behaviors in the infant-toddler classroom. Up until now, this involved regular weekly meetings to talk about some specific behavior problems and several strategies for dealing with them. Today, after observing Orlando and listening to Marianna, the consultant was considering a different approach.

In light of this dilemma, how should the consultant proceed? To answer this question, it is useful to examine the roles and verbal processes that a consultant might use at each stage of the consultation process. The types of consulting roles and stages in the consultation process were presented earlier. Table 9.4 outlines verbal processes or communication strategies used by skilled consultants to transfer knowledge and to elicit information from the consultee.

During the initial stages of consultation with Marianna, the consultant was concerned primarily with gaining rapport and establishing a relationship with her,

TABLE 9.4 Communication Strategies for Early Intervention Consultants

STRATEGY	GOAL	EXAMPLE
ACKNOWLEDGING	Indicates that the consultant is listening, interested, and nonjudgmental	Leaning toward the speaker, maintaining eye contact, nodding, and simple verbal messages such as "Yes," "Right," or "Mmm-hmm."
PARAPHRASING	Provides feedback to speakers about the essence of what was said	"You're not sure if you have the training or experience to work with him."
REFLECTING	Focuses on the speaker's feelings	"This situation makes you uncomfortable."
CLARIFYING	Seeks to ascertain the speaker's message	"Is that right?"
ELABORATING	Embellishes what the speaker says by adding detail	"Her ability to talk, both to reduce her frustration and to help her relate more successfully with others, is an important goal right now."
SUMMARIZING	Integrates and synthesizes all of the relevant information presented by the speaker.	"Well, for now, you'd like to see her move independently and play with her toys and work toward walking later."

Information from *Collaboration in the Schools: An Inservice and Preservice Curriculum for Teachers, Support Staff, and Administrators* by J. F. West, L. Idol, and G. Cannon, 1989, Austin, Tex.: Pro-ed.

so she functioned as a reflective observer or a facilitator (e.g., "You're not sure if you're doing the right things with Orlando."). Later on, after several consultation sessions, the consultant's role remained facilitative, but the emphasis changed to focus more specifically on identifying the nature of the problem and on determining the goals of consultation (e.g., "Tell me more about what Orlando does during circle time," or "It sounds like one of our goals might be to help Orlando understand the consequences of his behaviors. Is that right?"). Once several strategies had been identified to address common goals, the consultant's role and communication strategies centered around implementation issues (e.g., "What happened when you tried redirecting him as we discussed?"). During implementation, the consultant may play various roles, depending on the consultee's knowledge and skills and the nature of the problem. The consultant could begin by observing implementation in the classroom, but quickly move into another role—that of a technical adviser, modeler, or trainer. The final stage of consultation consists of evaluating the effectiveness of the intervention strategies that were implemented. During this phase, the consultant may return to roles that are more reflective and facilitative (e.g., "You handled Orlando beautifully during snacktime today."), or he or she may attempt to redirect or refine the intervention strategy (e.g., "Tomorrow, let's think about giving Orlando several choices during snacktime.").

Overcoming Consultation Constraints

Because consultation is an emerging service delivery model in early intervention, consultants frequently face barriers at many different levels, including state and local systems, programs, and individual classrooms (File & Kontos, 1992). Although many service providers now receive some form of training in consultation, putting these skills into practice may prove challenging. The challenges include both pragmatic issues such as caseload size, lack of time to consult, and funding patterns, as well as conceptual barriers that spring from different professional assumptions about the best way to organize and deliver services for young children. To overcome these barriers, File and Kontos (1992) suggested that future personnel preparation efforts be extended to include both early education professionals and service providers, as well as other consumers of consultation services. Moreover, all professionals involved in consultation should seek organizational support for consultation services from their administrators and develop a plan to grow professionally in consultation practice through supervision or peer mentorship.

TEAMING

Teaming is fundamental to the provision of services. The team approach, which achieves shared decision-making among parents and professionals and creates a wholesome system of checks and balances, is an important, underlying principle of federal legislation pertaining to early intervention and special education (Individuals with Disabilities Education Act, 1999). Furthermore, the team-based model of service delivery is widely recognized as a recommended practice in early intervention (Division for Early Childhood Task Force on Recommended Practices, 1993), largely because no one agency or discipline can meet the complex needs of young children with disabilities and their families.

A team usually consists of a child's parents or caregivers and professionals representing two or more disciplines (Rosin, Whitehead, Tuchman, Jesien, & Begun, 1993). The functions of the early intervention team are to provide cross-disciplinary evaluation and assessment, develop the Individualized Family Service Plan (IFSP), and implement and evaluate intervention and support services. Many authors have described the team approach as well as various models of team functioning, such as multidisciplinary, interdisciplinary, and transdisciplinary (Antoniadis & Videlock, 1991; Bailey, 1984; Bailey, McWilliam, & Winton, 1992; Briggs, 1993; McGonigel, Woodruff, & Roszmann-Millican, 1994; Maple, 1987; Rosin et al., 1993). The primary contribution of these models is to describe different ways in which team members relate to one another. Absent from these descriptions, however, are strategies to assist teams in achieving more effective functioning or a process by which they might move from one stage of development to the next. Moreover, these models may be less relevant today as a result of the shift to community-based programming, as child care providers, program administrators, and other human service professionals are now more likely to be part of the early intervention team. Second, early childhood special educators and other specialists may not be housed together under one roof or within a single organization. As a result, service providers face significant challenges in determining how to involve a key player who may not recognize his or her role as a team member, is unfamiliar with principles and practices related to teaming, or is unable to attend team meetings due to time or staffing constraints.

Recent changes in the field provide an opportunity for service providers to reexamine team functioning in view of expanding community contexts, the addition of multiprogram and multiagency team players, and the increasingly important role of families as active team members. The following sections present two team models. The first, the seven-stage model of team development (Drexler, Sibbet, & Forrester, 1992), is typical of the approach being used extensively in business and the corporate world to enhance team functioning. The second team model, the team-based model for change, was developed and tested by Bailey and his colleagues (Bailey et al., 1992; Winton, McWilliam, Harrison, Owens, & Bailey, 1992). This approach was designed specifically for the field of early intervention, as a method for promoting family-centered practices among members of these teams. Both approaches hold promising implications for community-based teaming in early intervention.

A Seven-Stage Model for Building Effective Teams

The seven-stage model for building effective teams (Drexler et al., 1992) is a process for bringing people together to form a team and help them to define a common ground for envisioning, implementing, and evaluating a strategic plan. In addition to achieving common goals related to a specific content area (e.g., becoming family-centered, implementing community-based services, increasing professionals' cultural sensitivity), the primary outcome of this process is to function more effectively as a team. This is an important outcome, since early intervention teams often have unstated, informal goals related to increasing their smooth functioning (Maple, 1987).

The seven stages of the Drexler, Sibbet, and Forrester approach are presented in Table 9.5, along with some of the issues a team must address at each stage. The process represents developmental stages of team formation, beginning with getting to know team members (i.e., orientation), and progressing to the development of a shared vision and common goals (i.e., trust building, goal and role clarification, commitment), and finally, implementing and evaluating a plan. At each stage of development, the team must address a key question (e.g., "Why am I here?"). The goal is to move the team from an unresolved to a resolved state. The seventh stage, renewal, is designed to help team members grow both personally and professionally and to renew their commitment to team ideals.

Team-Based Model for Change

The team-based model for change (Bailey et al., 1992; Winton et al., 1992) was developed to involve family members in early intervention teams and help them serve in meaningful ways. The model is based on the following assumptions about how change among team members occurs:

- Change is a difficult process.
- Change is a gradual, long-term process.
- Change is more likely to occur in small steps that blend new and existing ideas.

TABLE 9.5   Seven-Stage Team Building Model

Stage 1.   *Orientation:* "Why am I here?"

Stage 2.   *Trust Building:* "Who are you?"

Stage 3.   *Goal/Role Clarification:* "What are we doing?"

Stage 4.   *Commitment:* "How will we do it?"

Stage 5.   *Implementation:* "Who does what, when, where?"

Stage 6.   *Evaluation:* "How are we doing?"

Stage 7.   *Renewal:* "Why continue?"

Adapted from "The Team Performance Model," in *Team Building: Blueprints for Productivity and Satisfaction* (booklet) by A. Drexler, D. Sibbett, and R. Forrester, 1992, Alexandria, Va.: NTL Institute and University Associates.

TABLE 9.6   Moving a Team from an Unresolved to a Resolved State

STAGE	UNRESOLVED	RESOLVED
Orientation (Why am I here?)	▪ Disorientation ▪ Uncertainty ▪ Fear	▪ Purpose ▪ Personal fit ▪ Membership
Trust-building (Who are you?)	▪ Caution ▪ Mistrust ▪ Façade	▪ Mutual regard ▪ Forthrightness ▪ Spontaneous interaction
Goal/role clarification (What are we doing?)	▪ Apathy ▪ Explicit assumptions ▪ Façade	▪ Clear, integrated goals ▪ Identified goals
Commitment (How will we do it?)	▪ Dependence ▪ Resistance	▪ Shared vision ▪ Allocated resources ▪ Strategies/tools identified
Implementation (Who does what, when, where?)	▪ Conflict/confusion ▪ Nonalignment ▪ Missed opportunities	▪ Clear processes ▪ Alignment ▪ Effective execution
Evaluation (How are we doing?)	▪ Who are stakeholders? ▪ Who evaluates? ▪ Who needs results?	▪ Multiple strategies ▪ Criteria for success ▪ Results used for planning
Renewal (Why continue?)	▪ Boredom ▪ Burnout?	▪ Recognition ▪ Personal/professional development ▪ Staying power

Adapted from "The Team Performance Model," in *Team Building: Blueprints for Productivity and Satisfaction* (booklet) by A. Drexler, D. Sibbett, and R. Forrester, 1992, Alexandria, Va.: NTL Institute and University Associates.

- Training to promote change should focus on the entire team, not on the individual.
- Training to promote change should empower team members to identify their own change strategies and solutions.
- Parents and other consumers should have input about changes that will affect them.

The team-based model for change relies on an intensive four-day workshop format in which people work together within their existing teams to describe current practices and identify strategies for change with respect to family involvement. The process is guided by a facilitator who encourages self-reflection and shared decision-making through case studies and small- and large-group discussions. Over the course of the training session, six key questions are addressed:

1. What is our philosophy?
2. How will we involve families in child assessment?
3. How will we assess family needs and resources?
4. How will we involve families in team meetings and decision-making?
5. How will we write family goals and the IFSP?
6. How will we implement the IFSP and provide service coordination?

The outcome of the workshop is a specific plan developed by the early intervention team that includes goals, resources, and strategies for implementing family-centered practices upon return to their early intervention programs. To ensure success with this particular method of team training, Bailey and colleagues suggest that training organizers stress a shared decision-making approach and that administrators and family members be involved in team training efforts.

Challenges and Opportunities of the Team-Based Approach

Parents and professionals who serve on teams are presented with both challenges and opportunities. Common challenges include ensuring maximum participation from all team players and reducing negative effects when team members are absent from team meetings (Winton et al., 1992). To transform these challenges into opportunities, some early intervention teams have found it useful to alter their meeting places and times. For example, an IFSP meeting could take place at a child care center during naptime or during arrival and departure times to allow parents, child care teachers, and directors to attend the meetings.

Another challenge of creating effective teams in early intervention is identifying strong leadership potential (Brill, 1976; Friend & Cook, 1996). Leadership is necessary to give the team momentum and to monitor and guide the work of the team. In situations where a single leader has not emerged, it is sometimes useful to implement a system in which the leadership is rotated among some or all of the team members.

Another significant challenge to effective teaming occurs when there is dissatisfaction from one or more team members, but not the entire team, regarding team goals, roles, or process. In this case, the dissatisfaction of individual team members about how the team works can be turned into opportunities for self-reflection and an assessment of current team functioning and ideal practices. This process might begin by examining qualities of effective teams, as listed in Table 9.7.

To examine individual roles and styles of early intervention teams, an instrument such as the Parker Team Player Survey (Parker, 1991) may be administered. This survey provides a guideline for examining the style of team members, as shown in Table 9.8.

TABLE 9.7   Qualities of Effective Intervention Teams

1. Clear mission, purpose, and goals
2. Sufficient resources
3. Qualified team members
4. Open communication
5. Sufficient time devoted to team meetings
6. Effective problem-solving and conflict resolution strategies
7. Evaluation of individual and team performance
8. A climate of trust and support
9. Strong leadership
10. Organizational support

From "Team Talk: Communication Skills for Early Intervention Teams" by M. H. Briggs, 1993, *Journal of Childhood Communication Disorders, 15*(1), 33–40.

TABLE 9.8   Styles of Team Members

Contributor: Task oriented—trainer, mentor, disseminator of technical knowledge

Collaborator: Goal oriented—cheerleader, encourager, synthesizer of information

Communicator: Process oriented—monitor, consensus builder, listener, interdictor

Challenger: Values oriented—questioner, risk taker, seeker of creative solutions

Information from *Team Players and Teamwork* by G. M. Parker, 1991, San Francisco: Jossey Bass.

Team functioning and effectiveness can be further assessed through an examination of aspects of team culture, such as roles and rituals, and team artifacts such as IFSPs and assessment reports (Westby & Ford, 1993). Table 9.9 gives an example of questions for examining team structure.

Team members should look for evidence of clarity of mission, group cohesion, and parent participation in their team practices and products. Finally, from time to time, all teams must deal with basic differences among team members regarding philosophies, professional assumptions, and communication styles. These challenges, too, can be transformed into opportunities when team members realize that change is gradual and that it requires patience and a commitment to improving team functioning through team development activities.

TABLE 9.9   Questions for Evaluating Team Structure

- Who communicates most and how?
- Who has power and how is it exhibited?
- Who likes whom and what are the effects?
- How do team members' roles affect each other?
- How does work flow among members?
- What are peoples' status in relation to others?

Information from *Working in Teams* by M. Payne, 1982, London: Macmillan Press.

TRAINING

Training is a basic tool for improving the knowledge and skills of staff in order to ensure quality services for children and families. As communities continue to implement the Americans with Disabilities Act and the Individuals with Disabilities Education Act, local agencies increasingly view service providers as vital resources in planning and delivering training. In Vignette 9.1, we saw how child care providers may ask early interventionists to provide technical assistance, and how training is one strategy for building knowledge and skills. Community colleges also seek consultation and training from service providers as they expand their early childhood programs to address special education concerns. In many community colleges, service providers teach courses about children with special needs or co-teach early childhood courses. Local child care resource and referral agencies are another source of training for practitioners serving young children with disabilities and their families.

Within their own agencies, professionals may be team members, mentors, or supervisors, who provide training to colleagues, including those who are newly hired and others who may be taking on additional responsibilities or roles. In some places, early interventionists are members of interdisciplinary and multiagency community planning teams that coordinate services in the early intervention/ early childhood system. These teams make recommendations to reduce gaps and duplications in services and to make efficient use of scarce resources.

In some communities, community planning teams also plan and implement training opportunities for practitioners and families concerned with young children with and without special needs. In fact, it may be helpful to consider training as an ongoing process that starts prior to and continues throughout employment.

Under Part C of the Individuals with Disabilities Education Act, each state is required to have a Comprehensive System of Personnel Development (CSPD) that encourages interagency coordination and collaboration in training. Training has been viewed traditionally as a process that focuses on individuals from the same discipline or agency who are presumed to need the same set of competencies to do their jobs (Buckley & Mank, 1994). Yet, to be effective, training must do more than concentrate solely on the education of individuals or homogeneous groups. Training methods and content should instead address the multiple settings, agencies, funding sources, and stakeholders who work together in early intervention. Ideally, training promotes and is guided by the creative collaboration of families, professionals from various disciplines, community organizations, agencies, and universities.

What's missing in the way training is typically provided? In Vignette 9.3, one community's experiences provides a glimpse of how staff development often occurs.

VIGETTE 9.3 ALLEN COUNTY'S EXPERIENCE

Families and professionals in Allen County depend on a hodgepodge of training opportunities to develop and maintain their knowledge and skills in early education and early intervention. For example, every March the local Child Care Coalition sponsors a Day for Day Care, when child care providers attend workshops at the community college. Child care training credit is offered for participation in sessions led by local child care directors or teachers. The topics are chosen based on needs assessments completed the year before, and often include behavior management, developmentally appropriate practice, and resources for children with special needs. Although anyone can attend Day for Day Care, publicity is limited to the county child care network, and center- and home-based providers are usually the only participants.

The early interventionists in the county attend a two-day state conference every year. There they receive infant specialist licensure credit for sessions on many of the same topics offered at Day for Day Care. The topics are chosen by the conference's organizing committee based on the availability of speakers. The majority of participants are early childhood special educators who provide direct services to children and families, with only 10 percent being administrators. Therapists also go to the state conference, but are more likely to attend state and national meetings of their own discipline's professional organizations.

Allen County's elementary schools sponsor three days of in-service training for teachers seeking certificate renewal credit. Although the topic this year was early childhood inclusion, the sessions were not publicized or open to persons who are not school personnel. Following the teacher training, the schools hold a monthlong Spring Fling of weekly workshops for parents of children three to eight years old. This spring, the teacher-led sessions focused on home-school communication. A community college instructor from the Early Childhood Department was asked to lead a session, but the Spring Fling schedule conflicted with a night course she was teaching on early childhood curriculum.

> The community college course provides one of several preservice opportunities available locally. There are two major universities within a 45-mile radius of Allen County offering birth-kindergarten teacher licensure programs that reflect an inclusive focus on early childhood education. Interestingly, although more inclusive practicum sites are needed, the universities do not place students in Allen County, and have not explored the potential of developing sites there.
>
> P. J. Winton, J. A. McCollum, and C. Catlett (Eds.), 1997, *Reforming Personnel Preparation in Early Intervention: Issues, Models, and Strategies,* Baltimore: Paul H. Brookes Publishing Company, p. 54.

As is the case with the vast majority of in-service training, the staff development activities available to Allen County are not conducted in accordance with known components of effective training. The experiences of early intervention personnel and families illustrate a pattern of separating persons who seek staff development according to agency, discipline, job description, and whether they are engaged in preservice or in-service training. There is some history in Allen County of clustering events in the spring, but a system-wide view of training that is responsive to ongoing local needs is absent. Although training needs are similar among child care providers, early interventionists, and teachers, needs assessment is not coordinated across agencies, and training opportunities are not jointly sponsored. There is a lack of variety in training, resulting in only brief exposures to topics through onetime workshops that prove inadequate to support the implementation of changes at the local level. Although coordination with the community college is attempted, there seems to be no dialogue between community agencies and the nearby universities about either one's needs regarding personnel preparation. A critical shortcoming of Allen County's experience is the lost opportunity for diverse professionals and families to come together through staff development to create and sustain meaningful changes where they live and work.

A Plan for Staff Development

If community programs for children and families are to be viable, they must have an ongoing plan for recruiting and maintaining qualified and motivated staff. Edelman (1994) recommended nine survival skills for providers. These are:

1. Being able to think in terms of systems by seeing the process, rather than functions, and interrelationships, as opposed to linear cause-and-effect
2. Being a team player who shares respect, dialogue, vision, commitment, and language
3. Understanding the interrelationship between services and complex issues facing families and communities (e.g., violence, substance abuse, isolation)
4. Supporting families as caregivers and engaging families to shape programs
5. Acknowledging the power and influence of culture and honoring diversity in families

6. Providing professional skills within the framework of parent-directed decision-making and nurturing collaborative relationships to implement change
7. Sharing information and valuing information from other disciplines
8. Assuming the role of advocate for children and families
9. Becoming a change agent by recognizing the transformation of services, challenging the status quo, sharing visions, and working in partnerships

Training Challenges and Suggestions

We face numerous challenges as we consider how best to prepare and maintain a qualified workforce. Program staff are likely to be at various stages of career development. They have different experiences, learning styles, and goals for obtaining new knowledge and skills. They may have varying requirements and credit systems for training according to their discipline or agency. Training at the local and state levels often seems fragmented and seems to have little relevance to needs that arise in daily practice. The availability of resources, such as distance learning or trainers competent to address audiences from diverse disciplines and backgrounds, varies. Similarly, challenges in scheduling and locating space in which to provide training and conduct follow-up activities may seem overwhelming. Early interventionists and other professionals can use the following guidelines when providing training to others or selecting options for themselves:

- Emphasize training in early intervention that reflects the content and philosophical assumptions outlined in personnel preparation standards presented in the position statement by the Division for Early Childhood Task Force on Recommended Practices (1993). These include: (1) the uniqueness of early childhood as a developmental phase; (2) the significant role of families in early education; (3) the role of developmentally and individually appropriate practice; (4) the preference for service delivery in inclusive settings; (5) the importance of culturally competent professional behavior; and (6) the importance of collaborative interpersonal and interprofessional actions.
- Develop a system of ongoing collaboration across community agencies to assess training needs of staff and to plan for meeting them.
- Utilize multiple training formats and strategies based on adult learning theory. These may include university or community college coursework, correspondence courses, traditional workshops, on-site seminars, interactive video or self-instructional media packages, teleconferences, resource fairs, short- or long-term intensive institutes, study tours, lectures, panel presentations, question-and-answer sessions, or many other small- or large-group interactive formats.
- Provide joint training opportunities for staff from various agencies, disciplines, and levels of management, and emphasize participation by teams who work together.

- Obtain approval in advance to offer as many different kinds of training credit as possible, so that persons from various disciplines and agencies will be motivated to participate.
- Provide for the development of relationships among participants while emphasizing content and process, collaboration, and practical problem-solving. Require learners to make decisions and act rather than to just sit and think.
- Utilize participant journals, self-assessments or personal inventories, and written action plans to help participants evaluate the relevance of the information to themselves and develop plans for applying what they are learning.
- Provide time during the training to discuss what participants will do differently back in the community as a result of the training.
- Reflect and promote cross-cultural sensitivity.
- Employ real-life examples and case studies.
- Provide follow-up after the training to help participants transfer what they have learned to daily practice.

(See the appendix for a further discussion of innovative training models.)

Supervision and Mentorship

Tell me what you did, and how you felt about what you did.

Let me tell you what that suggests to me and then you can think it over and see what occurs to you. Okay?

That must have been really hard to take. They remind me of a father who cursed me out at the top of his lungs when I told him I had missed sending out an insurance reimbursement form.

Here's what I see as your strengths. . . . And these are the areas to work on. . . . Tell me what you think of what I've said, and if it makes sense to you, how do you think we could work on those areas?

—Shanok, 1991, pp. 16–19

What is supervision and mentorship? Most early education and intervention practitioners are unfamiliar with the term supervision as it relates to professional development. They may think of supervision as simply monitoring an individual's work performance. For professionals from medicine and the mental health fields, clinical supervision occurs naturally and has a very different meaning. The term mentor may be more familiar to most educators and more closely approximates the meaning of supervision as a method of collaboration. In the words of Pawl (1995): "Clinical supervision is a very special environment for teaching, created by the interaction between the supervisor and the supervisee. Just like any relationship, it always bears the stamp of each contributor and just like any relationship where one person bears greater responsibility than the other, the supervisor assumes the greater responsibility for the quality of what passes between them and for the basic parameters of the relationship." (p. 22)

Gallacher (1997) distinguishes between mentoring—a relationship between a more knowledgeable, experienced mentor and a less knowledgeable, less experienced mentee—and supervision, a relationship in which professional development is only one aspect of guidance in accomplishing organizational goals. In the majority of early education and intervention programs, however, it may be difficult to separate practices related to supervision and mentorship. Administrators of early childhood programs and experienced personnel frequently serve as both mentors and supervisors to less experienced staff members.

Roles of the Supervisor and Supervisee. Practiced correctly, supervision is beneficial to both the supervisor and the supervisee (Pawl, 1995). In other words, the "special environment for teaching" (p. 5) creates a relationship for learning that is bidirectional. This means that, no matter how seasoned a veteran professional may be, the potential to gain another perspective about a particular issue or to enlarge one's view of the world always exists. Supervision and mentorship may be particularly beneficial in helping professionals develop complex skills requiring problem-solving, critical thinking, and creativity (Gallacher, 1997). According to Fenichel (1991), experienced educators and administrators who function as supervisors are provided with opportunities to:

- Model a mutually respectful, collaborative relationship that parallels the professional-family relationship;
- Offer information and instruction in areas that are relevant and appropriate to the supervisee's needs;
- Support the supervisee, particularly as she deals with the more stressful aspects of work with young children and families; and
- Create and maintain a climate of intellectual inquiry, open communication, empathy, and support for long-term professional development.

For novice professionals, supervision and mentorship provide opportunities to:

- Deepen and broaden knowledge and skills;
- Reflect on professional experiences and practices;
- Develop a sense of professional identity and style through increased self-understanding;
- Examine the philosophy that underlies the policies and practices of a professional discipline or service system;
- Learn from an experienced professional who discusses successes and failures in the context of her own professional development (Fenichel, 1991).

Essential Features of Supervisory and Mentoring Relationships. What are the essential features of supervision and mentorship? The Zero to Three work group on Learning through Supervision and Mentorship identified three critical features of supervision that have evolved from various disciplines and traditions, and are relevant to the early education and intervention fields: reflection, collaboration, and regularity (Fenichel, 1991). Reflection requires the early interventionist to stand back from her work to examine its implications for young children and families as well as for her own professional identity. As part of this process, a supervisor offers an enlarged perspective, challenging the supervisee to consider the values and principles underlying her practices by asking, "What were you thinking about when you met with the family?" Reflection helps the novice interventionist understand the feelings associated with her work and to develop a "tolerance for ambiguity" (Fenichel, 1991), the realization that some problems pose human dilemmas that cannot be fully solved nor explained. In the course of supervision, an effective supervisor encourages reflection and responds in a variety of ways: by directing a supervisee to resource materials, by sharing reflections on her own professional experiences, by role-playing situations, or by providing instruction on specific strategies and techniques.

Collaboration could be considered the foundation of supervision and mentorship. The collaboration between novice and expert is based on shared power, on the recognition of the authority of the early intervention professional's own work experience, and on clear mutual expectations that delineate the boundaries and responsibilities of each participant in the supervisory relationship (Fenichel, 1991). Regularity, the third essential element of supervision and mentorship, requires a commitment on the part of the participants to meet on a regular basis. At the same time, it is important to note that supervision and mentorship may take different forms: a supervisor and supervisee may discuss how best to address a family's concern about their child over a cup of coffee, a group of preservice students may share their practicum experiences with an experienced field site supervisor, or staff may meet weekly with an infant mental health specialist to explore and reflect on home visiting practices. Ideally, professionals in early education and intervention will be introduced to the essential elements of supervision and mentorship as part of their field experiences in their preservice training programs. Once students enter the field as professionals, the practice of supervision and mentorship should continue throughout their careers to enhance professional development and improve the quality of services for young children and families.

Final Notes on Supervision and Mentorship The relationship between the supervisor and supervisee based on collaboration, mutual respect, and safety parallels the professional-family partnership found in effective practice. The notion that the supervisory relationship can set the tone for how professionals, in turn, relate to young children and families has been referred to as *parallel process*

(Fenichel, 1991; Pawl, 1995). Thus, because experiences and insights gained through supervision and mentorship directly affect consumers of early intervention services, supervisors bear a particular responsibility for ensuring that the supervisee develops an acute understanding of how relationships are the "medium through which all services are given" (Pawl, 1995, p. 22). Underscoring this important point is mounting evidence suggesting that the quality of supervision is tied to the quality of caregiving practices and the relationships between professionals and their clients (Pawl, 1995).

INTEGRATING AND EVALUATING COLLABORATIVE PROCESSES

Similarities and Distinctions Among Collaboration Models

Table 9.10 summarizes the key elements of each of the collaboration models presented in this chapter. At a glance, it is easy to identify the common elements of each of the models, as well as some unique features that distinguish them. Common to each is the notion that collaboration is a long-term, if not a lifelong, proposition. Professional development does not begin and end in graduate school. The need to work in a collaborative fashion with others continues as long as early education and intervention services are provided by professionals from a variety of backgrounds, disciplines, and agencies—with the ultimate goal of creating a coordinated and integrated system that is consumer-oriented, family-driven, and community-based. In addition, while the various collaborative roles and processes vary to some extent, building collaborative work relationships generally involves the following steps: getting to know someone and building trust, identifying goals for change, developing and implementing a plan, and evaluating these efforts. To make the collaborative process work, professionals must rely on a repertoire of roles (e.g., teacher, evaluator, coach) that change in response to client needs and the particular stage of the collaborative process (e.g., establishing rapport, assessing needs, suggesting different strategies).

The similarities among collaboration models help to explain why terms for these models often are used interchangeably. In actual practice, the models of collaboration frequently overlap. For example, a member of an early intervention team might serve as a consultant to another team member. As part of supervision, a director of an early intervention program might decide to implement training activities on a particular topic. Yet each of these models has evolved from different disciplines and traditions, and each has a slightly different purpose. To distinguish among the various approaches, it is useful to determine the recipient of collaboration, the specific goals for change, and available personnel and resources to address these needs. For example, if the recipient is a child care provider who needs classroom assistance in working with a child with disabilities,

TABLE 9.10   Key Elements of Collaboration Models

MODELS	DESCRIPTION	GOALS	PROVIDER ROLES	PROCESS
Technical assistance	An array of information and technology resources transferred by a specialist through a variety of methods, including dissemination, consultation, and training	Help clients identify areas in which change is needed; assist in implementing change; build capacity to sustain change over time	Evaluator Capacity-builder Facilitator Broker Educator Information specialist Helper Friend	1. Build trust 2. Assess needs 3. Develop a plan 4. Implement services 5. Evaluate 6. Amend plan
Consultation	Consultant and consultee working together to address a mutually identified goal for a client	Address client goals; increase consultee's capacity to solve problems independently in the future	Counselor Coach Partner Facilitator Teacher Modeler Observer Technical advisor Hands-on expert	1. Initiate consulting relationship 2. Assess needs 3. Set goals 4. Select strategies 5. Implement strategies 6. Evaluation
Teaming	Group consisting of a child's parent(s) or guardians and professionals from two or more disciplines	Promote shared decision-making regarding evaluation and assessment, development of the IFSP, and implementation and evaluation of interventions	Contributor Collaborator Communicator Challenger	1. Orientation 2. Building trust 3. Goal and role clarification 4. Commitment 5. Implementing a plan 6. Evaluation 7. Renewal
Training	Tools for improving knowledge, attitudes, and skills of early education/intervention professionals	Identify participant needs; provide opportunities for observation, practice, and structured feedback	Educator Evaluator Mentor Train-the-trainer	1. Preservice 2. Start-up support 3. Maintenance of effort 4. Periodic review and feedback 5. Transition
Supervision and mentorship	A special environment for leaning created by interactions between a supervisor and supervisee	Recognize, understand, and cope with professional challenges	Reflector Collaborator Mentor Catalyst	1. Establish a mentor relationship 2. Develop regular meeting times 3. Reflect on professional experiences and practices

consultation or technical assistance, rather than teaming or training, may be the most appropriate forms of collaboration. In addition to making these distinctions, professionals should strive for precision in the language they use to label collaborative processes in order to facilitate communication about these various approaches.

A Framework for Evaluating Collaboration

How can professionals determine if they have been successful in their efforts to collaborate? Like all good evaluations, a plan for evaluating collaboration should address the purpose of the evaluation, the audience for the evaluation results, and a set of criteria for determining if collaboration efforts were successful (Branham, 1992; Trohanis, 1986; Strata & Bricker, 1996). Articulating the specific goals of collaboration and the purpose of documenting its effectiveness should be viewed as essential first steps in any attempt to evaluate it. Specific evaluation strategies can then be incorporated into an evaluation framework consisting of three components: monitoring and accountability, documenting the processes, and outcomes related to collaboration. Monitoring is a useful tool for documenting the extent to which people actually participated in collaborative efforts and for projecting future needs. Examples of monitoring activities include documenting the number and nature of requests for training and technical assistance or tracking the number of consultative sessions or supervisory meetings one attends. Documenting the process of collaboration can be achieved by keeping a written log regarding the stages and phases of collaboration. Finally, a comprehensive evaluation must address the impact of collaboration on a variety of levels (program, professional, services for children and families). Again, the specific methods and instruments used to evaluate collaboration outcomes will depend, in large measure, on the goals of collaboration. The primary objectives should be to document consumer satisfaction with a particular form of collaboration (technical assistance, consultation, teaming, training, supervision and mentorship), along with specific aspects of collaboration that contributed to consumer satisfaction (training content, a skilled facilitator, a resource lending library). More challenging to document are the systemic changes resulting from collaboration efforts that influence the services and infrastructure of programs as well as human outcome—improvements for children and families (Kagan, Goffin, Golub, & Pritchard, 1995). Documenting these and other important outcomes of collaboration should be carried out in conjunction with ongoing, comprehensive program evaluation efforts.

FUTURE DIRECTIONS

As we approach the twenty-first century, we may see new forms of collaboration emerge or a refinement of those already in existence. Many of these ideas regarding forms of collaboration have their origin in the field of organizational transformation, a relatively new area of theory and practice designed to help organizations transform their purposes, structures, cultures, and strategies (Fletcher, 1990). The emphasis on organizational transformation is beginning to change our thinking about how to view the purposes of collaboration—from diagnosing the problem to envisioning the future, from improving services to reinventing services, from identifying goals and objectives to creating a mission statement, from making minor changes to implementing a major paradigm shift, from improving the organization to empowering the people who work there.

To support future collaborative efforts in early education and intervention, it is necessary to

- Educate students and professionals about various models of collaboration and the roles, goals, and processes associated with each;
- Test models of collaboration with people from other cultural groups and backgrounds and make adaptations to enhance the relevance and acceptability of these approaches;
- Obtain administrative support for early education and intervention personnel who must balance the need to collaborate with the direct service demands of their jobs;
- Create opportunities for family members and other nontraditional stakeholders, including individuals from historically underrepresented groups and diverse cultures, to participate actively in collaboration efforts;
- Conduct research to document outcomes related to particular forms of collaboration and to identify factors associated with the success or failure of these efforts;
- Identify leaders who can assist programs in making the necessary transformations to envision and create an ideal system of services for young children, families, and the professionals who work collaboratively to serve them.

REFERENCES

Antoniadis, A., & Videlock, J. L. (1991). In search of teamwork: A transactional approach to team functioning. *Infant-Toddler Intervention, 1*(2), 157–167.

Babcock, N. L., & Pryzwansky, W. B. (1983). Models of consultation: Preferences of educational professionals at five stages of service. *Journal of School Psychology, 21*, 359–366.

Bailey, D. B. (1984). A triaxial model of the interdisciplinary team and group process. *Exceptional Children, 51*, 17–25.

Bailey, D. B., McWilliam, P. J., & Winton, P. J. (1992). Building family-centered practices in early intervention: A team-based model for change. *Infants and Young Children, 5*(1), 73–82.

Bergan, J. R., & Kratochwill, T. R. (1990). *Behavioral consultation and therapy.* New York: Plenum.

Branham, L. A. (1992). An update on staff development evaluation. *Staff Development Practices, 13*(4), 24–28.

Briggs, M. H. (1993). Team talk: Communication skills for early intervention teams. *Journal of Childhood Communication Disorders, 15*(1), 33–40.

Brill, N. I. (Ed.). (1976). The internal life of the team, III. In *Team-work: Working together in the human services* (pp. 83–102). Philadelphia: J. B. Lippincott.

Brown, D., Pryzwansky, W. B., & Schulte, A. C. (1998). *Psychological consultation: Introduction to theory and practice* (3rd ed.). Boston: Allyn & Bacon.

Buckley, J., & Mank, D. (1994). New perspectives on training and technical assistance: Moving from assumptions to a focus on quality. *Journal of the Association for Persons with Severe Handicaps, 19*(3), 223–232.

Buysse, V., Schulte, A. C., Pierce, P. P., & Terry, D. (1994). Models and styles of consultation: Preferences of professionals in early intervention. *Journal of Early Intervention, 18*(3), 302–310.

Buysse, V., & Wesley, P. P. (1993). The identity crisis in early childhood special education: A call for professional role clarification. *Topics in Early Childhood Special Education, 13,* 418–429.

Caplan, G. (1970). *The theory and practice of mental health consultation.* New York: Basic Books.

Coleman, P. P., Buysse, V., Scalise-Smith, D. L., & Schulte, A. C. (1991). Consultation: Applications to early intervention. *Infants and Young Children, 4*(2), 41–46.

Conyne, K., & O'Neil, J. M. (1992). *Organizational consultation: A casebook.* Newbury Park, Calif.: Sage.

Dimock, H. G. (1981). *Intervention and collaborative change.* Guelph, Ontario: Centre for Human Resource Development.

Dimock, H. G. (1993). *Intervention and collaboration: Helping organizations to change.* San Diego: Pfeiffer.

Division for Early Childhood Task Force on Recommended Practices. (1993). *DEC recommended practices: Indicators of quality in programs for infants and young children with special needs and their families.* Reston, Va.: Author.

Drexler, A., Sibbet, D., & Forrester, R. (1992). The team performance model. In W. B. Reddy & Kaleel Jamieson (Eds.), *Team building: Blueprints for productivity and satisfaction.* Alexandria, Va.: NTL Institute and University Associates.

Edelman, L. (August, 1994). *Preparing learning for the present: Change and emerging roles.* Presentation at the Midwestern Consortium for Faculty Development. Minneapolis, Minn.: University of Minnesota.

Fenichel, E. (1991). Learning through supervision and mentorship to support the development of infants, toddlers, and their families. *Zero to Three, 12*(2), 1–8.

File, N., & Kontos, S. (1992). Indirect service delivery through consultation: Review and implications for early intervention. *Journal of Early Intervention, 16,* 221–233.

Fletcher, B. R. (1990). *Organization transformation theorists and practitioners.* New York: Praeger.

Friend, M., & Cook, L. (1996). *Interactions: Collaboration skills for school professionals.* White Plains, N.Y.: Longman.

Gallacher, K. K. (1997). Supervision, mentoring, and coaching: Methods for supporting personnel development. In P. J. Winton, J. A. McCollum, & C. Catlett (Eds.), *Reforming personnel preparation in early intervention: Issues, models, and practical strategies* (pp. 191–214). Baltimore: Paul H. Brookes.

Gallesich, J. (1982). *The profession and practice of consultation: A handbook for consultants, trainers of consultants, and consumers of consultation services.* San Francisco: Jossey-Bass.

Gallesich, J. (1985). Toward a meta-theory of consultation. *The Counseling Psychologist, 13,* 336–362.

Hansen, J. C., Himes, B. S., & Meier, S. (1990). *Consultation: Concepts and practices.* Englewood Cliffs, N.J.: Prentice Hall.

Harms, T., Cryer, D., & Clifford, R. M. (1997). *Infant/toddler environment rating scale* (rev. ed.). New York: Teachers College Press.

Havelock, R. (1973). *The change agent's guide to innovation in education.* Englewood Cliffs, N.J.: Educational Technology Publications.

Individuals with Disabilities Education Act, 20 U.S.C. §1400 *et seq.* (1999, January 5).

Kagan, S. L., Goffin, S. G., Golub, S. A., & Pritchard, E. (1995). *Toward systemic reform: Service integration for young children and their families.* Falls Church, Va.: National Center for Service Integration.

Kanter, R. M., Stein, B. A., & Jick, T. D. (1992). *The challenge of organizational change: How companies experience it and leaders guide it.* New York: The Free Press.

Kontos, S., & File, N. (1993). Staff development in support of integration. In C. A. Peck, S. L. Odom, & D. D. Bricker (Eds.), *Integrating young children with disabilities into community programs: Ecological perspectives on research and implementation* (pp. 169–186). Baltimore: Paul H. Brookes.

Loucks-Horsley, S., & Mundry, S. (1991). Assisting change from without: The technical assistance function. In J. R. Bliss, W. A. Firestone, & C. E. Richards (Eds.), *Rethinking effective schools: Research and practice* (pp. 112–127). Englewood Cliffs, N.J.: Prentice Hall.

Maple, G. (1987). Early intervention: Some issues in cooperative teamwork. *Australian Occupational Therapy Journal, 34*(4), 145–151.

McGonigel, M. J., Woodruff, G., Roszmann-Millican, M. (1994). The transdisciplinary team: A model for family-centered early intervention. In L. J. Johnson, R. J. Gallagher, & M. J. LaMontagne (Eds.), *Meeting early intervention challenges: Issues from birth to three* (2nd ed., pp. 95–131). Baltimore: Paul H. Brookes.

McLaughlin, M. W. (1991). The Rand change agent study: Ten years later. In A. R. Odden (Ed.), *Education policy implementation* (pp. 143–155). Albany: State University of New York.

Nugent, J. K. (1994). Cross-cultural studies of child development: Implications for clinicians. *Zero to Three, 15*(2), 1–8.

Parker, G. M. (1991). *Parker team player survey.* Tuxedo, N.Y.: Xicom.

Pawl, J. H. (1995). On supervision. In L. Eggbeer & E. Fenichel (Eds.), Educating and supporting the infant/family work force: Models, methods, and materials. *Zero to Three, 15*(3), 21–29.

Payne, M. (1982). *Working in teams.* London: Macmillan.

Peck, C. A., Furman, G. C., & Helmstetter, E. (1993). Integrated early childhood programs: Research on the implementation of change in organizational contexts. In C. A. Peck, S. L. Odom, & D. D. Bricker (Eds.), *Integrating young children with disabilities into community programs: Ecological perspectives on research and implementation* (pp. 187–205). Baltimore: Paul H. Brookes.

Richman, H., & Clifford, R. M. (1980). Toward a model of technical assistance. In R. M. Clifford & P. L. Trohanis (Eds.), *Technical assistance in educational settings* (pp. 13–18). Columbus, Ohio: Ohio State University.

Rosin, P., Whitehead, A., Tuchman, T., Jesien, G., & Begun, A. (1993). *Partnerships in early intervention: A training guide on family-centered care, team building, and service coordination.* Madison, Wisc.: Waisman Center.

Sallis, E. (1993). *Total quality management in education.* Philadelphia: Kogan Page.

Schulte, A. C. Osborne, S. S., & Kauffman, J. M. (1993). Teacher responses to two types of consultative special education services. *Journal of Educational and Psychological Consultation, 4*(1), 1–27.

Shanok, R. S. (1991). The supervisory relationship: Integrator, resource, and guide. *Zero to Three, 12*(2), 16–19.

Strata, E., & Bricker, D. (1996). Building a collaborative team. In D. Bricker & A. Widerstrom (Eds.), *Preparing personnel to work with infants and young children and their families* (pp. 321–345). Baltimore: Paul H. Brookes.

Sullivan, W. P. (1991). Technical assistance in community mental health: A model for social work consultants. *Research on Social Work Practice, 1*(3), 289–305.

Trohanis, P. L. (1982). Technical assistance and the improvement of services to exceptional children. *Theory into Practice, 21*(2), 119–128.

Trohanis, P. L. (1986). *Improving state technical assistance programs.* Chapel Hill: Frank Porter Graham Child Development Center, University of North Carolina at Chapel Hill.

Wesley, P. W. (1994). Providing on-site consultation to promote quality in integrated child care programs. *Journal of Early Intervention, 18*(4), 391–402.

West, J. F. (1985). *Regular and special educators' preferences for school-based consultation models: A statewide study* (Tech. Rep. No. 101). Austin: The University of Texas at Austin, Research and Training Institute on School Consultation.

West, J. F., Idol, L., & Cannon, G. (1989). *Collaboration in the schools: An inservice and preservice curriculum for teachers, support staff, and administrators.* Austin, Tex.: Pro-ed.

Westby, C. E., & Ford, V. (1993). The role of team culture in assessment and intervention. *Journal of Educational and Psychological Consultation, 4*(4), 319–341.

Winton, P. J., McWilliam, P. J., Harrison, T., Owens, A. M., & Bailey, D. B. (1992). Lessons learned from implementing a team-based model for change. *Infants and Young Children, 5*(1), 49–57.

CHAPTER TEN

TECHNOLOGY AND THE FUTURE

DEBORAH J. KRAVIK

OBJECTIVES

- To understand the use of assistive technology for young children with disabilities
- To understand the importance of exploratory behavior for infants and toddlers with disabilities and the outlet provided by adaptive toys, augmentative communication devices, and computers
- To apply the use of assistive technology to home and classroom situations for young children with disabilities
- To assess young children with disabilities for assistive technology needs
- To assess the environment of children with disabilities for specific technology needs
- To assist families in the selection of equipment, software, and other technologies for their children
- To locate and access services via technology for families of children with disabilities
- To understand and utilize computerized Individualized Family Service Plans
- To understand the impact of long distance learning relative to young children and families as well as service providers

ASSISTIVE TECHNOLOGY: DEFINITION, THE LAW, AND PHILOSOPHICAL BASIS

Assistive technology refers to the simple adaptation of toys and materials as well as the more complex development of sophisticated technical devices. A definition of assistive technology first appeared in the law in the Technology-Related Assistance for Individuals with Disabilities Act (PL 100-407), signed by President Ronald Reagan in 1988. PL 100-407 defined assistive technology as "any item, piece of equipment, or product system, whether acquired commercially off the shelf, modified, or customized, that is used to increase, maintain, or improve functional capabilities of children with disabilities" (Early Intervention Program, 1999, § 303.12).

The 1990 revision of the Individuals with Disabilities Education Act (IDEA) mandated responsibility to schools to provide assistive technology devices as well as services when appropriate. PL 100-407 and IDEA defined an assistive technology service as:

Any service that directly assists an individual with a disability in the selection, acquisition, or use of an assistive technology device, including:

- the evaluation of needs of an individual with a disability, including a functional evaluation of the individual's customary environment;
- purchasing, leasing, or otherwise providing for the acquisition of assistive technology devices by individuals with disabilities;
- selecting, designing, fitting, customizing, adapting, applying, maintaining, repairing, or replacing assistive technology devices;

- coordinating and using other therapies, interventions, or services with assistive technology devices, such as those associated with existing education and rehabilitation plans and programs;
- training or technical assistance for an individual with disabilities or the family, and for professionals (including individuals providing education and rehabilitation services), employers, or other individuals who provide services to, employ, or are otherwise substantially involved in the major life functions of individuals with disabilities.

—"New Federal Support," 1989, p. 3

In 1997 IDEA was reauthorized. It required consideration of assistive technology needs and services every time a new Individualized Education Plan (IEP) is written (Lance, 1998). As families and birth-to-three service providers participate on the IEP team, the child's current use of assistive technology as well as training requirements for users and staff should be considered during the transition to the new program.

Traditionally, children with disabilities have had more exposure to assistive technology than their typically developing peers. This is because technology has been used to serve as an equalizer. Parents and professionals have seen the effectiveness of assistive technology as a compensation mechanism for children with disabilities (Pierce, 1994). "Disabilities which limit mobility or cause developmental delays affect the physical, intellectual, social and emotional growth of a child" (Enders & Hall, 1990, p. 171). Every facet of a child's life is potentially affected by a limitation in mobility, whether it be physically based or cognitively based, because such limitations hinder the opportunity to explore the environment. The use of assistive technology devices has provided mobility, communication, and access to children with disabilities so that they might participate equally with their nondisabled peers. Switch toys allow a child to manipulate and explore the qualities of toys. Computers assist a child to engage in exploratory play. Wheelchairs or mobility devices may allow a child to move about to explore the same things nondisabled peers explore. Communication devices allow a child to have a voice to express needs and wants as well as to converse.

Armstrong and Jones (1994) acknowledge the current paradigm shift from viewing assistive technology as a useful tool for individual training based on a hierarchy of technology skill development to seeing it as "an effective tool to help children to be more active participants in typical routines" (p. 1). The shift has been toward viewing technology as an ongoing strategy to facilitate play and learning instead of as a device to be mastered. Assistive technology devices can be used in the home, in center-based programs, and in the community as a means to provide learning, communication, and social opportunities.

Play and Learning

An understanding of how infants and young children learn is essential to any discussion involving technology with children with disabilities. As Piaget's stages of development indicate, appropriate environmental experiences play a large role in cognitive development (Garwood & Fewell, 1983). Children's exploration of the environment facilitates learning. Play is the medium through which infants and toddlers experience their world (Bailey & Wolery, 1984; Enders & Hall, 1990; Linder, 1990; Musselwhite, 1986). It influences all domains of development (e.g., cognitive, social-emotional, communication, and motor).

It stands to reason that a child who is unable to explore and manipulate objects can now do so using technology. In Vignette 10.1, Dominic explored the effects of participating in his own birthday party and interacting with the other children.

VIGNETTE 10.1   DOMINIC AND HIS FRIENDS

Dominic is a two-year-old boy with multiple disabilities. He is involved in a home-based birth-to-three program and receives special instruction, occupational therapy, and physical therapy services. He requires round-the-clock nursing care, provided by a combination of home care nurses and his parents. He has three siblings: two brothers and a sister, ages five, four, and one, and will soon have another brother or sister. Dominic is gavage-fed, requires supplemental oxygen at times, and has a tracheostomy. It is unclear how well Dominic can see and hear, but he loves music and interaction with his parents and siblings. He likes to explore some textures. He is unable to sit unsupported and has limited control of his extremities. Dominic communicates by smiling, crying, and softly humming. He can roll from his back to his side while he is lying on the floor, and he sometimes rolls away to communicate his desire to discontinue an activity. Dominic is unable to actively participate in most family activities, and he reaches a state of overload quite easily.

This summer, Dominic's sister and brothers and their friends played outside frequently, and Dominic spent more time either alone or with a nurse. He missed the other children, and his face would visibly brighten when they came in to play with him. While working on the goals that were written by Dominic's mom, he and his teacher began to prepare for his upcoming birthday. During learning sessions, Dominic would touch, smell, and manipulate modeling clay and form it into a "cake." Magic candles that relight after they are blown out were placed in the "cake" and lit. Dominic already knew how to turn an adapted fan on and off with his switch to blow gentle breezes on himself at will. By pressing his switch, he now used the fan to blow out the candles again and again. He also practiced using the fan to blow pinwheels, which could later be given to all children as party favors. As Dominic became proficient at blowing out candles with the switch, the other children were invited in to play "birthday party" with him. With practice, as the children sang "Happy Birthday" to him, Dominic learned to blow the candles out at the appropriate time.

When the actual birthday arrived, a morning practice party was held to refresh Dominic's skills for his real party. As friends and family gathered around and sang "Happy Birthday" to him, Dominic blew out his own candles by activating the switch-adapted fan at the appropriate time in the song! The other children all clapped and cheered as Dominic smiled and hummed. Dominic was also able to participate in a weekend party with his relatives, taking an active role in his own birthday.

Typical and Atypical Development

For the infant and toddler, motor skills are the "primary vehicle for learning socialization" (Butler, 1988, p. 66). Piaget's theory of intellectual development was based on the belief that although the environment exerts an influence on the child, that influence occurs in the process of a child's actions upon the environment. "Piaget's central theme is that the infant is active; that is, he seeks contact with the environment. His curiosity does not let him wait for environmental events to happen; rather he searches them out and seeks increased levels of stimulation and excitement" (Ginsburg & Opper, 1979, p. 67). The child has a natural curiosity. It is in his nature to explore, participate in, and interact with his environment.

Disabilities in any area of development affect the manner in which the child plays and learns. Without opportunities to affect her world, a child may be severely limited in cognitive development as well as language development (Enders & Hall, 1990). How can the child with a disability seek out increased levels of stimulation? How can this child satisfy her curiosity? The child who has cerebral palsy may not be able to move around freely to explore. The child who views the world from a supine position gains a different understanding of events than the child who is able to view it from an upright position. The infant with a visual impairment may not be able to use visual cues in the same way another child can. Her perspective of the world may not include as large an area of exploration as that of another child. The child with a hearing impairment will not have the same opportunities to develop and engage in language as the typical child. The child with cognitive delays may not interpret cues from the environment or develop language in the typical fashion. Research has demonstrated quantitative and qualitative differences in the play of children with disabilities and children without disabilities (Linder, 1990). Limited access to the world of play deprives a child of crucial developmental opportunities.

Technology as a Learning Tool

One way to facilitate play in children with disabilities is to make toys and materials accessible to them. This is the role of adaptive switch devices, simple communication devices, and appropriate computer software and peripherals. Switches can provide access to toys, computers, augmentative communication devices, the daily living environment, leisure activities, and the social world. Infants and toddlers can be enticed to explore, interact, and be engaged through the creative use of adaptive equipment.

Using a computer-monitored adapted toy program Sullivan and Lewis (1993) gathered data that supported the use of technology in a systematic contingency curriculum. They suggested that switch-toy technology is developmentally appropriate for 2 -to-12-month-olds, based on the accepted Piagetian model of development and infant contingency learning research. Learned helplessness can be prevented by providing opportunities for control that can promote an attitude of expectancy of control over the environment, which in turn facilitates mastery motivation. "If motivation, attention, and fostering of engagement of the physical environment are considered important goals for the disabled infant, then switches, adapted toys, and other currently available technologies are the tools for achieving these goals and can be introduced at levels of cognitive functioning as early as 2 to 3 months" (Sullivan and Lewis, 1993, p. 75). Kinsley and Langone (1995) reviewed four studies that addressed the use of switch-adapted activities with young children with disabilities. In these studies, the researchers use adapted switch toys as contingent reinforcers. Such target behaviors as "increasing movement patterns" (p. 319) were identified. Although further replication of these studies is necessary, each supported the use of adapted switch toys as "powerful motivators for children who have disabilities" (p. 319).

Technology is a "means to provide new methods of access to play, language, and socialization, the primary developing domains of young children" (Behrmann, Jones, & Wilds, 1989, p. 68). When adaptations and technology are included creatively as intervention strategies, new opportunities are provided to facilitate play and learning. The development of these strategies should include typical children in natural settings. For example, computers or communication devices can provide a means of helping the child with disabilities to engage in activities with her typically developing peers.

Technology should be the tool or the strategy, rather than the goal. It is appropriate for a range of assistive technology options, rather than a single all-purpose device, to be considered to meet a child's current and future needs. For the child with a cognitive, physical, or sensory impairment or a developmental delay, the use of adaptive switches, communication devices, and/or a computer can provide the experience of influence over her world, fostering expectancy of participation and success. In the following sections, a variety of assistive technology devices will be discussed.

TYPES OF ASSISTIVE TECHNOLOGY

The most common types of assistive technology that are useful with the birth-to-three population are switches and switch toys, simple augmentative communication devices, and adapted computers. All can provide opportunities for the development of a sense of control and autonomy, language development, cognitive development, creative play, social interaction, and full participation in the physical and social environment (Burkhart, 1993; Hutinger et al., 1990; Musselwhite, 1986; Robinson, 1986). While more sophisticated devices are available, many are not appropriate for the very young child.

Switches

An adaptive switch is a device that allows alternative access to a battery-operated or electrical item. The switch provides an "interface between the child and a reinforcing device, so that the child can activate the device independently" (Musselwhite, 1986, p. 51). Switches can provide easier access to toys, augmentative communication devices, computers, mobility devices, tools, environmental controls, electrical devices, recreational equipment, items in the daily living environment, and more (Burkhart, 1987; Church & Glennen, 1992; Goossens', Crain, & Elder, 1994; Reichle, York, & Sigafoos, 1991).

Many types of switches can be constructed or purchased commercially, with a variety of activation methods (Church & Glennen, 1992; Goossens' & Crain, 1992; Musselwhite, 1986; Reichle et al., 1991). Some of the types of switches commonly used are listed in Table 10.1; several commercial versions are described in Table 10.2.

Appropriate switch selection depends on "the child's abilities, switch sensitivity, switch size, feedback, durability, and placement" (Hutinger, Johanson, Robinson, & Schneider, 1992, p. 19). Commercially available switches vary in sensitivity, or in the amount of pressure and/or movement required for activation. A knowledge of the child's physical abilities as they relate to the sensitivity of the switch will assist in selection.

Feedback refers to sound, light, or tactile information that is provided by the switch itself when it is activated. It may click, buzz, vibrate, light up, or play music as a signal that activation has occurred. These can be very useful features for children who have sensory or cognitive impairments. On the other hand, the feedback

TABLE 10.1   Types of Switches

Button switch
Pressure switch
Wobble switch
Sip-and-puff switch
Shadow switch
Joystick
Plate switch
String switch
Mercury switch
Grip switch
Sound-voice-activated switch
Infrared-beam switch

TABLE 10.2 Switches and Accessories

DEVICE	PRICE	VENDOR	DESCRIPTION
Battery Device Adapter	$8	AbleNet 1-800-322-0956 *www.ablenet.com*	An adapter that, when inserted in a device's battery compartment, allows activation of the device with a switch. For AA, C, or D batteries. Specify battery size when ordering.
Big Red Switch	$42	AbleNet 1-800-322-0956 *www.ablenet.com*	A durable, sensitive switch that is pressure-sensitive across its entire surface. 5" diameter.
Grip and Puff Switch	$46	Enabling Devices 1-800-832-8697 *www.enablingdevices.com*	A pneumatic switch that is activated by squeezing a vinyl grip
Jelly Bean Switch	$42	AbleNet 1-800-322-0956 *www.ablenet.com*	A 2½"-diameter version of the Big Red Switch
Joy Stick Switch	$50	Enabling Devices 1-800-832-8697 *www.enablingdevices.com*	A switch that can activate four different devices by pushing in four different directions
Judy Lynn Software Adaptor	$27	Judy Lynn Software 732-390-8845 *www.castle.net/judylynn*	A switch adapter for use with Judy Lynn software
L. T. Switch	$48	Don Johnston, Inc. 1-800-999-4660 *www.donjohnston.com*	A light-touch switch requiring limited strength for activation
PowerLink 2	$159	AbleNet 1-800-322-0956 *www.ablenet.com*	A control unit that allows a user to operate electrical appliances by switch activation. The PowerLink allows control in three modes: direct (when switch is operated); timed (at preset intervals of 1 to 60 seconds); or latch (with one-touch on and one-touch off).
Pull Switch	$25	Enabling Devices 1-800-832-8697 *www.enablingdevices.com*	A switch that activates a device by pulling on a wooden ball (specify ¼" or ⅛" jacks and plugs)
Rocking Plate Switch	$36 (large, 4 × 12") $27 (small, 1½ × 5")	Enabling Devices 1-800-832-8697 *www.enablingdevices.com*	A switch that can activate two devices separately (specify ¼" or ⅛" jacks and plugs)

(continued)

TABLE 10.2 **Continued**

DEVICE	PRICE	VENDOR	DESCRIPTION
Roller Switch Music Box	$33	Enabling Devices 1-800-832-8697 www.enablingdevices.com	A switch that plays music and/or activates a device by movement of a roller bar
Series Adaptor	$13	AbleNet 1-800-322-0956 www.ablenet.com	An adaptor that requires switches to be activated by two children simultaneously to operate a device
Slide Projector Control	$21	AbleNet 1-800-322-0956 www.ableNet.com	A control that advances slides on most Kodak carousels through single-switch operation
Specs Switch	$45	AbleNet 1-800-322-0956 www.ablenet.com	A 1⅜"-diameter version of the Big Red Switch
Vertical Wobble Switch	$41	Enabling Devices 1-800-832-8697 www.enablingdevices.com	A switch that activates a device through any swiping motion (specify ⅛" or ¼" jacks and plugs)
Vibrating Pillow Switch	$26	Enabling Devices 1-800-832-8697 www.enablingdevices.com	A soft pillow switch that vibrates. Can be used alone or connected to another device.

may be so stimulating to some children that they are distracted from the reinforcer and unable to focus on the intended activity. Instead, such children may get all the reinforcement they need from the switch click. A knowledge of the child and the switch will help determine how much feedback is reasonable and acceptable. Additional feedback, such as movement, light, sound, vibration, or any combination of these, is provided by the device being activated by the switch.

Durability of the switch is a necessary consideration when it is being used by young children. The switch may be dropped, thrown, stepped on, drooled on, or mouthed. It needs to be durable enough to be used in a variety of environments by a variety of children.

Choosing the appropriate size and placement of the switch and the device it will activate, and providing a comfortable and nondemanding position for the child, are critical elements in successfully providing access to an activity.

Switch Toys

Switch-adapted toy play offers a range of possibilities to children with varying skill levels. The development of an understanding of cause and effect can be facilitated through switch toys. Exploration of the properties of toys—sound, movement, color, light, and texture—can occur. Motor manipulation, visual tracking, motor development, choice selection, turn-taking, communication, imitation, matching, problem-solving, language development, social interaction, independent play, and concept development can be facilitated with switch-adapted toys (Hutinger et al., 1990; Musselwhite, 1986). The concepts of cause and effect, imitation, and turn-taking are vital pieces in the development of language. Activating switches can provide auditory, visual, tactile, and sensory stimulation. Using a variety of switches will aid in generalizing skills and will provide opportunities for higher skill development (Behrmann et al., 1989). Strategies should be individualized for each child, depending on her particular ability, interests, limitations, developmental level, and goals (Robinson, Rauschert & Schneider, 1988).

When a battery-operated toy is adapted with a switch, the child can easily control its action. For examples, a six-month-old child can make the train go by activating the switch and can practice his motor skills naturally by crawling after the train. The switch toy becomes the means to entice movement while giving opportunities to explore cause and effect. To move beyond cause and effect, or if the same action becomes too repetitive to hold the child's interest, switch toy can become a "new" toy that emphasizes new concepts by being covered with a puppet (King-DeBaun, 1995). Play will now have a new focus. Stories and play activities can be built around the new toy, and the child can direct appropriate action with the switch.

In Vignette 10.2, Dominic chooses one of two activities via technology.

VIGNETTE 10.2 THE POWER OF CHOICES

As Dominic became more proficient with switch activation and was ready to move beyond cause and effect, a method of indicating choices was needed. A choice switch was adapted with real objects so that he could indicate which of two activities he wanted. Two very different activities were selected initially. One side of the switch was connected via a battery interrupter to a toy bird that waddled, then stopped and squeaked, opening and shutting its beak as long as the switch was activated. Attached to the other side was a felt cutout of a character in the story "Brown Bear, Brown Bear." If Dominic chose that activity, a page of the story was read to him. Each activation resulted in another page being read. Often he would choose to hear several pages and then was ready for a break. He seemed to delight in his newfound power and would frequently change to the other activity as if to test whether his teacher would respond to his choice. Once he was confident that his selections would be honored, he stayed with a chosen activity for longer periods of time.

In this vignette, Dominic can be seen exerting influence over people, activities, and interactions. As they began to realize his abilities, his family and his nurses were also able to give him more opportunities to communicate his wishes and exercise choice. This is an important opportunity for a child whose disabilities are so severe that he constantly endures procedures being performed on his body.

A child's self-esteem can be enhanced by providing opportunities for his participation, control over the environment, and decision-making. In all cases, the child should play an active rather than a passive role. Access to switch-adapted toys can and should provide multisensory experiences with objects and people in the environment. The goal is access to play, not switch activation. Switch activation is the strategy that provides opportunities for play.

Augmentative Communication Devices

An augmentative communication device can be as simple as a picture that aids language expression or as complex as a multilevel electronic communication device. At the infant and toddler level, there are many single-message and 2–16-message devices available. They can be as inexpensive as an adapted talking picture frame. Most commonly used with young children are single-switch devices such as the BIGmack (Ablenet) and 4–8-message devices such as the talkPad (Frame Technologies) or the Cheaptalk (Enabling Devices) (see Table 10.3). The messages are quickly and easily recorded into the device, then activated when the child presses the message cell or a switch connected to it. King-Debaun (1995) described adapting a peekaboo book with simple vocal output to enable a child who is nonverbal or who is physically handicapped to participate with her parent in early reading experiences by pressing the page to activate the message. Simple communication devices can be used in a variety of play activities and can be changed in seconds. To make these developmentally appropriate, pictures should be attached to the cells so the child has a visual representation of the message inside.

Participation in small-group activities by all children can be enhanced through adapted play and communication devices. The young child's natural curiosity can be a catalyst for turn-taking and social interaction when an activity is set up appropriately. Play can be equalized and inclusion fostered with voice output. All children, with and without disabilities, should have the opportunity to communicate with the device. It is only then that the child who needs it can see that it truly can be used to communicate. The communicative intent of all who use it should be honored and responded to.

Play can be a means of building communication and direction-following concepts by using a simple communication device. Messages can easily be recorded to say "Build it up," "More blocks," "Uh-oh," "Crash," "My turn," and so on. Repetitive lines from stories or finger plays can be recorded for the child to play/say at the appropriate time.

In Vignette 10.3, Jackson uses a communication device to participate in a play group.

VIGNETTE 10.3   JACKSON TALKS TO HIS FRIENDS
Jackson, a two-and-a-half-year-old with Down syndrome and cerebral palsy, loved his friends at play group. He was usually one of the first to arrive with his dad. Jackson had a strong attachment to his

TABLE 10.3   Communication Devices

DEVICE	PRICE	VENDOR	DESCRIPTION
Alphatalker	$1595	Prentke-Romich 1-800-262-1990 *www.prentkeromich.com*	A communication device that allows for up to 32 messages on one board. Multiple boards with chained messages can convey a variety of messages. Accessed by direct selection, switches, or scanning.
BIGmack	$86	AbleNet 1-800-322-0956 *www.ablenet.com*	A single-message communication device that is activated with any switch
Cheap Talk 4 Direct*	$79	Enabling Devices 1-800-832-8697 *www.enablingdevices.com*	A communication device that allows the user to activate a choice of four prerecorded phrases (up to five seconds each)
Cheap Talk 8 Direct*	$95	Enabling Devices 1-800-832-8697 *www.enablingdevices.com*	Same as Cheap Talk 4 but with eight choices.
Dial Scan	$195	Don Johnston 1-800-999-4660 *www.donjohnston.com*	A rotary-scanning communication device that is activated by a switch. Speed and direction of scan can be set.
Shadow Talker	$110	Enabling Devices 1-800-832-8697 *www.enablingdevices.com*	A four-choice communication device that is activated by any body movement that creates a shadow over a choice station. Messages are prerecorded.
Voice-in-a-Box	$150	Wisconsin Assistive Technology Initiative 1-800-831-6391 *www.wati.org*	A 16-message communication device that is accessed by direct selection or a switch. Also available in 24- and 40-message models, and a 6-level/16-messages per level model.
talkPad	$99	Frame Technologies (920) 869-2979	A 4-message communication device that is easily recorded with human voice. In a lightweight, brightly colored, durable case.
One-Step Communicator	$99	AbleNet 1-800-322-0956 *www.ablenet.com*	A single-message communication aide that holds up to 20 seconds of memory.

*Cheap Talk 4 and Cheap Talk 8 are also available in scan versions or as switch modules.

father, and currently experienced intense separation anxiety whenever his dad moved away from him. As the other children drifted in one by one, Jackson would silently wave to greet them, but he rarely was able to get their attention. They would walk past him to find toys with which to play. Jackson was not able to walk, and he could only say a few words. He needed a way to greet his friends that would get their attention and entice them to come over to play with him.

A Cheap Talk 8 was on loan to Jackson's birth-to-three program. The teacher decided to program it for greetings. The messages "Hi, Buddy!," "See you later," and "I want to read a book now" (Jackson's favorite activity) were recorded, and the remaining message cells were hidden from view with a cardboard cutout. After modeling by his dad and the teacher, Jackson waved and pressed the cell for "Hi, Buddy!" when Kaila came in the door. At first, he did not get her attention. He continued to wave and activate the message "Hi, Buddy!" Finally, Kaila heard and saw Jackson, and she immediately came over and sat down to play with him and the new toy! Jackson was thrilled as he and Kaila looked at each other and took turns talking to each other with the aid of the Cheap Talk. After a little while, Jackson, seemingly satisfied, pressed the messages "See you later" and "I want to read a book now," waved to his dad, and crawled over to the book corner! This was Jackson's first exposure to any communication device.

In this vignette, Jackson was given a way to communicate very simple social messages to a variety of people. With his new power, he was able to more easily separate from his father. He now had his own way of talking to his peers and became less dependent on his father to facilitate the interaction. Jackson also began to use this device in his childcare setting at home with his brother and parents.

Technology is a "means to provide new methods of access to play, language, and socialization, the primary developing domains of young children" (Behrmann et al., 1989, p. 68). When adaptations and technology are included creatively as intervention strategies, new opportunities are provided to facilitate play and learning. The development of these strategies should include typical children in natural settings. Adapted toys, communication devices, and computers can provide a means of helping the child with disabilities to engage in activities with her typically developing peers.

Computers

The ability to operate simple switches is a prerequisite to computer access for young children. Computers can be used at early developmental levels with single-switch programs. The same type of switches used to operate toys can be used with computer software. Early switch-toy games were the precursors of more complex methods of accessing computers (Robinson, 1986, 1986–87). Computers can provide the next step in establishing a child's autonomous interaction with the environment. They are effective tools that, when included in the developmentally appropriate activities, can promote a child's ability to play, interact, communicate, problem-solve, and learn in many other ways. Even outdated Apple IIe and IBM computers can be useful with this age population. These can be acquired very inexpensively or for free as schools and companies upgrade their computers. By using public domain software, play activities can easily be adapted for very young children for home- or center-based use for less than $100 (the cost of a switch and a switch interface).

In Vignette 10.4, Kelsey gains a sense of self through her use of technology.

VIGNETTE 10.4 KELSEY AT PLAY

An outdated IBM computer had been donated by a local bank to 18-month-old Kelsey, who has muscular dystrophy, Because she has little strength in her extremities and is not able to scoot, crawl, or walk, she was unable to explore objects in her environment in typical ways. She was able to say some words or approximations, but was difficult to understand. Because of her limited strength, she was unable to pick up and play with toys that had any weight to them. When Kelsey's teacher made a home visit and brought her the Judy Lynn Software version of Fundamental Concepts to try for the first time, Kelsey greeted her by asking for the "pu" (computer). Kelsey was placed in her high chair in front of the computer. A Jelly Bean Switch (AbleNet) was plugged into a switch adapter (available from Judy Lynn Software), and the adapter was plugged into the joystick port in the back of the computer. The Jelly Bean Switch was small enough for Kelsey's tiny hands and for her high chair tray. A baby doll and a washcloth were also placed on her tray. "PeekaBoo" was selected from the software menu. The teacher first attempted to engage Kelsey in a game of peekaboo with the washcloth and the doll, and then with her own face. Kelsey was not interested and repeated "pu" in a demanding voice. She said "ba" for button, and the switch was given to her. As she pressed the switch, a screen slowly opened to reveal a face. Kelsey recognized the sing-song of the word "peekaboo" and repeated three nondescript syllables in the same intonation. Her delight was evident in her smile, and she clapped for herself when she uncovered the face by pushing her button. When Kelsey bored of this activity, she chose to color. Markers and paper were brought out and the game "Coloring" from the same software was used to color pictures. The same color markers that she chose on the computer were used by her teacher.

This vignette shows that, with the use of a switch and the computer, Kelsey was able to experience concepts that were developmentally appropriate for her age, despite the fact that she was so motorically challenged.

Lepper and Milojkovic (1986) identified instructional advantages of using the computer. With the computer, learning is interactive. Responses from the computer are immediate. Learning can be individualized, and responses can be given in a variety of modes, depending on the needs and learning style of the child. On the computer, the child can independently explore developmentally appropriate concepts. The computer, however, should not be substituted for interaction with adults or peers.

Research is emerging on the use of computers with children with disabilities who are under the age of three. The applications that have been reported so far are of three types: direct training of sensorimotor skills, contingency awareness, and communication and socialization (Butler, 1988). Butler (1988) reported the combined use of adaptive switches and computers to train "contingency awareness or cause-effect relationships in children as young as 3 months who had mentally retarding conditions such as Down syndrome" (p. 71). This understanding of cause and effect resulted in increased interest and involvement in their environment.

In Vignette 10.5, Emily learns to activate a switch to cause a change in the action on screen.

VIGNETTE 10.5   EMILY MAKES IT GO

The children trickled into the play-group room. On the floor, in the quiet corner, an Apple IIe computer was set up with the Dump Truck program on the Cause and Effect public domain software from Colorado Easter Seals. On the monitor appeared a dump truck, a hill, and a pile of dirt. The keyboard was completely hidden with a cardboard box covered with plain white adhesive-backed plastic. In the center was an AbleNet Big Red Switch attached to the box with Velcro. The switch was plugged into a switch adapter (Don Johnston, Inc.), which was then plugged into the game port in the back of the computer. On top of the monitor was a toy dump truck and a pile of cotton balls. It was the first time the computer had been available in the room.

Fourteen-month-old Emily, who has Down syndrome, was working on the motor objective "pulling to stand" and the communication objective "imitating sounds." She entered the room and immediately crept over to the computer. She studied the picture on the monitor with great interest, and slowly pulled herself up to stand by the cardboard box. She tapped the monitor several times and watched. Nothing happened. The teacher then showed Emily how to press the switch to cause the truck to dump its load and return for another load. Emily watched with fascination, then began tapping the switch. The teacher then "drove" the toy dump truck down to Emily's level and dumped the load of cotton balls while making a voiced lip-fluttering sound to emulate a truck noise. The teacher and Emily alternated between the activity on the computer and the toy play. Emily visibly made the connection between her switch activation and the movement on the monitor. She then became more interested in the toy play and began to push the truck along while imitating the teacher's truck sounds. Other children joined Emily in this activity as they arrived.

This vignette demonstrates Emily's awareness of the concept of cause and effect, her beginning imitation skills, and her interest in concrete objects. The visual action on the computer monitor provided a highly motivating activity that enticed Emily to pull to stand, to engage in turn-taking and imitation, and to produce environmental sounds.

Computer Access

Use of the regular keyboard with very young children is not developmentally appropriate. Alternative access to the computer for infants and toddlers can be achieved through a switch, a mouse, a trackball, the Muppet Learning Keys (Sunburst), the TouchWindow (Edmark), and IntelliKeys (IntelliTools). These operate in place of the standard keyboard and are more developmentally suited to young children (see Table 10.4). Some require software designed specifically for use with the particular alternative keyboard, while others work with overlays and can be programmed for activities individualized to the child's abilities and needs. Newer computers will be needed to run the more powerful animated software. The same factors must be considered when selecting an alternative keyboard as those considered when selecting switches (sensitivity, size, durability, feedback, and placement).

In Vignette 10.6, children use a TouchWindow to explore bubbles.

> **VIGNETTE 10.6   BUBBLE PLAY**
> At Playgroup, the day's theme revolved around bubbles. The children blew bubbles with wands and with switch-adapted bubble blowers, and played in whipped bubbles. The sensory pool contained a variety of items, including see-through balls, bubble-foam padding, and bubble pillows. For a gross motor activity, the children sat, crawled, walked, or jumped on bubble packing. They also reached way up high to catch the bubbles floating by. For language, all the activities focused on the words "pop," "bubble," and "my turn." Symbols (Mayer-Johnson) for these words were posted by every activity area. The Macintosh computer was loaded with Bubble Castle from the Reader Rabbit's Toddler CD (The Learning Company), an activity that allowed the children to engage in two-dimensional bubble play. The TouchWindow was attached to the monitor. Two-year-old Trevor and one-year-old Johnathan were busy touching the bubbles that floated around on the screen. As each bubble was touched, it popped and an animal dropped down to enter the castle. Trevor and Johnathan looked at each other excitedly when the bubbles popped.

TABLE 10.4   Computer Peripherals and Alternative Keyboards

DEVICE	PRICE	VENDOR	DESCRIPTION
Big Red Switch	$42.00	AbleNet 1-800-322-0956 *www.ablenet.com*	With a Computer Switch Interface, can be used to access single-switch software
Computer Switch Interface—Apple	$36.00	AbleNet 1-800-322-0956 *www.ablenet.com*	An adapter that allows a single switch to be connected to an Apple computer
Computer Switch Interface—Mac	$135.00	Don Johnston, Inc. 1-800-999-4660 *www.donjohnston.com*	An adapter that allows a single switch to be connected to a Mac computer
Computer Switch Interface—IBM	$99.00	Don Johnston, Inc. 1-800-999-4660 *www.donjohnston.com*	An adapter that allows a single switch to be connected to an IBM computer
IntelliKeys	$395.00	IntelliTools, Inc. 1-800-899-6687 *www.intellitools.com*	A light-touch keyboard that can be used with any standard keyboard software. Self-authoring software allows individualization for particular needs.
IntelliKeys with Mac Access Pac	$650.00	IntelliTools, Inc. 1-800-899-6687 *www.intellitools.com*	Includes the software Overlay Maker, IntelliPics, ClickIt!, and IntelliTalk
Microsoft EasyBall	$44.00	Don Johnston, Inc. 1-800-999-4660 *www.donjohnston.com*	Easy-to-use stationary mouse with a single button for click function. The child rolls the ball to move the cursor, then pushes the button.
Muppet Learning Keys	$129.95 (Apple II) $199.95 (Mac) $149.95 (DOS)	Sunburst 1-800-321-7511 *www.sunburst.com*	A touch-sensitive input device that allows users to access the computer without using the keyboard. Requires an Echo card and a color monitor.
Rollerball	$295.00	Don Johnston, Inc. 1-800-999-4660 *www.donjohnston.com*	Rolling ball replaces the mouse or cursor movement. Separate buttons perform click functions.
TouchWindow	$335.00	Edmark 1-800-426-0856 *www.edmark.com*	A touch-sensitive alternative input device. Software programs with overlays transform the surface into game boards and talking word boards. Requires an Apple IIe emulator card and works only with Mac software.

In this vignette, two boys explore a concept in a variety of ways. Using the computer with the TouchWindow allows direct selection that is developmentally appropriate for their ages and abilities.

The IntelliKeys is an user-friendly alternative keyboard that works with any software and can be used with switches, on either a Macintosh- or an IBM-compatible computer. Visual and auditory scanning with switch selection or direct selection is available. Commercial software or self-authored software can be run. There are many preprinted overlays for popular software programs for younger children with automatic setups for IntelliKeys and setups for printing overlays for Ke:nx. Easy-to-use authoring programs that allow individualized programming and overlay designing are also available.

Software for Very Young Children

Just as toys or communication devices provide the reinforcer with switches, software provides the reinforcer in computer activities. Software can provide the opportunity for exploratory play, interactive play, language development, storytelling, painting, and a variety of skills development (see Table 10.5). Careful software selection matched to the child's abilities, interests, and needs can provide a new avenue of access to the world.

Computer software for very young children has various functions, from exploration to more complex skill development. Many programs can be used with children at a variety of developmental levels. It is critical to consider the child's individual goals when selecting and planning computer activities. Skills and concepts can be introduced and reinforced, but the use of computers for drill and practice is not recommended (Hutinger, Robinson, & Schneider, 1995). Rather, activities and software should be implemented and utilized as one part of a comprehensive, integrated plan of intervention.

Computer games and activities may be designed specifically for development of an understanding of cause and effect at the simplest level, or they may involve fairly complex problem-solving at a much higher level. Behrmann (1984) identified three levels of learning for young children in which the computer is a useful strategy: cause and effect, choice-making, and matching. More recently, professionals report a wide range of goals that have successfully been addressed through computer activities, including exploration, communication, choice-making, play skills, cooperation, early math concepts, prereading skills, beginning problem-solving, cause and effect, attending skills, concept development, listening skills, classifying, object identification, picture identification, vocabulary development, fine motor skills, eye-hand coordination, visual motor skills, motor planning, social skills, and basic skill development (Church & Glennen, 1992; Hutinger et al., 1995; Fallon & Wann, 1994; Kinsley & Langone, 1995; Musselwhite, 1986). A recent survey of research replication sites in preschools reported that communication skill development is the most commonly cited use of computer activities with young children (Hutinger et al., 1995). Similar research with infants and toddlers is needed.

TABLE 10.5   Software for Young Children

DEVICE	PRICE	VENDOR	DESCRIPTION
Animals Coloring Book	$49.95	IntelliTools, Inc. 1-800-899-6687 *www.intellitools.com*	Colors are chosen by Intelli-Keys, a switch, or the mouse. The colors for the animal pictures are named as they are chosen. Creations can be printed.
Animated Toys	$35.00	Judy Lynn Software 732-390-8845 *www.castle.net/judylynn*	Single-switch access provides cause-and-effect and early scanning experiences
Arump!	$25.00	Creative Communicating 801-645-7737 *www.creativecomm.com*	A familiar rhyme provides the platform for practicing targeting skills using Touch Window, IntelliKeys, or the mouse
Baby Bear Nursery Series	$75.00	Creative Communicating 801-645-7737 *www.creativecomm.com*	Activities combine nursery rhymes, counting, and farm animal sounds with animation and colorful graphics
Baby Bear Series	$75.00	Creative Communicating 801-645-7737 *www.creativecomm.com*	Includes "Baby Bear's Bubble Bath," "Baby Bear Goes to School," and "Baby Bear Plays Outside"
Best of KidTECH	$59.00	Creative Communicating 801-645-7737 *www.creativecomm.com*	Includes one verse from six children's songs, including "Five Green and Speckled Frogs" and "I'm Bringing Home a Baby Bumble Bee"
BoardMaker	$399.00	Mayer-Johnson Co. 619-550-0084 *www.mayer-johnson.com*	Computerized library of picture communication symbols for creating overlays and communication displays
Circletime Tales Deluxe	$59.00	Don Johnston, Inc. 1-800-999-4660 *www.donjohnston.com*	Interactive nursery rhymes and activities in early literacy, counting, opposites, and directionality
ClickIt!*	$99.95	IntelliTools, Inc. 1-800-899-6687 *www.intellitools.com*	Software for customizing popular software to provide hotspots and scanning capabilities
Creature Antics	$85.00	Laureate 1-800-562-6801 *www.LaureateLearning.com*	Colorful animation and lively sounds by silly characters, accessible by keyboard, switch, mouse, or TouchWindow
Early Play	$30.00	Linda J. Burkhart 410-795-8834	Includes balloon play, clay, and blocks (requires IntelliPics software)
Eensy and Friends	$45.00	Don Johnston, Inc. 1-800-999-4660 *www.donjohnston.com*	Cause-and-effect activities that introduce concepts and early literacy
Five Green and Speckled Frogs	$95.00	Creative Communicating 801-645-7737 *www.creativecomm.com*	Activities involving cause and effect, numbers, number words, directionality, and beginning substitution

TABLE 10.5 **Continued**

DEVICE	PRICE	VENDOR	DESCRIPTION
Five Little Ducks	$59.00	Creative Communicating 801-645-7737 *www.creativecomm.com*	Cause-and-effect and beginning scanning activities teach 10 action verbs
Holidays Coloring Book	$49.95	IntelliTools, Inc. 1-800-899-6687 *www.intellitools.com*	Colors are chosen by IntelliKeys, a switch, or the mouse. The colors are named as they are chosen. Holiday theme creations can be printed.
Humpty Dumpty and Friends	$45.00	Don Johnston, Inc. 1-800-999-4660 *www.donjohnston.com*	Activities involving cause and effect, early exploration, opposites, and directionality
HyperStudio	$120.00– $130.00	Roger Wagner Publishing 1-800-497-3778 *www.hyperstudio.com*	Users can create and individualize programs in multimedia formats with text, sound, graphics, and video
IntelliPics*	$99.95	IntelliTools, Inc. 1-800-899-6687 *www.intellitools.com*	Creates activities from pictures by adding motion and sound
IntelliTalk*	$39.95 (Mac) $49.95 (Win)	IntelliTools, Inc. 1-800-899-6687 *www.intellitools.com*	Adds talking word processing to activities
JumpStart Baby	$20.00	Knowledge Adventure 1-800-542-4240 *www.knowledge*	Activities are filled with colors, sound, and music. Children can play hide-and-seek, sing nursery rhymes, do puzzles, and perform dressing activities.
JumpStart Toddler	$24.95	Knowledge Adventure 1-800-542-4240 *www.knowledge*	Enticing activities that introduce concepts in an exploratory manner
Just Grandma and Me	$40.00	Broderbund 1-800-474-8840 *www.broderbund.com*	Interactive software presenting early literacy experiences
KidPix Studio Deluxe	$69.96	Broderbund 1-800-474-8840 *www.broderbund.com*	Drawing, painting, and animation software for children's art projects. Includes colorful graphics and sound.
Little People Discovery Farm (CD-ROM)	$20.00	Fisher Price & Davidson 1-800-545-7677 *www.fisherprice.com*	Exploratory play featuring the little people from Fisher Price toys
Make It Go	$59.00	Creative Communicating 801-645-7737 *www.creativecomm.com*	Combines causes and effect with beginning scanning so children can play hide-and-seek, blow bubbles, find a puppy, etc.
Monkey's Jumping on the Bed	$95.00	Creative Communicating 801-645-7737 *www.creativecomm.com*	Activities involving cause and effect, colors, numbers, and matching

(continued)

TABLE 10.5   Continued

DEVICE	PRICE	VENDOR	DESCRIPTION
Old MacDonald's Farm	$75.00	Creative Communicating 801-645-7737 *www.creativecomm.com*	Children choose the animal that MacDonald sings about
Overlay-Maker*	$69.95 (Mac) $99.95 (Win)	IntelliTools, Inc. 1-800-899-6687 *www.intellitools.com*	Software for designing and customizing overlays for use with IntelliKeys and the computer. Can also design low-tech communication displays.
Press to Play Series	$45.00 each	Don Johnston, Inc. 1-800-999-4660 *www.donjohnston.com*	Cause-and-effect, exploratory play, and humorous multicultural activities
Reader Rabbit Playtime for Baby	$30.00	The Learning Company 1-800-543-9778 *www.learningco.com*	With parent's guidance, child can use mouse, keyboard, or TouchWindow to explore faces and feelings; play hide-and-seek, peek-a-boo, music, and imitation games; and listen to rhymes and stories
Reader Rabbit Toddler	$19.95	The Learning Company 1-800-543-9778 *www.learningco.com*	Early exploratory play using music, bubbles, animals, and other toddler activities
Ready for School Toddler (CD-ROM)	$20.00	Fisher Price & Davidson 1-800-545-7677 *www.fisherprice.com*	Concepts are explored using Fisher Price characters
Seasonal Activities I & II	$75.00 each	Creative Communicating 1-801-645-7737 *www.creativecomm.com*	The mouse, TouchWindow, or a switch can be used to explore seasonal activities.
Sesame Street Baby and Me	$30.00	The Learning Company 1-800-543-9778 *www.learningco.com*	With parent's guidance, child can interact with Sesame Street characters. Enlarged keyboard and hand-over-hand mouse movement facilitate typical early play and learning experiences.
Singalongs—volume I (CD-ROM)	$20.00	Fisher Price & Davidson 1-800-545-7677 *www.fisherprice.com*	Child can select familiar songs to hear and sing.
Songs and Play	$30.00	Linda J. Burkhart 410-795-8834	Includes "The Spider Song," "Five in a Bed," and "Big/Small/Fast/Slow" (requires IntelliPic software)
Storytime Just for Fun!	$125.00	Creative Communicating 801-645-7737 *www.creativecomm.com*	Digitized speech, colorful graphics, and animation provide interactive story experiences using IntelliKeys and IntelliPics (based on Pati King-Debaun's book of same title).

*Bundle price for all four software programs: Mac—$280.00, Win—$310.00; or Access Pac including all four software programs and IntelliKeys: Mac—$650.00, Win—$680.00.

In Vignette 10.7, Evelyn tries two programs for the first time.

VIGNETTE 10.7   EVELYN DISCOVERS HER VOICE

One-and-a-half-year-old Evelyn and her family have a Macintosh computer at home. Evelyn was born 12 weeks early and is doing quite well despite her complicated medical history. She is a quiet little girl who loves books but wants them read to her constantly. Otherwise, she has trouble focusing on activities for any length of time. Her mother is interested in expanding Evelyn's interests, increasing her vocalizations, and improving her ability to play with toys. Because Evelyn's mother is very interested in using the computer to capitalize on Evelyn's strength in attending to books, the TouchWindow was brought and set up with the program Old MacDonald's Farm (kidTECH). Evelyn is so tiny that her mom removed the keyboard from the computer desk, and Evelyn sat on the desk in the keyboard area with her mom behind her. As the program began, Evelyn's eyes got very big. When she saw the horse she exclaimed, "Oh!" When she saw the pig, she said, "pi." As the music played, Evelyn bounced up and down. When it stopped, she touched an animal to restart an activity.

Evelyn's mom then tried the exploratory program KeyWack (Stoneware Software). It can be used with a switch, the keyboard, or the TouchWindow. Whenever Evelyn touched the screen, she produced bright shapes and silly sounds. This led to lots of vocalizations, and Evelyn remained interested for far longer periods than she had before.

In this vignette, Evelyn demonstrates awareness of cause and effect, exploratory play, imitation, attending skills, choice-making, picture identification, communication, and eye-hand coordination skills on her computer at home. The computer activities provide motivation and reinforcement through graphics and animation. Any preschool skill can be reinforced by designing activities using carefully selected software. Speech synthesizer activities and vocal output foster language development. Problem-solving skills can be enhanced utilizing planning and sequencing programs (Robinson et al., 1988). Augmentative communication can be trained with software designed for that purpose. Authoring programs allow for the development of individualized overlays.

Technology and software development for infants and very young children, though still in its infancy, is rapidly expanding, and its possibilities are endless. More and more developmentally appropriate software for infants and toddlers is becoming available. Simple cause-and-effect software programs are being expanded to include exploratory play. For software to be appropriate, it must be multisensory and must address typical play of infants and toddlers. Linda T. Burkhart's programs, Early Play and Songs and Play, engage children in balloon play, clay exploration, block-building, and finger-play songs and actions. The kidTECH/SoftTouch software programs engage children in interactive songs frequently sung with very young children ("Five Green and Speckled Frogs," "Five Little Ducks," "Old MacDonald's Farm," "I'm Bringing Home a Baby Bumble Bee," etc.). Pati King-Debaun's Storytime Just for Fun! and Storytime Songbook include familiar songs and early literacy activities appropriate for 12-month-olds. Elaine Clark Center produces very simple and engaging software designed with infants and toddlers in mind. The Baby Bear Series follows Baby Bear in daily activities such as playing in the bath or the sandbox. The Baby Bear Nursery Series allows children to practice animal sounds or to expand concepts from the song "If You're Happy and You Know It." Most of this software is available with overlays for use with IntelliKeys. It can be used with a single switch or a TouchWindow.

The CD, or compact disk, is read by the computer without the necessity of storing the software on the computer's hard drive. While allowing interactive play on the computer, CD-ROM software does not use internal memory. This type of software can also be used in combination with switches and alternative access devices such as the TouchWindow and IntelliKeys. Commercially available software that is available on a disk or CD-ROM includes Ready for School Toddler, JumpStart Baby, and Reader Rabbit's Toddler in which toddlers can explore such activities as popping bubbles, singing songs, counting, sorting, matching shapes, and participating in stories. The Living Books Series provides opportunities for young children to explore stories interactively while experiencing them visually and auditorally. Software that is suitable for infants and toddlers is emerging at a rapid pace.

TECHNOLOGY ASSESSMENTS

A variety of technology assessment guides are available, and assessment techniques can be found in topical books and guides (Carl, Mataya, & Zabala, 1994; Church & Glennen, 1992; Goossens' & Crain, 1992; Hutinger et al., 1992; Levin & Scherfenberg, 1990; Wisconsin Assistive Technology Initiative, 1997). Ranging from interest surveys to formal assessment tools, they vary in many ways. Many resources that deal with implementation strategies also include informal strategies for assessing the child's needs and matching those needs to adaptive equipment (Burkhart, 1982; Goossens' & Crain, 1992; Musselwhite, 1986; Ray & Timms, 1993; Wright & Nomura, 1985).

In addition to defining assistive technology devices and services, PL 100-407 provided funding for states to develop comprehensive programs of assistive technology service delivery. States were to develop systems to provide a link between people with disabilities and assistive technology, and address the need to provide training to professionals, the users of assistive technology, and their families. Evaluation was also considered a major factor in providing quality assistive technology programs. As part of the training function, many states developed or adapted assessment guides for their service delivery programs that were then used statewide. In a study of professionals working with the early childhood special education population, ineffective assessment procedures were cited as a primary cause of abandonment or lack of implementation of assistive technology (Lesar, 1998).

The Assessment Team

Assessment of the use of technology involves a team approach, with the child and family as primary members in the decision-making process. The structure of the team is dictated by the child's physical and developmental needs, as well as the goals of intervention (Carl et al., 1994; Hutinger et al., 1992; Reed & Bowser, 1991; Wisconsin Assistive Technology Initiative, 1997). It is useful to include individuals who have sufficient knowledge of the child's abilities, needs, and communication skills. The nonverbal child may use very subtle cues to indicate pleasure, discomfort, interest, and disinterest. A person who has knowledge of these subtle indicators is a valuable team member. Again, the key to a good technology assessment is to consider the child first, then the device.

A team approach to the selection of equipment is essential for the success of the intervention. Table 10.6 lists candidates for inclusion on the team. At the very minimum, the team should include the child and the family, a child development specialist/teacher, and someone familiar with the technology. The latter may be someone chosen solely for this function or one of the other specialists who is also

TABLE 10.6   Technology Team Members

Child
Family
Occupational therapist
Child development specialist/teacher
Speech therapist
Assistive technology consultant
Family services coordinator
Administrator
Day care provider
Recreational therapist
Orientation and mobility specialist
Teacher of students with hearing impairments
Teacher of students with visual impairments
Therapist
Psychologist
Nurse
Advocate
Paraprofessional
Equipment vendor
Audiologist
Social worker
Funding representative

familiar with the technology. Other members are added as dictated by the child's and family's needs.

Assessing Individual Needs

The primary issue when assessing for possible technology use is the individual child (Hutinger et al., 1992), whose strengths, needs, interests, and motivation are to be addressed within the framework of the family and environments in which the child is expected to function. Choosing a piece of equipment is not a goal. Rather, determining the child's expectations in what environments and under what conditions is what leads the assessment process (Carl et al., 1994). The assessment team should focus on the following questions. What skills does the child have? What is the child having difficulty doing as well as her typical peers? What is hindering her performance? When and where does she need to demonstrate these abilities? under what conditions? What creative strategies can be implemented to address these difficulties? The choice of a piece of equipment is the last step in the process. Simple adaptations of materials and activities may be all that is needed in some cases.

Once it is determined that the goals of the child and the family can best be met by using assistive technology as a strategy, selection of the equipment begins. In this portion of the assessment, the determination of the best types of equipment to address the needs of the child occurs by carefully looking at the child's physical requirements, cognitive abilities, communication skills, motivation and interest levels, attention span, and movement patterns. Positioning of the child should guarantee that he is comfortable, is able to move independently, and has access to the reinforcer being activated by the switch. The child should not have to exert an excess amount of energy to maintain a stable position. His position should free him to engage in the desired activity. The inclusion of a physical and/or occupational therapist on the team is critical at this point.

Reliable movements that can be used to activate switches involve various body parts, such as the finger, hand, arm, trunk, leg, knee, foot, toe, head, chin, mouth, eyes, and facial muscles. Movements can be made on the right or left side of the body. They may consist of squeezing, pressing, waving, pulling, lifting, pushing, sucking, blowing, leaning, blinking, tilting, turning, flexing, or extending. Eye gaze may be the easiest reliable movement for one child. Consideration of the child's medical condition may preclude the use of certain pieces of equipment or reinforcers (i.e., some seizures are induced by flashing lights). Switches that are activated by reflex movements or controlled abnormal movements should never be selected. The movement chosen should be controlled by the child. It should involve an appropriate, voluntary, normal movement pattern (Goossens' & Crain, 1992).

Assessing the Environment

Careful assessment of all environments in which the child will be expected to use technology devices should be included in the assessment process. A child in a birth-to-three program may be served primarily in the home, at a center, at a day care, or at any combination of these settings. Awareness of the opportunities, limitations, and expectations in each setting is important in planning strategies for facilitating participation and generalization. For a child who participates in a center-based program or who attends a local day care center, selection and placement of equipment, positioning, and implementation strategies planned with an awareness of all the children in the setting will facilitate social interaction. In group settings, equipment will be used by all the children in the setting, not just the target child.

In Vignette 10.8, all the children help make the juice through the use of technology.

VIGNETTE 10.8   MAKING JUICE TOGETHER

On a hot summer day at Playgroup, the parents and children were preparing to have a snack. A blender was plugged into an AbleNet PowerLink2 and an AbleNet Big Red Switch was plugged into the PowerLink2. The teacher began to talk the children through the juice-making preparations. First she poured the frozen concentrated juice into the blender, and then added water from a pitcher. The older, more verbal children made comments about the process and the appearance of the juice in the blender. To help make the juice, each child took a turn mixing it by pressing the switch. The switch was passed from one child to another and placed on the table in a secure position in front of each one. As it was pressed, the children could see the change in color, hear the sound of the blender, and feel its vibration. Afterward, they tasted the juice. The typical children in the group spontaneously kept track and made sure each child had a turn, and were particularly concerned that those who had more difficulty calling attention to themselves for a turn were not excluded.

In this vignette, instead of simply drinking juice, all the children were invited to participate in the preparation. The switch and the power control unit provided the means by which they could participate while experiencing the multisensory properties of the activity. In a functional activity, each child exercised autonomy and productivity.

SELECTING MATERIALS

Material selection should only occur after a comprehensive technology assessment. Consideration of the purpose of the activity and the child's cognitive and physical abilities is important in selecting the switch. The appropriateness of a system for a particular child, whether it be for switch-toy play, communication, mobility, or computer play, involves examination of the unique needs of the child (Harrymann & Warren, 1992; Jensen & Bergman, 1992; Robinson, 1986; Wright & Nomura, 1985; York & Wiemann, 1991).

The selection of a switch and the switch-accessed activity should be made with the entire picture in mind. Do the switch system and activity invite participation and interaction with peers? How does the system fit in the family situation? Is the system easily accessible whenever the child wishes to use it or whenever it is appropriate to use it? How appropriate are the size, color, sensitivity, and feedback from the switch? Does the durability match its intended uses? These questions must be carefully answered within each setting in which the child will be using the switch system and activities: in the home, in peer groups, and in the community.

To maintain a holistic approach to the child and intervention, focus should be on the selection of toys and programs that provide auditory, visual, and tactile interaction as well as motor training. An important measure of effectiveness lies in the image of engagement and joy evidenced by the child.

Selection and placement of switches and reinforcers, and positioning of the child in the home setting must address the family's routines, preferences, goals, and space arrangements and limitations in order to promote family interaction and participation. Success should be assured for the child. When constructing a system, every attempt should be made to use developmentally appropriate materials and to provide as normal an appearance as possible.

Learning is experiential. Activities should be multisensory and developmentally appropriate, and should invite interaction with the toys, other children, and the facilitator. Design activities and create opportunities for guided exploration and play through switch access. Consider technology options to assist the infant to do what all children do in order to learn: see, hear, feel, taste, hold, bat, push, drop, and throw.

One of the benefits of using assistive technology with infants and toddlers is helping them learn "that they can play, communicate, interact, control their world, and do what all children their age can do" (Armstrong & Jones, 1994, p. 1). Infants and toddlers examine and explore toys through their senses. They see them, touch them, hold them, hear them, taste them, smell them, drop them, throw them, bat them, and manipulate them. Each toy has a unique input into the sensory system. Babies learn about objects by bringing them to their mouths and exploring their taste and texture. Older infants learn about contingency by throwing objects on the floor and then gesturing and/or vocalizing to persuade someone to interact and pick them up.

IMPLEMENTATION STRATEGIES

The use of adaptive devices and computers should never be a substitute for social interaction. Careful planning should ensure that the implemented strategies provide comprehensive experiences to effectively capture the exploratory nature of infants' and young children's play and learning. The role of the adult is to facilitate the child's opportunities to interact with the environment in as many ways as possible.

When using the computer as an avenue for providing experience, it is also important to offer three-dimensional, interactive experiences to accompany the computer activities (Hutinger et al., 1990). A variety of off-computer activities can be planned that reinforce and extend the experiences on the computer. The more exposure the child has in a variety of settings, the greater the chance for generalization of skills or concepts. In Vignette 10.5, Emily demonstrated skills both during computer play and during off-computer activities with the toys.

Social interaction opportunities should be built into switch-toy and computer activities at all levels. The goal of inclusion in community settings should be planned for at the very earliest stages of intervention, whether that intervention is in the home, in a child care setting, or a center. The facilitator may be the parent, the teacher or therapist, or an older sibling.

Switch Toys

In home or at a center, the switch and toy may be placed on the child's tray or high chair, on a table, or, as is often the case for infants and nonambulatory toddlers, on the floor. Securing the switch with Velcro to a surface is a quick and easy adaptation that provides stability. Many surfaces can be prepared with Velcro so that the switch can be easily transferred from location to location throughout the day and in different settings. Additional stabilizing aides include Blue-Tac and UltraStik, both from AbleNet, dycem, and pieces of nonslip drawer liner. It is useful to have more than one switch available to avoid excess setup time between activities. For instance, if a child uses a switch-activated voice output device to engage in conversation at the breakfast table, a family may find it easier to have another switch available in the play area for battery toys.

Subtle changes in presentation can be made for age appropriateness. Goossens' and Crain (1992) described a bib switch-mounting system constructed of terry cloth and Tempo Loop Display Fabric (Lockfast, Inc.). Burkhart (1987) described head mounts made of barrettes and headbands.

GUIDELINES FOR SUCCESSFUL TECHNOLOGY USE

Select battery-operated toys to which a baby or toddler might typically be attracted, remembering to engage as many senses as possible without overloading the child. Ensure that the child can reach the toy as well as the switch. Allow the infant or toddler to explore the toy visually, tactilely, orally, and auditorally, both with and without switch activation. Discuss attributes of the toy and its action (soft/hard, big/little, slow/fast, up/down, happy/sad, blue/red, hungry/thirsty, empty/full, etc.). Identify its parts or attributes such as color, texture, smell, or taste. A battery-operated black-and-white cow can be fun to play with as either a quiet, nonmoving toy or a walking, mooing, tail-swishing animal! Burkhart (1994) has suggested using cookie tin lids of varying sizes or hula hoops to contain moving toys so that they do not immediately "escape" from the child. Cafeteria trays, shoe-box lids, and many other household materials can accomplish the same task.

Much more can be addressed in switch-toy activities than just the concept of cause and effect. Functional goals including visual tracking, object permanence, play skills such as object play, relation of objects to each other, pretend play, sound production, labeling, motor and verbal imitation, turn-taking, choice-making, problem-solving, and communication skills can all be developed through switch-toy play in natural settings. For example, the moving cow may go into the barn and partially disappear as an activity in object permanence, or she may come out to eat from a bowl as the child visually tracks her progress. Identification of body parts may be addressed. Matching of animals to their sounds, counting skills, color matching, identification of actions, problem-solving, cooperative play, and many more skills can be effectively developed through well-designed activities utilizing switch toys as a strategy. Two or more children can engage in a block-building activity. As one child builds the blocks up high, counting each block as it is stacked, another child can activate the switch that drives the truck that knocks them down.

Augmentative Communication Devices

The speech therapist is essential in designing activities and selecting vocabulary for augmentative communication devices. Vocabulary should be chosen that is fun and invites interaction. Activities should be designed to provide both the need and the motivation to speak. Toddlers who are learning to pretend may enjoy playing a game in which they take turns with Mom or Dad pretending to fall asleep. The nonverbal child can "wake" snoring Dad by activating a single-message switch programmed to say, "Wake up!" With a four-message device, the game can be extended to include directives and messages with social comments such as "That's silly," "My turn," and "Nighty-night."

It is important that the communication devices be functionally used by both parties in the interaction so that the child understands that use of the device will be respected as communication. The adult models the use of the device and responds to the message the child conveys. In a play-group setting all the children, both verbal and nonverbal, should have the opportunity to communicate using the device. The communication, rather than the device, is the important feature. Sign language may also be used in conjunction with the device, just as it would be with voice.

Whenever possible, messages on communication devices should be programmed with a child's voice. Using lots of comments typically used by peers is a good motivator. "That's yucky!" or "Cool!" or "Mine!" are developmentally and socially appropriate comments that can be included on communication devices. Carefully listening to typical verbal infants and toddlers can give lots of clues for designing messages that are developmentally and socially appropriate.

Computers

As with switch toys, computers can be used with very young children as one part of a comprehensive strategy to develop a wide range of skills. The key to any well-designed plan is to provide access to activities in multiple, integrated settings using a variety of strategies and materials to expose a child to opportunities to learn. The child should be an active participant in the learning process. Computer activities for birth-to-three-year-olds should also involve a variety of related off-computer activities to provide opportunities to practice new skills (Hutinger et al., 1990).

Whenever possible, computers should be placed on the floor to ensure that the infant or toddler has easy access. Only the essential components of the computer need to be accessible to the child: the switch or alternative keyboard and the monitor. All other components can be removed or hidden from the child. If the computer is on a table, it should be a child-sized table, and appropriate child-sized seating should be available. If the regular keyboard is not detachable, a cardboard cover can easily be constructed, and the switch or alternate keyboard can be secured on the cardboard cover. If a TouchWindow is used, only the monitor with the window attached need be available to the child. All connecting cables should be removed from sight, and access to them should be prevented. The equipment should be stable, and specific positioning needs for each child should be addressed. Software should be loaded and ready to use. In addition to the computer and equipment setup, materials to reinforce activities on the computer should be available. If the activity portrayed on the monitor involves a baby, a baby doll should be available. If cars and blocks are involved, cars and blocks should be available during the computer activity. Babies and toddlers love to manipulate objects. Abstract concepts on the computer should be reinforced with manipulatives that resemble the pictured objects on the computer as closely as possible. The toys can duplicate actions that occur on the monitor. Visual attention, motor imitation skills, and concepts can be expanded by duplicating the action that occurred on the monitor with the toys that are available for the activity. Software is available that allows the user to print out the pictures that appear on the monitor. The printed material can be used for a wide variety of activities including coloring, painting, making a book, making a t-shirt, and making characters for youngsters to hold during story time. Books that reinforce the concepts from the computer activity should be available to the child. Toys that appear in the program can be used to expand play. With switch toys and computers as strategies for learning, every effort should be made to facilitate play in as natural a manner as possible. Young children should be enticed to participate in many activities that reinforce a concept and that provide opportunities for repetition and practice.

ISSUES AND CONCERNS
AROUND TECHNOLOGY USE

As new horizons in technology open new paths for enhancing development, it is necessary to be cognizant of some critical cautions. Each use of an adaptive device or system should be examined for its ability to provide maximum opportunity in the most natural manner possible. Each device or system should be usable by peers in inclusive settings and promote interaction. Use of the simplest, most natural techniques that promote independence should take precedence over more complex technology. Opportunities for socialization and skill development should be provided in a variety of situations using a repertoire of strategies. The primary aim of computer technology for young children with disabilities should be "to allow [them] access to the assistive technology which will be the most appropriate for their needs and to provide for the maximum participation of the young child in social and educational environments" (Wilds, 1989, p. 6).

Adaptive devices should be viewed as a means to an end rather than as a goal. They should enhance development rather than infringe on independence. Solutions utilizing technology should be innovative techniques to equip, entice, and encourage a child to interact with her environment, thereby promoting development to her fullest potential.

The home environment is also a major consideration for infants. Because the home is often the natural setting for birth-to-three-year-olds, utmost consideration should be given to the families' preferences when planning adaptations. The families should be included in the decision-making process from the very beginning.

FAMILIES AND TECHNOLOGY

In Vignette 10.9, Dominic and his family share some special times at home.

> **VIGNETTE 10.9   DOMINIC AND HIS MOM SHARE QUALITY TIME**
> Dominic's mother, Rita, reported that she was able to spend some quality time with him each night after the other children were in bed. Dominic's sleeping patterns are irregular, and he often has his days and nights mixed up. A string of Christmas lights was strung along his crib rail, and he was able to turn them on and off at will with a Big Red Switch and a PowerLink2. A tape player was added so that he could also turn music on and off at will. Each evening, Dominic's mother would spend some quiet time with him, talking and singing to him softly. It was during this time that Dominic would smile and hum and turn the lights off and on in a turn-taking activity with his mother. In addition to this beautiful time together for Rita and Dominic, a goal of participation in the family Christmas celebration was intended. As the family gathered around the Christmas tree, Dominic could actively participate by turning the tree lights on.

This vignette shows the importance of the family's priorities. In a household where other children are able to verbalize their needs, desires, and feelings, it is essential to provide opportunities for quality interaction time and strategies for participation for the child who cannot speak out.

Particularly in a home-based program, the family's comfort level with the technology will dictate the frequency of usage. How the technology is implemented to address the family's goals should be detailed in a clear manner. Just as the child may need to be enticed, the family may need to be engaged. Often, the family's intended use of technology may be for social and emotional purposes, rather than for the achievement of cognitive goals (Hutinger, 1994). The family's goals should take precedence and should be reflected on the Individualized Family Service Plan (IFSP). When excitement is transferred to the family, all will benefit. Siblings are wonderful instructional partners, and many welcome the shared responsibility as well as the interaction. Careful planning for implementation by the family is critical.

Professionals' goals for children often center around cognitive and motor development, while parents' goals for their children reflect goals that are social and emotional in nature (Hutinger, 1994). During this early time in their child's life, the family is often dealing with intricate grief feelings and is engaged in a period of great adjustment. Their hopes and dreams for their child must change as they come to an awareness that she will have difficulties that they had not anticipated or planned for. When asked what their dreams for their child are, they may respond that they really want her to have friends and to be able to play with other children. This dream should not be taken lightly by the professional. It is not necessarily inconsistent with the cognitive, communication, and motor goals that guide the teacher. The focus of all the goals can be functionally incorporated and may be well served using assistive technology as a strategy.

In Vignette 10.10, Kyle and his teacher use the computer to work on imitation, communication, and switch training as well as the social goals of the family by using eye contact to request the restart of an activity.

VIGNETTE 10.10   KYLE

Kyle is an adorable two-and-a-half-year-old boy who loves books and music. He is nonverbal and attempts to teach him to sign simple words have met with inconsistent results. He avoids eye-contact and interactive games, preferring to climb on a stool and watch the patterns of the sun through the leaves on the trees. His parents said it hurts them that Kyle doesn't look or smile at them. He enjoys rough play and can't seem to get enough. His parents feel that this is the only way Kyle is able to interact wih them meaningfully. They spend a lot of time swinging and bouncing him as he laughs and laughs. Usually, the adults wear out before he does!

During a home visit, Kyle's teacher set up an donated Apple IIe computer with a switch and the Laureate software program Creature Antics. The teacher held Kyle in her arms. She pressed the switch and the creature on the monitor bounced up and down. She then bounced up and down with Kyle. He laughed and tried to get her to bounce more by bouncing himself in her arms. Instead, she guided his hand to press the switch and pointed to the creature bouncing on the screen. When the creature bounced, so did they. If the creature wiggled or blinked, so did they. Next, the teacher guided Kyle's vision from the monitor to her face, using her index finger to point from the screen to her eyes. When Kyle briefly looked at her, she smiled and they repeated the activity from the monitor. Kyle picked this up fairly quickly, and soon began to press the switch and then request the physical movement by looking at his teacher.

In this vignette, the teacher is working on the cognitive goals of imitation and turn-taking. At the same time, she is also working on the family's priority of engaging in visual interaction with Kyle. The activity was repeated with Kyle's mom so she could experience his visual attention to her.

Assistive technology in the Birth to Three program and in the home can offer families "a degree of hope that their children can become active participants in society" (Hutinger et al., 1990, p. 7). In Vignette 10.3, Jackson engaged in cognitive, motor, communicative, social, and emotional behavior. His dad was thrilled to hear him say, "Hi, Buddy!" with a voice output device. What was even more thrilling was to watch other children come over and play with him. The interactions that flowed from a single, simple greeting were priceless. This incident became the springboard for Jackson's family's tireless pursuit to find a way for Jackson to communicate verbally.

Families may be hesitant to entertain the thought of using assistive technology with their child. It may connote for them a vision of helplessness and disability and thus, a picture of a child who is more severely disabled than they perceive their own child to be. Their child is a baby, after all, and may not have severe needs. Nor may their child's needs be visible to the eye. Technology may be viewed as necessary only for children with severe disabilities. While it is easier to comprehend the need for assistive technology for children with more involved disabilities, it is helpful for families to see how technology can be used with all young children and how it can facilitate play. Seeing a group of children playing at the computer or with a switch toy can help allay parents' fears that their child will become "technology dependent." Siblings are often natural demonstrators of how enticing adapted toys can be.

Parents and grandparents may fear that the use of a communication device will prevent a child from developing verbal speech. They need to know that when a child is able to experience the power of using a voice output device, speech will be facilitated rather than impeded.

Another roadblock to acceptance of technology use is the mystery behind it. Parents may not be sure what assistive technology is. The words may mean little without seeing what is meant by the term. Demonstrating what a switch is and how it works with a toy to engage their child and entice her to play and explore will give the words far more meaning than will an explanation. Actually seeing a variety of children playing with adapted toys will aid in understanding that assistive technology is a strategy that can facilitate play, interaction, learning, and active participation in the environment. An additional point that may encourage parents' acceptance and excitement is the fact that computers are used with younger and younger children in schools and preschools. Switch use, when seen as a forerunner to computer use, and adapted computer use, when seen as a means of providing a head start for a child with special needs, become vehicles for excitement rather than fear.

Families will feel more comfortable about assistive technology use if they have opportunities to see it in action. They may understand how technology can foster inclusion when they see all the children use a communication device in a play group. At home, when they see their child use a single-message switch to help read a story, acceptance and understanding of its value can be personally experienced.

SERVICE PROVIDERS AND TECHNOLOGY

Teachers and therapists may also share fears similar to parents'. Perhaps the greatest concern is how to make the technology work and how to incorporate it into intervention beyond the cause-and-effect level. The simplest way to overcome the fear is to attend a workshop or training session that includes, at the very least, demonstrations of devices. Opportunities to use the devices will be very helpful. Often, workshop presenters provide lists of resources that offer support at local, state, and national levels. In addition, other service providers who attend the same training become sources of support.

In Lesar's (1998) study, on-site workshops and consultation and technical support by specialists were cited as the most helpful training methods for professionals working with preschool children. Conferences and in-service courses were also listed as helpful. However, her study did not include early intervention specialists in Birth to Three programs because of the diversity of service delivery models.

The abundance of technical information and the variety of assistive technology devices on the market can be overwhelming to anyone! It is important from the start to recognize how rapidly the field of assistive technology advances and to realize that no one person is ever fully aware of all that is available. Everyone, even the expert, has gaps in information. It is impossible to keep abreast of all the new information about assistive technology. It is an ever-changing field. This can be a very comforting realization, as it removes a huge burden of responsibility from the individual service provider in the field. What is important is to focus on the information that is useful for a particular child or program and to follow best practice guidelines. It is not necessary to use state-of-the-art devices when simpler ones will do. Although a particular computer may be outdated, it may be quite functional for the purpose of the child being served.

Although a bigger and better device may be available tomorrow, today's version (or even yesterday's version) may be perfectly suitable. Low-end technology may be preferable to high-end technology. It is the child, the family, the goals, and the strategies that are most important.

Since the first step in assistive technology use is usually the most threatening for everyone, choosing a simple device, perhaps a basic switch toy, to incorporate into intervention is likely to be the most rewarding and successful. As Musselwhite (1997) is fond of saying, "We must eat the elephant in small bites!" Once some success has been experienced, a comfort level will follow. Capitalizing on a simple success can broaden awareness and comfort levels. Making plans to gradually add more technology into the Birth to Three program will ensure continued personal and program growth. Before spending program money to purchase devices, borrowing adapted toys from a toy lending library could provide necessary experience and avoid potentially costly mistakes and wasted money. State birth-to-three administrators are good resources for locating contact people at the local level who can share their experiences and suggestions. Service providers who are using assistive technology in their interventions can be great sources of information and support. Many states have assistive technology training opportunities in place.

THE COMPUTER AS A RESOURCE

In addition to facilitating learning opportunities for children, the computer is helpful to families and professionals in a variety of ways. Instant access to information, opportunities for communication, service plan development strategies, and continued participation in education are available through the computer.

Information and Communication

The Internet is a connection of computers and computer networks that allows users to share information. It includes networks of computer systems all over the world. In addition to sharing written information, the Internet provides the ability to send and receive e-mail messages, copy programs and data, use remote computers, and view information with text, pictures, sound, and video. Less expensive access to the Internet via the television screen, which will avoid the cost of a full computer system, will soon be available to more families.

A vast and rapidly expanding source of information for services providers and families is available on the Internet. Service providers who have access to the Internet can search for information on a particular disability from a medical, educational, or intervention standpoint. Local, national, and international resources can be accessed. Active discussions can be held with others from all over the world who have an interest in the same subject area. Experiences, strategies for intervention, and brainstorming can be shared among service providers, families, or any other interested individuals. Families can communicate directly with medical specialists, support organizations, and other parents, in addition to accessing information on their child's particular disability. New information is posted daily. Medical personnel, families, support organizations, research groups, and service providers can present queries about rare disabilities in an attempt to locate others with similar symptoms.

A very useful and comprehensive resource on the Internet for information specific to families of people with disabilities is the Family Village Web site. The address is http://www.familyvillage.wisc.edu/. This site is of particular value for those involved in Birth to Three programs. It offers the opportunity to find information, to locate resources, to receive training, to identify other families with similar needs, to learn how to access health care, and to chat with others. The Family Village is updated frequently and additions can be suggested by those who visit this site.

Individualized Family Service Plans

Computerized Individualized Family Service Plans can assist the service provider and the family to develop an appropriate, comprehensive plan for the family and child.

Distance Education

Distance education can be presented as interactive television, two-way audio, or one-way video at a central site. Online classes are available in the home or workplace. Students can earn graduate degrees or undergraduate credits. Colleges offer in excess of 30,000 courses via distance education ("Distance Education," 1998). Distance education can be a convenient way for those who work well independently to receive preservice and continuing course credit. More advanced courses may not be offered locally, and this technology allows access without the need for geographic proximity.

SUMMARY

This chapter provides information about the use of technology with and for infants and toddlers with disabilities and their families. Young children learn through play—through movement and active exploration and manipulation of objects in their environment—a learning strategy that is often unavailable to children with disabilities. Structuring the learning environment to include adaptations that provide access to exploration and manipulation can maximize a child's potential to become an active participant in her world. The use of technology can facilitate play and foster a sense of a capable self, as well as assist in the development of skills in every domain.

Inclusion of children with disabilities can be facilitated through the use of technology. Adapted devices can level the playing field by providing the ability and the means for a child to participate. They can provide a means of communicating with peers. Often, because the adapted toys are very attractive in terms of feedback, they tend to entice typical children to play with their disabled peers.

Careful assessment of the learner, the environments, and the tasks expected of the child within each environment will provide a firm basis for selecting possible technology devices to use. Assessment is a team process that is ongoing and should include the family. Implementation strategies include the provision of opportunities to learn new concepts in a variety of settings with a variety of materials.

Technology use should be planned as one part of a comprehensive strategy of facilitating play and learning. In all activities that include adaptations using technology, the device should be viewed as a tool to entice and encourage interactions with the toys and other children. This should be the primary focus of activities that provide multisensory, comprehensive experiences. Infants and tod-dlers should be viewed holistically with attention to the various aspects of their lives: at home, in the community, in peer groups, in therapy, and at school if intervention is center-based.

Families' stated goals for their child may differ from those of the service providers. The family may focus on social goals while the professional focuses on cognitive or communication goals. These goals are not mutually exclusive, and the goals identified by the parents should be primary. The use of technology can facil-itate all these goals simultaneously.

Technology changes daily, and no individual can possible be aware of all the technology that is available at any one time. Everyone is continually learning. A variety of trainings are available to address particular needs and interests. Service providers and families can and should take advantage of the trainings that fit their particular needs at a given time. Just as the information and technology change, so do the needs.

Information and resources are readily available for service providers and families on the Internet. Families can access information and software, as well as communicate with others throughout the world who have similar issues. Service providers can access information that may be useful in intervention in addition to locating resources and information for families.

The future holds great promise for creative technology use with infants and toddlers. Providing alternative opportunities for learning and mastering the envi-ronment for infants and young children with disabilities can maximize their poten-tial in exciting new ways, opening many new doors that were previously closed to those with disabilities. The early use of computers, augmentative communication devices, and adapted toys by young children can help provide them with opportu-nities for physical, cognitive, and social experiences on a level playing field.

The use of technology with very young children with disabilities can change others' perspectives of them. Rather than allowing a disability to limit a child, technology can maximize his potential. The earlier it is taken advantage of, the more far-reaching the results can be. Not only can the child's skills be addressed, but the family's and service provider's needs as well. Technology is useful for the child with the disability; for the family who needs and wants information, resources, software, and a parent network; and for the service provider who needs access to information, professional resources, and software.

RESOURCES

PROFESSIONAL ORGANIZATIONS
Council for Exceptional Children (CEC)
  1920 Association Drive
  Reston, VA 22091
  Phone (888) 232-7733
  Fax (703) 264-9494

www.cec.sped.org
Annual dues vary by state:
professional—$74.00–$85.00;
student—$32.50–$33.00
Publishes:
Exceptional Children
Teaching Exceptional Children

Technology and Media Division (TAM) of CEC
(address same as above)
Phone (800) 486-5773
www.tamcec.org
Annual subdivision dues
(in addition to CEC dues):
professional—$20.00;
student—$10.00
Publishes:
Journal of Special Education Technology
The TAM Newsletter

NEWSLETTERS
ACTTive Technology
Project ACTT—Macomb Projects
College of Education

27 Horrabin Hall
Western Illinois University
Macomb, IL 61455
Phone (309) 298-1634
Annual dues: $16.00

Closing the Gap
P.O. Box 68
Henderson, MN 56044
Phone (612) 248-3294
www.closingthegap.com
Annual dues: $31.00—(6 issues plus
the *Resource Directory*)
Publishes:
*Closing the Gap Resource
Directory* ($14.95
plus shipping)

REFERENCES

ACTT outreach training module 2: Birth to three component. (1992). (Available from Project ACTT, College of Education, Western Illinois University, Macomb, IL 61455)

Armstrong, J. S., & Jones, K. (1994, August–September). Assistive technology and young children: Getting off to a great start! *Closing the Gap, 13*(3), 1, 31–32.

Bailey, D., & Wolery, M. (1984). *Teaching infants and preschoolers with handicaps.* Columbus, Ohio: Merrill.

Baumgartner, L., Brassfield, J., Cooper, L., LeHew, S., Muller, L., & Shores, S. (1992, October). *Switches: Under construction.* (Available from Steven Shores, 201 Seventh Avenue N W, Puyallup, WA 98371)

Behrmann, M. M. (1984). A brighter future for early learning through high tech. *The Pointer, 28*(2), 23–26.

Behrmann, M. M., Jones, J. K., & Wilds, M. L. (1989). Technology intervention for very young children with disabilities. *Infants and Young Children, 1*(4), 66–77.

Burkhart, L. J. (1980). *Homemade battery-powered toys and educational devices for severely handicapped children.* Eldersburg, Md.: Author.

Burkhart, L. J. (1982). *More homemade battery devices for severely handicapped children with suggested activities.* Eldersburg, Md.: Author.

Burkhart, L. J. (1987). *Using computers and speech synthesis to facilitate communicative interaction with young and/or severely handicapped children.* Eldersburg, Md.: Author.

Burkhart, L. J. (1993). *Total augmentative communication in the early childhood classroom.* Eldersburg, Md.: Author.

Burkhart, L. J. (1994, October). *Augmentative communication and adaptive play for infants and toddlers.* Workshop conducted at the Closing the Gap conference, Minneapolis, Minn.

Butler, C. (1988). High tech tots: Technology for mobility, manipulation, communication, and learning in early childhood. *Infants and Young Children, 1*(2), 66–73.

Carl, D., Mataya, C., & Zabala, J. (1994). *What's the big IDEA? 1994: Assistive technology issues for teams in school settings.* (Available from Region IV Education Service Center, 7145 Tidwell Road, Houston, TX 77092)

Church, G., & Glennen, S. (1992). *The handbook of assistive technology.* San Diego: Singular.

Distance education: A learning tool for professionals and students. (1998). *CEC Today, 5,* (1), 1, 5, 15.

Early Intervention Program for Infants and Toddlers with Disabilities, 34 C.F.R. 303 (1999, July 1).

Enders, A., & Hall, M. (Eds.). (1990). *Assistive technology sourcebook.* Washington, DC: Resna.

Fallon, M. A., & Wann, J. A. S. (1994). Incorporating computer technology into activity-based thematic units for young children with disabilities. *Infants and Young Children, 6*(4), 64–69.

Federal laws strengthen: The core of current rights. (1991). *NICHCY News Digest, 1,* 4–9.

Garwood, S. G., & Fewell, R. R. (1983). *Educating handicapped infants.* Rockville, Md.: Aspen.

Ginsburg, H., & Opper, S. (1979). *Piaget's theory of intellectual development.* Englewood Cliffs, N.J.: Prentice Hall.

Goossens', C., & Crain, S. S. (1992). *Utilizing switch interfaces with children who are severely physically challenged.* Austin, Tex.: Pro-ed.

Goossens', C., Crain, S. S., & Elder, P. (1994). *Engineering the preschool environment for interactive symbol communication.* Birmingham, AL: Southeast Augmentative Communication Conference Publications.

Harrymann, S. E., & Warren, L. R. (1992). Positioning and power mobility. In G. Church & S. Glennen, *The handbook of assistive technology* (pp. 55–92). San Diego: Singular.

Hutinger, P. L. (1994). *Effective use of technology to meet educational goals of children with disabilities* (PR No. 180R10020, CFDA 84.180R). Macomb: Western Illinois University, Technology, Educational Media, and Materials for Individuals with Disabilities Program.

Hutinger, P. L., Clark, L., Flannery, B., Johanson, J., Lawson, K., Perry, L., Robinson, L., Schneider, C., & Whitaker, K. (1990). *Building ACTTive futures: ACTT's curriculum guide for young children and technology.* Macomb, Ill.: Macomb Projects.

Hutinger, P. L., Johanson, J., Robinson, L., & Schneider, C. (1992). *The technology team assessment process.* Macomb, Ill.: Macomb Projects.

Hutinger, P. L., Robinson, L., & Schneider, C. (1995). Annual survey of ACTT sites indicates common technology practices. *ACTTive Technology, 10*(1), 1, 3.

Jensen, A. S., & Bergman, J. S. (1992). Positioning the child for viable switch access. In C. Goossens' & S. S. Crain, *Utilizing switch interfaces with children who are severely physically challenged* (pp. 17–37). Austin, Tex.: Pro-ed.

King-DeBaun, P. (1995, October–November). Babes in bookland. *Closing the Gap, 14*(4), 1, 7, 36–38.

Kinsley, T. C., & Langone, J. (1995). Applications of technology for infants, toddlers, and preschoolers. *Journal of Special Education Technology, 12,* 312–324.

Lahm, E. A. (1989). Tools for a lifetime. *Exceptional Parent, 9,* 26–30.

Lance, D. (1998). Legal issues in assistive technology. *Closing the Gap, 17*(3), 1, 14, 19.

Lepper, M. R., & Milojkovic, J. D. (1986). The "computer revolution" in education: A research perspective. In P. Campbell & G. Fein (Eds.), *Young children and microcomputers* (pp. 12–23). Englewood Cliffs, N.J.: Prentice Hall.

Lesar, S. (1998). Use of assistive technology with young students with disabilities: Current status and training needs. *Journal of Early Intervention, 21*(2), 146–149.

Levin, J., & Scherfenberg, L. (1990). *Selection and use of simple technology in home, school, work, and community settings.* Minneapolis: Ablenet.

Linder, T. W. (1990). *Transdisciplinary play-based assessment.* Baltimore: Paul H. Brookes.

Malouf, D. B., Jamison, P. J., Kercher, M. H., & Carlucci, C. M. (1991). Computer software aids effective instruction. *Teaching Exceptional Children, 23,* 56–58.

Morris, K. J. (1989). Alternative computer access methods for young handicapped children. *Closing the Gap, 7,* 1, 15.

Musselwhite, C. R. (1986). *Adaptive play for special needs children.* Austin, Tex.: Pro-ed.

New federal support for technology services. (1989). *OSERS News in Print, 2,* 2–3.

Pierce, P. L. (1994). Technology integration into early childhood curricula: Where we've been, where we are, where we should go. In D. Bailey, V. Buysse, and P. Peirce, *Research synthesis on early intervention practices* [On-line]. Available: http://idea.uoregon.edu/~ncite/documents/techrep/tech11.html

Ray, J., & Timms, J. (1993, November). *A guide to computers and software for young children with disabilities.* (Available from Carolina Computer Access Center, 700 East Second Street, Charlotte, NC 28202)

Reed, P., & Bowser, G. (1991). The role of the occupational and physical therapist in assistive technology. In *Tech use guide: Using computer technology.* Reston, Va.: The Council for Exceptional Children.

Reichle, J., York, J., & Sigafoos, J., with invited contributors (1991). *Implementing augmentative and alternative communication: Strategies for learners with severe disabilities.* Baltimore: Paul H. Brookes.

Robinson, L. (1986). Designing computer intervention for very young handicapped children. *Journal of the Division for Early Childhood, 10,* 209–215.

Robinson, L. (1986–87, December–January). Computers provide solid learning base for preschool children. *Closing the Gap, 5*(5), 1, 18, 25.

Robinson, L. (1992a). From the editors. *ACTTion News, 7,* 2.

Robinson, L. (1992b). Integrating technology into birth to three programs. In *ACTT outreach training module 2: Birth to three component.* (Available from Project ACTT, College of Education, Western Illinois University, Macomb, IL 61455)

Robinson, L., Rauschert, M., & Schneider, C. (1988). Computer technology as a tool for preschool handicapped children. *Closing the Gap, 7,* 26–29.

Sullivan, M. W., & Lewis, M. (1993). Contingency, means-end skills, and the use of technology in infant intervention. *Infants and Young Children, 5*(4), 58–77.

Taber, F. M. (1986). Adaptive devices and the computer. *The Exceptional Parent, 6,* 29–30.

Wilds, M. L. (1989). Effective use of technology with young children. *NICHCY News Digest, 13,* 6–7.

Wisconsin Assistive Technology Initiative. (1997). *Assessing Students' Needs for Assistive Technology: A Resource Manual for School District Teams.* Amherst, Wisc.: Author.

Wright, C., & Nomura, M. (1985). *From toys to computers: Access for the physically disabled child.* San Jose: Author.

York, J., & Wiemann, G. (1991). Accommodating severe physical disabilities. In J. Reichle, J. York, & J. Sigafoos, with invited contributors, *Implementing augmentative and alternative communication* (pp. 239–255). Baltimore: Paul H. Brookes.